FOURTH EDITION

DEVELOPMENT AND SOCIAL CHANGE

Sociology for a New Century Series

SOCIOLOGY FOR A NEW CENTURY

FOURTH EDITION

DEVELOPMENT AND SOCIAL CHANGE

A Global Perspective

PHILIP McMICHAEL

Cornell University

PINE FORGE PRESS
An Imprint of Sage Publications, Inc.
Los Angeles • London • New Delhi • Singapore

For information:

Pine Forge Press
A SAGE Publications Company
2455 Teller Road
Thousand Oaks, California 91320
E-mail: order@sagepub.com

SAGE Publications Ltd.
1 Oliver's Yard
55 City Road
London EC1Y 1SP
United Kingdom

SAGE Publications India Pvt. Ltd.
B-42 Panchsheel Enclave
Post Box 4109
New Delhi 110–017
India

SAGE Publications Asia-Pacific
Pte. Ltd.
33 Pekin Street #02–01
East Square
Singapore 048763

Printed in the United States of America.

Library of Congress Cataloging-in-Publication Data

McMichael, Philip.
Development and social change: A global perspective/Philip McMichael. — 4th ed.
    p. cm. — (Sociology for a new century series)
Includes bibliographical references and index.
ISBN 978-1-4129-5592-8 (pbk.)
    1. Economic development projects—History. 2. Economic development—History. 3. Competition, International—History. I. Title.

HC79.E44M25 2008
306.309—dc22   2007026243

This book is printed on acid-free paper.

07   08   09   10   11   10   9   8   7   6   5   4   3   2   1

Acquisitions Editor:	Benjamin Penner
Associate Editor:	Elise Smith
Editorial Assistant:	Nancy Scrofano
Production Editor:	Sarah K. Quesenberry
Copy Editor:	Susan Jarvis
Proofreader:	Eleni Georgiou
Typesetter:	C&M Digitals (P) Ltd.
Marketing Manager:	Jennifer Reed

For Karen
with love and gratitude

Contents

About the Author

Philip McMichael grew up in Adelaide, South Australia, and he completed undergraduate degrees in Economics and in Political Science at the University of Adelaide. After traveling in India, Pakistan, and Afghanistan and doing community work in Papua New Guinea, he pursued his doctorate in sociology at the State University of New York at Binghamton. He has taught at the University of New England (New South Wales), Swarthmore College, and the University of Georgia and is presently International Professor of Development Sociology at Cornell University. Other appointments include Visiting Senior Research Scholar in International Development at the University of Oxford (Wolfson College), and Visiting Scholar, School of Political Science and International Relations at the University of Queensland. His book, *Settlers and the Agrarian Question: Foundations of Capitalism in Colonial Australia* (1984), won the Social Science History Association's Allan Sharlin Memorial Award in 1985. Philip edited *The Global Restructuring of Agro-Food Systems* (1994), *Food and Agrarian Orders in the World Economy* (1995), *New Directions in the Sociology of Global Development* (2005) with Frederick H. Buttel, and *Looking Backward and Looking Forward: Perspectives on Social Science History* (2005) with Harvey Graff and Lesley Page Moch. He has served as chair of his department, as director of Cornell University's International Political Economy Program, as chair of the American Sociological Association's Political Economy of the World-System Section, as President of the Research Committee on Agriculture and Food for the International Sociological Association, and as a board member of Cornell University Press. He and his wife, Karen Schachere, have two children, Rachel and Jonathan.

Foreword

S ociology for a New Century offers the best of current sociological thinking to today's students. The goal of the series is to prepare students and,
in the long run, the informed public for a world that has changed dramatically in the past three decades and one that continues to astonish.

This goal reflects important changes that have taken place in sociology.
The discipline has become broader in orientation, with an ever-growing
interest in research that is comparative, historical, or transnational in orientation. Sociologists are less focused on "American" society as the pinnacle of
human achievement and more sensitive to global processes and trends. They
also have become less insulated from surrounding social forces. In the 1970s
and 1980s, sociologists were so obsessed with constructing a science of
society that they saw impenetrability as a sign of success. Today, there is a
greater effort to connect sociology to the ongoing concerns and experiences
of the informed public.

Each book in this series offers in some way a comparative, historical,
transnational, or global perspective to help broaden students' vision. Students
need to comprehend the diversity in today's world and to understand the
sources of diversity. This knowledge can challenge the limitations of conventional ways of thinking about social life. At the same time, students need to
understand that issues which may seem specifically "American" (e.g., the
women's movement, an aging population bringing a strained social security
and health care system, racial conflict, national chauvinism) are in fact shared
by many other countries. Awareness of commonalities undercuts the tendency to view social issues and questions in narrowly American terms and
encourages students to seek out the experiences of others for the lessons they
offer. Finally, students need to grasp phenomena that transcend national
boundaries—trends and processes that are supranational (e.g., environmental
degradation). Recognition of global processes stimulates student awareness of
causal forces that transcend national boundaries, economies, and politics.

Reflecting the dramatic acceleration of the global economy, *Development and Social Change: A Global Perspective* explores the complex interplay between rich and poor countries over the post–World War II era. Its starting point is the view of international inequality predominant in the 1950s and 1960s. This thinking joined international organizations and Third World governments in a common ideology of state-managed economic and social change and championed the idea that, with a little help from rich countries and international organizations, poor countries could become developed countries, pulling themselves up by their own bootstraps. Reality, of course, fell far short of the vision that inspired development thinking, and this view—which McMichael calls the *development project*—gave way to a new initiative called the *globalization project*. Goals of integration with the world economy and openness to its forces supplanted goals of national development and "catching up with the West." McMichael's portrait of recent social change spotlights the long (and political) reach of markets and commodity chains and the many, often invisible, connections between producers and consumers worldwide, restores significance to the role of agriculture and food in development, incorporates social movements, and weaves ecology into the story to provide perspective on climate change.

Preface to the Fourth Edition

The fourth edition of this text updates the material in a world in transition. The original framework and perspective of the first edition remain intact, although the attempt to organize development as a global project is fraught with instability and possibly planet-threatening trends. The thread that weaves together the story of colonialism, developmentalism, and globalization is that development is a project of rule. It takes different forms in different historical periods, and these have been laid out as changing sets of political-economic relations, animated by powerful discourses of discipline and opportunity. While this text may have the appearance of an economic argument, it is important to note that the framework is essentially political and world-historical in that it attempts to make sense of the intersection between the development enterprise and power relations in ordering the world. The account of development focuses on social and political transformations, and the various ways in which development is realized through social and spatial inequalities. It also considers these processes from the perspective of social movements, and how their resistances problematize the dominant vision of economism as a form of rule and as an increasingly evident threat to ecological stability.

The conceptual framework posits "development" as a political construct devised to order the world and contain opposition by dominant actors such as metropolitan states, multilateral institutions, and corporate interests. Development and globalization are presented as projects with coherent organizing principles (e.g., economic nationalism, market liberalization), yet utopian in their vision and potential for accomplishment, since they are realized through inequality. The theoretical subtext is organized by the notion of extended Polanyian cycles of regulation and resistance. In the mid-twentieth century, a form of "embedded liberalism" (market regulation within a maturing nation-state system to contain labor and decolonization movements) informed social-democratic (developmentalist) goals within a Cold War context of economic and military aid to the Third World. This "development era" ended with a "counter-mobilization" of corporate interests dedicated to instituting a "self-regulating market" on a global scale from the 1970s onwards. The dominant ideology, neoliberalism, proposed market liberalization, privatization, freedom of capital movement and access, and so on. This project had a "test run" during the debt regime of the 1980s, and was fully implemented with the establishment of the World Trade Organization (WTO) in 1995. A *further* counter-mobilization—to the deprivations of the globalization project—has gathered momentum through maturing global justice movements in the 1990s, the Latin rebellion of the new century, and a growing "legitimacy deficit" for the global development establishment. This is symbolized in the collapse of the Washington Consensus following the 1997 Asian-originating global financial crisis, recovery of the trope of "poverty reduction" in the Millennium Development Goals (MDGs) initiative of 2000, stalemate at the WTO, and growing antipathy towards the World Bank and the International Monetary Fund (IMF) among countries of the global South. Neoliberalism is at a crossroads, complicated by serious security concerns (social—mushrooming slums, economic—financial volatility/ casualization of employment, political—terrorism, and ecological—global climate change). How the current cycle of opposition and creative development alternatives will unfold is yet to be determined.

This fourth edition has been revised to weave a stronger ecological theme into the story, make more visible the gendering of development, and pay attention to current trends that reformulate questions about development's future. Updating includes attention to the limits of the "development" lifestyle, "ecological footprints," global health questions, the "war on poverty," social reproduction issues, the "planet of slums" phenomenon, outsourcing, NGO-ization, African recolonization, the Latin rebellion against neoliberalism, the rise of China and India, and the ever-changing policy face of the development establishment as it seeks to retain or renew its legitimacy.

The subject of development is difficult to teach. Living in relatively affluent surroundings, students understandably situate their society on the "high end" of a development continuum—at the pinnacle of human economic and technological achievement. And they often perceive the development continuum and their favorable position on it as "natural"—a well-deserved reward for embracing modernity. It is difficult to put one's world in historical perspective from this vantage point. It is harder still to help students grasp a world perspective that goes beyond framing their experience as an "evolved state"—the inevitable march of progress.

In my experience, until students go beyond simple evolutionary views, they have difficulty valuing other cultures that do not potentially mirror their own. When they do go beyond the evolutionary perspective, they are better able to evaluate their own culture sociologically and to think reflexively about social change, development, and global inequalities. This is the challenge we face.

A Timeline of Developmentalism and Globalism

WORLD FRAMEWORK	Developmentalism (1940s–1970s)
POLITICAL ECONOMY	State-Regulated Markets (Keynesianism) Public Spending
SOCIAL GOALS	Social Contract and Redistribution National Citizenship
DEVELOPMENT [Model]	Industrial Replication National Economic Sector Complementarity [Brazil, Mexico, India]
MOBILIZING TOOL	Nationalism (Post-Colonialism)
MECHANISMS	Import-Substitution Industrialization (ISI) Public Investment (Infrastructure, Energy) Education Land Reform
VARIANTS	First World (Freedom of Enterprise) Second World (Central Planning) Third World (Modernization via Development Alliance)

MARKERS

		Cold War Begins (1946)	Korean War (1950–53)	Vietnam War (1964–75)	
	Bretton Woods (1944)	Marshall Plan (1946)		Alliance for Progress (1961)	
	United Nations (1943)		Non-Aligned Movement Forum (1955)	Group of 77 (G-77) (1964)	World Economic Forum (1970)

FIRST DEVELOPMENT DECADE   SECOND DEVELOPMENT DECADE

1940	1950	1960	1970

| INSTITUTIONAL DEVELOPMENTS | World Bank, IMF, GATT (1944)
US$ as Reserve Currency | PL-480 (1954) | UNCTAD (1964)
Eurodollar/offshore $ market |

COMECON (1947)

Globalism (1980s–)

Self-Regulating Markets (Monetarism)
Public Downsizing

Private Initiative and Global Consumerism
Multi-Layered Citizenship and Recognition

Participation in World Market
Global Comparative Advantage
[Chile, South Korea; NAFTA]

Markets and Credit

Export-Orientation
Privatization
Entrepreneurialism
Public and Majority-Class Austerity

National Structural Adjustment (Opening Economies)
Regional Free Trade Agreements
Global Governance

Oil Crises (1973, 1979)	Cold War Ends (1989)	"New World Order"	Imperial Wars (2001–)
	Debt Regime	WTO Regime	Climate Regime
New International Economic Order Initiative (1974)	Chiapas Revolt (1994)		World Social Forum (2001)
Group of 7 (G-7) (1975)	Earth Summit (1992)		MDGs (2000) Stern Report (2006)

"LOST DECADE"   "GLOBALIZATION DECADE"

1970	1980	1990	2000

GATT   NAFTA (1994)
Uruguay   WTO (1995)
Round
(1986–1994)

Offshore Banking   Structural Adjustment Loans   "Governance"/HIPC Loans

Glasnost/Perestroika

Acknowledgments

I wish to express my thanks to the people who have helped me along the way, beginning with my graduate school mentor: Terence Hopkins, James Petras, and Immanuel Wallerstein. Giovanni Arrighi played a critical role in encouraging me to cultivate "analytical nerve." For the first two editions, which include acknowledgment of the various people who were so helpful, special mention still goes to the original editor-in-chief, Steve Rutter, for his remarkable vision and his enthusiasm and faith in this project, as well as friends and colleagues who made significant contributions to improving this project—the late Fred Buttel, Harriet Friedmann, Richard Williams, Michelle Adato, Dale Tomich, Farshad Araghi, Rajeev Patel, Dia Da Costa, Gayatri Menon, and Karuna Morarji—and my undergraduate and graduate students (particularly my remarkable teaching assistants) at Cornell.

For this fourth edition, I have received continual encouragement from acquisitions editor Ben Penner, and associate editor Elise Smith. I extend my sincere thanks to them and to the production crew, especially Sarah Quesenberry, and my fellow Aussie, Sue Jarvis, who has done a wonderful job of copy editing. Nilay Yilmaz's well-presented figures complement Dana Perls' graphics from the third edition, for which I am grateful. I received thoughtful and provocative suggestions to improve this text from Tom Hall, Judi Kessler, Robert Forrant, Dennis McNamara, Ho-fung Hung, Steve Philion, Jennifer Edwards, Bob Torres, and Mazen Hashem—their collective good advice has certainly aided this revision, even if not always followed completely. I can only do so much.

Abbreviations

AGRA	Alliance for a Green Revolution in Africa
AoA	Agreement on Agriculture (WTO)
APEC	Asia-Pacific Economic Cooperation
BAIR	Bureaucratic-Authoritarian Industrializing Regime
BIP	Border Industrialization Program
CAFTA	Central American Free Trade Agreement
CBD	Convention on Biodiversity
CEDAW	Convention on the Elimination of All Forms of Discrimination Against Women
CGIAR	Consultative Group on International Agricultural Research
COMECON	Council for Mutual Economic Assistance
ECA	Export Credit Agency
ECLA	Economic Commission for Latin America
EOI	export-oriented industrialization
EPZ	export processing zone
EU	European Union
EurepGAP	Euro-Retailer Produce Working Group on Good Agricultural Practices
FAO	Food and Agricultural Organization (UN)
FDI	foreign direct investment
FLO	Fairtrade Labelling Organizations International
FTA	Free Trade Agreement
FTAA	Free Trade Area of the Americas
GAD	gender and development
GATS	General Agreement on Trade in Services
GATT	General Agreement on Tariffs and Trade
GDI	Gender Development Index
GDL	global division of labor
GDP	gross domestic product

GEF	Global Environmental Facility
GEM	gender empowerment measure
GNH	gross national happiness
GNP	gross national product
GPI	genuine progress indicator
HIPC	heavily indebted poor countries
HYV	high-yielding variety
ICT	information and communication technologies
IFI	international financial institutions
IMF	International Monetary Fund
IPR	intellectual property rights
ISI	import-substitution industrialization
LDC	least developed countries
MDGs	millennium development goals
NAC	new agricultural country
NAFTA	North American Free Trade Agreement
NAM	non-aligned movement
NEPAD	New Partnership for African Development
NGO	non-governmental organization
NIC	newly industrializing country
NIDL	new international division of labor
NIEO	new international economic order
NTE	non-traditional export
OAU	Organization for African Unity
OECD	Organisation for Economic Co-operation and Development
PRSP	poverty reduction strategy papers
SAL	structural adjustment loan
SAP	structural adjustment policies
SEZ	special economic zone
TFN	Transnational Feminist Network
TIE	Transnationals Information Exchange
TNB	transnational bank
TNC	transnational corporation
TPN	Transnational Policy Network
TRIMs	trade-related aspects of investment measures
TRIPs	trade-related intellectual property rights
UNCED	United Nations Conference on Environment and Development
UNCTAD	United Nations Conference on Trade and Development
UNDP	United Nations Development Program

UNEP	United Nations Environment Program
WEF	World Economic Forum
WHO	World Health Organization
WID	Women in Development
WSF	World Social Forum
WTO	World Trade Organization

1

Development and Globalization

Framing Issues

What Is the World Coming To?

These days we talk of globalization as a matter of fact, and often with approval. But approval cannot allay the anxiety associated with melting polar ice caps. We are becoming aware that there are limits to our way of life. Ecological limits are natural limits. However, there are also social limits. While over three-quarters of the world's population can access television images of the global consumer, not much more than a quarter have access to sufficient cash or credit to participate in the consumer economy. We are at a critical threshold: Whether consumer-based development remains a minority activity or becomes a majority activity among the earth's inhabitants, either way is unacceptable for social (divided planet) or environmental (unsustainable planet) reasons, or both. Development as we know it is in question.

Television commercials depict people everywhere consuming global commodities, but this is just an image. We know that 20 percent consume 86 percent of all goods and services, while the poorest 20 percent consume just 1.3 percent.[1] Distribution of, and access to, the world's material wealth is extraordinarily uneven. Almost half of the ex-colonial world dwells now in slums. Well over three billion of people cannot, or do not, consume as we do. While we may be accustomed to a commercial culture, other cultures and displaced peoples are non-commercial, not comfortable with commercial definition, or are simply marginal to commercial life. Contrary to media images, global consumerism is neither accessible to a majority of humans, nor a universal aspiration. Uruguayan writer Eduardo Galeano challenges these images:

> Advertising enjoins everyone to consume, while the economy prohibits the vast majority of humanity from doing so. . . . This world, which puts on a banquet for all, then slams the door in the noses of so many, is simultaneously equalizing and unequal: equalizing in the ideas and habits it imposes and unequal in the opportunities it offers.[2]

Holding up a mirror to our commercial culture, anthropologist Helena Norberg-Hodge describes how the Ladakhis of northern India, who subsist without money, perceive Western culture through contact with tourists, armed with cameras and seemingly infinite amounts of money for which they evidently do not have to work, "In one day a tourist would spend the same amount that a Ladakhi family might in a year. Ladakhis did not realize that money played a completely different role for the foreigners; that back home they needed it to survive; that food, clothing, and shelter all cost money—a lot of money. Compared to these strangers they suddenly felt poor." Artificial contact provokes invidious comparison with Western culture, and maybe aspirations to seek it. Terming this "the development hoax," Norberg-Hodge remarks that Ladakhis "cannot so readily see the social or psychological dimensions—the stress, the loneliness, the fear of growing old. Nor can they see environmental decay, inflation, or unemployment."[3]

Despite powerful images of a world converging on, or aspiring to, consumer culture, there are alternative currents of meaning, social organization, and ecological practices. How the differences will be resolved is a major issue that frames the twenty-first century. It speaks directly to the key issue of our time, namely the possibility of irreversible global climate change, which *The Economist* has called "a potential time bomb capable of wreaking global havoc."[4] The world has a short time span within which it must learn to transform its energy-use patterns, in order to reduce greenhouse gas emissions by up to 90 percent. Current levels of consumption of goods and services are unsustainable. In addition, they are quite inequitable: not only do Ethiopians, on average, emit about one-300th of the carbon dioxide generated by the average American, but also those who tread lightly on the earth are more vulnerable to the impact of climate change: "The effort to tackle climate suffers from the problem of split incentives: those who are least responsible for it are the most likely to suffer its effects." The race against time involves preventing a 2 percent rise in global average temperatures above preindustrial levels, as this is regarded by the international scientific community as a threshold for "critical positive feedbacks," wherein climate change would self-accelerate.[5]

The prospect of rendering the planet uninhabitable should, and will, be a call to action on the part of the global community. The terms of the response will be telling. There are three large obstacles to overcome, all of which spotlight tensions within the current global development model.

¦ First is the objective obstacle of *inequality* between and within nations. Wealthy nations located in temperate regions are less vulnerable to ecological changes and have resources to protect citizens from natural disasters (flooding, drought, temperature extremes). Their wealthiest citizens have the resources to ensure that they are the last affected.[6] In the 1990s, while 90 percent of natural disaster fatalities resulted from hydro-meteorological events (such as droughts, floods, hurricanes, and windstorms), 97 percent of natural disaster-related deaths occurred in the global South. Computer modeling relating African rain patterns and ocean temperatures suggests that the crisis in Darfur, originating in a massive drought, is the "first climate change war."[7] George Monbiot observes, "asking wealthy people in the rich nations to act to prevent climate change means asking them to give up many of the things they value—their high-performance cars, their flights to Tuscany and Thailand and Florida—for the benefit of other people."[8]

¦ The second obstacle is the subjective consequence of *uneven development*. For example, while University College London researchers and the British Meteorological Office objectively reported in 2005 that "the Amazonian forest is currently near its critical resiliency threshold,"[9] subjectively, Brazil's president Lula claimed the right to exploit the forest for Brazilian development, reminding the global North of its own path of development: "The wealthy countries are very smart, approving protocols, holding big speeches on the need to avoid deforestation, but they already deforested everything."[10] Such statements combine the desire for sovereignty with a strategy of leverage. Brazil was already a recipient of a global fund to contain rainforest destruction. In the same month (February 2007), the Chinese Foreign Ministry claimed wealthier countries should take the lead in reducing greenhouse gas emissions. Following President George H. W. Bush's declaration at the Rio Earth Summit (1992) that the American lifestyle was not negotiable, the Chinese refused mandatory emissions limits to preserve their economic growth.[11] Until the world's governments can agree to modify, or reverse, their growth rivalries (linked to legitimacy and military security), neither of the unevenly divided world regions will take the drastic steps necessary to agree on an equitable and sustainable path toward sufficiency.

The third obstacle is the *economism* that frames solutions to social and ecological crises. The discourse of development was founded in economic language, institutions, and rules. Activity that commands a price, or generates cash, counts overwhelmingly as the measure of development, despite a range of other valued cultural practices that reproduce social and ecological relations, for which money is meaningless. The international community only began to take the global warming threat seriously when the British government released the Stern Report (November 2006), the financial calculation of which showed the cost of not addressing this threat would dwarf the cost of investing now in preventing catastrophic climate change. However, as some have noted, the choice before us is not economic, but rather moral: "we must make that decision on the grounds of how much we value people and places as people and places, rather than as figures in a ledger."[12]

The ecological threshold we face today is a stark challenge to development thinking and the promise of prosperity from an unbridled world market, stated a decade ago by former World Trade Organization (WTO) director-general Renato Ruggiero, "More than ever before, the world's prosperity . . . rests on maintaining an open international economy based on commonly agreed rules . . . by opening their economies . . . countries accelerate their development."[13]

More than ever before, the world's survival rests on developing a different set of international protocols, ones driven by principles of sufficiency rather than accelerating development along the path of insatiable consumption of dwindling resources. This is the development challenge faced by the global community, and at base it means giving greater priority, and value, to resources that do not need to be priced—such as biodiversity, habitat, the global commons (air, water, forests, wetlands, local knowledges, etc.), cooperation, health, literacy, unpaid labor, and so on. If the "developed world" wants the "developing world" to conserve the planet's tropical rainforests for their global ecological function, then it is reasonable to expect a reformulation of the meaning of value. Not only does the development paradigm privilege monetary relations and measures, often at the cost of non-monetary resources, but also it is busy encouraging the conversion of resources like water (in bottles), air (tradable pollution permits), survival networks of the poor (micro-credit), and even love (the global care industry) into commodities.[14] However, nature appears to be reminding us now that we need to revalue what we share as humans, rather than what we consume, in order to survive. And, as we shall see below, across the world there are a multitude of social experiments in reducing the human impact on the environment, involving re-embedding the market in more secure/durable sociocultural values and advocating for the so-called "life economy" at various scales of social and political organization.[15]

The question of scale is important here because the political organization of the world is so much an artifact of the consumer lifestyle. Scaling down (spatially and in consumption terms) may be one necessary response to the ecological challenge, but it cannot occur without reconfiguring trade and financial rules, governance protocols, and multilateral regimes protecting the "global commons." Proposals for these kinds of shifts in the organizational ecology of the world community have already emerged. They are spurred by the political, social and ecological tensions generated by a "Fast World" consumer culture steadily drawing down the earth's ecological capital, at the expense of distant populations' habitats, human rights, survival, and possibilities of sustainable development. Consumer boycotts, anti-sweatshop, and child labor movements, labeling initiatives, "green capitalism," and so forth express these tensions. They reveal mutual dependencies in a seriously unequal global community, and question the impact of powerful corporations and accommodating governments at a time when development is identified as consumption of increasingly valued, if not scarce, resources.

The Global Marketplace

Much of what we consume today has global origins. Even when a product has a domestic "Made in . . ." label, its journey to market probably combines components and labor from production and assembly sites around the world. Sneakers, or parts thereof, might be produced in China or Indonesia, blue jeans assembled in the Philippines, a cell phone or portable media player put together in Singapore, and a watch made in Hong Kong. The fast food eaten by North Americans may include chicken diced in Mexico or hamburger beef from cattle raised in Costa Rica. And, depending on taste, our coffee is from Southeast Asia, the Americas, or Africa. We may not be global citizens yet, but we are certainly global consumers.

The global marketplace binds us all. The Japanese eat poultry fattened in Thailand with American corn, using chopsticks made with wood from Indonesian or Chilean forests. Canadians eat strawberries grown in Mexico with fertilizer from the United States. Consumers on both sides of the Atlantic wear clothes assembled in Saipan with Chinese labor, drink orange juice from concentrate made with Brazilian oranges, and decorate their homes with flowers from Colombia or Egypt. The British and French eat green beans from Kenya, and cocoa from Ghana finds its way into Swiss chocolate. Consumers everywhere are surrounded, and often identified by, world products.

One of the most ubiquitous, and yet invisible, world products is coltan, a metallic ore used in consumer electronics products such as computers and cell phones, in addition to nuclear reactors. It comes predominantly from the Congo, where recent militarized conflict over this valuable resource has caused nearly 4 million deaths, and its mining has negative environmental consequences for forests and wildlife. Such ethical issues, similar to those associated with "blood diamonds," have driven some electronics corporations to mine coltan elsewhere in Africa.[16]

Commodity Chains and Development

The global marketplace is a tapestry of networks of commodity exchanges that bind producers and consumers across the world. In any one network, there is a sequence of production stages, located in a number of countries at sites that provide inputs of labor and materials contributing to the fabrication of a final product. Sociologists call the networks **commodity chains.** The chain metaphor illuminates the interconnections among producing communities dispersed across the world. And it allows us to understand that, when we consume a product, we often participate in a global process that links us to a variety of places, people, and resources. While we may experience consumption individually, it is a fundamentally social (and environmental) act.

Not everything we consume has such global origins, but the trend toward these worldwide supply networks is powerful. Our food, clothing and shelter, in addition to other consumer comforts, have increasingly long supply chains, otherwise known as the "ecological footprint." Take food, for example. Britain was the first nation to deliberately "outsource" a significant part of its food supply to its empire in the 1840s. In spite of the fact that its climate is ideal for fruit production, 80 percent of pears and almost 70 percent of apples consumed by Britons now come from Chile, Australia, the United States, South Africa, and throughout the European Union.[17] The concept of "ghost acres," originating in a Netherlands study, refers to additional land offshore used to supply the diet of a nation—the Dutch use almost double the human average of hectares of arable land for supplying food. Britons are estimated to use about 4.1 million hectares of "ghost acres" to grow mainly animal feed.[18] "Ghost acres," implying an ecological footprint, include "food miles," referring to distances traveled by food, and implicating carbon emissions from the use of fossil fuels. As Lang and Heasman suggest, "This form of global sourcing . . . is not only energy-inefficient, but it is also doubtful whether it improves global 'equity,' and helps local farmers to meet the goals of sustainable development."[19] More goods and services are produced on this transnational scale every year, confirming that development as we know it has assumed global proportions. And the "ghost acres" often comprise land cultivated in the ex-colonial regions for export agriculture—encouraged by development agencies as providing jobs for Mexicans or Kenyans, or Indonesians, and foreign exchange for their national coffers to retire debt or purchase technology, or even foodstuffs to compensate for food exported. In this way, global integration transforms development along global lines, deepening cross-national dependencies.

As former WTO director Renato Ruggiero (quoted above) said, globalization is now perceived as indispensable to development. This is a powerful idea informing development policies made by national governments and international development agencies, such as the World Bank. Most governments across the world participate in an opening of their economies to global competition or, in the case of the European Union, synchronizing their macroeconomic policies by adopting a common currency, the euro, to streamline the European economy and give it a global competitive edge. This initiative gathered steam when the United States, Canada, and Mexico signed the North American Free Trade Agreement (NAFTA) in 1994, providing the United States with a huge open market as a home base. The point is that *development* and *globalization* have become synonymous for business and political elites across the world.

The dilemma is that large corporations have become global players, countries specialize to produce for the global market, and global consumers are addicted to goods and services from that market. More specifically, humans (especially those with large ecological footprints) are living beyond their ecological means. A 2005 Scientific Report to the Royal Society in London warned that "almost two-thirds of the natural machinery that supports life on Earth is being degraded by human pressure."[20] The World Wildlife Fund (WWF) reported in October 2006 that calculations on declining planetary capacity to provide food, fiber and timber, and absorb carbon dioxide, indicate that humanity is using 25 percent more resources than are renewed naturally in a year. Such "ecological overshoot" began in 1987. The report concludes, "Effectively, the earth's regenerative capacity can no longer keep up with demand—people are turning resources into waste faster than nature can turn waste back into resources. Humanity is no longer living off nature's interest, but is drawing down its capital. This growing pressure on ecosystems is causing habitat destruction or degradation and is threatening both biodiversity and human wellbeing."[21] The WWF's measure of the ecological footprint (extent of human demand in hectares per person less resources needed to provide raw materials plus land for building and absorbing carbon emissions) places the United Arab Emirates as the most profligate, followed by the United States and the European Union, with the least profligate countries being Bangladesh, Somalia, Afghanistan, and Malawi.[22] Figure 1.1 aggregates ecological footprints by region.

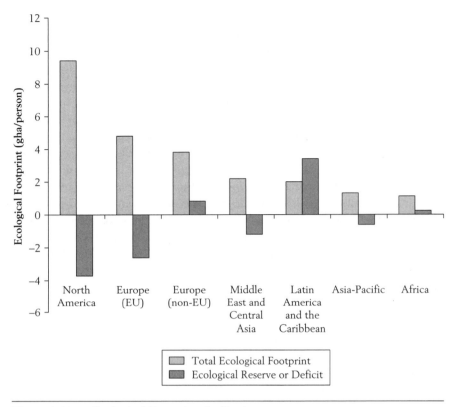

Figure 1.1   Ecological Footprints by Region

Source: http://worldwildlife.org/news/livingplanet/pdfs/living_planet_report.pdf (p. 28).

At the same time, global inequality is deepening. Since 1970, the gap between the richest, and the poorest 20 percent of the world's population has more than doubled (now standing at about 89:1). By 2000, there were three people who owned more wealth than the total income of the 48 "poorest" countries in the world.[23] In 2006, the Helsinki-based World Institute for Development Economics Research of the United Nations University (UNU-WIDER) reported that the richest 2 percent of adults in the world owned more than half of global household wealth, that the richest 1 percent of adults owned 40 percent of global wealth in 2000, and that the richest 10 percent of adults owned 85 percent of global wealth, whereas 50 percent of the world adult population owned barely 1 percent.[24] More to the point, perhaps, is that there are now "global classes" and "national classes," marked by the inequalities produced on a global scale—thus, "even the middle that has been created in Latin America is hardly a middle at all. In the United

States, the median income is about 90 percent of the average income. In Brazil, the median is only about 30 percent of the average, and that is typical for most Latin American countries—because such a huge share of income goes to the rich, they skew the average upward."[25]

The marriage of development and globalization is spawning quite uneven offspring, as some regions and populations survive and prosper and others decline. It is an integrated outcome—that is, rather than a world in which some remain on the margins in a frugal, or subsistence condition, untouched by globalization and waiting to join the party (or not), virtually all peoples are now subject to mechanisms of integration (markets, media, credit, land and other resource appropriation, food requisitioning for paying consumers, education systems, bio-prospecting, dam-building displacement, and so forth). Such mechanisms of integration serve as transmission belts of enrichment or impoverishment in country after country. The creation of a worldwide belt of slums, containing about one-sixth of the world's population (1 billion) is one measure of this process. And it has dramatized the point that development is not simply about production, but also includes **social reproduction**, whereby people (mainly women) provide unpaid services through networks of mutual aid, care, child-rearing, and basic survival tactics to get by and/or supplement household income.

Global Interdependencies

In today's world, the interdependencies among people, communities, and nations are ever present. When we consume, we consume an image (an aesthetic symbol) as well as materials and labor from many places in the global marketplace. Just as all humans eventually breathe the same air and drink the same water, so consumers enjoy the fruits of others' labor. At this point in time, most laborers do not enjoy the revenues from consumption, since most of these revenues remain in the world centers of consumption.

The *global labor force* is dispersed among the production links of these commodity chains (see, for example, Figure 1.2). In the United States-based athletic shoe industry, the initial labor is related to the symbolic side of the shoe design—and marketing. This step remains primarily in the United States. Then there is the labor of producing the synthetic materials—of dyeing, cutting, and stitching; and of assembling, packing, and transporting. These forms of labor are all relatively unskilled and are often performed by women, especially South Koreans, Taiwanese, Chinese, Indonesians, and Filipinos. Athletic shoe companies *subcontract* with these labor forces through local firms in regional production sites, chasing sites where labor is cheap and/or stable, and environmental regulations are minimal.

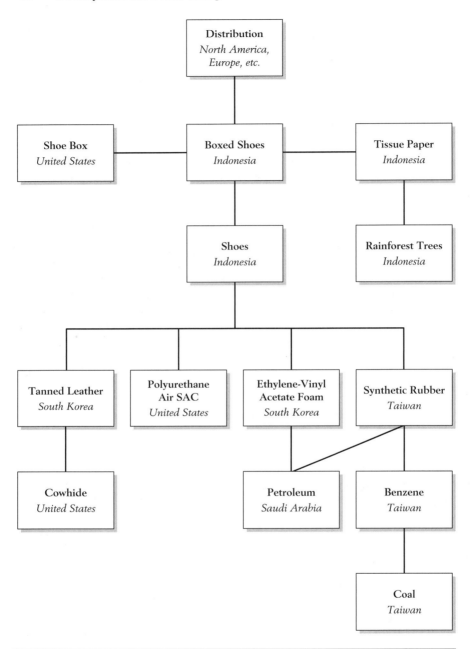

Figure 1.2   A Commodity Chain for Athletic Shoes

Source: Adapted from Bill Ryan and Alan During, "The Story of a Shoe," *World Watch*, March/April 1998.

Relocating production is a routine part of any competitive firm's operations today. Any shopper at The Gap, for example, knows that this clothing retailer competes by changing its styles on a short-term cycle. Such flexibility requires access through subcontractors to labor forces, increasingly feminized, which can be intensified or let go as orders and fashion changes. People who work for these subcontractors often have little security (or rights), being one of the small links in this global commodity chain stretching across an unregulated global workplace. Job security varies by commodity, firm, and industry, but rising employment insecurity across the world reflects the uncertainties of an increasingly competitive global market comprising a hierarchy of labor (of costs and skills).

We hear a lot of discussion about whether the relocation of jobs from the United States, Europe, and Japan to the "developing countries" (outsourcing) is a short-term or a long-term trend. The topic raises some questions:

- First, are "mature" economies shedding their manufacturing jobs and becoming global centers of service (e.g., education, retailing, finance, insurance, design and marketing)?
- Second, do those jobs that shift "South" descend a wage ladder toward the cheapest labor—for example, in the American South, or Southern Europe, or Southern Africa, or the Caribbean, or China, or Vietnam?
- Third, is this stratification of the world into low- and high-wage regions, among and within nations, where young women are overwhelmingly represented in the low-wage sectors, temporary or permanent?
- Fourth, is this relocation of jobs, or investment, a method of "pollution" migration, as energy-intensive processing of raw materials ("ecological debt") is relocated from North to South?

We examine such questions in the following chapters because the redistribution of jobs and natural capital, on a global scale and in opposite directions, is an indicator of a profound transformation underway in the world, a transformation that is redefining the parameters and meaning of development.

Global interdependencies extend to food. Increasing quantities of fruits and vegetables are being grown under corporate contract by peasants and agricultural laborers around the world. Chile exports grapes, apples, pears, apricots, cherries, peaches, and avocados to the United States during the winter months. Caribbean nations produce bananas, citrus fruits, and frozen vegetables, and Mexico supplies North American supermarkets with tomatoes, broccoli, bell peppers, cucumbers, and cantaloupes. Thailand grows pineapples and asparagus for the Japanese market, China produces organic fruits and vegetables for European markets, and Kenya exports strawberries, mangoes, and chilies to Europe, and so on. In short, the global fruit and salad bowl is seemingly bottomless. In an era when much of this production is organized by huge food companies and global supermarkets (e.g., Wal-Mart, Tesco, Carrefour, Ahold) that subcontract with growers and sell in consumer markets across the world, growers face new conditions of work.

From the early 1990s, the average share of supermarkets in food retailing in much of South America and East Asia (other than China and Japan), Northern-Central Europe, and South Africa rose from roughly 10–20 percent (1990) to 50–60 percent by the early 2000s. By comparison, supermarkets had a 70–80 percent share in food retail in the United States, United Kingdom, and France in 2005. A "second wave" spread to parts of Southeast Asia, Central America, and Mexico, and Southern-Central Europe, where shares of food retailing rose from 5–10 percent in 1990 to 30–50 percent by the early 2000s. A "third wave," reaching 10–20 percent of food retailing by 2003, occurred in parts of Africa (especially Kenya), remaining parts of Central and South America and Southeast Asia, and China, India, and Russia—these last three being the current frontrunner destinations.[26]

As discussed in Chapter 2, New World people (in the Caribbean and the Americas) and non-Europeans (Asians and Africans) have been producing specialized agricultural products for export for some time, but the scale and profitability of export food production have expanded greatly in recent decades as the number and concentration of world consumers have grown, carefully nurtured nowadays by global supermarket chains. Such firms must remain flexible to compete in the global marketplace. Not only does this need for flexibility bring growers across the world into competition with one another as firms cut costs, but it also means that the produce itself must meet high, and increasingly privatized (corporate), standards of quality and consistency to maintain market image and a predictable supply of products desirable to consumers elsewhere. Most contract growing of fruits and vegetables is performed by women. Women are considered more reliable and attentive as workers than men; they are also trained to monitor plant health and growth and to handle fruit and work efficiently. Employers presume that women are more suited to the seasonal and intermittent employment practices (e.g., harvesting, processing, and packing) necessary to mount a flexible operation.[27]

We are hearing increasing discussion now about the implications of "globetrotting" food. New questions are being raised about whether the relocation of global food production from the North to the South is a short-term or a long-term trend, and whether this indeed is a "comparative advantage" for the "undeveloped world" or simply a process of "recolonization."

- First, short of drastically improving fuel efficiencies of sea and air freight, how can the world sustain the expansion of food miles in the face of rising emissions of carbon dioxide?
- Second, and related, where is the rationality of displacing local agriculture with agri-exporting from the global South, so that food miles intensify as the South imports more basic staples to make up its food deficit?
- Third, can the "export of sustainability"[28] from the global South, as a result of the relocation of industrial agriculture there to take advantage of inexpensive land and labor and relatively lax environmental laws, be sustained in the face of global warming?

These are also questions we tackle in the chapters to come, as they signal some of the apparent new limits to the globalization of patterns of development on which our lifestyle depends, suggesting new challenges and directions for development.

The Lifestyle Connection

Globalization is ultimately experienced locally. But that experience does not automatically link other experiences to our own, nor does it specify them. To put it simply, as we consume the experience of distant producers, so they produce our experience. This is what may be called "the lifestyle connection," a term that, at first approximation, connects lifestyles across the world of producers and consumers, but also embodies the inequalities in this relationship. It is a relationship mediated by public policies and transnational corporations that together organize the global marketplace. That is, while we tend to experience the global market as something natural, it is actually an unequal political construct, embedded within corporate networks and supply chains that straddle the world and shape the composition and rules of exchange we know as "trade."

Along many of the commodity chains that sustain our lifestyle are people who experience globalization in quite different ways. Many are not consumers of commodities: at least two-thirds of the roughly 6 billion people in the world do not have access to consumer cash or credit.[29] Even so, they are often the producers of what we consume, and their societies are shaped as profoundly by the global marketplace as ours. In addition to the transformation of local production systems to service the global market, there is also the intensive conversion of the environment into "resources" that profoundly affects the sustainability of local habitats and the planet itself.

One of the most dramatic transformations underway is in the "animal protein" complex. When we consume shrimp, or chicken, or pork, or beef, chances are that we are simultaneously consuming mangrove swamps (habitat for people who fish and shrimp for a living) or biologically rich rainforests (habitat for indigenous peoples), which are being flattened for fields of soy for expanding feedlot operations around the world. Beef consumption, long identified with dietary modernity (whether beef steak for the rich or hamburger for the poor), is being overtaken by chicken and pork consumption. Whereas, between the 1960s and the 1990s, the forests of Central America were leveled for grazing cattle destined for hamburger meat, more recently South America pastures (notably in Argentina and Brazil) have been converted into beef supply zones for supermarkets in Europe and the Middle East. At the same time, South American forestland is being converted into vast soyfields to supply the European, Chinese, and Japanese beef, chicken, and pork industries. The Asian consumer class has outstripped that of the United States and Europe combined, and Asia is now the leading edge of the "global livestock revolution." Two-thirds of the increase in meat consumption is located in the global South, supplied primarily with Brazilian soybeans. China, once home to and net exporter of soybeans, is now the world's largest importer of soybeans and oils.[30]

The rising levels of consumption of animal protein (beef, poultry, pork, fish, and shrimp) by global consumers divided into high and low incomes,

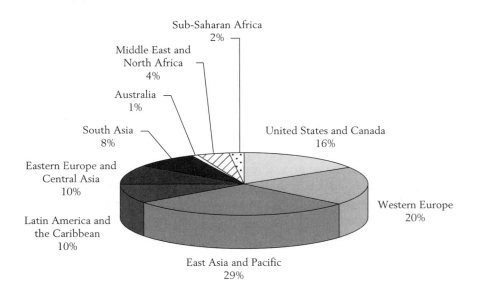

Figure 1.3   Share of Global Consumer Classes by Region

Source: WorldWatch, State of the World 2004 (Washington, DC: Worldwatch, p. 7).

demanding specialty cuts (including fresh fish and shrimp) and processed meats respectively, have a multi-layered ecological impact. Both cattle and shrimp farming have irreversible ecological effects on soil, hydrological cycles, and forests, and on coastal mangrove swamps, in South America and South and Southeast Asia respectively. In the case of shrimp, as mangroves' fragile biodiversity deteriorates, shrimp aquaculture proliferates, along with new ecological vulnerabilities, ranging from fresh water pollution and depletion to the disease outbreaks familiar in other forms of industrially farmed livestock.[31] In climatic terms, "it takes up to 16 times more farmland to sustain people on a diet of animal protein than on a diet of plant protein. . . . The emerging meat-eaters of the emerging economies—especially China—are driving industrial agriculture into the tropical forests of South America, sending greenhouse gases skyward in a dangerous new linkage between the palate and the warming of the planet."[32] A 2006 Food and Agricultural Organization (FAO) Report titled *Livestock's Long Shadow* notes, "the livestock sector generates more greenhouse gas emissions as measured in CO_2 equivalent—18 percent—than transport. . . . The environmental costs per unit of livestock production must be cut by one half, just to avoid the level of damage worsening beyond its present level."[33]

Meat consumption further specifies the "lifestyle connection" in access to food by social classes. Cattle consume more than one-third of the world's grain, and animal protein consumption in general bids cereals and land away from the world's poor. Roughly 95 percent of global soybean production, and a third of commercial fishing, are consumed by animals rather than humans, and a "quarter of the earth's landmass is used as pasture for livestock farming," while grain fed to U.S. livestock roughly equals the amount of food consumed by the combined populations of India and China.[34] The substitution of feed crops for food crops redistributes food from low- to high-income populations.

Then there is factory farming, which is unhealthy for environments and bodies (both animal and human). In the United States, for example, "animal factories produce 1.3 billion tons of manure each year. Laden with chemicals, antibiotics, and hormones, the manure leaches into rivers and water tables, polluting drinking water supplies and causing fish kills in the tens of millions."[35] In terms of human health, "Animals in cramped conditions easily catch and transmit bacteria, which may then be passed to humans. Farmers routinely use antibiotics to combat infectious diseases, but in so doing may be contributing to growing antibiotic resistance among humans."[36] The related global threat of an avian flu pandemic, fanned by transnational human mobility, is rooted in the ecology of rising densities of urban populations and factory farming systems.[37]

CASE STUDY

Consuming the Amazon

In a recent report, *Eating Up the Amazon*, Greenpeace noted that, "Europe buys half the soya exported from the Amazon state of Matto Grosso, where 90% of rainforest soya is grown. Meat reared on rainforest soya finds its way on to supermarket shelves and fast food counters across Europe." As its website claimed, "nuggets of Amazon forest were being served up on a platter at McDonald's restaurants throughout Europe." Following this dramatic report, McDonald's slapped a moratorium on purchasing soya grown in newly deforested regions of the rainforest, and entered into an alliance with Greenpeace, and other food retailers, to develop a zero deforestation plan, involving the government in monitoring the integrity of the forest and of its inhabitants, some of whom had been enslaved and subjected to violence. The global soy traders, Cargill, ADM, Bunge, Dreyfus, and Amaggi, made a two-year commitment to the alliance.

What is all this about? Quite simply, like many Non-Governmental Organizations (NGOs) today, Greenpeace made the lifestyle connection and ecological relation (embodied in chicken nuggets) explicit. Documenting the ways in which the Brazilian soy boom, with all its social and environmental consequences, is a product of the fast food diet, Greenpeace made visible what is routinely invisibilized by an impersonal marketplace. By tracing the soy chain—with the aid of satellite images, aerial surveillance, classified government documents, and on-ground observation—Greenpeace reconstructed the geography of the soy trade, bringing the ethical dimensions of their diet to consumers' notice. While traders can escape the notice of the consuming public, retailers have become "brand sensitive" in an era in which information technology has created a new public space, and consumers have the ability to choose not to consume products with baggage.

In this case, what is the value of fast food compared with the value of preserving one of the richest and most biologically diverse rainforests on the planet—especially given that the scientific journal, *Nature*, recently warned that 40 percent of the Amazon rainforest will disappear by 2050 if current trends continue?

Source: Greenpeace, *Eating Up the Amazon*, 2006. Available at www.greenpeace.org.

The Development Lifestyle

So far we have focused on the connection between our lifestyle and conditions in the "developing world." But what about our lifestyle? It is *relatively* comfortable, to say the least. With only 6 percent of the world adult population, North America holds 34 percent of household wealth (in monetary terms). Europe and high-income Asia-Pacific countries also have disproportionate wealth, whereas the overall share of wealth of Africans, Chinese, Indians, and other lower-income countries in Asia is substantially less than their population share, sometimes by a factor of more than ten.[38] We have already noted that our lifestyle implicates, through ecological footprints and resource appropriations, the lifestyles of people elsewhere. We are indeed in "the age of high mass consumption"—the final stage of development economist W. W. Rostow's famous five stages of economic growth. Aside from the looming question of whether this final stage is terminal in an age of global warming, the assumption in the development industry is that we have arrived, and the "developing world" is just that. That is, it still has a way to go to match the Gross National Product (GNP) measures of the "developed world." The consequence of this assumption is that those societies still have some work to do *en route*. This ought to be a questionable stance by now. Not only is the "developed world" implicated in these problems, but this working assumption assumes away other problems associated with affluence.

Most of us know that money cannot really buy happiness, but standardizing development measures reinforces the belief that there is a high correlation between GNP and social wellbeing. There is evidence of a negative relationship between income and happiness. For example, in Asia, residents of wealthy countries such as Japan and Taiwan regularly report the highest proportion of unhappy people, while countries like the Philippines, with the lowest incomes, report the highest number of happy people.[39] Clive Hamilton, executive director of the Australian Institute think-tank, notes,

> The evidence shows that, beyond a certain point, increased income does not result in increased wellbeing. . . . The direct evidence on the relationship between income levels and happiness is extensive. In the United States, there is virtually no difference in reported satisfaction between people with incomes of $20,000 and $80,000. . . . In poor countries such as Bangladesh, wealthier people have higher levels of wellbeing than poor people. But in rich countries, having more income makes surprisingly little difference . . . [and] despite a trebling of real incomes during the period, fewer Americans in the 1990s [were] satisfied with their incomes than was the case in the 1950s.[40]

It is well established that social health in the United States has declined over the last three decades, as poverty and income inequity, teenage suicide, and lack of health insurance have increased. The UN Development Program's Human Poverty Index ranks the United States last among 17 industrial (OECD) countries with respect to indicators of poverty, illiteracy, longevity, and social inclusion.[41] Meanwhile, a 2007 UNICEF report on the wellbeing of children and adolescents in 21 wealthy countries ranked Britain last, right behind the United States. One commentator observed, "What is so striking is not only the lack of security and contentment that has been identified, but the vast gap between British children's experience and those of young people in other developed countries. The United Kingdom's only partner in crime is America, which must lead one to question how successful the "Anglo-Saxon" economic model can ever be at tackling inequality and discontent."[42]

Common to the Anglo-Saxon cultural economy, and increasingly found in affluent settings across the world, is the explosion of obesity, beginning in childhood, costing billions in health care, and exacerbated by poor diet and fast-track and/or sedentary lifestyles. In 2004, the FAO published a major study on the narrowing of urban diets, with increasing consumption of animal protein, edible oils, salt and sugar, and declining dietary fiber, associated with rising consumption of brand-name processed and store-bought food found to contribute to an increasing prevalence of non-communicable (dietary) diseases and obesity, and described by the World Health Organization (WHO) as "one of the greatest neglected public health problems of our time."[43] This global public health issue compounds the problem of malnutrition associated with global inequality. As Figure 1.4 shows, there are now two forms of malnutrition: processed food and sedentary lifestyle malnutrition; and malnutrition from lack of adequate nutritious

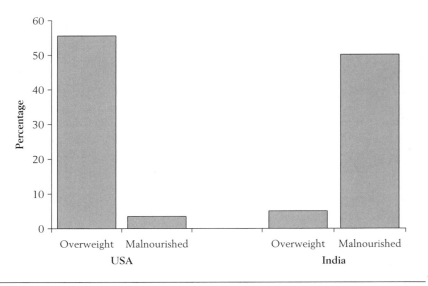

Figure 1.4   Percentage of Population Malnourished and Overweight

Source: Adapted from *New Internationalist* 353 (2003): 20.

food supplies. Not only are producers and consumers linked across space by commodity chains, but these links have mirror images, so to speak, at each end of the world.

The stage of "high mass consumption" is clearly not without its dilemmas. In this context, new measures of development, or progress, have emerged. Some, such as the Gender Development Index (GDI), recording differences in life expectancy, earned income, and literacy, and the Gender Empowerment Measure (GEM), registering female proportions of administrators, managers, politicians, and professionals, engender development standards. Others account for broader contributions to wellbeing than aggregate sales of goods and services—that is, social and natural relations that are not commodified. Thus, in 1972, the King of Bhutan coined Gross National Happiness (GNH) as a qualitative benchmark combining material and spiritual development in emphasizing equality, preservation of cultural values, environmental sustainability, and good governance. The Index of Sustainable Economic Welfare, or the Genuine Progress Indicator (GPI), offers a quantifiable national balance sheet that includes the benefits *and costs* of economic growth. Weighted for inequality of income, job security, the value of unpaid household and community work, emotional intimacy, unemployment, environmental quality and sustainability, public health provisions, and so on, it evaluates the shortcomings of the standard GDP measure—for example, where "GDP counts the value of timber from native forests as a benefit and stops there, the GPI also counts the environmental costs of logging."[44] Clive Hamilton reports, "Despite the differences in national circumstances (between the United Kingdom, the United States, and Australia), there is a very consistent and startling pattern: while GDP per capita has risen steadily since the 1950s, the more comprehensive measure of national prosperity, GPI, has risen much more slowly and has stagnated or declined since the 1970s."[45] It is in this context that the phenomenon of "downshifting" has taken hold in the wealthy countries, as people take leave of the consumer treadmill and pursue a more balanced and rewarding life.

In her book *The Overspent American* (1999), Juliet Schor reports that 19 percent of the adult U.S. population has downshifted, "voluntarily switching to lower paid jobs, choosing to reduce their hours of work, and deciding to stay at home and look after their children."[46] This sentiment is reflected in the rising discussion of "degrowth economics," a provocative term designed to counter the prevailing economic orthodoxy of unbridled "growth" that translates into "development" today, and to create "integrated, self-sufficient and materially responsible societies in both the North and the South." Using a dramatic metaphor to make the point, Serge Latouche claims, "Growth economics, like HIV, destroys societies' immune systems against social ills. And growth needs a constant supply of new markets to survive, so, like a drug dealer, it deliberately creates new needs and dependencies that did not exist before."[47]

The proliferation of alternative conceptions and practices reflects our times, as people (re)discover values other than market values in individual and collective attempts to redefine the meaning of development. As we will see, such redefinition preoccupies the social justice and sovereignty movements springing up across the world.

The Project of Development

Development is a highly contested concept today. Contention revolves around four questions:

- What is the goal of development on an increasingly finite planet?
- What are the core values of development (who decides)?
- Why is development realized through inequality?
- What is an appropriate scale of development?

Officially, "development" is still measured at the national scale (GDP/GNP measures), yet development increasingly has become a global and private undertaking, with assistance from international institutions, states, and non-governmental organizations (NGOs). Without really defining what development comprises, but rather focusing on its ethical goals, the 1991 UN *Human Development Report* states,

> The basic objective of human development is to enlarge the range of people's choices to make development more democratic and participatory. These choices should include access to income and employment opportunities, education and health, and a clean and safe physical environment. Each individual should also have the opportunity to participate fully in community decisions and to enjoy human, economic, and political freedoms.[48]

Development, understood ultimately as economic growth, is a political goal rather than a natural process. We know this, for example, from observing existing communities of forest dwellers, who fashion their lives around managing natural *cycles* rather than pursuing growth *trends*. With the rise of European capitalism, state bureaucrats pursued economic growth to finance their needs for military protection and administrative legitimacy. But "development," as such, was not yet a universal strategy. It became so only in the mid-twentieth century, as newly independent states constituted a community of nations, embracing development as an antidote to colonialism, with widely varying success.

The mid-twentieth century **development project** (1940s–1970s), an internationally orchestrated program of *national* economic growth, with foreign financial, technological, and military assistance under the conditions of the Cold War, managed the aftermath of collapsing European and Japanese empires within the idealistic terms of the United Nations and its focus on governments implementing a human rights-based social contract with their citizens. This book traces the implementation of this project, noting its partial successes and ultimate failure, in its own terms, to equalize conditions across the world, and its foreshadowing of its successor, the globalization project, in laying the foundations of a global market that progressively overshadowed the states charged with development in the initial post–World War II era.

The **globalization project** (1970s–2000s), liberalizing trade and investment rules, and privatizing public goods and services, has privileged corporate rights over the social contract and redefined development as a private undertaking. Coinciding with the market triumphalism associated with the collapse of the Soviet empire in 1989, the globalization project perhaps reached its zenith in 1994–95. In that year, following recovery from bankruptcy a dozen years prior, Mexico's entry into the rich nations' club, the Organisation for Economic Co-operation and Development (OECD) was undercut by a crisis of its currency, the *peso*, coinciding with a dramatic uprising in its impoverished southern state, Chiapas. At the time, the Inter-American Development Bank observed, "The resumption of economic growth has been bought at a very high social price, which includes poverty, increased unemployment and income inequality, and this is leading to social problems."[49] From then on, the neo-liberal doctrine ("market freedoms") underlying the globalization project has been met with growing contention, symbolized by the anti-neoliberal social revolt in Latin America over the last decade, and the growing weight and assertiveness of China (and India) in the world political economy. Whether the global market will remain as dominant as in the past is still to be determined, so what a post-globalization project may look like is still on the drawing board—undoubtedly to be heavily influenced by the climate change emergency.

Further Reading

Diamond, Jared. *Collapse: How Societies Choose to Fail or Succeed*. New York: Penguin, 2005.

Flannery, Tim. *The Weather Makers: The History and Future Impact of Climate Change*. Melbourne: Text Publishing, 2005.

Patel, Raj. *Stuffed and Starved: Markets, Power and the Hidden Battle for the World Food System*. London: Portobello Books, 2007.

Perrons, Diane. *Globalization and Social Change: People and Places in a Divided World*. London: Routledge, 2004.

Select Websites

Eldis Gateway to Development Information: www.eldis.org

Global Exchange: www.globalexchange.org

New Internationalist: www.newint.org

Stern Report: www.hm-treasury.gov.uk/independent_reviews/stern_review_economics_climate_change/sternreview_index.cfm

United Nations Development Program: www.undp.org

PART I

The Development Project
(Late 1940s to Early 1970s)

2

Instituting the
Development Project

Development emerged during the colonial era. While it may have been experienced by nineteenth century Europeans as something specifically European, over time it came to be viewed as a universal necessity. Understanding why this was so helps to answer the question "what *is* development?"

In the nineteenth century, *development* was understood philosophically as the improvement of humankind. Practically, development was interpreted by European political elites as social engineering of emerging national societies. It meant formulating government policy to manage the social transformations attending the rise of capitalism and industrial technologies. So development was identified both with industrialization and with the regulation of its disruptive social effects. These effects began with the displacement of rural populations by land enclosures for cash cropping, creating "undesirables" such as menacing paupers, restless proletarians, and unhealthy factory towns.[1] Development, then, meant balancing technological change and class structuring with social intervention—understood idealistically as assisting human social evolution and perhaps realistically as managing citizen-subjects experiencing wrenching social transformations.

Unsurprisingly, this social engineering impulse framed European colonization of the non-European world. Not only did the extraction of colonial resources facilitate European industrialization, but also colonial administrators managed subject populations as they in turn experienced their own version of wrenching social transformations. Under these circumstances, where native peoples appeared backward to Europeans, development assumed an additional meaning: the proverbial "white man's burden."

Development thus became an extension of modern social engineering to the colonies as they were incorporated into the European orbit. Subject populations were exposed to a variety of new disciplines, including forced labor schemes, schooling, and segregation in native quarters. Forms of colonial subordination differed across time and space, but the overriding object was either to adapt or marginalize colonial subjects to the European presence. In other words, *development was a power relationship*. For example, British colonialism introduced the English "Lancaster school" factory model to the city of Cairo in 1843 to consolidate the authority of its emerging civil service. Egyptian students learned the new disciplines required of a developing society that was busy displacing peasant culture with plantations of cotton for export to English textile mills and managing an army of migrant labor building an infrastructure of roads, canals, railways, telegraphs, and ports.[2] Across the colonial divide, industrialism was transforming both English and Egyptian society, producing new forms of social discipline among laboring populations and middle-class citizen-subjects. And, while industrialism produced new class inequalities within each society, colonialism racialized international inequality.

Non-European cultures were irrevocably changed through colonialism, and the postcolonial context was founded on inequality. When newly independent states emerged, political leaders had to negotiate an unequal international framework not of their making but through which their governments acquired political legitimacy. How that framework emerged is the subject of this chapter. But first we must address the historical context of colonialism.

Colonialism

Our appeal to history begins with a powerful simplification. It concerns the social psychology of European colonialism, built largely around stereotypes that have shaped perceptions and conflict for at least five centuries. (*Colonialism* is defined and explained in the box on the next page, and the European colonial empires are depicted in Figure 2.1.) One such perception was the idea among Europeans that non-European native people or colonial subjects were "backward," trapped in stifling cultural traditions. The experience of colonial rule encouraged this image, as European and non-European cultures were compared within a relationship in which Europe had a powerful social-psychological advantage rooted in its missionary and military-industrial apparatus. This comparison was interpreted, or misinterpreted, as European cultural superiority. It was easy to take the next step and view the difference as "progress," something the colonizers had, and could impart to their subjects.

What Is Colonialism?

Colonialism is the subjugation by physical and psychological force of one culture by another—a colonizing power—through military conquest of territory and stereotyping the relation between the two cultures. It predates the era of European expansion (fifteenth to twentieth centuries) and extends to Japanese colonialism in the twentieth century and, most recently, Chinese colonization of Tibet. Colonialism has two forms: colonies of settlement, which often eliminate indigenous people (such as the Spanish destruction of the Aztec and Inca civilizations in the Americas); and colonies of rule, where colonial administrators reorganize existing cultures by imposing new inequalities to facilitate their exploitation. Examples of this are the British creation of local landlords, zamindars, to rule parts of India; the confiscation of personal and common land for cash cropping; depriving women of their customary resources; and the elevation of ethnoracial differences (such as privileging certain castes or tribes in the exercise of colonial rule). The outcomes are, first, the cultural genocide or marginalization of indigenous people; second, the introduction of new tensions around class, gender, race, and caste that continue to disrupt postcolonial societies; third, the extraction of labor, cultural treasures, and resources to enrich the colonial power, its private interests, and public museums; fourth, the elaboration of ideologies justifying colonial rule, including notions of racism, and backwardness; and fifth, various responses by colonial subjects, ranging from death to submission and internalization of inferiority to a variety of resistances—from everyday forms to sporadic uprisings to mass political mobilization.

Such a powerful misinterpretation—and devaluing—of other cultures appears frequently in historical accounts. It is reflected in assumptions made by settlers about indigenous people they encountered in the Americas and Australasia. Europeans perceived the American Indians and Australian

Aborigines as people who did not "work" the land they inhabited. In other words, they had no right of "property"—a European concept in which property is private and alienable. Their displacement from their ancestral lands is a bloody reminder of the combined military power and moral fervor with which European colonization was pursued. It also foreshadowed the modern practice of rupturing the unity of the human and natural world which characterized non-European cultures.

In precolonial Africa, communities relied on ancestral ecological knowledges and earth-centered cosmologies to sustain themselves and their environment. These methods were at once conservative and adaptive because, over time, African communities changed their composition, scale, and location in a long process of settlement and migration through the lands south of the equator. European colonists in Africa, however, saw these superstitious cultures as static and as only occupying, rather than improving, the land. This perception ignored the complex social systems adapted first to African ecology and then to European occupation.[3] Under these circumstances, Europeans viewed themselves as bearing civilization to the nonwhite races. French historian Albert Sarraut, ignoring non-European inventions such as gunpowder, the compass, the abacus, moveable type printing, and the saddle, claimed,

> It should not be forgotten that we are centuries ahead of them, long centuries during which—slowly and painfully, through a lengthy effort of research, invention, meditation and intellectual progress aided by the very influence of our temperate climate—a magnificent heritage of science, experience and moral superiority has taken shape, which makes us eminently entitled to protect and lead the races lagging behind us.[4]

The ensuing colonial exchange was captured in the postcolonial African saying, "When the white man came he had the Bible and we had the land. When the white man left we had the Bible and he had the land." Under colonialism, when non-Europeans lost control of their land, their spiritual life was compromised insofar as it was connected to their landscapes. It was difficult to sustain material and cultural integrity under these degrading extractive processes and conditions. At the same time, European colonization of natural resources converted land, water, cultivars, and food into economic categories, discounting their complex regenerative capacities and ecological interdependencies.

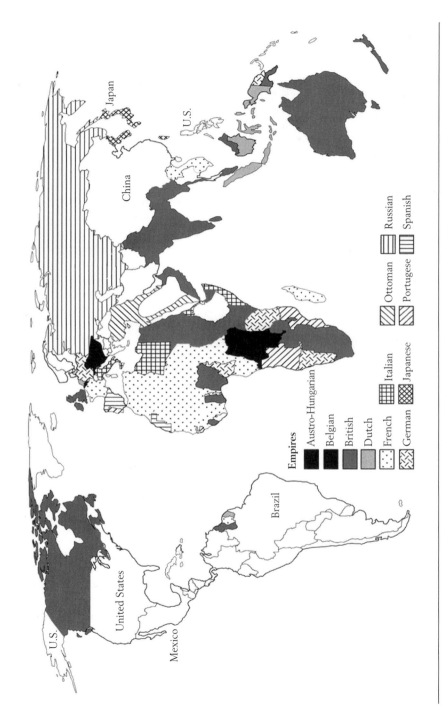

Figure 2.1 European Colonial Empires at the Turn of the Twentieth Century

What Are Some Characteristics of Precolonial Cultures?

All precolonial cultures had their own ways of satisfying their material and spiritual needs. Cultures varied by the differentiation among their members or households according to their particular ecological endowments and social contact with other cultures. The variety ranged from small communities of subsistence producers (living off the land or the forest) to extensive kingdoms or states. Subsistence producers, organized by kin relations, usually subdivided social tasks between men, who hunted and cleared land for cultivation, and women, who cultivated and processed crops, harvested wild fruits and nuts, and performed household tasks. These cultures were highly skilled in resource management and production to satisfy their material needs. They generally did not produce a surplus beyond what was required for their immediate needs, and they organized cooperatively—a practice that often made them vulnerable to intruders because they were not prepared for self-defense. Unlike North American Indians, whose social organization provided leadership for resistance, some aboriginal cultures, such as those of Australia and the Amazon, lacked leadership hierarchies and were more easily wiped out by settlers. By contrast, the Mogul empire in seventeenth century India had a complex hierarchical organization based on local chiefdoms in which the chief presided over the village community and ensured that surpluses (monetary taxes and produce) were delivered to a prosperous central court and "high culture." Village and urban artisans produced a range of metal goods, pottery, and crafts, including sophisticated muslins and silks. Caste distinctions, linked to previous invasions, corresponded to divisions of labor, such as trading, weaving, cultivating, ruling, and performing unskilled labor. Colonizers typically adapted such social and political hierarchies to their own ends—alienating indigenous cultures from their natural ecologies, and their political systems from their customary social functions, incubating tensions that have been inherited by postcolonial states.

Sources: Bujra (1992); Rowley (1974).

Development thus came to be identified as the destiny of humankind. The systematic handicapping of non-Europeans in this apparently natural and fulfilling endeavor remained largely unacknowledged, just as non-European scientific, ecological, and moral achievements, and legacies in European culture, were generally ignored. Being left holding the Bible was an apt metaphor for the condition of non-Europeans who were encouraged to pursue the European way, often without the resources to accomplish this task—of "development."

The Colonial Division of Labor

From the sixteenth century, European colonists and traders traveled along African coasts to the New World and across the Indian Ocean and the China seas seeking fur, precious metals, slave labor, spices, tobacco, cacao, potatoes, sugar, and cotton. The principal European colonial powers—Spain, Portugal, Holland, France, and Britain—and their merchant companies exchanged manufactured goods such as cloth, guns, and implements for these products and for Africans taken into slavery and transported to the Americas. In the process, they reorganized the world.

The basic pattern was to establish in the colonies specialized extraction and production of raw materials and primary products that were unavailable in Europe. In turn, these products fueled European manufacturing as industrial inputs and foodstuffs for its industrial labor force. On a world scale, this specialization between European economies and their colonies came to be termed the **colonial division of labor** (see Figure 2.2 on page 42).

While the colonial division of labor stimulated European industrialization, it forced non-Europeans into primary commodity production. Specialization at each end of the exchange set in motion a transformation of social and environmental relationships, fueled by a dynamic relocation of resources and energy from colony to metropolis: an **unequal ecological exchange**.[5] Not only were the colonies converted into exporters of raw materials and foodstuffs, but also they became "exporters of sustainability."[6]

CASE STUDY

The Colonial Division of Labor and Unequal Ecological Exchange

The ecological dimension of the colonial division of labor reminds us that industrialism is premised on transforming nature from a regenerative system to mere "raw material." Prior to industrial society and colonialism, the majority of humans depended on their local ecosystem to supply their various needs via a multiplicity of locally produced materials, harvesting just what was necessary. Overharvesting resources wastes energy, reducing an ecosystem's capacity and thereby threatening the sustainability of the human community. The colonial division of labor depended on overharvesting. Here, trade across ecosystemic boundaries focused extractive activities on those few resources profitable to the traders. Stephen Bunker and Paul Ciccantell, in their research on Amazonian ecology, observe, "Extractive economies thus often deplete or seriously reduce plants or animals, and they disrupt and degrade hydrological systems and geological formations [which] serve critical functions for the reproduction of other species and for the conservation of the watercourses and land forms on which they depend. Losses from excessive harvesting of a single species or material form can thus ramify through and reduce the productivity and integrity of an entire ecosystem."

The early Portuguese colonists, enslaving indigenous labor, extracted luxury goods from the Amazon such as cacao, rosewood, spices, caymans, and turtle eggs—all of which had high value to volume ratios in European markets. Wealthy Europeans prized turtle oil for perfume and lighting their lamps, but wasteful harvesting of turtle eggs for the oil severely depleted protein supplies and Amazonian aquatic environments on which populations depended for their material reproduction. English and French colonies of the eighteenth century imposed monocultures of sugar, tobacco, coffee, and tea. Mimi Sheller observes, "In consuming the Caribbean . . . Europe was itself transformed."

By the nineteenth century, European and North American extraction focused on industrial inputs such as rubber, further disrupting Amazonian habitats and ecology and exposing local industry to competition from commodities imported cheaply in the ample cargo space on the return leg of the rubber transport ships. As demand for rubber intensified later in the century, rubber plantations were established in Southeast Asia and Africa, by the British and the Americans respectively—in turn transforming those ecologies by introducing monocultures, and also impoverishing the Amazonian economy as feral rubber extraction declined.

Why does the developmentalist focus on human exchange through trade ignore the exchange with nature?

Sources: Bunker and Ciccantell (2005:34–47); Sheller (2003:81).

The colonial division of labor, as cause and consequence of economic growth, exposed non-European cultures and ecologies to profound disorganization, given the precipitous way in which colonies were converted into supply zones of labor and resources. Local crafts and mixed farming systems were undermined, alienating land and forests for commercial exploitation and rupturing the ecological balance. Not only did non-European cultures surrender their handicraft industries in this exchange, but also their agriculture was often reduced to a specialized **export monoculture**, where local farmers produced a single crop, such as peanuts or coffee, for export, or plantations (sugar, cotton, tea, rubber, bananas) were imposed on land appropriated from those who became plantation laborers. Systems of export agriculture interrupted centuries-old patterns of diet and cultivation, creating the all-too familiar commercial food economy, in which "what was grown became disconnected from what was eaten, and for the first time in history, money determined what people ate and even if they ate."[7]

Handicraft decline was often deliberate and widespread. Perhaps the best-known destruction of native crafts occurred through Britain's conquest of India. Until the nineteenth century, Indian cotton muslins and calicos were luxury imports into Europe (as were Chinese silks and satins). By that time, however, the East India Company (which ruled India for the British Crown until 1858) undermined this Indian craft and, in its own words, "succeeded in converting India from a manufacturing country into a country exporting raw produce."[8] The company had convinced the British government to use tariffs of 70 to 80 percent against Indian finished goods and to permit virtually free entry of raw cotton into England. In turn, British traders flooded India with cheap cloth manufactured in Manchester. Industrial technology (textile machinery and steam engine) combined with political power to impose the colonial division of labor, as British-built railway systems moved Indian raw cotton to coastal ports for shipment to Liverpool and returned across India with machine-made products, undermining a time-honored craft.

Social Reorganization Under Colonialism

The colonial division of labor devastated producing communities and their craft- and agriculture-based systems. When the British first came to India in the mid-eighteenth century, Robert Clive described the textile city of Dacca as "extensive, populous, and rich as the city of London." By 1840, Sir Charles Trevelyan testified before a British parliamentary committee that the population of Dacca "has fallen from 150,000 to 30,000, and the jungle and malaria are fast encroaching upon the town. . . . Dacca, the Manchester of India, has fallen off from a very flourishing town to a very poor and small town."[9]

While native industries declined under colonial systems, local farming cultures lost their best lands to commercial agriculture supplying European consumers and industries. Plantations and other kinds of cash cropping proliferated across the colonial world, producing specialized tropical exports ranging from bananas to peanuts, depending on local agri-ecologies (see Table 2.1). Non-European societies were fundamentally transformed through the loss of resources and craft traditions as colonial subjects were forced to labor in mines, fields, and plantations to produce exports sustaining distant European factories. This was a *global* process, whereby slaves, peasantries, and laborers in the colonies provisioned European industrial classes with cheap colonial products such as sugar, tea, tropical oils, and cotton clothing. European development was realized through a racialized global relationship, "underdeveloping" colonial cultures.

Colonial systems of rule focused on mobilizing colonial labor. For example, a landed oligarchy (the *hacendados*) ruled South America before the nineteenth century in the name of the Spanish and Portuguese monarchies, using an institution called *encomienda* to create a form of native serfdom. Settler colonialism also spread to North America, Australasia, and southern Africa, where settlers used military, legal, and economic force to wrest land from the natives for commercial purposes using slave, convict, and indentured labor. As the industrial era matured, colonial rule (in Asia and Africa) grew more bureaucratic. By the end of the nineteenth century, colonial administrations were self-financing, depending on military force and the loyalty of local princes and chiefs, tribes, and castes (the British presence never exceeded 0.5 percent of the Indian population).[10] Native rulers were bribed with titles, land, or tax-farming privileges to recruit male peasants to the military and to force them into cash cropping to pay the taxes supporting the colonial state.

Male entry into cash cropping disrupted patriarchal gender divisions, creating new gender inequalities. Women's customary land-user rights were often displaced by new systems of private property, circumscribing food production, traditionally women's responsibility. Thus British colonialism in Kenya fragmented the Kikuyu culture as peasant land was confiscated and men migrated to work on European estates, reducing women's control over resources and lowering their status, wealth, and authority.

In India, production of commercial crops such as cotton, jute, tea, peanuts, and sugar cane grew by 85 percent between the 1890s and the 1940s. In contrast, in that same period, local food crop production declined by 7 percent while the population grew by 40 percent, a shift that spread hunger, famine, and social unrest.[11] Using tax and irrigation policies to force farmers into export agriculture, Britain came to depend on India for almost 20 percent of its wheat consumption by 1900. Part of the reason that "Londoners were in fact eating India's bread" was the destruction of Indian food security by modern technologies converting grain into a commodity. New telegraph systems transmitted prices set by London grain merchants, prying grain reserves from villages along railway networks for export to Britain. Thus new global market technologies undermined the customary system of grain reserves organized at the village level as protection against drought and famine. For example, during the 1899–1900 famine, 143,000 peasants in Berar starved to death as the province exported tens of thousands of cotton bales in addition to 747,000 bushels of grain.[12]

Table 2.1   Selected Colonial Export Crops

Colony	Colonial Power	Export Crop
Australia	Britain	Wool, wheat
Brazil	Portugal	Sugar, coffee
Congo	Belgium	Rubber, ivory
Egypt	Britain	Cotton
Ghana	Britain	Cocoa
Haiti	France	Sugar
India	Britain	Cotton, opium, tea
Indochina	France	Rice, rubber
Indonesia	Holland	Rubber, tobacco
Ivory Coast	France	Cocoa
Kenya	Britain	Coffee, tea, sisal
Malaya	Britain	Rubber, palm oil
Senegal	France	Peanuts
South Africa	Britain	Gold, diamonds

Starvation in the colonies was not simply due to conversion of resources into export commodities. British rule in India, for example, converted the "commons" into private property or state monopolies. Forest and pasture commons were ecological zones of nonmarket resources to which villagers were customarily entitled—village economy across monsoonal Asia "augmented crops and handicrafts with stores of free goods from common lands: dry grass for fodder, shrub grass for rope, wood and dung for fuel, dung, leaves, and forest debris for fertilizer, clay for plastering houses, and, above all, clean water. All classes utilized these common property resources, but for poorer households they constituted the very margin of survival."[13] By the end of the 1870s, Britain had enclosed all Indian forests, previously communally managed. Ending communal access to grassland resources ruptured "the ancient ecological interdependence of pastoralists and farmers," and age-old practices of extensive crop rotation and long fallow, to replenish soils, declined with the expansion of cotton and other export monocrops.[14] Export monocultures displaced indigenous irrigation systems with canals, blocking natural drainage, exacerbating water salinity and pooling water in swamps, as host for the dreaded malarial anopheline mosquito. A British engineer reported to the 1901 Irrigation Commission, "Canals may not protect against famines, but they may give an enormous return on your money."[15]

The colonial division of labor developed European capitalist civilization (with food and raw materials) at the same time that it undermined non-European cultures and ecologies. As European industrial society matured, the exploding urban populations demanded ever-increasing imports of sugar, coffee, tea, cocoa, tobacco, and vegetable oils from the colonies, and the expanding factory system demanded ever-increasing inputs of raw materials such as cotton, timber, rubber, and jute. The colonists forced more and more subjects to work in cash cropping, employing a variety of methods such as enslavement, taxation, land grabbing, and recruitment for indentured labor contracts.

As the African slave trade subsided, the Europeans created new schemes of forced, or indentured, labor. Indian and Chinese peasants and handicraftsmen, impoverished by colonial intervention or market competition from cheap textiles, scattered to sugar plantations in the Caribbean, Fiji, Mauritius, and Natal; to rubber plantations in Malaya and Sumatra; and to British East Africa to build the railways that intensified the two-way extraction of African resources and the introduction of cheap manufactured goods. In the third quarter of the nineteenth century alone, more than one million indentured Indians went overseas. Today, Indians still outnumber native Fijians; they also make up 50 percent of the Guyanese population and 40 percent of the residents of Trinidad. In the same period, 90,000 Chinese indentured laborers went to work in the Peruvian guano fields, and 200,000 went to California to work in the fruit industry, on the gold fields, and on the railways.[16] Displacement of colonial subjects from their societies and their dispersion to resolve labor shortages elsewhere in the colonial world have had a lasting global effect—most notably in the African, Indian, and Chinese diasporas. This cultural mosaic underlines modern expressions of race, ethnicity, and nationality—generating ethno-political tensions that shape national politics across the world today, and question the modernist ideal of the secular state.

Colonialism Unlocks a Development Puzzle

Colonialism was far-reaching and multidimensional in its effects. We focus here on the colonial division of labor because it isolates a key issue in the development puzzle. Unless we see the interdependence created through this division of world labor, it is easy to take our unequal world at face value and view it as a natural continuum, with an advanced European region showing the way for a backward, non-European region. But viewing world inequality as relational (interdependent) rather than as sequential (catch-up), calls the conventional modern understanding of "development" into question. The conventional understanding is that individual societies experience or pursue development in sequence, on a "development ladder." If, however, industrial growth in Europe depended on agricultural monoculture in the non-European world, then development was more than simply a national process, even if represented as such. What we can conclude from the colonial encounter is that development historically depended on the unequal relationships of colonialism, which included an unequal division of labor and unequal ecological exchanges—both of which produced a legacy of "underdevelopment" in the colonial and postcolonial worlds. Persisting global inequality today, in material and governance terms, prompts the charge of "recolonization."

The secular-modernist ideal is contradicted by colonial racialized rule, where industrial and/or military techniques organized labor forces, schooling and urban and rural surveillance, and supervised hygiene and public health.[17] European exercise of power in the colonies revealed the hard edge of power in the modern state, premised on racial humiliation.[18] Such methods produced resistances among subject populations, whether laborers, peasants, soldiers, or civil servants. These tensions fed the politics of decolonization, dedicated to molding inchoate resistance to colonial abuses into coherent, nationalist movements striving for independence.

Decolonization

As Europeans were attempting to "civilize" their colonies, colonial subjects across the Americas, Asia, and Africa engaged the European paradox—a discourse of rights and sovereignty juxtaposed against their own subjugation. In the French sugar colony of Haiti, the late eighteenth century "Black Jacobin" revolt powerfully exposed this double standard. Turning the rhetoric of the French Revolution successfully against French colonialism, the rebellious slaves of the Haitian sugar plantations became the first to gain their independence, sending tremors throughout the slaveholding lands of the New World.[19]

Resistance to colonialism evolved across the next two centuries, from the early nineteenth century independence of the Latin American republics (from Spain and Portugal) to the dismantling of South African apartheid in the early 1990s. Although decolonization has continued into the present day (with the independence of East Timor in 2002 and the Palestinians still struggling for a homeland), the worldwide decolonization movement peaked as European colonialism collapsed in the mid-twentieth century, when World War II sapped the power of the French, Dutch, British, and Belgian states to withstand anticolonial struggles. Freedom was linked to overcoming the deprivations of colonialism. Its vehicle was the *nation-state,* which offered formal political independence. Substantively, however, the sovereignty of independent states was shaped by the cultural and economic legacies of colonialism.

Colonial Liberation

Freedom included overcoming the social-psychological scars of colonialism. The racist legacy of colonialism penetrated the psyche of colonist and colonized and remains with us today. In 1957, at the height of African independence struggles, Tunisian philosopher Albert Memmi wrote *The Colonizer and the Colonized,* dedicating the American edition to the (colonized) American Negro. In this work (published in 1967), he claimed,

> Racism . . . is the highest expression of the colonial system and one of the most significant features of the colonialist. Not only does it establish a fundamental discrimination between colonizer and colonized, a *sine qua non* of colonial life, but it also lays the foundation for the immutability of this life.[20]

To overcome this apparent immutability, West Indian psychiatrist Frantz Fanon, writing from Algeria, responded with *The Wretched of the Earth*, a manifesto of liberation. It was a searing indictment of European colonialism and a call to people of the former colonies (the Third World) to transcend the mentality of enslavement and forge a new path for humanity. He wrote,

> It is a question of the Third World starting a new history of Man, a history which will have regard to the sometimes prodigious theses which Europe has put forward, but which will also not forget Europe's crimes, of which the most horrible was committed in the heart of man, and consisted of the pathological tearing apart of his functions and the crumbling away of his unity. . . . On the immense scale of humanity, there were racial hatreds, slavery, exploitation and above all the bloodless genocide which consisted in the setting aside of fifteen thousand millions of men. . . . Humanity is waiting for something other from us than such an imitation, which would be almost an obscene caricature.[21]

Decolonization was rooted in a liberatory upsurge, expressed in mass political movements of resistance. In Algeria (much as in Palestine today), the independence movement incubated within and struck at the French occupation from the native quarter. The use of terror, on both sides, symbolized the bitter divide between colonizer and colonized (portrayed in Gillo Pontecorvo's classic film *Battle of Algiers*) and resonates today in Al Qaeda attacks against symbols of corporate and state military power and Western affluence.

CASE STUDY

The Tensions and Lessons of the Indian Nationalist Revolt

Mahatma Gandhi's model of nonviolent resistance to British colonialism affirmed the simplicity and virtue in the ideal-typical premodern solidarities of Indian village life. Rather than embrace the emerging world of nation-states, Gandhi argued, didactically, that Indians became a subject population not because of colonial force but through the seduction of modernity. Gandhi's approach flowed from his philosophy of transcendental (as opposed to scientific or historical) truth, guided by a social morality. Gandhi disdained the violent methods of the modern state and the institutional rationality of the industrial age, regarding machinery as the source of India's impoverishment, not only in destroying handicrafts but in compromising humanity:

> We notice that the mind is a restless bird; the more it gets the more it wants, and still remains unsatisfied. . . . Our ancestors, therefore, set a limit to our indulgences. They saw that happiness is largely a mental condition. . . . We have managed with the same kind of plough as existed thousands of years ago. We have retained the same kind of cottages that we had in former times and our indigenous education remains the same as before. We have had no system of life-corroding competition. . . . It was not that we did not know how to invent machinery, but our forefathers knew that if we set our hearts after such things, we would become slaves and lose our moral fibres.

Gandhi's method of resistance included wearing homespun cloth instead of machine-made goods, foreswearing use of the English language, and mis-trusting the European philosophy of self-interest. Gandhi viewed self-interest as undermining community-based ethics, and advocated the decentralization of social power, appealing to grassroots notions of self-reliance, proclaiming,

> Independence must begin at the bottom. Thus, every village will be a republic or *panchayat* having full powers. It follows, therefore, that every village has to be self-sustained and capable of managing its affairs even to the extent of defending itself against the whole world.

While Gandhi's politics, anchored in a potentially reactionary Hindu religious imagery, galvanized rural India, Indian nationalism actually rode to power via the Indian National Congress and one of its progressive democratic socialist leaders, Jawaharlal Nehru. Nehru represented the formative national state, viewing the Gandhian philosophy as inappropriate to the modern world but recognizing its mobilizing power. Infusing the national movement with calls for land reform and agrarian modernization to complement industrial development, Nehru declared, "It can hardly be challenged that, in the context of the modern world, no country can be politically and economically independent, even within the framework of international interdependence, unless it is highly industrialized and has developed its power resources to the utmost."

Together, Gandhi and Nehru are revered as fathers of independence and the Indian national state, respectively. Note that the struggle against empire was woven out of two strands: an *idealist* strand looking back and looking forward to a transcendental Hinduism anchored in village-level self-reliance, as well as a *realist* strand looking sideways and asserting that Indian civilization could be rescued, contained, and celebrated in the form of a modern state.

Did Nehru and Gandhi's opposing visions of development at the time of Indian independence foreshadow today's rising tension between maximum economic growth and sustainability?

Source: Chatterjee (2001:86, 87, 91, 97, 144, 151).

Other forms of resistance included militarized national liberation struggles (e.g., Portuguese African colonies, French Indo-China) and widespread colonial labor unrest. British colonialism faced widespread labor strikes in its West Indian and African colonies in the 1930s, and this pattern continued over the next two decades in Africa as British and French colonial subjects protested conditions in cities, ports, mines, and on the railways. In this context, development was interpreted as a pragmatic effort to preserve the colonies by improving material conditions—and there was no doubt that colonial subjects understood this and turned the promise of development back on the colonizers, viewing development as an entitlement. British Colonial Secretary MacDonald observed in 1940, "If we are not now going to do something fairly good for the Colonial Empire, and something which helps them to get proper social services, we shall deserve to lose the colonies and it will only be a matter of time before we get what we deserve."[22] In these terms, eloquent international appeals to justice in the language of rights and freedom by the representatives of colonized peoples held a mirror up to the colonial powers, demanding freedom.

A new world order was in the making. From 1945 to 1981, 105 new states joined the United Nations (UN) as the colonial empires crumbled, swelling UN ranks from 51 to 156. The extension of political sovereignty to millions of non-Europeans (more than half of humanity) ushered in the era of development.[23] This era was marked by a sense of almost boundless idealism, as governments and people from the First and Third Worlds joined together in a coordinated effort to stimulate economic growth; bring social improvements through education, public health, family planning, and transport and communication systems to urban and rural populations; and promote political citizenship in the new nations. Just as colonized subjects appropriated the democratic discourse of the colonizers in fueling their independence movements, so leaders of the new nation-states appropriated the idealism of the development era and proclaimed equality as a domestic and international goal, informed by the UN Universal Declaration of Human Rights (1948).

The UN declaration represented a new world paradigm of fundamental human rights of freedom, equality, life, liberty, and security to all, without distinction by race, color, sex, language, religion, political opinion, national or social origin, property, birth, or other status. The declaration also included citizenship rights—that is, citizens' rights to the social contract: everyone was "entitled to realization, through national effort, and international co-operation and in accordance with the organization and resources of each State, of the economic, social and cultural rights indispensable for his dignity and the free development of his personality."[24]

Decolonization and Development

Decolonization gave development new meaning, linking it to the ideal of sovereignty, the possibility of converting subjects into citizens, and the pursuit of economic development for social justice. Already independent Latin American states adopted similar goals, and in fact offered a new model for national industrial development.

Latin American political independence occurred in the 1820s as the older Spanish and Portuguese empires declined. During the nineteenth century, Latin American commercial development centered on the prosperity gained through agricultural and raw material exports to Europe. Because of the profitability of export agriculture, Latin American political systems came to be dominated by powerful coalitions of landowners and urban merchants. The Latin American republics clothed their oligarchic regimes with the French and U.S. revolutionary ideologies of **liberal-nationalism,** which informed nineteenth-century European nation building via national education systems, national languages and currencies, and modern armies and voting citizens. These ideologies also informed the twentieth-century movements in Asia and Africa for decolonization, coinciding with the rise of the United States to global power and prosperity. Eager to reconstruct the post–World War II world to expand markets and the flow of raw materials, the United States led an international project, inspired by a vision of development as a *national* enterprise to be repeated across a world of sovereign states.

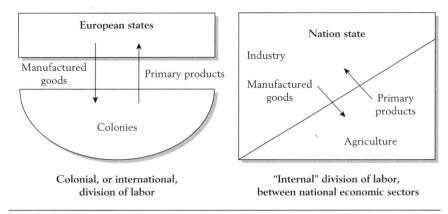

Figure 2.2   Distinguishing Between an International and a National Division of Labor

U.S. development modeled this vision, being "inner-directed" compared with the "outer-directed" British imperial model (as "workshop of the world"). In spite of the relentless destruction of native American cultures as the continent was claimed (*internal colonialism*), U.S. origins in the revolt of the North American colonies against British colonialism in the late eighteenth century informed an "anticolonial" heritage. Once the slave plantation was abolished, the New South was incorporated into a national economic dynamic based in interdependent agricultural and industrial sectors. Figure 2.2 depicts the difference between the colonial and the national division between industry and agriculture.

The division of labor between industry and agriculture which had defined the global exchange between colonial powers and their colonies was now *internalized* within the United States. Chicago traders, for instance, purchased Midwestern farm products for processing, in turn selling machinery and goods to those farmers. This idea of city and countryside prospering together is a *model*—that is, it *prescribes an ideal version,* even if the reality does not quite match up. On the American plains, for example, farmers "ripped open enormous areas of prairie grasslands" and enjoyed high yields so long as crops drew down the "vast storehouse of accumulated organic fertility just below the surface." As this rich topsoil was consumed, the land frontier extended in a cycle of unsustainable growth, until reaching its ecological limits in the "dustbowl" crisis of the 1930s. The solution was publicly supported agro-industrialization, centered on commodity stabilization programs. Specialized monocropping encouraged an excessive use of industrial inputs, such as chemical fertilizers, whose corrosive effect on soils produces the "fertilizer treadmill." As we shall see, the U.S. export of capital-intensive industrial farming has become the norm for agricultural modernization ever since, with global ecological consequence.[25]

Postwar Decolonization and the Rise of the Third World

In the era of decolonization, the world subdivided into three geopolitical segments. These subdivisions emerged after World War II (1939–1944) during the Cold War, dividing the capitalist Western (**First World**) from the communist Soviet (**Second World**) blocs. The **Third World** included the postcolonial bloc of nations. Of course, there was considerable inequality across and within these subdivisions, as well as within their national units. The subdivision of the world is further explained in the box below.

In this era, the United States was the most powerful state economically, militarily, and ideologically. Its high standard of living (with a per capita income three times the West European average), its anticolonial heritage, and its commitment to liberal domestic and international relations lent it the legitimacy of a world leader, and the model of a developed society.

How We Divide the World's Nations

Division of the nations of the world is quite complex and extensive, and it depends on the purpose of the dividing. The basic division made (by French demographer Alfred Sauvy in 1952) was into three worlds: The First World was essentially the capitalist world (the West plus Japan), the Second World was basically the socialist world (the Soviet bloc), and the Third World was the rest—mostly former European colonies. The core of the Third World was the group of nonaligned countries steering an independent path between the First and Second Worlds, especially China, Egypt, Ghana, India, Indonesia, Vietnam, and Yugoslavia. In the 1980s, a Fourth World was named to describe marginalized regions. The United Nations and the development establishment use a different nomenclature: developed countries, developing countries, and least developed countries—this terminology echoes **"modernization" theory**, which locates countries on a continuum, or "development ladder," traversed as a country develops an industrial economy, rational-legal administrative structures, and a pluralist-representative political system. The counterpoint, **"dependency" analysis**, does not quibble with these goals, but argues that development creates "underdevelopment" because countries inhabit unequal interdependencies structured by the colonial relation, beginning with the division of labor. **"World-systems" analysis** builds on the dependency concept to argue that a single division of labor is the organizing principle of the centuries-old world-economy, and shapes the differential fortunes of its member states which, along with their firms, compete via "endless accumulation."

Ranged against the United States were the Soviet Union and an assortment of Eastern European communist states. This Second World was considered the alternative to First World capitalism. The Third World, the remaining half of humanity—most of whom were still food-growing rural dwellers—was represented in economic language as impoverished or, in Fanon's politico-cultural language, as the "wretched of the earth."

Whereas the First World had 65 percent of world income with only 20 percent of the world's population, the Third World accounted for 67 percent of world population but only 18 percent of its income. While some believe the gap in living standards between the First and Third Worlds registers differential rates of growth, others believe that much of it was a result of colonialism.[26] Still others are skeptical of distinguishing cultures via a uniform standard based on income levels, since non-Western cultures value non-cash-generating practices.

Economic disparity between the First and Third Worlds generated the vision of development that would energize political and business elites in each world. Seizing the moment as leader of the First World, President Harry S. Truman included in a key speech on January 20, 1949, the following proclamation:

> We must embark on a bold new program for making the benefits of our scientific advances and industrial progress available for the improvement and growth of underdeveloped areas. The old imperialism—exploitation for foreign profit—has no place in our plans. What we envisage is a program of development based on the concepts of democratic fair dealing. . . . Only by helping the least fortunate of its members to help themselves can the human family achieve the decent, satisfying life that is the right of all people. Democracy alone can supply the vitalizing force. . . .[27]

The following year, a Nigerian nationalist echoed these sentiments:

> Self-government will not necessarily lead to a paradise overnight. . . . But it will have ended the rule of one race over another, with all the humiliation and exploitation which that implies. It can also pave the way for the internal social revolution that is required within each country.[28]

Despite the power differential between the United States and the African countries, the shared sentiments affirmed the connection between decolonization and development, where sovereign states could pursue national economic growth with First World assistance. The program of development pursued by new nations, "dependence" in independence, marked the postcolonial experience.

President Truman's paternalistic proclamation confirmed this understanding in suggesting a new paradigm for the postwar era: the division of humanity into developed and undeveloped regions. This division of the world projected a singular destiny for all nations. Mexican intellectual Gustavo Esteva commented,

> Underdevelopment began, then, on January 20, 1949. On that day, two billion people became underdeveloped. In a real sense, from that time on, they ceased being what they were, in all their diversity, and were transmogrified into an inverted mirror of others' reality: a mirror that defines their identity . . . simply in the terms of a homogenizing and narrow minority.[29]

In other words, the proclamation by President Truman divided the world between those who were modern and those who were not. *Development/ modernity* became the discursive benchmark. This was a way of looking at the world, a new paradigm, suggesting that the ex-colonial world could also develop, with help.

This new paradigm inscribed First World power and privilege in the new institutional structure of the postwar international economy. In context of the Cold War between First and Second Worlds (for the hearts and resources of the ex-colonial world), "development" was simultaneously the restoration of a capitalist world market to sustain First World wealth, through access to strategic natural resources, and the opportunity for Third World countries to emulate First World civilization and living standards. Because development was both blueprint for the world of nation-states *and* a strategy for world order, we shall call this enterprise the **development project.** The epithet *project* emphasizes the political content of development, as an organizing principle rather than an end in itself.

The power of the new development paradigm arose in part from its ability to present itself as universal, natural, and therefore uncontentious—obliterating its colonial roots. In a postcolonial era, Third World states could not repeat the European experience of developing by exploiting the labor and resources of other societies. Development was modeled as a national process, initiated in European states. Its aura of inevitability devalued non-European cultures and discounted what the West learned from the non-European world. Gilbert Rist observed of postcolonial states, "Their right to self-determination had been acquired in exchange for the right to self-definition,"[30] suggesting that in choosing the Western-centered future for the world, they legitimized (or naturalized) it. Of course, each state imparted its own particular style to this common agenda, drawing on regional cultures such as African socialism, Latin American bureaucratic authoritarianism, or Confucianism in East Asia.

Ingredients of the Development Project

The development project was a political and intellectual response to the condition of the world at the historic moment of decolonization. Under these conditions, development assumed a specific meaning. It imposed an essentially economic (reductionist) understanding of social change. In this way, development could be universalized as a market culture common to all, driven by the nation-state and economic growth.

The Nation-State

The **nation-state** was to be the framework of the development project. Nation-states were territorially defined political systems based on the government–citizen relationship that emerged in nineteenth century Europe. Colonialism exported this political model (with its military shell), framing the politics of the decolonization movement, even where national boundaries made little sense. The UN Economic Commission for Africa, for example, argued in 1989 that African underdevelopment derived from its arbitrary postcolonial geography, including 14 landlocked states, 23 states with a population below 5 million, and 13 states with a landmass of fewer than 50,000 hectares each.[31] The following insert illustrates the effects of these arbitrarily drawn boundaries.

How Was Africa Divided Under Colonialism?

The colonial powers inflicted profound damage on that continent, driving frontiers straight through the ancestral territories of nations. For example, we drew a line through Somalia, separating off part of the Somali people and placing them within Kenya. We did the same by splitting the great Masai nation between Kenya and Tanzania. Elsewhere, of course, we created the usual artificial states. Nigeria consists of four principal nations: the Hausa, Igbo, Yoruba, and Fulani peoples. It has already suffered a terrible war which killed hundreds of thousands of people and which settled nothing. Sudan, Chad, Djibouti, Senegal, Mali, Burundi, and of course Rwanda are among the many other states that are riven by conflict.

Source: Quoted from Goldsmith (1994:57).

During the 1950s, certain leading African anticolonialists doubted the appropriateness of the nation-state form to postcolonial Africa. They knew that sophisticated systems of rule had evolved in Africa before colonialism. They advocated a pan-African federalism whose territories would transcend the arbitrary borders drawn across Africa by colonialism. However, decisions about postcolonial political arrangements were made in London and Paris where the colonial powers, looking to sustain spheres of influence, insisted on the nation-state as the only appropriate political outcome of decolonization. Indeed, a British Committee on Colonial Policy advised the prime minister in 1957 that, "During the period when we can still exercise control in any territory, it is most important to take every step open to us to ensure, as far as we can, that British standards and methods of business and administration permeate the whole life of the territory."[32] An African elite, expecting gains from decolonization—whether personal or national—prepared to assume power in the newly independent states. The power its members assumed was already mortgaged to the nation-state system: a vehicle of containment of political desires and of extraction of resources via European military and economic aid, investment, and trade—the paradox of sovereignty.

Pan-Africanism was unsuccessful; nevertheless, it did bear witness to an alternative political and territorial logic. Some of Guinea's rural areas were in fact attached as hinterlands to urban centers in other states, such as Dakar in Senegal and Abidjan in the Ivory Coast. Considerable cross-border smuggling today is continuing testimony to these relationships. Fierce civil wars broke out in Nigeria in the 1960s and in Ethiopia in the 1970s, states such as Somalia and Rwanda collapsed in the early 1990s and, at the birth of the twenty-first century, conflict in the Congo among armies of six different nations threatened a more general repartition of Africa. These eruptions all included ethnic dimensions, rooted in social disparities and cross-border realities. In retrospect, they suggest that the pan-African movement had considerable foresight. Ideas about the limits to the nation-state organization resonate today in new macro-regional groupings.

Economic Growth

The second ingredient of the development project was economic growth. A mandatory UN System of National Accounts institutionalized a *universal quantifiable* measure of national development. The UN Charter of 1945 proclaimed "a rising standard of living" as the global objective. This "material wellbeing" indicator is measured in the commercial output of goods and services within a country: capita gross national product (GNP), or the national average of per capita income. While per capita income was not the sole measure of rising living standards (health, literacy, etc.), the key criterion was measurable progress toward the "good society," popularized by economist and U.S. presidential adviser Walt Rostow's idea of the advanced stage of "high mass consumption."[33]

In the minds of Western economists, development required a kind of jump start in the Third World. Cultural practices of wealth sharing and cooperative labor—dissipating individual wealth, but sustaining the community—were perceived as a *traditional* obstacle to making the transition. The solution was to introduce a market system based on private property and accumulation of wealth. A range of modern practices and institutions designed to sustain economic growth, such as banking and accounting systems, education, stock markets and legal systems, and public infrastructure (transport, power sources) was required.

The use of the *economic growth* yardstick of development, however, is fraught with problems. Average indices such as per capita income obscure inequalities among social groups and classes. Aggregate indices such as rising consumption levels, in and of themselves are not accurate records of improvement in quality of life. Running air conditioners is measured as increased consumption, but it also releases harmful hydrocarbons into the warming atmosphere. Economic criteria for development have normative assumptions that often marginalize other criteria for evaluating living standards relating to the quality of human interactions, physical and spiritual health, and so on. The emphasis on converting human interactions into measurable (and taxable) cash relations discounts the social wealth of nonmonetary activities (nature's processes, cooperative labor, people growing their own food, performing unpaid household labor and community service). Wolfgang Sachs observed provocatively of early 1940s comparative statistical measurement of "economic growth,"

> As soon as the scale of incomes had been established, order was imposed on a confused globe: horizontally, such different worlds as those of the Zapotec people of Mexico, the Tuareg of north Africa, and Rajasthanies of India could be classed together, while a vertical comparison to "rich" nations demanded relegating them to a position of almost immeasurable inferiority. In this way, "poverty" was used to define whole peoples, not according to what they are and want to be, but according to what they lack and are expected to become. Economic disdain had thus taken the place of colonial contempt.[34]

Framing the Development Project

Perhaps the most compelling aspect of the development project was a powerful perception by planners, governmental elites, and citizens alike that development was destiny. Both Cold War blocs understood development in these terms, even if their respective paths of development were different. Each bloc took its cue from key nineteenth century thinkers. The West identified free-enterprise capitalism as the endpoint of development, based in Jeremy Bentham's utilitarian philosophy of the common good arising out of the pursuit of individual self-interest. Communist orthodoxy identified the abolition of private property and central planning as the goal of social development, deriving from Karl Marx's collectivist dictum: "from each according to their ability, and to each according to their needs."

Although the two political blocs subscribed to opposing representations of human destiny, they shared the same modernist paradigm. *National industrialization* would be the vehicle of development in each.

National Industrialization: Ideal and Reality

"National industrialization" had two key assumptions. First, it assumed that development involved the displacement of agrarian civilization by an urban-industrial society. For national development policy, this meant a deliberate shrinking of the agricultural population as the manufacturing and service sectors grew. It also meant the *transfer of resources* such as food, raw materials, and redundant labor from the agrarian sector as peasants disappeared and agricultural productivity grew. Industrial growth would ideally feed back and technify agriculture. These two national economic sectors would therefore condition each other's development, as in the U.S. case discussed earlier in this chapter and illustrated in Figure 2.2.

Second, the idea of national industrialization assumed a *linear direction* for development—that is, playing catch-up with the West. Soviet dictator Joseph Stalin articulated this doctrine in the 1930s, proclaiming, "We are fifty or a hundred years behind the advanced countries. We must make good this distance in ten years. Either we do it or they crush us."[35] Stalin's resolve came from the pressures of military (and therefore economic) survival in a hostile world. The Soviet Union industrialized in one generation, "squeezing" the peasantry to finance urban-industrial development with cheap food.

Across the Cold War divide, industrialization symbolized success. Leaders in each bloc pursued industrial development to legitimize their power; the reasoning was that, as people consumed more goods and services, they would subscribe to the prevailing philosophy delivering the goods and support their governments. *Development is not just a goal; it is a method of rule.*

CASE STUDY

 National Development and the Building Blocks
of the Global Economy

The Cold War compelled leaders of each bloc to accelerate economic growth to secure their rule, including economic aid and access to markets or resources. These competing spheres of influence were effectively political and economic empires.

In the Second World, Soviet self-reliant industrialization and collectivized agriculture extended to East Central Europe, to reduce Eastern Europe's traditional agricultural exports to Western Europe and to encourage industrial self-reliance. The Council for Mutual Economic Assistance (COMECON) coordinated trade among bloc members, and organized infrastructural energy projects for the bloc at large.

In the First World, integration among market economies was basic, but documents from the U.S. State Department and the Council for Foreign Relations reveal World War II plans for organizing a grand investment sphere "strategically necessary for world control," including the entire Western Hemisphere, the former British empire, and the Far East. The United States opened these areas via export credits (loans tied to imports of U.S. technology) and by encouraging foreign investment as (multinational) firms outgrew national borders.

In this way, economic integration "internationalized" domestic economies, either through patterns of foreign ownership, economic/military aid, or through the interdependence of commodity chains. But empires are based on power hierarchies—thus State Department official George F. Kennan wrote in 1948: "We have 50 percent of the world's wealth, but only 6.3 percent of its population. . . . In this situation we cannot fail to be the object of envy and resentment. . . . Our real task in the coming period is to devise a pattern of relationships which will allow us to maintain this position of disparity." The question that lies just below the surface in both the development and the globalization eras is the following: how can the empire of a superpower be reconciled with the ideals of a system of sovereign nation-states? Is it because of inequality among states, where some are more equal than others, or because an imperial power defines the rules of an unequal international order, or both?

Sources: Chomsky (1994); Kaldor (1990:62, 67); Robinson (1996:1).

The competitive—and legitimizing—dynamic of industrialization framed the development project across the Cold War divide. Third World states climbed on the bandwagon. The ultimate goal was to achieve Western levels of affluence. If some states chose to mix and match elements from either side of the Cold War divide, well and good. The game was still the same: catch-up. Ghana's first president, Kwame Nkrumah, proclaimed, "We in Ghana will do in ten years what it took others one hundred years to do."[36]

Economic Nationalism

Decolonization involved a universal nationalist upsurge across the Third World, assuming different forms in different countries depending on the configuration of social forces in each national political system. Third World governments strove to build national development states—whether centralized like South Korea, corporatist like Brazil, or decentralized and populist like Tanzania. The **development state** organizes economic growth by mobilizing money and people. It uses individual and corporate taxes, along with other government revenues such as export taxes and sales taxes, to finance public building of transport systems and to finance state enterprises such as steel works and energy exploration. And it forms coalitions to support its policies. State elites regularly use their power to accumulate wealth and influence in the state—whether through selling rights to public resources to cronies or capturing foreign aid distribution channels. As Sugata Bose remarked of the Indian state, "Instead of the state being used as an instrument of development, development became an instrument of the state's legitimacy."[37]

Import-Substitution Industrialization

Just as *political* nationalism pursued sovereignty for Third World populations, so *economic* nationalism sought to reverse the colonial division of labor—as governments encouraged and protected domestic industrialization with tariffs and public subsidies, reducing dependence on primary exports ("resource bondage").

Economic nationalism was associated with Raul Prebisch, an adviser to the Argentine military government in the 1930s. During that decade's world Depression, world trade declined and Latin American landed interests lost political power as shrinking primary export markets depleted their revenues. Prebisch proposed an industrial protection policy. Import controls reduced expensive imports of Western manufactured goods and shifted resources into domestic manufacturing.[38] This policy was adopted in the 1950s by the

UN Economic Commission for Latin America (ECLA), under Prebisch's lead as executive secretary.

Import-substitution industrialization (ISI) framed initial economic development strategies in the Third World as governments subsidized "infant industries." The goal was a cumulative process of domestic industrialization. For example, a domestic automotive industry would generate parts manufacturing, road building, service stations, and so on, in addition to industries such as steel, rubber, aluminum, cement, and paint. In this way, a local industrial base would emerge. ISI became the new economic orthodoxy in the postwar era.[39] In formally promoting economic nationalism, ironically ISI substantively resulted in encouraging direct investment by foreign firms.

States like Brazil redistributed private investment from export sectors to domestic production, establishing a development bank to make loans to investors and state corporations in such central industries as petroleum and electric power generation. When the domestic market was sufficiently large, multinational corporations invested directly in the Brazilian economy—as they did elsewhere in Latin America during this period. Latin America characteristically had relatively urbanized populations with expanding consumer markets.[40]

By contrast, the South Korean state centralized control of national development and the distribution of industrial finance. South Korea relied less on foreign investment than Brazil and more on export markets for the country's growing range of manufactured goods. Comprehensive land reforms equalized wealth among the rural population, and South Korean development depended on strategic public investment decisions that more evenly distributed wealth among urban classes and between urban and rural constituencies.

Foreign Investment and the Paradox of Protectionism

When states erected tariffs in the development era, multinational corporations hopped over and invested in local, as well as natural resource, industries. For Brazil, in 1956, foreign (chiefly U.S.) capital controlled 50 percent of the iron and rolled-metal industry, 50 percent of the meat industry, 56 percent of the textile industry, 72 percent of electric power production, 80 percent of cigarette manufacturing, 80 percent of pharmaceutical production, 98 percent of the automobile industry, and 100 percent of oil and gasoline distribution. In Peru, a subsidiary of Standard Oil of New Jersey owned the oil that represented 80 percent of national production, and Bell Telephone controlled telephone services. In Venezuela, Standard Oil produced 50 percent of the oil, Shell another 25 percent, and Gulf one-seventh. In what Peter Evans has called the "triple alliance," states such as Brazil actively brokered relationships between foreign and local firms in an attempt to spur industrial development.

Sources: de Castro (1969:241–42); Evans (1979).

To secure an expanding industrial base, Third World governments constructed political coalitions among different social groups to support rapid industrialization—such as the Latin American **development alliance**.[41] Its social constituency included commercial farmers, public employees, urban industrialists, merchants, and workers dependent on industrialization, organized into associations and unions. Policy makers used price subsidies and public services such as health and education programs, cheap transport, and food subsidies to complement the earnings of urban dwellers, attract them to the cause of national industrialization, and realize the *social contract*.

The development alliance was also a vehicle of *political patronage*, whereby governments could manipulate electoral support. Mexico's Institutional Revolutionary Party (PRI), which controlled the state for much of the twentieth century, created corporatist institutions such as the Confederation of Popular Organizations, the Confederation of Mexican Workers, and the National Confederation of Peasants to channel patronage "downward" to massage loyalty "upward." Political elites embraced the development project, mobilizing their national populations around the promise of rising living standards, and expecting economic growth to legitimize them in the eyes of their emerging citizenry.

In accounting for and evaluating the development project, this book gives greatest attention to the Western bloc, since Western affluence was the universal standard of development and modernity, and this has been extended under the guise of the globalization project to the ex-Second World following the collapse of the Soviet empire in 1989.

Summary

The idea of development emerged during, and within the terms of, the colonial era. This global hierarchy informed the understanding of development as a European achievement. Meanwhile, colonialism disorganized non-European societies by reconstructing their labor systems around specialized, and ecologically degrading, export production, and disorganizing the social psychology of colonial subjects. Exposure of non-European intellectuals, workers, and soldiers to the European liberal discourse on rights fueled anti-colonial movements for political independence.

The political independence of the colonial world gave birth to the *development project*, a blueprint for national political-economic development as well as a "protection racket," insofar as international aid, trade and investment flows were calibrated to military aid from the West to secure Cold War perimeters and make the "free world" safe for business. Third World states become at once independent, but collectively defined as "underdeveloped."

The pursuit of rising living standards, via industrialization, inevitably promoted Westernization in political, economic, and cultural terms as the non-European world emulated the European enterprise. The influential terms of the development project undercut Frantz Fanon's call for a non-European way, qualifying the sovereignty and diversity that often animated the movements for decolonization. It also rejected the pan-African insight into alternative political organization. Both of these ideas have re-emerged recently, and they have a growing audience.

The remainder of this book explores how these ideals have worked out in practice, and how they have been reformulated. The next chapter examines the development project in action.

Further Reading

Davis, Mike. *Late Victorian Holocausts: El Niño Famines and the Making of the Third World*. London: Verso, 2001.

Escobar, Arturo. *Encountering Development: The Making and Unmaking of the Third World*. Princeton, NJ: Princeton University Press, 1995.

Evans, Peter. *Dependent Development: The Alliance of Multinational, State, and Local Capital in Brazil*. Princeton, NJ: Princeton University Press, 1979.

Fanon, Frantz. *The Wretched of the Earth*. Harmondsworth, UK: Penguin, 1967.

Leys, Colin. *Underdevelopment in Kenya: The Political Economy of Neo-Colonialism*. Berkeley: University of California Press, 1975.

3

The Development Project

International Relations

W hen countries became independent nation-states, they joined the international relations of the development project. But how could a national strategy simultaneously be international?

- First, the colonial division of labor's legacy of "resource bondage" was embedded in Third World social structures, where trading classes of landowners and merchants, enriched by primary goods exports, would favor this relationship. And, of course, the First World still needed to import raw materials and agricultural goods and to market its industrial products.
- Second, as newly independent states industrialized, they purchased First World technology, for which they paid with loans or foreign exchange earned from primary exports.
- Third, nation-states formed within an international framework, with the normative, legal, and financial relationships of the United Nations (UN) and the Bretton Woods institutions integrating states into universal political-economic practices.

National economic growth depended, then, on the stimulus of these new international economic arrangements. The UN declared the 1960s and 1970s "Development Decades" to mobilize international development cooperation. In this chapter, we examine the construction of the Bretton Woods system and look at how its multilateral arrangements shaped national development strategies. We then examine the ways the development project reshaped the international division of labor.

What Are the Ingredients of the Development Project?

The development project was an internationally organized strategy for pursuing nationally managed economic growth. As colonialism collapsed, political elites of newly independent states embraced development as an enterprise for growth, revenue generation, and legitimacy. The Western experience provided the model, and an international institutional complex supplied financial and technical assistance for national development across the world, protected by Cold War military relations. Some ingredients were:

- an organizing concept with universal claims (e.g., development as rising living standards, rationality, and scientific progress);
- a national framework for economic growth;
- an international framework of aid (military and economic) binding the developing world to the developed world, and securing continuing access to its natural and human resources;
- a growth strategy favoring industrialization;
- an agrarian reform strategy encouraging agro-industrialization;
- development-state initiatives to manage investment and mobilize multi-class political coalitions into a development alliance supporting industrial growth; and
- realization of development through new inequalities, embedded in states and spread through markets along regional, class, gender, racial, and ethnic lines.

The International Framework

The pursuit of national economic growth depended on international relations, both material and political-legal. Material supports included foreign aid, technology transfer, stable currency exchange, and international trade. Aid and trade relationships followed well-worn paths between ex-colonial states and their postcolonial regions. Complementing these historic relationships were the Bretton Woods institutions and the political, military, and economic relationships of the new superpower, the United States, as it sought to contain a rival Soviet empire.

Following the severe 1930s Depression and the devastation of World War II (1939–1945), the United States spearheaded two initiatives to reconstruct the world economy: the bilateral **Marshall Plan** and the multilateral **Bretton Woods** program. The development project emerged within the Marshall Plan, formalized under the Bretton Woods program. It did not become a fully fledged operation until the 1950s, the peak decade of Third World political independence.

U.S. Bilateralism: The Marshall Plan

In the post–World War II years, the United States focused on European reconstruction as the key to stabilizing the Western world and securing capitalism. European grain harvests in 1946 would reach only 60 percent of prewar levels. Scarcity of labor skills and certain goods depleted transport and communication networks, and countless refugees posed enormous problems. There was also a growing popular desire for social reform.[1] Returning from Europe in 1947, U.S. Assistant Secretary of State for Economic Affairs Will Clayton stated,

> Communist movements are threatening established governments in every part of the globe. These movements, directed by Moscow, feed on economic and political weakness. . . . The United States is faced with a world-wide challenge to human freedom. The only way to meet this challenge is by a vast new programme of assistance given directly by the United States itself.[2]

In these political circumstances, the United States hoped to use financial aid to stabilize discontented populations and rekindle economic growth in strategic parts of the world. Central to this strategy was containing communism—primarily in Europe, where the Soviet Union had laid claim to territories east of Berlin, but also in the Far East, where communism had gained ground, first in China and then in North Korea. The United States courted nations' allegiance to the Western free enterprise system with financial assistance. In 1950, Secretary of State Dean Acheson proposed to concentrate assistance in Western Europe, to counter Soviet rule over Eastern Europe: "We cannot scatter our shots equally all over the world. We just haven't got enough shots to do that. . . . If anything happens in Western Europe the whole business goes to pieces."[3]

Meanwhile, the United Nations had organized a multilateral program of international relief. U.S. bilateral initiatives—increasingly important in the Cold War—complemented and sometimes contradicted these multilateral initiatives. The Marshall Plan was a bilateral transfer of billions of dollars to Europe and Japan, serving U.S. geopolitical goals in the Cold War. The plan restored trade and price stability, and expanded production, to undercut socialist movements and labor militancy. Dollar credits, allowing recipients to purchase U.S. goods, and a massive rearmament effort closely integrated these countries' economies with that of the United States, solidifying political loyalty to the Western "free world."

Europeans desired social peace and full employment, to be achieved through closely regulated national economies, but the U.S. government wanted an open world economy. The Marshall Plan solved this dilemma, using bilateral aid to facilitate international trade and encourage U.S. direct investment in European national economies. Since Europe ran a serious trade deficit with the United States (which imported little from Europe), an ingenious "triangular trade" was established to enable Europe to finance imported American technology and consumer goods. This arrangement enabled U.S. access to raw materials from European colonial territories, paying in dollars deposited in European accounts in London banks. From these accounts, European states financed imports from the United States. In turn, U.S. investments in colonial and postcolonial territories stimulated demand for European manufactured goods. The triangle was complete.[4]

Multilateralism: The Bretton Woods System

The idea for an international bank was part of the plan to reconstruct the world economy in the 1940s. Trade was to be restored by disbursing credit to regions devastated by war or colonialism. The famous July 1944 conference of 44 financial ministers at Bretton Woods, New Hampshire provided the opportunity to create such an international banking system. Here, the U.S. Treasury steered the conference toward chartering the foundation of the "twin sisters": the **World Bank** and the **International Monetary Fund (IMF)**.

Each institution was based on member subscriptions. The World Bank would match these subscriptions by borrowing money in international capital markets to raise money for development. The IMF was to disburse credit where needed to stabilize national currency exchanges. Once the ministers approved formation of these Bretton Woods institutions, the conference president, Henry Morgenthau, foresaw

> the creation of a dynamic world economy in which the peoples of every nation will be able to realize their potentialities in peace . . . and enjoy, increasingly, the fruits of material progress on an earth infinitely blessed with natural riches. This is the indispensable cornerstone of freedom and security. All else must be built upon this. For freedom of opportunity is the foundation for all other freedoms.[5]

These were the key sentiments of the development project: multinational universalism, viewing nature as an unlimited resource, and a liberal belief in freedom of opportunity as the basis of political development. Human satisfaction was linked to rising living standards.

The functions of the Bretton Woods agencies were as follows:

- to stabilize national finances and revitalize international trade (IMF);
- to underwrite national economic growth by funding Third World imports of First World infrastructural technologies;
- to expand Third World primary exports to earn foreign currency for purchasing First World exports.

The World Bank's mandate was to make large-scale loans to states for national infrastructural projects such as dams, highways, and power plants. These projects supported national economic integration and growth, complementing smaller scale private and public investments. In its first 20 years, two-thirds of the Bank's loans purchased inputs to build transportation and electric power systems. Indeed, its *Eleventh Annual Report* stated, "Most of the Bank's loans are for basic utilities . . . an essential condition for the growth of private enterprise." At the same time, the Bank invested in large-scale cash crop agriculture, such as cacao, rubber, and livestock, deepening the legacy of the colonial division of labor.[6]

The Bretton Woods institutions lubricated the world economy by moving funds to regions that needed purchasing power. Expanded trade stimulated economic growth across the First World–Third World divide. At the same time, these agencies disseminated the technologies of the development project, tempting Third World states to adopt the capital-intensive methods of the West. Whereas Europe had taken several centuries to industrialize, Third World governments expected to industrialize rapidly with multilateral loans, substituting capital-intensive for labor-intensive production technologies despite substantial populations already displaced from customary habitats.

The Bretton Woods system was unveiled as a universal and multilateral attempt to promote rising living standards on a global scale. Of the 45 nations in attendance at Bretton Woods, 27 were from the Third World. Nevertheless, the system had a predictable First World bias. First, control of the World Bank was dominated by the five biggest shareholders (beginning with the United States), whose representatives appointed their own executive directors to the board. The remaining seven directors represented the remaining member states. This asymmetry, including overwhelming male representation, still exists; in the 1990s, the 10 richest industrial states controlled 52 percent of the votes, and 45 African countries controlled just 4 percent of the votes. Second, the president of the World Bank is selected by the U.S. administration, and the managing director of the IMF is appointed by the largest European nations (the United Kingdom, France, and Germany).[7] Third, the Bank finances only foreign exchange costs of approved projects, encouraging import dependence (in capital-intensive technologies) in development priorities. Finally, the IMF adopted a "conditionality" requirement, requiring applicants to have economic policies that met certain criteria for them to obtain loans. International banks and other lenders inevitably adopted IMF conditionality as their loan criterion for Third World countries. In this way, Third World development priorities were tailored toward external (i.e., First World) evaluation.[8]

World Bank lending, however effective, reflected First World priorities. The Bank emphasized what were considered to be productive investments, such as energy and export agriculture, rather than social investments, such as education, health services, water and sanitation facilities, and housing. In addition, as a global agency, the Bank found it more convenient to invest in large-scale, capital-intensive projects that might, for example, have common technological inputs and similar appraisal mechanisms.[9] Not only has the Bank sponsored Western **technology transfer**, but it has also established an *institutional presence* in Third World countries. When the Bank finances infrastructural projects, these are often administered through agencies with semi-autonomous financial and political power within host countries, as the case study shows.

CASE STUDY

Banking on the Development Project

The World Bank has always been the premier global development institution. In providing loans and expertise, it has considerable influence over domestic development policy. For example, in the late 1950s, as a condition for further power loans, the Bank insisted that the Thai government establish the Electrical Generating Authority of Thailand (EGAT). EGAT then supervised a series of loans for large-scale dams, from 1964 (the Bhumibol hydroelectricity project) through the 1970s and 1980s. Thousands of Thai peasants were displaced and resettled under the terms of the dam project, often on poorer lands and at considerable cost to their livelihood. Given EGAT's semi-autonomous status, however, the agency was immune to demands for compensation by these displaced peasants. Such semi-autonomous agencies (parastatals) often override domestic political process in the name of technical efficiency.

In Malaysia, a similar parastatal, called the Federal Land Development Authority (FELDA), was created by the Bank to administer three loans between 1968 and 1973. The purpose was to finance the clearing of sections of tropical rainforest and the resettling of 9,600 families who would grow oil palms and rubber trees. By 1982, by the Bank's own account, FELDA had developed 1.3 million acres (6.5 percent of Malaysian forest cover in the 1970s) and resettled 72,600 families. And in Colombia, between 1949 and 1972, more than 70 percent of Bank loans supported such autonomous development agencies. Despite the likelihood that Bank projects would short-circuit the political process, Third World elites embraced them in the name of development. India's first prime minister, Nehru, referred to the

Bank-financed Rihand dam project as one of "the temples of modern India" in generating power for the Singrauli region, India's "Switzerland."

The question is whether the embrace of Western-style large-scale infrastructural projects was development, an instrument of legitimacy for ruling elites, or a Trojan horse for foreign interests—or all three.   🌐

Source: Rich (1994:75).

In examining how the development project issued from the Bretton Woods institutions, we have focused on the World Bank as the key multilateral agency responsible for underwriting Third World development. In addition to its parastatal influence, the Bank framed development priorities via onsite project agencies and by encouraging large-scale power generation and transport projects, stimulating industrialization on a Western scale. The Bank also channeled loans into intensive agriculture, requiring fossil fuel, energy-dependent technical inputs such as chemical fertilizers, pesticides, and hybrid seeds. In addition, it catalyzed development project norms, creating the Economic Development Institute in 1956, which trained Third World officials (soon to be prime ministers or ministers of planning or finance in their own countries) in the theory and practice of development.[10] Finally, Bank lending became a model for other multilateral banks and aid agencies, as they determined priorities for assistance.

In short, multilateralism, Bank style, characterized the Bretton Woods system—Bank policy set the parameters for development. Third World elites by and large embraced these parameters since they were in no position to present an alternative to free enterprise. When governments adopted socialist policies, loan funds rapidly dried up.

Politics of the Postwar World Order

As the realm of free enterprise expanded, the political dynamics of the Cold War deepened. While the United States and the Soviet Union were busy dividing the world, the countries of the Third World came together to assert their own international presence. We explore the interplay of all these forces in the following sections.

Foreign Aid

An examination of the patterns of Western foreign aid shows that patterns of development assistance contradicted the universalism of the development project. All states could not be equal, as some were more significant than others in the maintenance of order in the world market system. Western aid concentrated on undercutting competition from states or political movements that espoused rival (i.e., socialist) ideologies of development. Economic and military aid and trade to stabilize geopolitical regions prioritized regionally powerful states such as South Korea, Israel, Turkey, and Iran. These states functioned as military outposts in securing the perimeters of the "free world" and in preventing a "domino effect" of defections to the Soviet bloc.

Cold War rivalry governed much of the political geography of the development project. The Soviet Union was expanding economic and political relations with Third World states, especially newly independent states in Asia and Africa. Political rivalry intensified in 1956, when the Soviet Union built Egypt's Aswan Dam. This Soviet initiative followed U.S. pressure on the World Bank not to fund the project, in opposition to the "Arab socialism" of Egypt's new leader, Gamal Abdel Nasser. By 1964, the Soviet Union had extended export credits to about 30 states, even though eight received most aid. Under the Soviet aid system, loans could be repaid in local currencies or in the form of traditional exports, a program that benefited states short of foreign currency. Not only was the Soviet Union offering highly visible aid projects to key states such as Indonesia and India, but aid policies also clearly favored states pursuing policies of central planning and public ownership in their development strategies.[11]

For the United States and its First World allies, then, the development project was more than a transmission belt for Western technology and economic institutions. So long as the Third World—a vital source of strategic raw materials and minerals—was under threat from a political alternative, First World security was at stake. In 1956, this view was articulated clearly by Walt Rostow, the influential development economist:

> The location, natural resources, and populations of the underdeveloped areas are such that, should they become effectively attached to the Communist bloc, the United States would become the second power in the world. . . . Indirectly, the evolution of the underdeveloped areas is likely to determine the fate of Western Europe and Japan, and therefore, the effectiveness of those industrialized regions in the free world alliance we are committed to lead. . . . In short, our military security and our way of life as well as the fate of Western Europe and Japan are at stake in the evolution of the underdeveloped areas.[12]

The United States' foreign aid patterns between 1945 and 1967 confirm this view of the world. Yugoslavia, for instance, received considerable aid as the regional counterweight to the Soviet Union. Elsewhere, aid to geopolitically strategic states (including Iran, Turkey, Israel, India, Pakistan, South

Vietnam, Taiwan, South Korea, the Philippines, Thailand, and Laos) matched the total aid disbursement to all other Third World countries.[13]

The Non-Aligned Movement

Parallel with this world ordering was an emerging Third World perspective that advocated a more independent vision. As decolonization proceeded, the composition of the United Nations shifted toward a majority of non-European member states. In 1955, the growing weight of the Third World in international politics produced the first meeting of "nonaligned" Asian and African states at Bandung, Indonesia, forming the **Non-Aligned Movement (NAM)**. Key players were the leaders of Indonesia (Sukarno), India (Nehru), Ghana (Nkrumah), Vietnam (Ho Chi Minh), Egypt (Nasser), and China (Zhou Enlai). The NAM used its collective voice in international fora to forge a philosophy of noninterference in international relations. President Nyerere of Tanzania articulated this position in terms of economic self-reliance:

> By non-alignment we are saying to the Big Powers that we also belong to this planet. We are asserting the right of small, or militarily weaker, nations to determine their own policies in their own interests, and to have an influence on world affairs. . . . At every point . . . we find our real freedom to make economic, social and political choices is being jeopardized by our need for economic development.[14]

The subtext of this statement, following the final Bandung communiqué, involved questioning the legitimacy of the model of development embedded in the multilateral institutional order. The first bone of contention was the paucity of multilateral loans. By 1959, the World Bank had lent more to the First World ($1.6 billion) than to the Third World ($1.3 billion). Third World members of the UN pressed for expanded loans, with concessions built in, proposing that a Special United Nations Fund for Economic Development (SUNFED) perform these multilateral development functions. The First World's response was to channel this demand toward the Bank, where a new subsidiary, the International Development Association (IDA), was established to make loans at highly discounted rates (called "soft loans") to low-income countries. Between 1961 and 1971, the IDA lent $3.4 billion, representing about one-quarter of total Bank lending. In addition, several regional banks modeled on the World Bank were established— including the Inter-American Development Bank (IDB) in 1959, the African Development Bank (AfDB) in 1964, and the Asian Development Bank (ADB) in 1966.[15]

The Group of 77

International trade remained contentious. The **General Agreement on Tariffs and Trade (GATT)**, founded in 1947, enabled states to negotiate reciprocal trade concessions. Because the GATT assumed a level playing field, despite colonialism, Third World representatives saw it as discriminatory, as they were unable to make such reciprocal concessions.[16] In fact, during the 1950s, the Third World's share of world trade fell from one-third to almost one-fifth, with declining rates of export growth associated with declining terms of trade.[17]

Third World pressure, led by Latin America, founded the **United Nations Conference on Trade and Development (UNCTAD)** in 1964. UNCTAD was the first international forum at which Third World countries, formed into a caucus group called the **Group of 77 (G-77)**, collectively demanded economic reform in the world economy. They declared that reform should include stabilizing and improving primary commodity prices, opening First World markets to Third World manufactures, and expanding financial flows from the First World. Once UNCTAD was institutionalized, it served as a vehicle for Third World demands.

While UNCTAD had a limited world-economic impact, its scholar/planner members infused international agencies with a "Third Worldist" perspective. Perhaps its most concrete influence was on the World Bank under its president, Robert McNamara (1968–1981), who refocused "poverty" on quality of life issues rather than simply income measures. "Growth with equity" was the new catchcry, and for a while planners embraced the idea of investing in "basic needs," such as elimination of malnutrition and illiteracy, and reducing infant mortality. Infrastructural lending continued, but new Bank funds were directed into poverty alleviation projects, with rural development and agricultural expenditure rising from 18.5 percent of Bank lending in 1968 to 33.1 percent in 1981.[18]

We now take leave of the institutional side of the development project and examine its impact on the international division of labor.

Remaking the International Division of Labor

If the development project was an initiative to promote Third World industrialization, then it certainly had some success. The result was uneven, however, and in some respects industrialization was quite incomplete. Nevertheless, by 1980 the international division of labor had been remade, if not reversed. Overall, exports from the Third World included more manufactured goods than raw materials, and the First World was exporting 36 percent more primary commodities than the Third World.[19]

The Newly Industrializing Countries (NICs)

The average growth rate for the Third World in the 1960s was 4.6 percent; however, six Third World **newly industrializing countries (NICs)**[20] grew at rates of 7 to 10 percent.[21] These six countries were Hong Kong, Singapore, Taiwan, South Korea, Brazil, and Mexico. The rise of the NICs revealed two sides of the development project. On one hand, NICs fulfilled the expectation of rising living standards and upward mobility in the international system, *legitimizing the development project*. The other middle-income countries—especially Malaysia, Thailand, Indonesia, Argentina, and Chile—expected to follow the same path. On the other hand, the NICs also demonstrated the *selectivity* of the forces released by the development project. They cornered the bulk of private foreign investment.[22] Much of this was concentrated in developing export production facilities in textiles and electronics in South Korea, Taiwan, Mexico, and Brazil. In 1969, for instance, most of the foreign investment in electronic assembly centered on the Asian NICs—Hong Kong, South Korea, Taiwan, and Singapore.[23] Between 1967 and 1978, the share of manufactured exports from the NICs controlled by transnational corporations (TNCs) was 20 percent in Taiwan, 43 percent in Brazil, and 90 percent in Singapore.[24] Distribution of industrial growth in the Third World was also highly concentrated. Between 1966 and 1975, more than 50 percent of the increase in value of Third World manufacturing occurred in only four countries, while about two-thirds of the increase was accounted for by only eight countries: Brazil, Mexico, Argentina, South Korea, India, Turkey, Iran, and Indonesia.[25]

Across the Third World, countries and regions differed in their levels of industrialization. The manufacturing portion of the gross domestic product (GDP) in 1975 was 5 percent in Africa, 16 percent in Asia, and 25 percent in Latin America and the Caribbean.[26] By 1972, the Organisation for Economic Co-operation and Development (OECD) reported, "It has become more and more clear that measures designed to help developing countries as a group have not been effective for [the] least developed countries. They face difficulties of a special kind and intensity; they need help specifically designed to deal with their problems."[27] The idea of a universal blueprint was clearly fading.

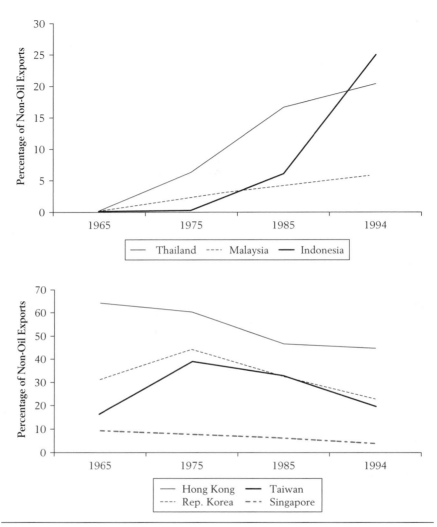

Figure 3.1   Textiles, Clothing, and Footwear Exports From Newly
Industrializing Countries

Sources: Adapted from graphs in Ransom (2001:103); data retrieved from UNCTAD (1996:118–119).

CASE STUDY

The NICs — Exceptions That Disproved the Rules?

The NICs demonstrated both the success of, and departures from, the model
of national development. Economic growth was expected to stimulate democracy, but the NICs experience compromised this. Nor were they an arbitrary

grouping of middle-income states; geopolitical relations contributed to their industrial success. In the Bretton Woods system, all states may have been equal, but some states were more equal than others in their global position.

Hong Kong and Singapore have functioned historically as *entrepôts* (port cities) in South China and the Malaccan Straits respectively. In the late twentieth-century, they served as vital centers of marketing, financial, and producer services, coordinating the regional entrepreneurial networks of the Chinese diaspora.

Within the context of the Cold War, the other four states—Taiwan, South Korea, Mexico, and Brazil—held strategic regional geopolitical positions. Their higher rates of economic growth were fueled by Western economic assistance. Military aid and preferential access to the U.S. market helped sustain authoritarian regimes that stabilized economic growth conditions through investment coordination and the political control of labor, whether repressive forms in East Asia or corporatist forms in Latin America. During the period óf maximum growth, South Korea and Taiwan garrisoned U.S. troops, given their proximity to North Korea and China respectively, and Taiwan, South Korea, Mexico, Singapore, and Brazil were distinguished by one-party or military rule. The term "bureaucratic-authoritarian industrial-izing regime" (BAIR) described this type of government. The former prime minister of Singapore, Lee Kuan Yew, justified the BAIR regime in his pater-nalistic way: "I do not believe that democracy necessarily leads to develop-ment. I believe that what a country needs to develop is discipline more than democracy. The exuberance of democracy leads to indiscipline and disor-derly conduct which are inimical to development." He may have meant that when different classes put conflicting demands on the state—industrialists seeking propitious business conditions, workers demanding higher wages, farmers requesting subsidies—ruling elites have less flexibility.

What does it mean to consider the NICs as showcases of development when their industrial success and leadership depended on conditions not exactly predicted in the development model? 🌍

Sources: Cumings (1987); *The Economist* (August 27, 1995:15).

The European First World lost its core manufacturing position in this period. Japan and a middle-income group of Third World states improved their share of world manufacturing, from 19 to 37 percent.[28] In agriculture, the Third World's share of world agricultural exports fell from 53 to 31 percent between 1950 and 1980, while the American granary consolidated its critical role in world agricultural trade.[29] By the 1980s, the United States was producing 17 percent of the world's wheat, 63 percent of its corn, and

63 percent of its soybeans; its share of world exports was 36 percent in wheat, 70 percent in corn, and 59 percent in soybeans.[30] On the other side of the globe, between 1961 and 1975 Third World agricultural self-sufficiency declined everywhere except in centrally planned Asian countries (China, North Korea, and Vietnam). In all regions except Latin America, self-sufficiency dropped below 100 percent. Africa's self-sufficiency, for instance, declined from 98 percent in 1961 to 79 percent in 1978.[31]

Two questions arise:

- Why did commercial agriculture concentrate in the First World, while manufacturing dispersed to the Third World?
- Is there a relation between these trends?

The answer lies in the political structures of the development project. While ISI protected Third World "infant" industries, farm subsidies protected First World agriculture under the terms of the GATT. These policies complemented one another via American food surplus aid mechanisms, substantially reshaping the international division of labor. Central to this process was a "food-aid regime," which demonstrated the profoundly international character of the development project as a strategy of ordering the world under the guise of promoting development.

CASE STUDY

South Korea in the Changing International Division of Labor

South Korea is arguably the most successful of the middle-income NICs, transforming its economy and society in the space of a generation. In 1953, agriculture generated 47 percent of its gross national product (GNP), whereas manufacturing generated less than 9 percent. By 1981, these proportions had switched to 16 percent and 30 percent respectively. At the same time, the contribution of heavy and chemical industries to total industrial output matured from 23 percent in 1953–1955 to 42 percent in 1974–1976. How did this happen?

South Korea depended on injections of American dollars following the Korean War in the early 1950s, as it pursued the ISI strategy. By 1973, its government's Heavy Industry and Chemicals Plan encouraged industrial maturity in shipbuilding, steel, machinery, and petrochemicals, and complemented ISI with export-oriented industrialization, beginning with labor-intensive consumer goods such as textiles and garments. From the early

1960s to the early 1980s, manufactured goods rose from 17 to 91 percent of exports, as increasingly sophisticated electronics goods emerged, and as Korean manufacturers gained access to foreign markets.

South Korea exemplifies a development state whose success depended on a rare flexibility in policy combined with the unusually repressive political system of military ruler Park Chung Hee (1961–1979). Koreans worked extremely long hours only to find their savings taxed away to support government investment policies. Industrial labor had no rights. Confucianism promoted consensus, and the authority of education and the bureaucracy, providing a powerful mobilizing cultural myth. A frontline position in the Cold War helped, as the United States opened its markets to Korean exports.

Meanwhile, cheap U.S. food exports were key. Before 1960, virtually no Western-style bread was consumed in Korea—rice is cherished, and at that time, the country was self-sufficient in food. By 1975, however, South Korea was only 60 percent food self-sufficient, and by 1978 it belonged to what the U.S. Department of Agriculture calls "the billion dollar club." That is, South Korea was purchasing $2.5 billion worth of American farm commodities, primarily wheat. The government provided free lunch bread to schoolchildren, and thousands of Korean housewives attended sandwich-making classes, financed by U.S. "counterpart funds" from its food aid program.

The South Korean farming population fell by 50 percent as urban industry attracted rural migrants. From 1957 to 1982, more than 12 million migrated to work in industrial cities like Seoul and Pusan. Rural migration, however, was not because rice farming modernized—it remained extremely small scale, retaining an average farm size of 1 hectare (2.471 acres), closely husbanded by the state with farm credit and price supports.

Since the South Korean "miracle" depended significantly on the subsidy to its industrialization strategy provided by cheap American food (lowering wage costs), and on access to U.S. markets for its manufactured exports, was its development ultimately a domestic or an international process? 🌍

Sources: Chung (1990:43); Evans (1995); Harris (1987:31–36); Wessel (1983: 172–173).

The Food-Aid Regime

In the postwar era, the United States set up a food-aid program to channel food surpluses to Third World countries. Surpluses arose out of the U.S. agro-industrial model, heavily protected by tariffs and subsidies (institutionalized in the GATT). Farmers specialized in one or two commodities (such as corn, rice, sugar, and dairy products) and, with technological support from the public purse, routinely overproduced. Farm subsidies set prices for farm goods above their price on the world market. The resulting surpluses subsidized Third World wage bills with cheap food. It was a substantial transfer of agricultural resources to the Third World urban-industrial sectors. This **food-aid regime**[32] set in motion the rural–urban prescriptions of development economists, with a difference: operating on a global, instead of a national, scale.

The Public Law 480 Program

To dispose of farm surpluses, the U.S. government instituted the **Public Law 480 Program (PL-480)** in 1954. It had three components: commercial sales on concessionary terms—discounted prices in local currency (Title I); famine relief (Title II); and food bartered for strategic raw materials (Title III). The stated goal was "to increase the consumption of U.S. agricultural commodities in foreign countries, to improve the foreign relations of the U.S. and for other purposes." By 1956, almost half of U.S. economic aid was in the form of food aid. In 1967, the U.S. Department of Agriculture reported, "One of the major objectives and an important measure of the success of foreign policy goals is the transition of countries from food aid to commercial trade."[33]

Title I sales anchored this food aid regime, accounting for 70 percent of world food aid (mostly wheat) between 1954 and 1977. By the mid-1960s, food aid accounted for one-quarter of world wheat exports, determining the prices of traded foods. Management of food surpluses stabilized prices, and this in turn stabilized two key, and mutually conditioning, parts of the development project: the American agricultural economy; and Third World government industrial plans.

Food Dependency

Under the aid program, wheat imports supplied burgeoning Third World urban populations. At the same time, governments established distribution programs to channel aid to urban consumers (and reward the so-called "development alliance" of manufacturers, labor unions, urban professionals, and middle classes). Cheap food thus supported consumer purchasing power and subsidized the cost of labor, stabilizing urban politics and improving the Third World environment for industrial investments.

The impact of food aid varied across the world, depending on the resources of particular countries and their development policies. South Korea was a success story largely because the government centralized management of its rice culture and the supply of labor to the industrial centers. By contrast, urbanization in Colombia followed the collapse of significant parts of its agriculture under the impact of food aid and commercial imports of wheat, as the government did not protect its farmers. Stimulated by the food aid program, imports of discounted wheat grew tenfold between the early 1950s and 1971, reducing by half the prices obtained by Colombian farmers. They reduced their wheat production by about two-thirds, and other food crops—such as potatoes and barley—virtually disappeared. Displaced peasants entered the casual labor force, contributing to the characteristic urban underemployment and low-wage economy of Third World countries.[34]

Between 1954 and 1974, major recipients of U.S. food aid were India, South Korea, Brazil, Morocco, Yugoslavia, South Vietnam, Egypt, Tunisia, Israel, Pakistan, Indonesia, Taiwan, and the Philippines (see Figure 3.2). Usually, it was cheaper and easier for governments to import wheat to feed their growing urban populations than to bankroll long-term improvements in the production, transportation, and distribution of local foods.[35] Food aid allowed governments to purchase food without depleting scarce foreign currency, but it built "food dependency."

Shipments of food were paid for in counterpart funds—that is, local currency placed in U.S. local bank accounts as payment—in India, for example, the United States owned over one-third of the rupee supply by the 1970s.[36] These funds could be spent only by U.S. agencies within the recipient country, on a range of activities such as infrastructural projects, supplies for military bases, loans to U.S. companies (especially local agribusiness operations), locally produced goods and services, and trade fairs. Counterpart funds were also used to promote *new diets* among Third World consumers in the form of school lunch programs and the promotion of bread substitutes. U.S. Senator George McGovern predicted in 1964,

> The great food markets of the future are the very areas where vast numbers of people are learning through Food for Peace to eat American produce. The people we assist today will become our customers tomorrow. . . . An enormous market for American produce of all kinds will come into being if India can achieve even half the productivity of Canada.[37]

Across the Third World (with the exception of Argentina), wheat importing rose from a base of practically zero in the mid-1950s to almost half of world food imports in 1971. By 1978, the Third World was receiving more than three-quarters of American wheat exports. At the same time, Third

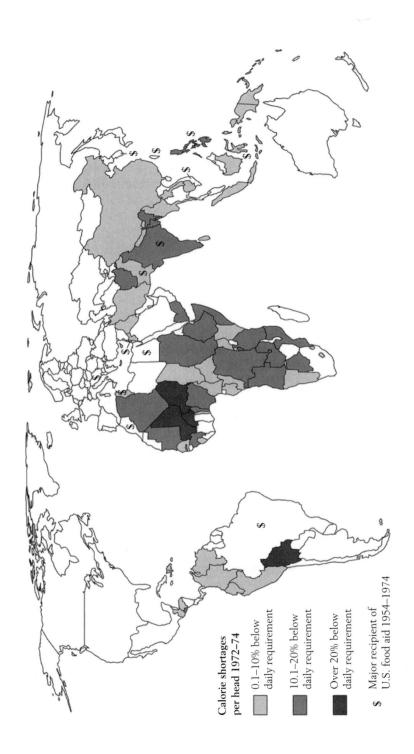

Figure 3.2   Food Shortage Regions and Food Aid Recipients

Source: Michael Kidron and Ronald Segal, *The State of the World Atlas.* London: Pan, 1981.

Calorie shortages
per head 1972–74

0.1–10% below
daily requirement

10.1–20% below
daily requirement

Over 20% below
daily requirement

$ Major recipient of
U.S. food aid 1954–1974

World per capita consumption of wheat rose by almost two-thirds, and per capita consumption of all cereals except wheat increased 20 percent while per capita consumption of traditional root crops declined by more than 20 percent.[38] In Asian and Latin American urban diets, wheat progressively replaced rice and corn. Wheat (and rice) imports displaced maize in Central America and parts of the Middle East and millet and sorghum in West Africa. Subsidized grain imports also undercut the prices of traditional starches (potatoes, cassava, yams, and taro). Thus, traditional "peasant foods" were replaced by the new "wage foods" of grains and processed foods consumed by urban workers.[39]

The rising consumption of imported wheat in Third World countries was linked to two far-reaching changes:

- the increasingly tenuous condition of peasant agriculture, as government-organized urban food markets enabled subsidized wage foods to outcompete peasant foods; and
- the expansion of an industrial labor force, as small producers (outside the agro-export sector) left the land for low-wage jobs in the rapidly growing cities.

In the conventional development model, these social trends occur within a national framework. In reality, via the development project, they occurred within an international political-economic framework as First World farmers supplied Third World industrial workers, thus remaking the international division of labor.

Remaking Third World Agricultures

The intent of the PL-480 program was to create future markets for commercial sales of U.S. grains as consumers shifted to wheat-based diets. Consumption of final products (bread) was complemented by expanding consumption of other surplus agricultural goods, such as feed grains and agricultural technology. Behind this stood the massive state-sponsored expansion in American agricultural productivity, outstripping manufacturing from the 1950s to the 1970s. Disposal of surpluses was a matter of government policy. At this point, it is important to reflect on the longer-term consequences of a short-term "food-empire" strategy. Such public support of "petro-farming"—where petroleum fuels industrial agriculture via mechanization, inorganic fertilizers, pesticides, herbicides and seed varnishes, abandoning agriculture's natural biological base—undermines nature's intrinsic ecological qualities over time. In the process, intensive agriculture annually loses 2 million acres of farm land to erosion, soil salinity, and flooding, in addition to consuming groundwater 160 percent faster than it can be replenished.[40] Marc Reisner, referring to the American West in *Cadillac Desert,* wrote: "Westerners call what they have established out here a civilization, but it would be more accurate to call it a beachhead. . . . And if history is any guide, the odds that we can sustain it would have to be regarded as low."[41] This agribusiness model remains one of the key exports stemming from the era of the development project.

The Global Livestock Complex

During the food-aid regime, surplus grain was sufficiently cheap and plentiful to feed livestock rather than people. Expanding supplies of feed grains stimulated the growth of commodity chains linking specialized feed producers with specialized animal protein producers across the world. Beyond a wheat-based diet, more affluent Third World consumers shifted up the food chain, from grain to animal protein (beef, poultry, pork, and shrimp). Such "dietary modernization" is as much the result of policy as it is the consequence of rising incomes. Beef consumption is stratified between high-end, grain-fed beef steak and low-end grass-fed hamburger for the global fast food industry, marking the class distinctions among modern consumers. The "hamburger connection" has its counterpart to petro-farming's ecological impact in deforestation. For example, between 1960 and 1990, over 25 percent of the Central American rainforest was converted to pasture for cattle which were, in turn, converted into hamburgers for an expanding fast-food industry in the United States. The contributions of beef production to global warming, via carbon dioxide, nitrous oxide and methane, are significant, as Jeremy Rifkin reminds us:

> Global warming is the inverse side of the Age of Progress. It represents the millions of tons of spent energy of the modern era. . . . Altered climates, shorter growing seasons, changing rainfall patterns, eroding rangeland, and spreading deserts may well sound the death knell for the cattle complex and the artificial protein ladder that has been erected to support a grain-fed beef culture.[42]

American grain-processing industries followed the movement of cattle from open-range feeding to grain feeding (75 percent by the early 1970s, as grass-feeding was outsourced to the Third World). The grain companies that formerly sold and processed wheat diversified into processed feeds (corn, barley, soybeans, alfalfa, oats, and sorghum) for cattle and hog feedlots as well as poultry motels. Consumption of animal protein became identified with "the American way of life," as meat accounted for one-quarter of the food bill by 1965.[43] Poultry consumption more than tripled between the 1930s and 1970, and beef consumption roughly doubled between the turn of the century and 1976.[44] Under the auspices of Marshall Plan export credits for U.S. agribusiness products, this agrifood model spread to Europe and Japan. Looking ahead, factory farms in the United States today annually produce well over 1 billion tons of manure, laden with chemicals, antibiotics, and hormones, which leach into rivers and water tables.[45] The animal protein culture—a marker of modernity—is also symbolic of the chemical technology that compromises the health of humans, animals, and the environment.

Through the food aid program, exports of feed grains also flourished as animal protein consumption spread among Third World middle classes. The U.S. Feed Grains Council routinely channeled counterpart funds into the development of local livestock and poultry industries. Loans went to more than 400 agribusiness firms to establish subsidiary operations in 31 countries and to finance trade fairs and educational programs introducing livestock feeds and feeding techniques. By 1966, feed grains were the biggest single earner of export dollars for food companies.[46] In 1969, for example, four South Korean firms entered into joint ventures with U.S. agribusinesses (including Ralston-Purina and Cargill) to acquire technical and marketing expertise. The 1970 PL-480 annual report stated these enterprises would use counterpart funds "to finance construction and operation of modern livestock feed mixing and livestock and poultry production and processing facilities. As these facilities become fully operational, they will substantially expand the market for feedgrain and other feed ingredients."[47]

CASE STUDY

Food and Class Relations

The growing feed grains trade traces changing social diets, and therefore the transformation of social structures.

Animal protein consumption reflects rising affluence as middle-class Third Worlders embraced First World diets beyond those staple (grain, primarily wheat) diets promoted directly through food aid. (Ernst) Engel's law correlated the dietary move from starch to grain to animal protein and fresh vegetables with rising incomes. Rather than reflecting individual choice and mobility, however, dietary differentiation reflects who controls production of certain foods, and how consumption patterns distribute among social classes.

Consider Egypt, where, in 1974–1975, the richest 27 percent of the urban population consumed four times as much animal protein as the poorest 27 percent. Rising incomes, complemented by U.S. and Egyptian government subsidies, fostered a switch from legumes and maize to wheat and meat products. From 1970 to 1987, livestock production outstripped crop production on an order of ten to one (1 kilogram of red meat requires 10 kilograms of grain). Egypt's grain imports exploded as it became the world's largest importer after Japan and China. Tim Mitchell notes that dependence on imported grain stems from a shift to meat consumption:

> Rather than importing animal feed directly, though, Egypt has diverted domestic production from human to animal consumption . . . the Egyptian government, supported by large American loans, has encouraged this diversion by subsidizing the import of staples for consumers, heavily taxing the production of staples by farmers, and subsidizing the production of meat, poultry and dairy products. . . . Egypt's food problem is the result not of too many people occupying too little land, but of the power of a certain part of that population, supported by the prevailing domestic and international regime, to shift the country's resources from staple foods to more expensive items of consumption.

Engel's law appears to operate globally, as different classes dine on different parts of the food chain, but the difference is an effect of the development *project*. As wealthy consumers dine "up" on animal protein, the working poor dine either on food aid grains or the low end of the food chain: low-protein starchy diets.

While it seems *natural* for those with rising incomes to consume animal protein, can we separate meat consumption from the political mechanisms and social inequalities that support such indirect consumption of feed grains, displacing direct consumption of grains and other staple foods?   🌍

Sources: Gardner and Halweil (2000); Mitchell (1991).

With livestock production expanding throughout the Third World, specialized feed grain supply zones (primarily of maize and soybeans) concentrated in the First World and in "middle-income" countries such as Brazil and Argentina. Between the late 1940s and 1988, world production of soybeans increased sixfold. At the same time, maize production was revolutionized as a specialized, capital-intensive agro-industry, outstripping the value of the world wheat trade by a factor of six.[48] A global livestock complex formed, through links, made by the grain companies, between livestock operations and crop farming elsewhere in the world.

The Green Revolution

The other major contribution to the remaking of Third World agriculture was the **green revolution**, associated with a "package" of plant-breeding agricultural technologies originally developed by the Rockefeller Foundation in Mexico—increasing production of corn, wheat, and beans in the two decades after 1943 by 300 percent—and in a combined venture with the Ford Foundation in the Philippines in the 1960s, then in tropical centers in Nigeria and Colombia. In 1971 it culminated in the formation of the Consultative Group on International Agricultural Research (CGIAR), sponsored by the Food and Agricultural Organization (FAO), the United Nations Development Program (UNDP), and the World Bank, with research facilities and gene banks across the world.[49] The green revolution was also the principal medium through which the U.S. model of chemical agriculture was introduced into the Third World—a technology transfer involving specific political choices and consequences.

Green revolution advocacy symbolized the idealized prescriptions of the development project, with its focus on output, despite known social and ecological consequences.[50] However interpreted, the U.S. consequences included displacement of millions of rural Americans as landholdings concentrated and corporate farming took over, converting family farmers to "contract farmers" dependent on chemical inputs and corporate processors. In the development narrative, rural population shrinkage is inevitable as agriculture "modernizes." The question is: why shrink rural populations in historical settings where they were so predominant, meaning where industry was either capital-intensive or not extensive, or both? The social fact of slumdwellers comprising nearly 50 percent of the twenty-first century Third World population gives credence to this question.

"Productivism" has been a central development theme. It was promoted heavily by the U.S. land-grant university system, with an extension program geared to a model of commodity-specific research, supporting large, capitalized farmers.[51] Within the development project, the "entire argument for increasing yields was framed by the specter of increasing population." This argument lent moral and political legitimacy to a technological solution (despite the consequences), it represented population as an independent variable (we have seen how the case study of Egypt questions this) and, finally, the green revolution program appealed to "economic nationalism," a central ingredient of developmentalism at the time.[52]

Even more compelling were the political implications of the Chinese model where, following the 1949 communist revolution, about 45 percent of total cultivated land monopolized by landlords was redistributed to small and landless peasants. Collectivization of land mobilized underemployed surplus labor and investment in water management and local enterprises, and extended basic health and rural education through a decentralized process supplemented with central government assistance—albeit with a goal of squeezing agriculture to finance industrial growth and centralized administration.

In this period, much of "China's good growth, reduction in rural poverty and excellent performance on the human development indicators can be traced to the initial egalitarian land reform."[53] Whether or not this vast social experiment ultimately succeeded, the Chinese model loomed large in countries like India, where Prime Minister Nehru said: "We know for a fact that some other countries have rapidly increased their food production in the last few years without any tremendous use of fertilizers. How has China done it? China's resources in this respect are not bigger than ours. China is at the same time laying greater stress on industrial development and heavy industry than we are. Surely it should not be beyond our power to do something China can do."[54] However, institutional reforms desired by the Indian central government required compliance by state governments, generally dominated by landlords and merchants unfavorable to land reform and labor cooperatives. The revolution would change color, from red to green.

Meanwhile, the United States, with its counterpart funds, was encouraging India to substitute green revolution technology for land redistribution. In 1965 the *New York Times* commented, "To prod developing countries in the right direction . . . India is already being told, for instance, that loans and grants from the Agency for International Development for economic development as well as for Food for Peace shipments will depend in part on the amount of foreign exchange she sets aside each year for fertilizer imports or the equivalent in new fertilizer plants."[55] Pressure to extend chemical agriculture stemmed from the conversion of wartime nitrogen production (for bombs) to inorganic fertilizer, displacing nitrogen-fixing legumes and manure, and the development of insecticides, stemming from World War I nerve gases, with advances in petroleum refining and organic chemistry.[56]

"Petro-farming"—marrying the chemical industry with the energy sector—both enabled and encouraged proliferation of green revolution technology, with the FAO (in the name of the UN's Freedom from Hunger campaign), providing extension services for the disposal of surplus inorganic fertilizer across the Third World, intensifying agricultural dependence on the energy sector.[57] This political choice has been explained thus: "it was not that native crop varieties were low yielding inherently. The problem with indigenous seeds was that they could not be used to consume high doses of chemicals. The Green Revolution seeds were designed to overcome the limits placed on chemically intensive agriculture by the indigenous seeds."[58]

The new high-yielding varieties (HYVs) of hybrid seeds were heavily dependent on disease- and pest-resisting chemical protections in the form of fungicides and pesticides. Intensive irrigation and fertilization were necessary to optimize macro-nutrient yields, eliminating traditional leafy greens (micro-nutrients such as vitamin A) now redefined as "weeds" and targeted by herbicides. The HYVs promoted industrial farming, geared to producing "wage foods" for urban consumers, displacing agro-ecological methods of crop-rotation, geared to "peasant foods," and compromising soil fertility. In 1984, an Indian farmer commented on the stronger, healthy soils promoted by manure-based fertilizer: "chemical fertilizer makes the crop shoot up . . . whereas organic manure makes for strength. Without strength, no matter how much fertilizer you put, the field won't give output; this is what we have determined from experience."[59] The hybrid seed ruptured the ecological cycle of natural regeneration and renewal, replacing it with linear flows of purchased inputs and commodified outputs, and incorporating farmers into the "chemical treadmill."[60] Long-term social and ecological impacts have been blamed for as many as 100,000 farmer suicides in India between 1993 and 2003.[61]

CASE STUDY

The Green Revolution and "Development Subjectivity"

One of the underexplored dimensions of development is the way people experience it, and why development has so much appeal beyond the legitimizing role it serves for political-economic elites. Most studies, including this one, foreground the social-structural changes, leaving changes in systems of thought and subjectivity in the background. This is perhaps because of the ingrained rationalism of the categories through which we conceptualize the world, categories such as "market," "class," "peasant," and "urban" that sociologize individuals and their relationships.

In examining the adoption of green revolution technology in the Colombian coffee industry, Christopher London shows how coffee growers rethink their subjective identity in the process of technification of coffee production. London's archetype grower, Santiago Mejía, reproduces in his production practices and in his self-understanding the essential ingredients of the conception of development advocated by the National Federation of Coffee Growers of Colombia (FEDECAFE). In an interview, Mejía expresses the shift in his beliefs, devaluing farming with the traditional coffee variety, *pajarito*, now that he has adopted the scientific practices of FEDECAFE-style technification:

Before . . . [we planted] *pajarito* because there wasn't any other more productive variety, so indisputably it had to be the one we used. What else could a coffee grower sow? . . . One cultivated *pajarito* in a rustic manner, rudimentary, with whatever resources one happened to have because he didn't have anyone who could say "we have a much better system," or that "it's already been tested and proved" like the extension agents do. . . . So, for that reason we and our grandfathers had to do it that way because it was the first thing that appeared. But as all things evolve so one has to be in agreement with development.

London observes that, in embracing the new agricultural technology, the grower embraces, to a greater or lesser extent, the modern mentality, where "his own past . . . is seen as being primitive and better for having been left behind. One has to be in agreement with development."

While there are powerful institutions such as the state, development agencies, the market, and private property that shape the possibilities and understandings of development, under what conditions do subjects either accept official versions of development or reject them as forms of rule and explore alternative practices of development?

Source: London (1997).

The expansion of green revolution agriculture embodied the two sides of the development project: the national and the international. From a *national* perspective, governments sought to improve agricultural productivity and the delivery of maize, wheat, and rice to urban centers. In the context of the food-aid regime, this *import-substitution* strategy either supplemented food aid or complemented its competitive effects on local farmers. The green revolution produced dramatic yields, but they have been highly concentrated in a few ecologically advantaged regions of the Third World. Asia and, to a much lesser degree, Latin America have captured the benefits from the new grain varieties, while Africa has charted few gains. Maize, emphasized early, was not a very successful green revolution crop. The major wheat-producing countries in the Third World—India, Argentina, Pakistan, Turkey, Mexico, and Brazil—planted the bulk of their wheat acreage in the new hybrid varieties, accounting for 86 percent of the total green revolution wheat area by the 1980s. Meanwhile, six Asian countries—India, Indonesia, the Philippines, Bangladesh, Burma, and Vietnam—were cultivating more than 87 percent of the rice acreage attributed to the green revolution by the 1980s. Because little commercial wheat or rice is grown in much of Africa, the green revolution largely bypassed that continent, even as Africa experienced soaring imports of wheat, to complement dietary changes among the affluent classes.[62]

From an *international* perspective, the food aid program helped to spread green revolution technology. Counterpart funds routinely promoted agribusiness and green revolution technologies, complemented with loans from institutions such as the United States Agency for International Development (USAID) and the World Bank.[63] These agencies aimed to weave First World agricultural technologies into Third World commercial farming.

The green revolution was realized through the increase of rural income inequalities. In parts of Latin America, such as Mexico, Argentina, Brazil, and Venezuela, as well as in irrigated regions of India (Punjab and Haryana), this high-input agriculture nurtured processes of economic differentiation among, and often within, farming households. Within households, typically women have less commercial opportunity. Hybrid seeds and supporting inputs had to be purchased; to buy them, participants needed a regular supply of money or credit. Women, particularly poor women, tended to be excluded—not only because of the difficulty of obtaining financing but also because of institutional traditions in extension traditions of transferring technology to male heads of households.

Among farming households, the wealthier ones were more able to afford the package—and the risk—of introducing the new seed varieties. They also prospered from higher grain yields, often with easier access to government services than their poorer neighbors who lacked the political and economic resources to take full advantage of these technologies.

The rising incomes and higher yields of the wealthier households give them a competitive advantage over their poorer neighbors. Rising land values often hurt tenant farmers by inflating their rent payments, forcing them to rent their land to their richer neighbors or to foreclose to creditors. Finally, the mechanical and chemical technologies associated with the green revolution either reduce farmhand employment opportunities for poor or landless peasants (where jobs were mechanized) or degrade working conditions where farmhands are exposed to toxic chemicals, such as herbicides.[64]

Antirural Biases of the Development Project

Within the framework of the development project, Third World governments strove to feed growing urban populations cheaply, for political support, for lowering wages, and for national security. The term **urban bias** has been coined to refer to the systematic privileging of urban interests, from health and education services through employment schemes to the delivery of food aid.[65] This bias was central to the construction of development alliances based in the cities of the Third World. But it also expressed the modernist belief in peasant redundancy.

Urban bias did not go unnoticed in the countryside, which was neither silent nor passive. Growing rural poverty, rural marginalization, and persistent peasant activism over the question of land distribution put **land reform** on the political agenda in Asia and Latin America. When the Cuban Revolution redistributed land to poor and landless peasants in 1959, land reforms swept Latin America. Between 1960 and 1964, Brazil, Chile, Costa Rica, the Dominican Republic, Ecuador, Guatemala, Nicaragua, Panama, Peru, and Venezuela all enacted land reforms. The Alliance for Progress (1961)—a program of nationally planned agrarian reform coordinated across Latin America—provided an opportunity for the United States to support land reforms as part of a strategy to undercut radical insurgents and stabilize rural populations. Land reforms attempted to reproduce the American family farm model, first introduced in the late 1940s in East Asia, at that time under occupation by U.S. military forces. These land reforms were a model in two senses: first, as interventions to quell peasant militancy; and second, as a method of reducing tenancy and promoting smallholder owner occupancy.[66]

The land reform movement, however, focused on redistributing land not already absorbed into the agribusiness complex. In effect, the reforms exempted commercialized farmland and dealt with what was left, including frontier lands. Indeed, alongside the strengthening of the agribusiness sector, considerable "re-peasantization" occurred during this period. In Latin America, two-thirds of the additional food production between 1950 and 1980 came from frontier colonization, and the number of small farmers with an average of two hectares of land grew by 92 percent. Overall, arable land increased by as much as 109 percent in Latin America and 30 percent in Asia but possibly declined in Africa.[67] Resettlement schemes on frontiers, including forests, were typically financed by the World Bank, especially in Indonesia, Brazil, Malaysia, and India, and they usually privileged males, as household heads—"one of the principal mechanisms of exclusion of women as direct beneficiaries."[68] These strategies sometimes simply relocated rural poverty and resembled "a war against the earth's rapidly dwindling tropical forests." In Brazil between 1960 and 1980, for example, roughly 28 million small farmers were displaced from the land by the government's sponsorship of industrial farming to enhance foreign exchange earnings from agricultural exports, notably soy products. The displaced farmers spilled into the Amazon region, burning the forest to clear new and often infertile land.[69]

Persistent rural poverty through the 1960s highlighted the urban bias of the development project. At this point, the World Bank devised a new poverty alleviation program, a multilateral scheme to channel credit to smallholding peasants and purportedly to stabilize rural populations where previous agrarian reforms had failed or been insufficient. The Bank itself acknowledged that almost half of its 82 agricultural projects between 1975 and 1982 were unsuccessful in alleviating poverty. Instead, the outcomes included leakage of credit funds to more powerful rural operators, displacement of hundreds of millions of peasants, and the incorporation of surviving peasant smallholders, via credit, into commercial cropping at the expense of basic food farming.[70]

The lesson we may draw from this episode of reform is that neither the resettlement of peasants nor their integration into monetary relations is always a sustainable substitute for supporting agro-ecological methods that preserve natural cycles of regeneration of land, water, and biodiversity. The assumptions of the development project heavily discriminated against the survival of peasant culture, as materially impoverished as it may have seemed.

Through a combination of food dumping, and institutional support of commercial and export agriculture, the long-term assault on peasant agriculture begun in the colonial era has intensified. Priority given to import and production of "wage foods"—stressing soil fertility and hydrological cycles—undermines the viability of household food production as a livelihood strategy for peasants and a subsistence base for the rural poor. The result has been a swelling migration of displaced peasants to overcrowded urban centers of Latin America, Asia, and Africa, creating a "planet of slums."[71]

Summary

The development project was multilayered, as national strategies of economic growth dovetailed with international programs of multilateral and bilateral assistance. The Third World *as a whole* was incorporated into a *singular* project, despite national and regional variations in available resources, starting point, and ideological orientation.

Military and economic aid programs shaped the geopolitical contours of the "free world," integrating Third World countries into the Western orbit. They also shaped patterns of development through technological transfer and food subsidies to industrialization programs. Food aid was significant in securing geopolitical alliances as well as in reshaping the international division of labor. As development economists predicted, Third World industrialization depended on the transfer of rural resources. But this transfer was not confined to national arenas, as exports of First World food and agricultural technology constituted a *global* rural–urban exchange.

The international dimension is as critical to our understanding of the development processes during the postwar era as is the variety of national forms. We cannot detail such variety here, and that is not the point of this story. Rather, the focus is on understanding how the development project set in motion a *global* dynamic that embedded national policies within an international institutional and ideological framework. This framework was theoretically in the service of national economic growth policies. But on closer examination, the reverse was also true. Social changes within Third World countries put their own local face on what was ultimately a common global process of development embedded in unequal relations, and technology transfer, between the First and Third Worlds.

In this chapter, we have examined one such example of these transfers, and we have seen how they condition the rise of new social structures. First World agricultural expansion was linked with the rise of new industrial classes in the Third World. At the same time, the export of green revolution technology to Third World regions stimulated social differentiation among men and women and among rural producers, laborers, and capitalist farmers. Those peasants unable to survive the combined competition of cheap foods and high-tech farming in the countryside migrated to the cities, further depressing wages. Not surprisingly, this scenario stimulated a massive relocation of industrial tasks to the Third World, reshaping the international division of labor. This is the subject of Chapter 4.

Further Reading

Gupta, Akhil. *Postcolonial Developments: Agriculture in the Making of Modern India*. Durham, NC: Duke University Press, 1998.
Kloppenburg, Jack R., Jr. *First the Seed: The Political Economy of Plant Biotechnology, 1492–2000*. Cambridge, UK: Cambridge University Press, 1988.
Rich, Bruce. *Mortgaging the Earth: The World Bank, Environmental Impoverishment and the Crisis of Development*. Boston: Beacon, 1994.

Select Websites

Consultative Group on International Agricultural Research (CGAIR): www.cgiar.org
Food and Agriculture Organization (FAO), UN: www.fao.org
International Monetary Fund (IMF): www.imf.org
United Nations Conference on Trade and Development (UNCTAD): www.unctad.org
The World Bank: www.worldbank.org

PART II

From National Development to Globalization

4

Globalizing National Economy

The development project promised rising standards of living, based in producing "national products" in an industrializing economy linking national manufacturing and agricultural sectors. The development state would partner private enterprise, assisted by multilateral and bilateral aid. But aid programs were more than simply complementary to national economies. In promoting technology transfer, trade in goods and services, and foreign investment, aid programs also constructed global economic relations woven into national economic spaces. Recall that the "economic nationalism" of the development project was an ideal, not a guarantee. The conversion of segments of domestic production to export production deepened the participation of national economies in the world market. This chapter focuses on the socioeconomic dimensions of this transformation, which continues today (therefore some accounts are quite contemporary). It is part of a two-chapter transition in the storyline of this book—from development to globalization project and beyond. The following chapter, on the debt crisis, explores the political dimensions of this transformation.

The development project was about reconstructing a world market, albeit subordinated to the development concerns of nation-states. The Cold War marked the rise of an American-centered world economy in which U.S. governments deployed military and economic largesse to secure an informal empire as colonialism receded. With the West focused on *containing* Soviet and Chinese power, the development project settled on the twin economic foundations of *freedom of enterprise* and the U.S. dollar as the *international currency*. Bilateral disbursements of dollars wove together the principal national economies of the West and Japan and, as the dollar source, the U.S. Federal Reserve System led those countries' central banks in regulating an international monetary system.[1]

Within this arrangement, Third World political elites pursued national development targets shaped by geopolitical security concerns, expressed in substantial military and financial aid packages. Countries differed in their resource endowments and their political regimes—ranging from military dictatorship to one-party states to parliamentary rule. Nonetheless, despite a vision of convergence through development, divergent forces soon appeared. These included a growing, rather than diminishing, gap between First and Third World living standards and a substantial differentiation among states within the Third World, as the newly industrializing countries "took off." *In combination,* these divergent developments signaled a deepening integration of production relations across, rather than within, nation-states. The development "fast track" was emerging in the web of economic relations across national borders as a new form of global economy emerged, leaving the national experiment behind.

Third World Industrialization in Context

The rise of the NICs appeared to confirm that the colonial legacy was in retreat and that industrialization would inevitably expand into the Third World. Each of the NICs, with some variation, moved through low-value industries (processed foods, clothing, toys) to higher-value industries (steel, autos, petrochemicals, machinery). Whereas the Latin American NICs (Mexico and Brazil) began the early phase in the 1930s, graduating to the more mature phase in the 1950s, the Asian NICs (Taiwan and South Korea) began manufacturing basic goods in the 1950s and did not upgrade until the 1970s. The other regional variation was that the Asian NICs financed their import-substitution industrialization (ISI) via the export of labor-intensive products because they lacked the resource base and domestic markets of the Latin NICs.[2]

With the exception of Hong Kong, most of the NICs had strong development states guiding public investment into infrastructure development and industrial ventures with private enterprise. The South Korean state virtually dictated national investment patterns.[3] Industrialization depended on the size of domestic markets as well as access to foreign exchange for purchasing First World capital equipment technologies. As technological rents rose, Latin NICs adopted the **export-oriented industrialization (EOI)** model of the Asian NICs to earn foreign exchange.

Widespread EOI signaled a significant change in strategies of industrialization, increasingly organized by TNC investment and marketing networks. For First World firms, EOI became a means of relocating the manufacturing of consumer goods, and then machinery and computers, to the Third World. Third World states welcomed the new investment with corporate concessions and a ready supply of cheap, disorganized labor. At the same time, First World consumption intensified with easy credit and a mushrooming of shopping malls and fast food in the 1970s. The *global consumer* and the *global labor force* reproduced each other.[4]

Third World manufacturing exports outpaced the growth in world manufacturing trade during this period, increasing their share of world trade from 6 to 10 percent between 1960 and 1979. The NICs accounted for the bulk of this export growth, its composition broadening from textiles, toys, footwear, and clothing in the 1960s to more sophisticated exports of electronics and electrical goods (First World bound), as well as machinery and transport equipment (Third World bound), by the 1970s.[5] Asian NIC development was achieved by rooting industrialization in the world economy. Thus,

> Mexico, Brazil, Argentina, and India . . . accounted for over 55% of all Third World industrial production but only about 25% of all Third World manufactured exports (narrowly defined). Hong Kong, Malaysia, Singapore and South Korea . . . were responsible for less than 10% of Third World production but 35% of all Third World manufactured exports (narrowly defined).[6]

The Asian NICs' export orientation was exceptional for geopolitical reasons. First, the East Asian perimeter of the Pacific Ocean was a strategic zone in the Cold War security system. Military alliances opened U.S. markets to exports, often of goods assembled for U.S. corporations. Second, Japan's historic trade and investment links with this region deepened as Japanese firms invested in low-wage assembly production offshore. In each case, the Asian NICs reaped the benefits of access to the near-insatiable markets of the United States and Japan. The global and regional contexts have been as influential in their growth as domestic policy measures and economic cultures.

The World Factory

The expanding belt of export industries in the Third World, led by the NICs, provides a clue to a broader transformation occurring within the world at large. There was a new "fast track" in manufacturing exports, superseding the traditional track of exporting processed resources. It heralded the rise of the **world factory**: proliferating export platforms producing *world*, rather than national, products. Often, the production steps are separated and distributed among geographically dispersed sites in assembly-line fashion, producing and assembling a completed product. World products (automobiles, cell phones, computers, jeans, or electronic toys) emerge from a single site or a global assembly line of multiple sites organizing disparate labor forces of varying skill, cost, and function.[7]

The phenomenal growth of export manufacturing using labor-intensive methods in the East Asian region, as well as regions such as Mexico's border-industrial zone, signaled the rise of *a global production system*. In Asia, the stimulus came from the relocation of the Japanese industrial model of hierarchical subcontracting arrangements to sites across the region. The Mexican Border Industrialization Program (BIP) paralleled this "decentralization" of industrial production, whereby unfinished components would come to this new industrial enclave for assembly to be sold on the world market as a world product. In 1965, the Mexican government implemented the BIP to allow entirely foreign-owned corporations to establish labor-intensive assembly plants (known as *maquiladoras*) within a 12 mile strip south of the border. Concessions to firms employing Mexican labor at a fraction of U.S. wages and paying minimal taxes and import duties to the Mexican government were part of a competitive world factory strategy. In 1967, the Mexican minister of commerce stated, "Our idea is to offer an alternative to Hong Kong, Japan, and Puerto Rico for free enterprise."[8] The *maquiladoras* earn about one-third of Mexico's scarce foreign currency income.

U.S. firms establishing assembly plants in the BIP concentrated on garments, electronics, and toys. By the early 1970s, 70 percent of the operations were in electronics, following a global trend of U.S. firms relocating electronic assembly operations to southern Europe, South Korea, Taiwan, and Mexico, seeking low-cost labor in response to Japanese penetration of the transistor radio and television market. The 168 electronics plants established by 1973 on the Mexican border belonged to firms such as General Electric, Fairchild, Litton Industries, Texas Instruments, Zenith, RCA, Motorola, Bendix, and National Semiconductor. There were also 108 garment shops, sewing swimsuits, shirts, golf bags, and undergarments; some subsidiaries of large companies such as Levi Strauss; and other small sweatshops (unregulated workplaces) subcontracted by the large retailers.[9]

The cost calculus driving the relocation of manufacturing to the Third World includes avoidance of stringent environmental regulations. Over a quarter of factory operators in the city of Mexicali, close to the California border, cited Mexico's lax environmental enforcement as a condition of relocation. The impact is both physical and environmental. Electronics factories commonly include open containers of carcinogenic acids and solvents, emitting toxic fumes; this results in chronic illness, such as headaches, sore throat, and drowsiness, among the workforce. California's Silicon Valley includes 29 sites listed on the Environmental Protection Agency's Superfund list of most contaminated toxic dumps—such environmental hazards accompany the world-scale proliferation of semiconductor manufacturing. Chemical discharges from *maquiladoras,* into open ditches adjacent to shantytowns have been linked to cancer, birth defects, and brain damage, and factories in EPZs have been associated with the dumping of pollutants into local waters, affecting drinking water and fisheries.[10]

CASE STUDY

The Chinese World Factory

Looking ahead to the present, China has become perhaps the prime location for the "world factory." The government anticipated this development by establishing "special economic zones" (SEZs) in coastal regions in the 1980s to attract foreign investment. By the mid-1990s, when the East Asian NICs had emerged as "middle-income countries" with relatively high-skilled labor forces, China was the preferred site for foreign investors—especially Korean and Taiwanese investors, with rising labor costs at home. In 1995, the ratio of factory wages in China to South Korea/Taiwan to Japan was approximately 1:30:80.

In her investigations of shoe factories (such as Reebok and Nike) in Dongguan City, sociologist Anita Chan observes that vast concrete industrial estates have mushroomed on former rice paddies. Local farmers now live off the rents from the factories, while tens of thousands of migrants from China's poorer hinterland swell the low-wage workforce. Twelve-hour shifts (with enforced overtime) and seven-day workweeks are common, with managers using militaristic methods to break in and control the migrant labor force (in addition to requiring a deposit of two to four weeks' wages and confiscation of migrant ID cards). Between 1980 and 2001, 380,000 foreign-owned exporting plants were established in China, as the Chinese proportion of world exports from such plants grew from 1 percent to almost 50 percent, and China became synonymous with the "world factory."

Today China produces about half of the world's shoes and a proliferating array of electronic items, toys, and garments for the global economy. While this may appear to be China's "industrial revolution," to the extent that a substantial portion is export manufacturing, it is also a global industrial revolution. And, to the extent that this global industrial revolution depends on a moving belt of world factories (from Hong Kong to Mexico, to China, and now to Vietnam, India, and Bangladesh), including labor and capital-intensive work, the notion of a national "development ladder" is rendered increasingly problematic, especially as this "world factory" model depends on disposable labor (expendable generations of young women). Even if some foreign manufacturers integrate with local firms, surpassing simple processing, how can we square such "development" with the human casualties from the sweatshops along the way?

Sources: Boyd (2006); Chan (1996:20); Faison (1997:D4); Greider (2001); Myerson (1997); Perrons (2005); Sachs (2005).

The global proliferation of low-wage assembly marked the strategic use of export platforms chiefly in the Third World by competing TNCs from the United States, Europe, and Japan and, later, from some Third World countries. As these companies seek to reduce their production costs to enhance their global competitiveness, so export platforms have spread. Thus the NICs' strategy of export-oriented industrialization sparked the world factory phenomenon: from sweatshops in Los Angeles to subcontractors in Bangladesh, Ireland, Morocco, and the Caribbean.

The Strategic Role of Information Technologies

The world factory system is nourished by the technologies of the "information age." Especially important in the latest of these revolutions is the semiconductor industry. Semiconductors—notably the integrated computer chip—are the key to the new information technologies that undergird the accelerating globalization of economic relations. Advances in telecommunication technologies enable firms headquartered in global cities such as New York, London, or Tokyo to coordinate production tasks distributed across sites in several countries. Information technologies allow rapid circulation of production design blueprints among subsidiaries, instructing them in retooling their production to accommodate changing fashion or reorganize production methods in their offshore plants. Thus we find **global assembly lines** stretching from California's Silicon Valley or Scotland's Silicon Glen to assembly sites in Taiwan, Singapore, Malaysia, or Sri Lanka.[11] What *appears* to be an expansion of industrial exporting, from a national (accounting) perspective, is increasingly a globally organized production system. As participants in global assembly lines, nations may specialize in producing just airplane wings, or automobile dashboards, or shoe soles, or buttonholes. And, to the extent that the export platforms are substitutable, nationally located production loses permanence.

How has this come about? Microelectronics. This was a leading industry in establishing the world factory, given the low skill in much electronic assembly and the dispersion of electronics *production* to export platforms across the world. In turn, electronic *products* such as computers and digital telecommunications technology enable the global dispersion and coordination of production and circulation in other industries, from banking to textiles to automobiles. Thus information technology globalizes the production of goods and services, in both senses. In particular, it has enabled the proliferation of the **export processing zone (EPZ)**.

The Export Processing Zone

Export processing zones, or free trade zones (FTZs), are specialized manufacturing export estates with minimal customs controls, and they are usually exempt from labor regulations and domestic taxes. EPZs serve firms seeking lower wages and Third World governments seeking capital investment and foreign currency to be earned from exports. The first EPZ appeared at Shannon, Ireland in 1958; India established the first Third World EPZ in 1965 and, as early as the mid-1980s, roughly 1.8 million workers were employed in a total of 173 EPZs around the world. By the century's end, more than 800 EPZs employed millions of workers.[12]

The dynamics of EPZs run counter to the development project since they favor export market considerations over the development of domestic markets (local production capacity and consumption). Export processing zones typically serve as *enclaves*—in social as well as economic terms. Often physically separate from the rest of the country, walled in with barbed wire, locked gates and special security guards, EPZs are built to receive imported raw materials or components and to export the output directly by sea or air. Workers are either bused in and out daily or inhabit the EPZ under a short-term labor contract. Inside the EPZ, whatever civil rights and working conditions that hold in the society at large are usually denied the workforce. As noted in 1983, "Free trade zones . . . mean more freedom for business and less freedom for people."[13] It is a workforce assembled under conditions analogous to those of early European industrial history to enhance the profitability of modern, global corporations.

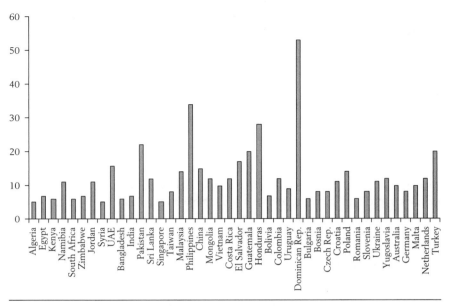

Figure 4.1   Number of EPZs by Selected Country, 2003

Source: International Labor Organization (ILO, 2003).

Export processing zones provided an early portal for Third World women to enter the global workforce, just as English and American farm girls staffed the textile mills in the initial Industrial Revolution. The new "factory girls" earned in one week approximately what their First World counterparts earned in one hour. In the early 1980s, 80–90 percent of zone workers were female, between 16 and 25 years old. Women were regarded as best suited to the tasks because of their "natural patience" and "manual dexterity"—a personnel manager of a Taiwanese assembly plant claimed, "Young male workers are too restless and impatient to be doing monotonous work with no career value. If displeased, they sabotage the machines and even threaten the foreman. But girls, at most they cry a little."[14] Appealing to Orientalist perceptions on the part of Western manufacturers, a Malaysian investment brochure stated, "The manual dexterity of the oriental female is famous the world over. Her hands are small and she works fast with extreme care. Who, therefore, could be better qualified by nature and inheritance to contribute to the efficiency of a bench-assembly production line than the oriental girl."[15] On balance, much of the world's now 27 million strong EPZ labor force has comprised women.[16] Between 1975 and 1995, garment production spawned 1.2 million jobs in Bangladesh, with women taking 80 percent (with considerable impact on Islamic culture). In 1998, the International Labor Organization estimated 2,000 EPZs employed 27 million workers, 90 percent of whom were female. In Mexico, young women accounted for roughly 78 percent of the *maquiladora* workforce in 1979, some 85 percent in the mid-1990s, and 54 percent in 2004.[17] The shifting gender proportions of the labor force (here, "defeminization") mark the generalization of the *maquila* system throughout Mexico, with upgrading of work beyond simple assembly, and higher proportions of female workers in simple assembly zones (Indonesia, Mauritius, Tunisia, Sri Lanka, and the Philippines).[18] The construction of global assembly work on the foundation of a feminized labor force nevertheless remains a constant, as sweatshops cycle through countries in search of lower wages and appropriate location. Absent rights and regulations render such labor vulnerable to super-exploitation, with employees often being forced to work overtime (sometimes up to 48 hours) to meet rush orders, under debilitating conditions. The following description of a worker at an electronics *maquiladora* near Tijuana captures the conditions of sweatshop labor.

> Her job was to wind copper wire on to a spindle by hand. It was very small and there couldn't be any overlap, so she would get these terrible headaches. After a year some of the companies gave a bonus, but most of the girls didn't last that long, and those that did had to get glasses to help their failing eyes. It's so bad that there is constant turnover.[19]

While sweatshops may register on some indicators of development, Raquel Grossman notes that retirement from failing eyesight leaves such young women betwixt and between the factory culture and their previous life, compelled to work in the "entertainment industry," whether in bars and restaurants, or the sex trade.[20]

The foreign companies that employ EPZ workers obtain concessions, such as free trade for imports and exports, infrastructural support, tax exemptions, and locational convenience for re-export. For example, for *maquila* investment in Sonora, one of the poorest border states, the Mexican government's most favorable offer was 100 percent tax exemption for the first 10 years and 50 percent for the next 10.[21] In short, the EPZ is typically an island in its host country, separated from domestic laws and contributing little to the host economy, other than mostly dead-end jobs and foreign currency earned via export taxes levied by host states. It belongs instead to an archipelago of production sites across the world (concentrated in Latin America, the Caribbean, and Asia), serving world markets.

The Rise of the New International Division of Labor (NIDL)

The formation of a global labor force began during the development project. The effects of urban bias, agrarian class polarization accelerated by the green revolution, and cheap food imports combined to expel peasants from the land. From 1950 to 1997, the world's rural population decreased by some 25 percent, and roughly half of the world's population dwells in and on the margins of sprawling cities.[22] European depeasantization was spread over several centuries, with pressure on cities relieved through immigration to settler colonies in the Americas and Australasia. But for Third World societies, this process has been compressed into a few generations, a little longer for Latin America. Rural migrants overwhelm the cities, generating what has been termed a "planet of slums."[23]

Depeasantization does not by itself create a global labor force; it simply swells the ranks of displaced people lacking means of subsistence and needing wage work. Wage work for a global labor force stems from the *simplification* of First World manufacturing work and *relocation* of these routine tasks as low-cost jobs to form a global assembly line linking sites across the world.

Initially, First World mass production developed around large production runs using assembly lines of work subdivided into specialized tasks. Simplification *deskills* work on the assembly line, presaging the global assembly line. As the world factory emerged, such tasks as cutting, sewing, and stitching in the garment or footwear industries or assembly, machine tending, or etching in the electrical, automobile, or computer chip industries relocated to cheap labor regions. At the same time, the technologies to coordinate those tasks generated a need for new skilled labor, such as managerial, engineering, or design labor, often retained in the First World. This produced a *bifurcation of the global labor force*, with skilled labor concentrating in the First World, and unskilled labor concentrating in the Third World. TNCs coordinated this bifurcation via their "internal" labor hierarchies as early as the 1970s, as detailed in the following description.

> Intel Corporation is located in the heart of California's "Silicon Valley." . . . When Intel's engineers develop a design for a new electronic circuit or process, technicians in the Santa Clara Valley, California plant will build, test, and redesign the product. When all is ready for production of the new item, however, it doesn't go to a California factory. Instead, it is air freighted to Intel's plant in Penang, Malaysia. There, Intel's Malaysian workers, almost all young women, assemble the components in a tedious process involving hand soldering of fiber-thin wire leads. Once assembled, the components are flown back to California, this time for final testing and/or integration into a larger end product. And, finally, they're off to market, either in the United States, Europe, or back across the Pacific to Japan.[24]

In the 1970s, the relocation of deskilled tasks to lower-wage regions of the world was so prevalent that the concept of a **new international division of labor** (**NIDL**) was coined to describe this development. NIDL referred to an apparent decentralization of industrial production from the First to the Third World. The conditions for this movement were defined as endless supplies of cheap Third World labor, the new technical possibility of separating and relocating deskilled manufacturing tasks offshore, and the rise of transport and informational technologies to allow coordination of global production systems.[25]

CASE STUDY

Gendering the Global Labor Force

"Endless supplies of cheap Third World labor" needs definition. Where labor-intensive work is disproportionately feminized, labor supply depends on complex patriarchal and subcontracting hierarchies. Labor-intensive export platform industries prefer young, unmarried, and relatively educated women. While employers argue that women are suited to the jobs because of their dexterity and patience, the qualities assumed of female employees are required as much by the construction of the jobs as by patriarchal and repressive cultural practices reproduced within the factories, sweatshops, and home work units. Job construction also depends on changing conditions; as Laura Raynolds shows for Dominican Republic plantations, in times of recession displaced men may displace women via the use of local patronage networks, with work regendered to reward masculine competition.

Women are typically subjected to long work days and lower wages compared with men. High turnover, lack of union rights, sexual harassment, and poor health characterize the female workforce that has mushroomed across the Asian, Central American, and Middle Eastern regions. Under these conditions, patriarchal states, competing for foreign investment, encourage women to enter the workforce at the same time as the new female workforce may be under official (especially Islamic) scrutiny for loose morals, and governments withhold maternity benefits, child care, and education opportunities on the grounds that they are "secondary workers" in a male-dominated labor market. Rural families propel, and sometimes sell, their teenage girls into labor contracts, viewing their employment as a daughterly duty or a much-needed source of income. Fuentes and Ehrenreich quote Cynthia Enloe: "the emphasis on family is absolutely crucial to management strategy. Even recruitment is a family process. Women don't just go out independently to find jobs. . . . Discipline becomes a family matter since, in most cases, women turn their paychecks over to their parents. Factory life is, in general, constrained and defined by the family life cycle."

Where young women and children work in family production units (as in China today), subcontractors rely on patriarchal pressures to discipline the workers. In the workplace, teenage girls are often forced to take birth control pills to eliminate maternity leave and payments or are forced to have abortions if they get pregnant. Labor contractors and managers routinely demand sexual favors from young women for awarding jobs, giving rise to a "factory harem mentality." The endless nature of the supply of female labor comes from their short working life in many of these jobs—because of the eye–hand coordination of girls that peaks at age 16; the physical deterioration from low wages, poor health, and nutrition; the high turnover due to harassment; the steady experience of having the life sucked out of them by long working hours and no advancement in skills; and the steady stream of new cohorts of younger women to follow, whether from the countryside, the children of the working poor, or international traffickers in labor. These are some of the compelling conditions that enable a particular kind and scale of casual labor to form around the world to supply the brand owners the brands to sell to the global consumer.

What kind of development is realized through the manipulations of (international and national) gender inequalities? 🌐

Sources: Agarwal (1988); Fernandez-Kelly (1983:129); Fuentes (1983); Kernaghan (1995); Ong (1997); Pyle (2001); Raynolds (2001).

With global bifurcation of labor skills, skilled labor became concentrated in the First World, extending to enterprising states such as the East Asian NICs (South Korea, Taiwan, Singapore, and Hong Kong), which used public investment to upgrade workforce skills. The upgrading was necessary as their wage levels were rising in relation to other countries hosting export production, such as Malaysia, Indonesia, and the Philippines. In 1975, if the hourly wage for electronics work in the United States was measured at 100, the relative value for equivalent work was 12 in Hong Kong and Singapore, 9 in Malaysia, 7 in Taiwan and South Korea, 6 in the Philippines, and 5 in Indonesia and Thailand.[26] This wage differentiation forced the East Asian NICs to upgrade their segment of the global labor force.

East Asian countries improved their competitiveness by specializing in more sophisticated export manufacturing for First World markets, using skilled (more male) labor rather than semiskilled and unskilled labor. After upgrading their labor force, the NICs attracted skilled labor inputs as a regional growth strategy. As the skilled work came, these states became headquarters, or cores, of new regional divisions of labor patterned on the production hierarchy between Japan and its East and Southeast Asian neighbors.

An East Asian division of labor in the semiconductor industry for U.S. firms formed by 1985, through the upgrading of the production hierarchy.

Final testing of semiconductors (capital-intensive labor involving computers with lasers) and circuit design centers were located in Hong Kong, Singapore, and Taiwan; wafer fabrication in Malaysia; and assembly in Malaysia, Thailand, the Philippines, and Indonesia. In the 1970s, semiconductors were assembled in Southeast Asia and then flown back to the United States for testing and distribution, but by the 1980s Hong Kong imported semiconductors from South Korea and Malaysia to test them for re-export to the First World and for input in Hong Kong's fabled watch assembly industry.[27]

Patterns of global and regional sourcing have since mushroomed across the world, particularly under the stimulus of informatics. Firms establish subsidiaries offshore or extensive subcontracting arrangements in labor-intensive consumer goods industries such as garments, footwear, toys, household goods, and consumer electronics. The Nike Corporation produces most of its athletic shoes through subcontracting arrangements in South Korea, China, Indonesia, and Thailand; product design and sales promotion are reserved for its U.S. headquarters, where the firm "promotes the symbolic nature of the shoe and appropriates the greater share of the value resulting from its sales."[28] In these senses, the legacy of the world factory revolution has been an initial global bifurcation of labor skills—made increasingly complex by global subcontracting arrangements, as firms have entered into joint ventures to organize their supplies, reduce their costs, and position their final assembly operations for global and/or regional marketing.

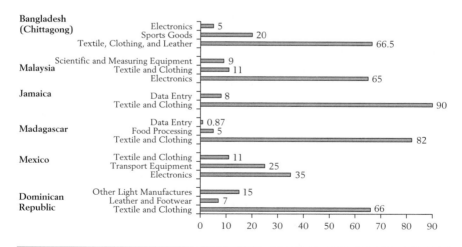

Figure 4.2   Percentage of Workforce Involved in Making Products, Provisions, and Services Exported From Selected EPZ Host Countries, 1994

Sources: International Confederation of Free Trade Unions (1995, www.cftu.org); International Labor Organization (1995, www.ilo.org).

From the NIDL to a Global Labor Force

The rise of global subcontracting transformed the tidy bifurcation of labor between the First World (skilled) and the Third World (unskilled labor), captured in the NIDL concept, into a bifurcation of labor everywhere. Why did this shift take place? First, it occurred because of upgrading by firms in the NICs beyond low-skill assembly work. The second reason is that global subcontracting threatens (by relocation) organized labor in the global North, weakening some unions and casualizing some labor. Bifurcation is the separation of a core of relatively stable, well-paid work from a periphery of casual, low-cost labor, wherever. We see it occurring in tertiary education, across and within institutions, where teaching is divided between tenured professors and part-time lecturers. This relationship has no particular geography, although its most dramatic division remains a North–South one.

 CASE STUDY

Global Subcontracting in Saipan

One of the production sites used over the past two decades as a supplier in global subcontracting is the tiny island of Saipan in the western Pacific. Saipan has been a U.S. territory since 1945, and the islanders are American citizens. In the early 1980s, new federal rules for the garment industry allowed duty-free (and virtually quota-free) imports from Saipan into the United States as well as liberal foreign investment conditions. Companies involved in garment production on Saipan have included The Gap, Geoffrey Beene, Liz Claiborne, Eddie Bauer, and Levi Strauss. Saipan has strategic importance. While its exports make up only about 1 percent of all clothing imports into the United States, they account for roughly 20 percent of sales for some large American companies.

Saipan has a "comparative advantage": although the "Made in USA" label can legitimately be used here, the island was exempted from the federal minimum wage in 1976. The commonwealth government has maintained a minimum wage of $2.15 an hour since 1984 (compared with the federal minimum of $4.25 on Guam, 120 miles to the south).

Despite the label, more than half the labor force is foreign—predominantly Chinese, who expect to work in the United States but find themselves in Saipan barracks surrounded by barbed wire and patrolled by uniformed guards. The clothing factories resemble sweatshops, recently attracting the attention of American labor unions and investigators from the U.S.

Department of Labor and the Occupational Safety and Health Administration. Inspectors found Chinese workers whose passports were confiscated and who worked 84-hour weeks at subminimum wages. Workers filed a class action suit against their employers in 1999. Four U.S. retailers (Nordstrom, Gymboree, Cutter and Buck, and J. Crew) settled with 50,000 current and former workers, committing to monitor improvements in wages and working conditions. Other lawsuits followed, with one company, Levi Strauss, agreeing to new codes requiring improved conditions, to be implemented also in other sites in Myanmar and China.

How can codes of corporate conduct be enforced in sweatshops when host governments are complicit, employers are often subcontractors, union organization is often disallowed, and firms can move on to the next cheap labor site at the drop of a hat?

Sources: Dickinson and Schaeffer (2001:212); Fickling (2003); Shenon (1993:10); *The Economist* (June 3, 1995:58); Udesky (1994).

The Saipan case study illustrates the dark side of subcontracting—exploitation commonly experienced by unprotected labor throughout the world. In 1999, the United Nations estimated there were about 20 million bonded laborers worldwide, with half that number in India. Similarly, the International Labor Organization estimates about 80 million children younger than age 14 working across the world in conditions hazardous to their health—in farming, domestic labor, drug trafficking, fireworks manufacturing, fishing, brick making, carpet weaving, sex work, stone quarrying, and as soldiers. Many of these children work 14-hour days in crowded and unsafe workplaces.[29] Regardless of whether transnational corporations offer better conditions than local firms, the global subcontracting system eliminates and/or severely weakens regulation of employment conditions.

As firms restructure and embrace **lean production** (see box below), they may trim less skilled jobs and fulfill them through subcontracting arrangements that rely on casual labor, often overseas. The U.S. automobile sector outsourced so much of its components production from the late 1970s that the percentage of its workforce belonging to unions fell from two-thirds to one-quarter by the mid-1990s. Not only did outsourcing bifurcate auto industry labor, but the expansion of this nonunion workforce also eroded wages, such that between 1975 and 1990, the low-wage workforce grew by 142 percent, from 17 to 40 percent of the automobile workforce. And for the U.S. workforce as a whole, industrial restructuring reduced real average weekly earnings by 18 percent from the mid-1970s to the mid-1990s. Meanwhile, union density fell from 25 to 14.5 percent across the period 1980 to 1995.[30]

What Is Lean Production?

Lean production combines information technologies, craft work, and archaic or repressive forms of work organization, including self-employment, subcontracting, and piece-rate work. Responding to "just-in-time" supply patterns, it bifurcates labor forces between stable cores of full-time employment and unstable peripheries of "flexible," part-time, or temporary workers, sometimes drawing on the labor of slumdwellers. The hierarchy, with its casual base, offers production flexibility and the possibility of disciplining core workers with the threat of outsourcing.

Temporary and part-time labor is a defining feature of the twenty-first century labor market. By 1995, the largest employer in the United States was no longer General Motors but Manpower, Inc., a firm coordinating "temps." And by 2007, Manpower, Inc. had 4,400 offices in 73 countries, serving 400,000 clients ranging from small enterprises to the largest TNCs. The U.S. labor market represents a model of lean production, where companies hire part-time employees without traditional full benefits, creating millions of second-class jobs (most workers prefer full-time work). Women comprise 70 to 90 percent of the temps in the global North. By a European Union requirement, European governments are relaxing labor laws and generating new part-time jobs, at the rate of 10 percent a year, to improve the flexibility of European firms competing in the world market.

Sources: Cooper and Kuhn (1998:A1); Moody (1999:97–99); www.manpower.org.

From 1970 to 1994, manufacturing employment fell 50 percent in Britain, 8 percent in the United States, 18 percent in France, and 17 percent in Germany, with many of these being "low-tech" jobs, such as footwear, textiles, and metals. In 1995 alone, the U.S. apparel industry lost 10 percent of its jobs and, with jobs lost in the fabrics industry, accounted for 40 percent of manufacturing jobs lost that year. More than 50 percent of the U.S. clothing market is accounted for by cheap imports from Asia and Latin America. Around 65,300 U.S. footwear jobs disappeared in the 1980s—for example, Nike ceased making athletic shoes in the United States and relocated most of its production to South Korea and Indonesia. In the early 1990s, a worker, usually female, in the footwear industry in Indonesia earned $1.03 per day compared with an average wage in the U.S. footwear industry of $6.94 per *hour*.[31] The gap left by the relocation of manufacturing to the Third World has partially been filled by postindustrial work (retailing, health care, security, finance, restaurants), some of which is performed by migrant labor—creating cycles of ethnic tension during times of economic downturn. Temporary and part-time employment (one-third of

U.S. employees in 1995) and multiple jobs have become a common pattern for low-skilled workers.

Manufacturing labor has lost considerable organizational, as well as numerical, power to corporate strategies of restructuring, leading to the qualitative restructuring of work discussed in the box on lean production. After a decade of conservative government restructuring of the British labor force (weakening union rights, eliminating minimum wages, reducing jobless benefits), Britain in the 1990s became a new site for offshore investment from Europe—mostly in part-time jobs (electronic assembly, apparel, clerical tasks) undertaken by women at considerably lower wages than would be paid in Europe.[32] Typically, "Third World" working conditions are just as likely to appear in the global centers via the practice of lean production. Garment sweatshops are a recurring phenomenon—for example, in New York City—and a range of "Third World" jobs has spread in First World cities over the past two decades. In other words, the *global labor force* is well entrenched everywhere.

Global integration habitually marginalizes people and their communities, as jobs are automated, shed, or relocated by corporations under global competitive pressures. Competition compels firms not only to go global but also to keep their sourcing flexible, and therefore their suppliers—and their workers—guessing. The women's wear retailer Liz Claiborne, which divides its sources mainly among the United States, Hong Kong, South Korea, Taiwan, the Philippines, China, and Brazil, claims, "The Company does not own any manufacturing facilities: all of its products are manufactured through arrangements with independent suppliers. . . . The Company does not have any long-term, formal arrangements with any of the suppliers which manufacture its products."[33] As the world market has been corporatized, firms that once organized paternalistic "company towns," have shed that responsibility as they have reached out to the more abstract (flexible and expendable) global labor force.

CASE STUDY

The Corporatization of World Markets

Export markets concentrate in the global North, where markets are much denser than Southern markets and consumer culture is well entrenched. Export, or world, markets are typically organized by TNCs. UN data reveal that transnational corporations account for two-thirds of world trade. Fifty of the largest 100 economies are run by TNCs—for instance, General

Motors is larger than Thailand, Norway, or Saudi Arabia, and Toyota is larger than Israel or Greece. TNCs control most of the world's financial transactions, (bio)technologies, and industrial capacity—including oil and its refining, coal, gas, hydroelectric and nuclear power plants, mineral extraction and processing, home electronics, chemicals, medicines, wood harvesting and processing, and more.

The top five TNCs in each major market (such as jet aircraft, automobiles, microprocessors, and grains) typically account for between 40 and 70 percent of all world sales, with the 10 largest corporations in their field controlling 86 percent of telecommunications and 70 percent of the computer industry. UNCTAD in 2002 reported that sales by foreign subsidiaries were twice the value of world exports of goods and services, and that 60,000 TNCs owned over 820,000 subsidiaries, with about 45.5 million employees (compared with 17.5 million in 1982). The combined annual revenues of the 200 largest corporations exceeded those of the 182 states with 80 percent of the world's population. Corporate tax rates have declined significantly in most Northern states (from 30 to 7 percent of U.S. government funds since the early 1950s), shifting tax burdens to lotteries, personal income, and sales.

The combined sales of the largest 350 TNCs in the world total about one-third of the combined GNPs of all industrialized countries and exceed the individual GNPs of *all* Southern countries. The majority of these firms are headquartered in France, Germany, Japan, the United Kingdom, and the United States, accounting for 70 percent of all transnational investment and about 50 percent of all the companies themselves. Wal-Mart is now the largest corporation in the world and the largest importer of Chinese-made products, with annual revenues of $220 billion, $7 billion in profits. Wal-Mart has more than 1 million nonunionized employees (three times the number of General Motors), a large proportion of whom are employed part-time (with minimal benefits).

Under these circumstances of globalization, the framework and content of development appear to have been redefined—not in terms of governments pursuing social equity in the national citizen-state, but in terms of the corporate pursuit of efficiency and choice for the global consumer-citizen.

If the consumer-citizen represents at most one-third of the world's population, what kind of development (and globalization) do we have?

Sources: Alperovitz (2003:15); Baird and McCaughan (1979:135–136); Beams (1999); Brown (1993:47); Daly and Logan (1989:67), Ellwood (1993:5; 2001:55–63); Hightower (2002); Karliner (1997:5); Korten (1996:323); Martin and Schumann (1997:12); Perrons (2005:69); *The Economist* (July 16, 1994).

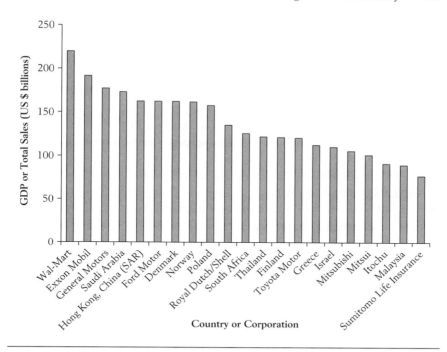

Figure 4.3   Corporate Versus Country Economic Graph

Sources: Sales: *Fortune* (July 22, 2002). Gross domestic product: *Human Development Report* (United Nations, 2002).

As corporations shuffle the global employment deck, Northern citizens experience declining real wages (a trend since 1972), rising poverty rates, increased family stress and social disorder, rising public health costs, and so on. The feminization of work involves lowering wages and job conditions and, in addition to declining social services, has overstressed mechanisms of social reproduction—for which women typically take most responsibility.[34] Proposed retraining schemes to help workers adjust to a shifting employment scene are often ineffectual, as most replacement jobs are low paid and low- or no-benefit service work.[35]

The loss of jobs is not simply an international economic transfer; it "hollows out" a nation's economic base and erodes social institutions that stabilize the conditions of employment and habitat associated with those jobs. A century of institution building in labor markets, in corporate/union relations, and in communities can disappear overnight when the winds of the market are allowed to blow across uneven national boundaries. Those who have work find they are often working longer hours to make ends meet, despite remarkable technological advances.

Agricultural Globalization

With the food aid regime and the green revolution both incorporating Third World countries into international circuits of food and agribusiness technologies, the **"world farm"** emerged alongside the "world factory." In this process, many Third World country development profiles switched from a focus on modernizing agriculture as a domestic industry towards developing agriculture as a world industry. A **second green revolution** facilitated this switch.

As we saw in Chapter 2, beginning in the 1960s, the green revolution encouraged agribusiness in the production of wage foods for urban consumers in the Third World. Beyond that national project, agribusiness technology has spread from basic grains to other grains—especially feedstuffs—to livestock, and to horticultures of fresh fruits and vegetables. Further, agribusiness has created feed-grain substitutes such as cassava, corn gluten feed, and citrus pellets, and biotechnology is creating plant-derived "feedstocks" for the chemical industry. This kind of agriculture depends on hybrid seeds, chemical fertilizers, pesticides, animal antibiotics, and growth-inducing chemicals, specialty feeds, and, most recently, genetically modified plants. It is a specialized, high-input agriculture servicing high-value markets, in addition to food processing and agrochemical firms. It extends green revolution technology from basic to consumer foods and agro-industrial inputs, and has been termed the second green revolution.[36] A distinguishing development feature is that, whereas the first green revolution was a *public* initiative geared to *national* markets, its successor was a *private* initiative increasingly geared to *global* markets.

The second green revolution serves high-income consumers everywhere with relatively affluent diets. It involves, most notably, substituting feed crops for food crops and the exacerbation of social inequalities (in terms of access to land and basic foods). In Mexico, for example, U.S. agribusiness firms promoted hybrid sorghum seeds among Mexican farmers in the late 1950s, buoyed by a support price in 1965 favoring sorghum over wheat and maize (first green revolution products). As sorghum production doubled (supplying 74 percent of feedstuffs), wheat, maize, and even bean production began a long decline. In the 1970s, meat consumption rose among wealthier Mexicans, with increases of 65 percent in pork, 35 percent in poultry, and 32 percent in beef. At the same time, no meat was available for about one-third of the population.[37] Conversion of crop land to feed livestock is now a global enterprise with supply chains of corn, soymeal, and cassava stretching across the world to feed a proliferating factory farm complex, realizing development through new dietary inequalities.

The factory farm complex depends on feed supply chains, whose early symbolic product was the "world steer."[38] Produced in a variety of locations with global inputs (standardized genetic lines) for global sale (standardized packaging), the world steer extends the agro-industrial model on a world scale. Whether pasture fed (hamburger), or lot fed (beefsteak), production of the world steer incorporates flows of imported semen, pasture seeds, chemical fertilizers, herbicides, feed grains, medicines, and antibiotics supplied from around the world by transnational firms. Pastures, or feed crops, routinely displace food crops, reinforcing inequality in the supply regions by undermining mixed farming and peasant self-provisioning (livestock traditionally provide food, fuel, fertilizer, transport, and clothing, and consume crop stubble). Globally supplied beefsteak and hamburger carry a hidden cost, both social and environmental (as discussed in Chapter 1).

The second green revolution also contributes to the globalization of markets for high-value foods such as off-season fresh fruits and vegetables. This market is one of the most profitable for agribusinesses. As global markets have deepened and transport technologies have matured, "cool chains" maintain chilled temperatures for transporting fresh fruit and vegetables grown in the Third World to supermarket outlets across the world. U.S. firms such as Dole, Chiquita, and Del Monte moved beyond their traditional commodities such as bananas and pineapples into other fresh fruits and vegetables, joined by British firms Albert Fisher and Polly Peck. By coordinating producers scattered across different climatic zones, these firms reduce the seasonality of fresh fruits and vegetables. Year-round produce availability is complemented with exotic fruits such as breadfruit, cherimoya (custard apple), carambola (star fruit), feijoa (pineapple guava), lychee, kiwi, and passionfruit; vegetables such as bok choy, cassava, fava beans, and plantain; and salad greens such as arugula, chicory, and baby vegetables.[39]

In this new division of world agricultural labor, transnational corporations typically subcontract with or hire peasants to produce specialty horticultural crops and off-season fruits and vegetables for export processing (canning, freezing, gassing, boxing, juicing, and dicing) to supply expanding consumer markets located primarily in Europe, North America, and the Asia-Pacific. As the conversion of agriculture into a global, increasingly feminized industry proceeds, it impinges on women's livelihoods, their food security, and that of their families. Most food consumed across the world is produced by women, accounting for 45 percent in Latin America, 65 percent in Asia, and 75 percent in sub-Saharan Africa. Women's lack of security and rights in land means that commercialization easily erodes women's role in and control of food production. As small farming is destabilized, women must work in the agribusiness sector on plantations and in processing plants, as planters, pickers, and packers, feminizing the global agricultural labor force, and adding to women's workday, despite income benefits and associated "empowerment."

CASE STUDY

Global Labor in Agriculture and the Question of Food Security

The global fruit and vegetable industry depends on flexible contract labor arrangements. Coordination of multiple production sites, for a year-round supply of fresh produce, is achieved through information technologies. These supply chains disconnect producers and consumers with interesting consequences: consumer ignorance of (gendered) conditions under which their goods are produced, as well as producer experience of growing food for (firms for) distant consumers rather than for their own communities.

Deborah Barndt's research retraces the journey of the tomato from Mexico to the ubiquitous fast-food and retailing outlets of North America. Naming it "Tomasita," to underline its labor origins in ethnic and gendered terms, she describes the Sayula plant of one of Mexico's largest agro-exporters, Santa Anita Packers, where, in the peak season, Sayula employs more than 2,000 pickers and 700 packers. The improved seed varieties originate in Mexico but are developed and patented in Israel or the United States. Such seeds need heavy doses of pesticides, but the company did not provide any health and safety education or the protective gear. Perhaps a more visually striking indicator of monocultural production is the packing plant, employing hundreds of young women whom the company moved by season from one site to another as a kind of "mobile *maquiladora*" . . . the only Mexican inputs are the land, the sun, and the workers. . . . The South has been the source of the seeds, while the North has the biotechnology to alter them . . . the workers who produce the tomatoes do not benefit. Their role in agro-export production also denies them participation in subsistence agriculture, especially since the peso crisis in 1995, which has forced migrant workers to move to even more scattered work sites. They now travel most of the year—with little time to grow food on their own plots in their home communities . . . with this loss of control comes a spiritual loss, and a loss of a knowledge of seeds, of organic fertilizers and pesticides, of sustainable practices such as crop rotation or leaving the land fallow for a year—practices that had maintained the land for millennia.

In this way the food security of northern consumers is obtained through the food *in*security of Mexico—converted from a food self-sufficient nation (national food system dismantled in 1982) to one that imports one-third of its food needs (staple grains). Displaced maize farmers (especially indigenous women) move to the new *agromaquilas* or to North American orchards or plantations, where they can earn in a day what they earn in a week in Mexico.

What are the long-term consequence of a global food system that destabilizes peasant communities and exacerbates southern food dependency for no good reason other than profit and a year-round supply of tasteless tomatoes? 🌐

Source: Barndt (1997:59–62).

The New Agricultural Countries (NACs)

As was the case in manufacturing, agribusiness investments first became concentrated in select Third World countries (e.g., Brazil, Mexico, Argentina, Chile, Hungary, and Thailand), known as the **new agricultural countries (NACs)**.[40] They were analogous to the NICs insofar as their governments promoted agro-industrialization for urban and export markets. As the development project has receded, agro-exporting has intensified. Such agro-exports have been called **nontraditional exports (NTEs)** because they either replace or supplement the traditional tropical exports of the colonial era. Nontraditional exports tend to be high-value foods such as animal protein products and fruits and vegetables, or low-value feed grains.

Thailand's traditional role in the international division of labor as an exporter of rice, sugar, pineapples, and rubber is now complemented with an expanding array of nontraditional primary exports: cassava (feed), canned tuna, shrimp, poultry, processed meats, and fresh and processed fruits and vegetables. Former exports such as corn and sorghum are now mostly consumed domestically in the intensive livestock sector. Raw agricultural exports, which accounted for 80 percent of Thailand's exports in 1980, now represent 30 percent; processed food makes up 30 percent of manufactured exports. Thailand is a model NAC.[41] Viewed as "Asia's supermarket," Thailand expanded its food processing industry on a foundation of rural smallholders under contract to food processing firms. Food companies from Japan, Taiwan, the United States, and Europe use Thailand as a base for regional and global export-oriented production. For example, Japanese firms form joint ventures with Thai agribusinesses to expand feed (soybeans and corn) and aquaculture supply zones for Japanese markets. Thailand's agro-exports are linked to the affluent markets in the Pacific Rim (Japan, South Korea, and Taiwan), and these markets brought over 60 percent of Thailand's foreign exchange in the 1990s. Thai poultry production is organized around small growers who contract with large, vertically integrated firms. To facilitate this, the Thai government organized a complex of agribusinesses, farmers, and financial institutions with state ministries to promote export contracts, distributing land to landless farmers for contract growing and livestock farming.[42] Thailand's mature feed industry, coupled with low-cost labor, helped Thai poultry producers compete with their U.S. (and now Chinese) counterparts in the Japanese market. Thailand is the world's largest producer of farmed shrimp[43]—symbolizing how consumer affluence and the NAC phenomenon reproduce one another.

Just as the NICs served as platforms for global supply chains in manufacturing, so the NACs have served global sourcing. It sustains the feedlots of far-flung intensive livestock operations. Three agribusiness firms headquartered in the United States have meat-packing operations across the world, raising cattle, pigs, and poultry on feedstuffs supplied by their own grain marketing subsidiaries elsewhere in the world. Cargill, headquartered in Minnesota, is the largest grain trader in the world, operating in 70 countries with more than 800 offices or plants and more than 70,000 employees. It has established a joint venture with Nippon Meat Packers of Japan, called Sun Valley Thailand, from which it exports U.S. corn-fed poultry products to the Japanese market. ConAgra, headquartered in Nebraska, owns 56 companies and operates in 26 countries with 58,000 employees. It processes feed and animal protein products in the United States, Canada, Australia, Europe, the Far East, and Latin America. Tyson Foods, headquartered in Arkansas, runs a joint venture with the Japanese agribusiness firm C. Itoh, which produces poultry in Mexico, supplied with U.S. feedstuffs, for both local consumption and export to Japan.[44]

Whether it is poultry from Thailand, green beans from Kenya, tomatoes from Mexico, soybeans from Brazil, or farmed salmon from Chile, second green revolution technologies, and nontraditional exporting, have converted agriculture across the world towards the "world farm," serving the global market rather than the national project.

Global Sourcing and Regionalism

Global sourcing is a strategy used by transnational corporations and host governments alike to improve their world market position and secure predictable supplies of inputs. Because of the formation of an infinitely available global labor force, firms reorganize marketing strategies to segment consumer markets. This means substituting flexible for standardized mass production, using smaller and less specialized (multitasking) labor forces. Whether **flexible production** is actually replacing mass production is not entirely clear. In fact, flexible—or lean—production is reorganizing mass

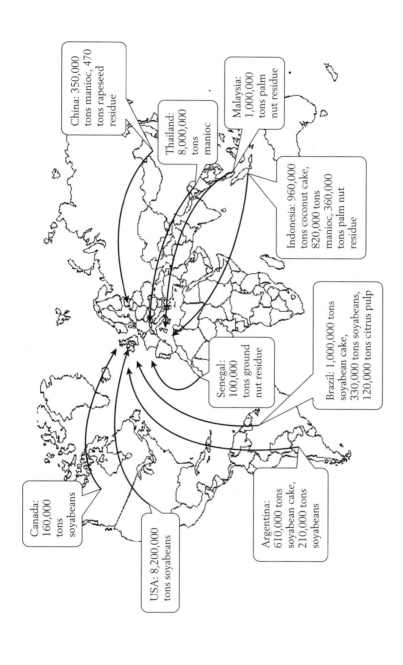

Figure 4.4 Europe's Global Sourcing of Animal Feed Ingredients

Source: Tim Lang, "Dietary Impact of the Globalization of Food Trade," *International Forum on Globalization News 3* (1998):10–12.

production to allow the segmentation or differentiation of consumer markets. Marketing now drives production, and a system of "mass customization" has developed to allow firms to mass produce essentially similar products with multiple variations to suit individual needs—the sneaker industry, with its endless variations in style, is a clear case in point.

The size of market segments depends on social class incomes. Recently, we have seen a considerable stratification of consumption—in the broad quality range of cars and clothing items, as well as in the segmentation of the beef market (steak/hamburger). With a global market, firms are increasingly under pressure to respond to changing consumer preferences as the life span of commodities declines (with rapidly changing fashion and/or technologies). Shifting consumer tastes require greater flexibility in firms' production runs, use of inputs, use of inventory, and selling strategies.

In the 1980s, the Toyota Company introduced the just-in-time (JIT) system of "flexible mass production."[45] With JIT (premised on informatics), simultaneous engineering replaces the sequencing of mass production—the "just-in-case" system in which materials are produced on inflexible assembly lines to supply standardized consumer markets. By contrast, simultaneous engineering allows quicker changes in design and production, so firms can respond to volatile consumer markets. The Gap, for example, changes its inventory and "look" every six weeks. As the company's Far East vice president for offshore sourcing remarked, "The best retailers will be the ones who respond the quickest, the best . . . where the time between cash register and factory shipment is shorter."[46]

The JIT system promotes both global *and* regional corporate strategies. In the clothing industry, shoes and garments commodity chains can be dispersed globally and centrally coordinated by the parent firm. In the garments trade, a global fashion designer typically purchases a Paris-designed shirt for US$3 to $4 in Bangladesh, Vietnam, or Thailand and sells the shirt in the European market at five to 10 times its price. In the shoe trade, Vietnamese workers make about US$400 a year stitching sneakers, while corporate celebrities are paid US$10 million to $20 million a year to "sell" these products. Changing fashions favors flexible subcontracting arrangements in the "field," where flexible labor costs are so cheap. In more capital-intensive sectors, where automated technologies are less transferable, firms tend to invest in regional sites so they can respond quickly to local/regional market signals as fashions change.[47]

Recent concentration of investment flows in the denser First World regions of the world market reflects this corporate strategy. These are the regions with the largest markets, where an integrated production complex based on the JIT principle has the greatest chance of success. So firms locate near the big markets, where strategic countries act as nodes for trade and investment circuits. Thus countries such as Mexico and Malaysia become important investment sites precisely because of the new regional complexes of the North American Free Trade Agreement (NAFTA) and the Asia-Pacific Economic Cooperation (APEC).

NAFTA encouraged U.S., Japanese, and European firms to invest in food-processing operations in Mexico, consolidating its status as an NAC supplying the North American market—similar to Thailand's "regional supermarket" role. Firms such as Coca-Cola, PepsiCo, General Foods, Kraft, Kellogg's, Campbell's, Bird's Eye, Green Giant, Tyson Foods, C. Itoh, Nestlé, and Unilever have invested in fruits and vegetables, meat, dairy products, and wheat milling to supply regional markets.[48]

CASE STUDY

Regional Strategy of a Southern Transnational Corporation

We tend to think of TNCs as Northern in origin. The Charoen Pokphand (CP) Group was formed in Bangkok in 1921 by two Chinese brothers to trade in farm inputs. In the 1960s, CP expanded into animal feed production, and from there to vertically integrated poultry production, providing inputs (chicks, feed, medicines, credit, extension services) to farmers and in turn processing and marketing poultry regionally in East Asia. In the 1980s, CP entered retailing, acquiring a Kentucky Fried Chicken (KFC) franchise for Thailand, and now controls about one-quarter of the Thai fast-food market as an outlet for its poultry, including 715 Seven-Eleven convenience stores. By the mid-1990s, CP was Thailand's largest TNC and Asia's largest agro-industrial conglomerate, with 100,000 employees in 20 countries. It was an early investor in China, establishing a feed mill in Shenzhen in 1979, in a joint venture with Continental Grain. In 1995, CP was operating 75 feedmills in 26 of China's 30 provinces; controlled the KFC franchise rights for China, operating in 13 cities; and its poultry operations accounted for 10 percent of China's broilers, producing 235 million day-old chicks per annum.

Today, CP has investments in fertilizers, pesticides and agro-chemicals, vehicles, tractors, supermarkets, baby foods, livestock operations in poultry and swine, milk processing, crop farming and processing, seed production, aquaculture, and jute-backed carpets, as well as in telecommunications, real estate, retailing, cement, and petrochemicals. CP produces poultry in Turkey, Vietnam, Cambodia, Malaysia, Indonesia, and the United States, as well as animal feed in Indonesia, India, and Vietnam; through a public joint venture, CP is involved in China's fourth and sixth largest motorcycle manufacturing operations and in the development of an industrial park and satellite town in Shanghai. CP's current initiative is in shrimp farming, where it controls 65 percent of the Thai market and is the world's largest producer of farmed shrimp. It has used joint ventures to expand shrimp farming to Indonesia, Vietnam, China, and India, which are likely to replace Thailand as the regional source of shrimp since they are cheaper sites for an industry beset by ecological stress.

When we see the extent of a TNC's concentration of power over regional or global economic activity, where is this kind of development going, and whose future does it serve?

Source: Goss et al. (2000).

New strategies of regional investment partly explain the repatterning of investment flows in the 1990s. As that decade began, foreign direct investment (FDI) in the Third World increased as global FDI declined.[49] Just as in the 1970s, when the NICs were the locus of world economic expansion, the majority of foreign investment concentrated in regionally significant states such as China, Mexico, Indonesia, and South Korea. These states are significant because they have large and growing domestic markets and/or they are located near other large, affluent markets in East Asia and North America. Meanwhile, there is a new vision of economic regionalism underway in the *Plan Puebla de Panama* complex: an industrial corridor linking the south of Mexico to Panama to mobilize the pool of displaced, cheap, indigenous labor.[50]

Different firms have different production strategies, whether regional or global, depending on the need for proximity (e.g., automated technologies or fresh vegetables) or on sourcing from cheap labor zones (e.g., low-skill labor processing). In the service industry, regional strategies may be necessary to accommodate cultural preferences. McDonald's, for instance, may sell Big Macs and Happy Meals in Vienna, Indonesia, and South Korea, but in Vienna it caters to local tastes in blended coffee by selling "McCafes"; in Jakarta, rice supplements French fries on the menu; and in Seoul, McDonald's sells roast pork with soy sauce on a bun. However, the low- to mid-value retailer Wal-Mart has broad, standardized consumer segments in mind, a spokesperson remarking, "With trade barriers coming down, the world is going to be one great big marketplace, and he who gets there first does the best."[51] McDonald's, the firm with the global brand, deploys flexible menus to retain local market share, while Wal-Mart sees the consumer world as its oyster.

World capitalism has tendencies toward both global and regional integration. Regional integration may anticipate global integration since it promotes trade and investment flows among neighboring countries. But it also may reflect a defensive strategy by firms and states that distrust the intentions of other firm/state clusters. At present, the global economy is subdivided into three macroregions, centered on the United States, Japan, and Germany/Western Europe—each with hinterlands in Central and Latin America, Southeast Asia, and Eastern Europe/North Africa, respectively. But within those macroregions, there are smaller free trade agreements in operation, often based on greater economic affinity among the members in terms of their GNPs and wage levels. How the future will unfold—with global or regional integration as the dominant tendency—is not yet clear.

Summary

This chapter has examined the emergence of a global production system. Specialization in the world economy, rather than replication of economic activities within a national framework, has emerged as the new criterion of "development." NICs and NACs have served increasingly as export platforms for TNCs, which bring technologies of flexible manufacturing and the second green revolution, respectively. As a result, the "world factory" and the "world farm" phenomena have proliferated across the Third World, producing world products for the global consumer class. As jobs have relocated from First World factories to Third World EPZs, a process of labor casualization has occurred, as organized labor in the former has been forced to yield to the competitive low-cost and unorganized labor of the latter, via the exploitation of information technology by TNCs. The formation of a global labor force has involved political decisions that unravel the social compact with First World labor, and cycle Third World labor into sweatshops. Women predominate in the low-skill, low-paid jobs, and "defeminization" occurs as labor organizes, wages rise and/or industrial upgrading takes place in the NICs and their immediate followers. This patterning represents a transition between state-managed national economic growth in the development project, and the international market networks anticipating the globalization project. It displaced the ideal of national replication with a new global hierarchy of labor mapped on to regional divisions of labor among states.

In effect, a new global economy was emerging, beyond trade among national economies. The global economy was embedded in those parts of national societies producing or consuming world commodities. It is organized chiefly by transnational corporate webs of economic activity, linking sites of labor differentiated along skill and gender/ethnic lines. For any one state, the corporate-based global economic system is unstable and beyond its ability to control or regulate. Development has begun to shed its national identity and to change into a global enterprise in which individual states must participate—but quite tenuously, as we shall see.

Further Reading

Bonnano, Alessandro, Lawrence Busch, William Friedland, Lourdes Gouveia, and Enzo Mingione, eds. *From Columbus to ConAgra: The Globalization of Agriculture and Food*. Lawrence: University Press of Kansas, 1994.

Gereffi, Gary, and Miguel Korzeniewicz, eds. *Commodity Chains and Global Capitalism*. Westport, CT: Praeger, 1994.

Hoogvelt, Ankie. *Globalization and the Postcolonial World: The New Political Economy of Development*. London: Macmillan, 1987.

Nash, June, and Maria Patricia Fernández-Kelly, eds. *Women, Men, and the International Division of Labor*. Albany: State University of New York Press, 1983.

Sklair, Leslie. *Assembling for Development: The Maquila Industry in Mexico and the United States*. Boston: Unwin Hyman, 1989.

Select Websites

Gender Equality and Development (UNESCO): www.unesco.org/shs/gender

Institute for Agriculture and Trade Policy (USA): www.agobservatory.org/agribusiness.cfm

International Labor Organization (UN): www.ilo.org/public/english/dialogue/sector/themes/epz.htm

Multinational Monitor (USA): www.multinationalmonitor.org

5

Demise of the Third World

The consolidation of a global economy helped undo the Third World as a political entity, preparing the way for the globalization project. More than economic integration, the laying of the foundations of globalization was an exercise of First World power in shifting international development discourse and practice from "economic nationalism" to "world market participation." This involved more than two decades of military and financial disciplining of Third World initiatives that restricted foreign corporate access to Third World resources and markets and threatened default on First World loans. Beginning, perhaps, with the installation of General Suharto in Indonesia (1965), United States-led Western intervention introduced a new model of development, premised on an open-door policy across the Third World, culminating in the debt regime in the 1980s. This regime imposed financial disciplines via structural adjustment, completing the rollback of economic nationalism and the political dismantling of the Third World.

Within the Third World, the separation of the newly industrializing countries (NICs) from their Third World peers led to a reevaluation of the economic nationalism of the development project, undermining Third World unity. Export-oriented industrialization fueled rapid economic growth, legitimizing a new "free market" model of development, and in the 1980s this was represented as the solution to the debt crisis. Development, which had been defined as nationally managed economic growth, was redefined in the World Bank's *World Development Report 1980* as "participation in the world market."[1]

The redefinition prepared the way for superseding economic nationalism and embracing globalization. *The global economy was emerging as the unit*

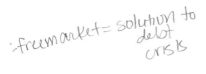

free market = solution to debt crisis

117

of development. This was made possible by the rise of a global banking system in the 1970s, spurred on by a process of financial liberalization that eased the cross-border movement of money. Money became increasingly "stateless" and easier to borrow. In the 1970s, Third World states borrowed from global banks as if there were no tomorrow. Banks lent money as if there were no risks in bankrolling Third World governments. In the 1980s, this mountain of debt crumbled as interest rates were hiked to relieve an over-subscribed dollar. The resulting debt crisis drastically reframed the development agenda: the World Bank and the International Monetary Fund (IMF) imposed new loan-rescheduling conditions on indebted states, compelling them to look outward rather than inward for their development stimulus.

This chapter surveys the various ways in which the debt crisis transformed the development project into a globalization project. It is essentially about the transition between projects and suggests that this transition had several related political and economic strands, including the following:

- elaboration through military and economic aid of a cold war empire of containment,
- defeat of a final effort at Third World unity (the New International Economic Order initiative),
- financial deregulation and the rise of a global money market,
- First World sponsorship of profligate borrowing by often corrupt Third World elites, and
- financial disciplining of indebted countries by the Bretton Woods institutions, bringing extensive austerity and Third World charges of a "lost decade."

The Empire of Containment and the Political Decline of the Third World

Just as the Third World was born as a political entity, so it died as a political entity, symbolizing the rise and fall of the development project. An early symbolic blow to Third World economic nationalism came in the form of a CIA-led coup in 1953 against Iranian Prime Minister Mossadegh after he nationalized British oil holdings. By the time of Indian Prime Minister Jawaharlal Nehru's death in 1964, the nonalignment strategy of Third Worldism was weakening. Third World regimes and nationalist movements aligned with one or both of the superpowers. In addition, China's model appeared to depart from the bureaucratic-industrial model of the Soviet Union, reversing urban bias and mobilizing (and investing in) the peasantry via the Great Leap Forward in the 1950s. The United States, concerned that the Chinese experiment would overshadow the Indian model of state-guided (nevertheless capitalist) development, moved to strengthen its alliance with India to anchor the Western development project. Another key figure in the Non-Aligned Movement (NAM), Indonesian President Sukarno, nurtured a state- and military-sponsored form of independent development, supported by a complex coalition of nationalist, Muslim, and communist parties, forming what he called a "Guided Democracy."[2]

In 1965, President Sukarno and his brand of economic nationalism were overthrown in a bloody coup, including a pogrom claiming between half a million and a million lives—mostly members of Indonesia's huge and popular Communist Party (the PKI). The CIA reported, "In terms of the numbers killed, the massacres rank as one of the worst mass murders in the 20th century." General Suharto, the leader of the coup, used the pretext of an internecine struggle between the Indonesian army and the PKI to unleash a violent "year of living dangerously."[3] Declassified documents reveal that a British Foreign Office file in 1964 called for the defense of Western interests in Southeast Asia because it is "a major producer of essential commodities. The region produces nearly 85 percent of the world's natural rubber, over 45 percent of the tin, 65 percent of the copra and 23 percent of the chromium ore." Two years earlier, a CIA memo recorded an agreement between British Prime Minister Harold Macmillan and U.S. President John F. Kennedy to "liquidate president Sukarno, depending on the situation and available opportunities."[4]

Not unlike the U.S. government's awarding of private contracts to rebuild Iraq in 2003, following regime change, Time-Life, Inc. sponsored a 1967 meeting in Geneva between General Suharto, his economic advisers, and corporate leaders representing "the major oil companies and banks, General Motors, Imperial Chemical Industries, British Leyland, British-American Tobacco, American Express, Siemens, Goodyear, the International Paper Corporation, and US Steel." With Ford Foundation help, General Suharto reformulated a development partnership with foreign investment. Billed "To Aid in the Rebuilding of a Nation," the conference nevertheless invited the corporations to identify their interest in the Indonesian economy. James Linen, president of Time-Life, Inc., expressed the *birth of this new global order* when he observed in his opening remarks, "We are here to create a new climate in which private enterprise and developing countries work together . . . for the greater profit of the free world. This world of international enterprise is more than governments. . . . It is the seamless web of enterprise, which has been shaping the global environment at revolutionary speed."[5]

These events marked a turning point in the trajectory of Third World nationalism, forging a new discourse of *global development partnership* between states and corporations. Such intervention was consistent with the containment policy articulated for that region by U.S. President Eisenhower in 1959:

> One of Japan's greatest opportunities for increased trade lies in a free and developing Southeast Asia. . . . The great need in one country is for raw materials, in the other country for manufactured goods. The two regions complement each other markedly. By strengthening Vietnam and helping insure the safety of the South Pacific and Southeast Asia, we gradually develop the great trade potential between this region . . . and highly industrialized Japan to the benefit of both. In this way freedom in the Western Pacific will be greatly strengthened.[6]

The war waged in Vietnam by a United States–led coalition during the next two decades confirmed this policy, and it was followed by strategic interventions in Chile, El Salvador, Nicaragua, Panama, Granada, and Iraq, as well as disbursements of military and economic aid to secure the perimeter of the "free world" and its resource empire. Militarization was critical, securing and prying open the Third World to an emerging project of global development orchestrated by the United States as the dominant power.

The New International Economic Order

The Vietnam War (early 1960s to 1975) came to symbolize global inequality. The world was deeply divided over the war, as a confrontation between foreign high-tech and peasant armies, as well as between the ideologies of free enterprise and socialism, and as an issue of empire versus sovereignty. Just as today's terrorism is linked to poverty, so communism and/or national liberation struggles were linked to underdevelopment at this time. This was the time of the "second-generation Bandung regimes," displaying a more left-wing Third Worldism than the first-generation regimes that pioneered the NAM at Bandung in 1955 and informing a radical dependency theory that explained the failures of the development project as a result of "neocolonialism"—that is, the "informal" exploitation of the postcolonial world by a First World empire.[7]

Between 1974 and 1980, national liberation forces came to power in 14 different Third World states, perhaps inspired by the Vietnamese resistance. The possibility of a united South presented itself in two forms in this decade: first, the formation of the **Organization of Petroleum Exporting Countries (OPEC)**, representing the possibility of Third World control over strategic commodities such as oil; and second, the 1974 proposal to the United Nations (UN) General Assembly by the G-77 for a **New International Economic Order (NIEO)**.[8] This proposal demanded reform of the world economic system to improve the position of Third World states in international trade and their access to technological and financial resources.

The NIEO included the following program:

- opening northern markets to southern industrial exports;
- improving the terms of trade for tropical agricultural and mining products;
- providing better access to international financing; and
- facilitating more technology transfers.[9]

The NIEO initiative included a "dependency perspective," namely, that First World structural power stunted Third World development. The United Nations Conference on Trade and Development (UNCTAD) demanded further tariff reductions on Third World manufactured exports by the First World, which reduced protection only on exports from transnational corporation (TNC) production sites. Despite exceeding the UN growth target of 5 percent per annum for the second development decade, economic and social indices showed that most Third World countries had not achieved the rising living standards promised by the development project. Refocusing on *basic needs* via the elevation of rural development funding for 700 million smallholders, in 1974 the World Bank reported,

> It is now clear that more than a decade of rapid growth in underdeveloped countries has been of little or no benefit to perhaps a third of their population. Paradoxically, while growth policies have succeeded beyond the expectations of the first development decade, the very idea of aggregate growth as a social objective has increasingly been called into question.[10]

Third World representatives argued that focusing on inequalities within the Third World as the source of poverty neglected global inequalities. Of course, both sets of relationships were responsible and mutually conditioning, but the interpretive stakes were high. Algerian president Houari Boumedienne told the UN General Assembly in 1974,

> Inasmuch as [the old order] is maintained and consolidated and therefore thrives by virtue of a process which continually impoverishes the poor and enriches the rich, this economic order constitutes the major obstacle standing in the way of any hope of development and progress for all the countries of the Third World.[11]

neo-Keynesian
G-77's
new International economic order

The NIEO was a charter of economic rights and duties of states, designed to codify global reform along neo-Keynesian lines (public initiatives). It demanded reform of international trade, the international monetary system (to liberalize development financing and debt relief), and technological assistance. It also proclaimed the economic sovereignty of states and the Third World right to collective self-reliance.[12] Although the NIEO included the Second World, the Soviet Union declined involvement on the grounds that the colonial legacy was a Western issue.

Widely perceived as *"the revolt of the Third World,"* the NIEO initiative was indeed the culmination of collectivist politics growing out of the NAM. But it was arguably a movement for reform at best, and at worst a confirmation of dependency insofar as the proposal relied on Northern concessions that would, in turn, increase external revenues available to Third World elites. Interestingly enough, its prime movers were the presidents of Algeria, Iran, Mexico, and Venezuela—all oil-producing nations distinguished by their very recently acquired huge oil rents, as opposed to the impoverished "least developed countries" (LDCs) and the NICs.[13]

Coinciding with the G-77's proposal for global reform was a strengthening of a First World core: the formation of the **Group of Seven (G-7)** states. The finance ministers of the United States, the United Kingdom, France, and West Germany met first in 1973. By 1975, Japan, Italy, and Canada were included in annual secret meetings, setting the Northern agenda. This followed agreement by the central bankers of the G-10 (the G-7 plus Sweden, the Netherlands, and Belgium) to use the Bank for International Settlements (BIS) to organize a "lender of last resort" function in the event of economic crises that might threaten the world-economic order.[14] Until 1986, the G-7 played a key role behind the scenes in *crisis management*, providing First World backbone, ensuring that the NIEO and its symbolic politics would not amount to much.

The First World response combined moral themes with governance. But the master theme was really time. In the short run, Third World unity fragmented as the prospering OPEC states and the NICs showed greater interest in *upward mobility* in the international order. In the long run, the redistributive goals of the NIEO would be overridden by the new doctrine of **monetarism** that ushered in the 1980s debt crisis through drastic restrictions in credit and social spending by governments. A U.S. official articulated the expectation that differentiation among Third World states would promote a form of *embourgeoisement,* as prospering states distanced themselves from their poorer neighbors.[15] The shift to "participation in the world market" as a new development strategy enabled the First World to sidetrack the Third World solidarity, asserting private market solutions to development problems.

The moral of this story is that Third World elites attempted to assert political unity in the world just as economic disunity grew with the divergence of middle-income and poorer states. To understand that process, we examine financial globalization below. In the meantime, the NIEO goal of redistributing wealth from First to Third Worlds actually came to pass, in a way. Although much of the wealth was oil money, recycled through bank loans to the Third World, it nevertheless met demands of political elites for development financing (including rising costs of imported fuel and rising military expenditure—one-fifth of Third World borrowing). Much of this money was concentrated in the middle-income states and further undercut political unity. The marked differentiation in growth patterns of countries intensified in the ensuing debt crisis of the 1980s, consolidating global power relations between North and South.

Global Finance

Transnational banks (TNBs) formed in the 1970s via a burgeoning offshore capital market. The TNBs were banks with deposits outside the jurisdiction or control of any government, usually in tax havens in places such as Switzerland, the Bahamas, or the Cayman Islands. TNBs made massive loans from these deposits to Third World governments throughout the 1970s. International bank lending, at $2 billion in 1972, peaked in 1981 at $90 billion, then fell to $50 billion in 1985 as a debt crisis followed the orgy of overextended loans.[16] To learn why this financial globalization occurred, we need to look at the duality of the Bretton Woods system, where *national* economic growth depended on the *international* circulation of American dollars.

Bretton Woods maintained stable exchanges of currency between trading states. Stabilization was accomplished by the American dollar's role as the international reserve currency, with the multilateral financial institutions (the World Bank and the IMF) and the U.S. Federal Reserve Bank making disbursements in dollars. At the same time, fixed currency exchanges stabilized domestic interest rates and, therefore, national economies. Governments could thus implement macroeconomic policy "without interference from the ebb and flow of international capital movements or flights of hot money," said J. M. Keynes, the architect of the postwar world economic order.[17] Within this stable monetary framework, Third World countries pursued development programs with some predictability.

The Offshore Money Market

Foreign aid and investment underwrote national economic growth during the 1950s and 1960s, breeding a growing offshore dollar market (accessed also by the Soviet Union). This was the so-called Eurocurrency market, initially centered in London's financial district. Depositing earnings in this market, TNCs evaded Bretton Woods currency stabilizing controls on cross-border movements of capital.

Eurodollar deposits ballooned as U.S. military and economic spending expanded abroad during the Vietnam War. As overseas dollar holdings ballooned, dwarfing U.S. gold reserves, they became a U.S. liability if cashed in for gold. With mounting pressure on the dollar, President Nixon burst the balloon by declaring the dollar nonconvertible in 1971. This ended the gold-dollar standard by which all currencies were *fixed* to a gold value through the U.S. dollar. From then on, currencies would *float* in relative value, with the dollar as the dominant (reserve) currency, a dollar standard more volatile than the dollar-gold standard, since it fluctuated with U.S. policies. The termination of the Bretton Woods system of fixed currency exchanges was the beginning of the end of the development project.

Just as the rise of the development project was politically managed under American political and economic leadership, so the demise of the development project was politically managed. In the early 1970s, against the wishes of Western Europe and Japan, the United States unilaterally liberalized international financial relations. Removal of exchange controls protected the autonomy of U.S. policy, separating it from financial claims in offshore markets. Floating exchange rates allowed the United States to shift the adjustment burden associated with its large deficits on to other states and investors via their speculative purchases of dollars or American assets, or revaluation of their own currencies.

The deregulation of the international financial system signaled a change in the balance of forces. *Internationally,* U.S. power was waning with the emergence of rival economies, the bloodletting of the Vietnam War, and mounting financial deficits associated with the war and overseas corporate investments. *Domestically,* conservative forces—including an increasingly coherent neoliberal coalition—and multinational corporate interests favored financial liberalization—as a mechanism to reassert U.S. power in the post–Bretton Woods era.[18]

Deregulation introduced an era of uncontrolled—and heightened—capital mobility as currency speculators bought and sold national currencies. Financial markets, rather than trade, began to determine currency values, and speculation on floating currencies destabilized national finances. By the early 1990s, world financial markets traded roughly $1 trillion daily in various currencies, all beyond the control of national governments.[19] The loss of currency control by governments threatens their political-economic sovereignty. Speculation destabilizes currency values, thus compromising planning. In 1992, Citicorp's former chairman described the currency traders, facing 200,000 trading room monitors across the world, as conducting "a kind of global plebiscite on the monetary and fiscal policies of the governments issuing currency." He found this system to be "far more draconian than any previous arrangement, such as the gold standard or the Bretton Woods system, because there is no way for a nation to opt out."[20]

Banking on Development

Fueled by the 1973 spike in oil prices engineered by OPEC, the offshore capital market grew from $315 billion in 1973 to $2,055 billion in 1982. The seven largest U.S. banks saw their overseas profits climb from 22 to 60 percent of their total profits in the same time period.[21] By the end of the 1970s, trade in foreign exchange was more than 11 times the value of world commodity trade. The instability of currencies, and therefore of profitability conditions, forced TNCs to diversify their global operations to reduce their risk.[22] In this way, the financial revolution, combined with a flood of petro-dollars, consolidated *a global production system*. With the First World in an oil price-induced recession, global banks turned to Third World governments, eager to borrow and considered unlikely to default. By encouraging massive borrowing, the banks brokered the 1970s expansion in the middle-income Third World countries, which functioned now as the engine of growth of the world economy.

In the early 1970s, bank loans accounted for only 13 percent of Third World debt, while multilateral loans made up more than 33 percent and export credits accounted for 25 percent.[23] At the end of the decade, the composition of these figures had reversed, with banks holding about 60 percent of the debt. The departures from the original development model are summarized in the following box.

Departures From the Development Model in the 1970s

The 1970s was a decade of transition, as the development project unwound. First, financial deregulation challenged national sovereignty by opening national markets to cross-border capital flows which, along with currency speculation, destabilized macroeconomic planning. Second, unregulated private bank lending displaced official, multilateral lending to Third World states, but this kind of debt financing was unsound—too much money was lent on the assumption that countries could not go bankrupt. When the debt crisis hit, austerity measures undid many of the gains of the development project. Third, TNCs produced more and more manufactured goods and agricultural products for world, rather than domestic, markets. Fourth, development discourse in the early 1970s targeted poverty alleviation, acknowledging the shortcomings of the development decades; however, by the 1980s, the discourse switched to "world market participation" as the key to development.

Willing private lenders represented a golden opportunity for Third World states to exercise some autonomy from the official financial community. Until now, they had been beholden to powerful First World states for foreign aid and to multilateral agencies for funding of their development programs. Even though official lending rose through the 1970s, from $8 billion to $45 billion,[24] global bank loans came with no strings attached, and with easy repayment terms since there was so much money to lend. By 1984, all nine of the largest U.S. banks were lending more than 100 percent of their shareholders' equity in loans to Mexico, Brazil, Argentina, and Venezuela, while Lloyds of London lent a staggering 165 percent of its capital to such countries.[25]

Loans typically served several functions. Political elites sought to legitimize rule with grand public development projects represented in nationalist terms, to strengthen their militaries, and to enrich their patronage networks with lucrative contracts resulting from loans. In Brazil, between 1964 and 1985, a string of military generals pursued the characteristic Latin American nationalist model, using loans to build the public sector in steel, energy, and raw material production. With debt financing, Brazil transformed itself from a country earning 70 percent of its export revenue from one commodity—coffee—into a major producer and exporter of a multiplicity of industrial goods—including steel, aluminum, petrochemicals, cement, glass, armaments, and aircraft—and processed foodstuffs such as orange juice and soybean meal. Rio de Janeiro and São Paulo have new subway systems, railroads take ore from huge mines deep in the interior to new ports, and major cities are linked by a modern telecommunications network.[26]

Of the 21 Latin American nations, 18 were ruled by military regimes in the 1970s, committed to investing in huge infrastructural projects, particularly in the energy sector. At the same time, between 1976 and 1984, the rise in public foreign debt roughly matched a parallel outflow of private capital to banks in New York, the Cayman Islands, and other financial havens.[27] The composition of Latin American borrowing shifted dramatically between the 1960s and the late 1970s, as official loans fell from 40 to 12 percent, private foreign direct investment fell from 34 to 16 percent, and foreign bank and bond financing rose from 7 to 65 percent.[28] Much of this expansion was organized by public- or state-owned enterprises (like a national postal service), and much of it generated export earnings. Between 1970 and 1982, the average share of gross domestic investment in the public sector of 12 Latin American countries rose from 32 to 50 percent. State managers borrowed heavily to finance the expansion of public enterprise. Often, this was done to establish a counterweight to the foreign investor presence in these economies—which, for example, accounted for about 50 percent of the Brazilian and 28 percent of the Mexican manufacturing sectors in 1970.[29]

During the 1970s, public foreign debt grew twice as fast as private foreign debt in Latin America. In Mexico, state enterprises expanded between 1970 and 1982 from 39 to 677 under the rule of the Institutional Revolutionary Party (PRI). By 1978, foreign loans financed 43 percent of the Mexican government's budget deficit and 87 percent of state-owned companies. All across Latin America, public largesse supplemented and complemented foreign and local private investment, and even subsidized basic goods and services for the largely urban poor. Regarding the Argentine military's holding company, Fabricaciones Militares, an Argentine banker claimed, "No one really knows what businesses they are in. Steel, chemicals, mining, munitions, even a whore house, everything."[30]

As public foreign debt grew in the Third World, regimes reached beyond the ideal terms of the development project, borrowing to enrich their patronage networks, strengthen power through militarization or grand projects, or simply make up lost ground. During the 1970s, state enterprises across the Third World enlarged their share of the gross domestic product (GDP) by almost 50 percent. Because it was so uncontrolled, *debt financing inflated the foundations of the development state.* Borrowing was an effective counterweight to corporate foreign investment, even when it enabled states to insist on joint ventures with foreign companies.[31] But it also deepened the vulnerability of Third World development states to banks and multilateral managers, who appeared on the scene in the 1980s.

 CASE STUDY

Containment and Corruption—Incubating the Debt Crisis

Assigning blame for the debt crisis is complicated. Certainly the old colonial tactic of surrogate rule died hard—for much of the development era, the military was the rule rather than the exception in the Third World, where the West bankrolled dictators as client regimes in the Cold War. Powerful military leaders, such as Ferdinand Marcos of the Philippines, Chile's Augusto Pinochet, and Saddam Hussein of Iraq, ruled through fear and squandered the national patrimony. It was estimated that 20 percent of loans by non-oil-exporting countries went to imports of military hardware—that is, militarizing the development project.

In the Congo, the CIA helped bring President Mobutu to power in 1965 for a rapacious 31-year rule. Mobutu renamed his country Zaire, authenticating his rule in African nationalist terms, but he traded away Zaire's vast natural resources, including a quarter of the world's copper and half its cobalt, for bank loans totaling billions of dollars and half of U.S. aid to sub-Saharan African in the late 1970s. From the spoils, he stashed $4 billion by the mid-1980s, in addition to a dozen European estates to which he traveled on chartered Concorde flights. Under his rule, Zaire gained 500 British double-decker buses, the world's largest supermarket, and an unwanted steelworks. Deposed in 1996, Mobutu's family inherited his fortune, and the country inherited his $12 billion debt.

Two years later, when General Suharto was forced to resign, his severance pay was estimated at $15 billion—13 percent of Indonesia's debt—owed mostly to the World Bank. During Suharto's dictatorship of 30 years, the World Bank loaned more than $30 billion, some of which went into constructive literacy programs, while more than $630 million underwrote the regime's infamous "transmigration" program to colonize the archipelago, including massacres in East Timor. In 1997, a secret World Bank memorandum from Jakarta disclosed a monumental development scandal: that "at least 20 to 30 percent" of the Bank's loans "are diverted through informal payments to GOI [Government of Indonesia] staff and politicians."

If containment encouraged military rule and corruption was rife, how did it serve development, and why should the burden of debt repayment be borne disproportionately by the citizen-subjects of these Third World states?

Sources: Pilger (2002:19–20); Roodman (2001:5–6, 27).

The Debt Regime

The 1980s debt crisis confirmed the demise of the Third World as a political bloc, instituting a new era of *global governance* in which individual national policies were subjected to external, rule-based procedures that strengthened the grip of the First World, through the international financial institutions (the IMF and the World Bank). The debt crisis spawned the **debt regime**. The subdivision of the Third World enabled global political and economic elites to argue that the international economic order was not responsible for the crisis centered in Latin American and African states, given the success of the Asian NICs. Debt stress elsewhere in the Third World, they claimed, stemmed from failure to copy the NICs' strategy of export diversification in the world market. Although represented as examples of market virtue (to justify **neoliberal** ideology), the NICs were in fact state-managed economies. And we now know that the debt crisis was visited upon East and Southeast Asia a decade later, in the 1997 regional financial collapse.

The export-led strategy informed a 1989 World Bank report, *Sub-Saharan Africa: From Crisis to Sustainability*. It pointed out that, regardless of whether the world market, or the environment, could absorb such a proliferation of exports,

> Declining export volumes, rather than declining export prices, account for Africa's poor export revenues. . . . If Africa's economies are to grow, they must earn foreign exchange to pay for essential imports. Thus it is vital that they increase their share of world markets. The prospects for most primary commodities are poor, so higher export earnings must come from increased output, diversification into new commodities and an aggressive export drive into the rapidly growing Asian markets.[32]

Debt was not unique to the 1980s. From 1955 to 1970, several countries (including Argentina, Brazil, Chile, Ghana, Indonesia, Peru, and Turkey) had their debt rescheduled—sometimes several times—to ease the conditions of payment. And debt servicing (paying off the interest) was consuming more than two-thirds of new lending in Latin America and Africa by the mid-1960s. The difference now was the combination in the 1970s of inflated oil prices and unsecured lending by the banks, deepening debt vulnerability.[33]

The debt crisis began in 1980 when the U.S. Federal Reserve Board moved to stem the fall in the dollar's value from its over-circulation in the 1970s lending binge. The United States reduced dollar circulation with an aggressive monetarist policy. The contraction of credit raised interest rates as banks competed for dwindling funds. Lending to Third World states slowed, and shorter terms were issued—hastening the day of reckoning on higher cost loans. Some borrowing continued, nevertheless—partly because of rising oil prices. Higher oil prices actually accounted for more than 25 percent of the total debt of the Third World. Previous debt had to be paid off too, especially the greater debt assumed by overconfident oil-producing states such as Nigeria, Venezuela, and Mexico.[34]

Third World debt totaled $1 trillion by 1986. Even though this amount was only half the U.S. national debt in that year, it was significant because countries were devoting new loans entirely to servicing previous loans.[35] Unlike the United States, cushioned by the dollar standard (the *de facto* international reserve currency preferred by countries and traders), Third World countries were unable to continue debt servicing—their dollar reserves lost value as real interest rates spiked, First World recession reduced consumption of Third World products, and Third World export revenues collapsed as primary export prices dived 17 percent relative to First World manufactured exports.[36]

The World Bank estimated the combined average annual negative effect of these "external" shocks in 1981–1982 to be 19.1 percent of GDP in Kenya, 14.3 percent in Tanzania, 18.9 percent in the Ivory Coast,

8.3 percent in Brazil, 29 percent in Jamaica, and more than 10 percent in the Philippines.[37] Third World countries were suddenly mired in a *debt trap:* debt was choking their economies. To repay the interest (at least), they had to drastically curtail imports and drastically raise exports. But reducing imports of technology jeopardized growth. Expanding exports was problematic, as commodity prices were at their lowest in 40 years due in part to the export glut. Some commodities lost markets to First World substitutes. Since the mid-1970s sugar price boom, the soft drink industry had steadily replaced sugar with fructose corn syrup, a biotechnological substitute. Other substitutes included glass fiber for copper in the new fiber-optic telecommunications technology, soy oils for tropical oils, and synthetic alternatives to rubber, jute, cotton, timber, coffee, and cocoa.[38] The market alone could not solve these problems.

Debt Management

The chosen course of action was debt management. The Bretton Woods institutions were back in the driver's seat, even though 60 percent of Third World debt was with private banks. The IMF took charge because its original task was to evaluate a country's financial condition for borrowing (which broke down in the 1970s). The IMF now had a supervisory status that individual banks did not have in the financial system at large.

Debt management took several forms. Initial stabilization measures focused on financial management (lowering imports to reduce imbalance of payments). **Structural adjustment policies (SAPs)** followed: a comprehensive restructuring of production priorities and government programs in a debtor country. Working with the World Bank and its structural adjustment loan (SAL), the IMF levied restructuring conditions on borrowers in return for loan rescheduling. By the mid-1980s, loan conditions demanded *policy restructuring,* whereby debtor states received prescriptions for political-economic reforms, including austerity measures, to stimulate economic growth and regular debt service. The debt managers drew on the Chilean model of the 1970s, where a military junta experimented with monetarist policies, slashing social expenditures to reduce debt. In 1989, the executive director of the United Nations Children's Fund (UNICEF), James P. Grant, observed,

> Today, the heaviest burden of a decade of frenzied borrowing is falling not on the military or on those with foreign bank accounts or on those who conceived the years of waste, but on the poor who are having to do without necessities, on the unemployed who are seeing the erosion of all that they have worked for, on the women who do not have enough food to maintain their health, on the

infants whose minds and bodies are not growing properly because of untreated illnesses and malnutrition, and on the children who are being denied their only opportunity to go to school. . . . It is hardly too brutal an oversimplification to say that the rich got the loans and the poor got the debts.[39]

Under this regime, the responsibility for irredeemable debt fell on the borrowers, not the lenders—unlike U.S. bankruptcy law at the time. Debt was defined as an individual liquidity problem (shortage of foreign currency) rather than a systemic problem.[40] That is, the debt managers placed the blame on the policies of the debtor countries rather than on the organization of the global financial system. Why? First, the IMF had the power to insist that debt rescheduling (including further official loans) was possible only if countries submitted to IMF evaluation and stabilization measures, including World Bank structural adjustment loans. Second, despite attempts at debt strikes (e.g., by Peru), collectively, debtors were in a weak bargaining position, given the differentiation among Third World states in growth and debt. Furthermore, an individual solution for debt rescheduling was often preferred by indebted governments to the uncertainty of a collective debtors' strike.

Mexico was the first "ticking bomb" in the global financial structure, with an $80 billion debt in 1982. Over 75 percent of this was owed to private banks (U.S. bank loans were more than 50 percent exposed in Mexico). Mexican political forces were divided between a "bankers' alliance" and the "Cárdenas alliance"—representing a nationalist coalition rooted in the labor and peasant classes.[41] The outgoing president, José López Portillo, allied with the latter group, linked the huge capital flight from his country ($30 billion between 1978–1982) to the international financial order, recommending controls on "a group of Mexicans . . . led and advised and supported by the private banks who have taken more money out of the country than the empires that exploited us since the beginning of time." Portillo opposed debt management proposals by nationalizing the Mexican banking system and installing exchange controls against capital flight, shocking the international financial community when he declared in his outgoing speech,

The financing plague is wreaking greater and greater havoc throughout the world. As in Medieval times, it is scourging country after country. It is transmitted by rats and its consequences are unemployment and poverty, industrial bankruptcy and speculative enrichment. The remedy of the witch doctors is to deprive the patient of food and subject him to compulsory rest. Those who protest must be purged, and those who survive bear witness to their virtue before the doctors of obsolete and prepotent dogma and of blind hegemonical egoism.[42]

Portillo's conservative successor, Miguel De La Madrid, campaigned on guaranteeing a reversal, forcing Portillo to concede to an IMF accord, initiated by the U.S. government and the Bank of International Settlements. To effect the bailout, the IMF put up $1.3 billion, foreign governments $2 billion, and the banks $5 billion in "involuntary loans." In 1986, Mexico was rewarded for resisting a regional effort to form a debtors' club.[43]

The Mexican bailout became a model, primarily because Mexico effectively implemented the austere measures the IMF demanded in return for debt rescheduling. As in Mexico, in other middle-income nations (e.g., Brazil, Thailand, Turkey) it has been documented that development alliance constituencies—particularly ruling elites and middle classes who benefited from the original loans—used their political power to shift repayment costs on to the working poor via austerity cuts in social services. As World Bank chief economist Stanley Fischer noted in 1989, "Most of the burden has been borne by wage earners in the debtor countries."[44]

Reversing the Development Project

As countries adopted debt regime rules and restructured their social economies, they reversed the development project. These rules had two key effects. First, they institutionalized the definition of development as "participation in the world market," focusing on export intensification. Second, rescheduling "conditions" brought dramatic adjustments in economic and social priorities within indebted countries, overriding the original development goal of managed national economic growth. Under these circumstances, social protections evolved from line-item subsidies in national policies to the status of "emergency funds"—pioneered by the World Bank as **Social Funds** to soften the impact of austerity in the Caribbean, Latin America, and Africa. These "social safety nets," such as the Bolivian Fondo de Emergencia Social, and the Egyptian Social Fund, were administered by NGOs through decentralized feeding and micro-credit programs that nonetheless bypassed communities with the least resources to propose programs, and neglected gender differences.[45] In the meantime, rescheduling bought time for debt repayment, but it came at a heavy cost.

Adjustment measures included the following:

- drastic reduction of public spending (especially on social programs, including food subsidies);
- currency devaluation (to inflate prices of imports and reduce export prices, thereby improving the balance of trade);
- export intensification (to earn foreign exchange);
- privatization of state enterprises (to "free" the market); and
- reduction of wages to attract foreign investors and reduce export prices.

Most of these measures fell hardest on the poorest and least powerful social classes—those dependent on wages and subsidies. While some businesses and export outfits prospered, poverty rates climbed. Governments saw their development alliances crumble with deindustrialization and shrinking funds for subsidizing urban constituencies.

CASE STUDY

Social Reproduction Under the Debt Regime

The austerity measures of the debt regime intensified social reproduction strategies as families split up to obtain employment, or subsistence in the countryside, and working women in particular scrambled to pool household resources to get by. On the basis of research in Mexico City, Lourdes Benería observed that, "the privatization of survival . . . in the face of decreasing governmental services and subsidies, the family had become the only source of support." As formal employment for males dwindled, women found ways to stretch their work inside and outside the home, to counterbalance loss of male income and social services and to respond to new fees for education and health care. SAPs simultaneously ignored and depended on the elasticity of women's reproductive labor. In her rich ethnography of the 1980s, *Mexican Lives,* Judith Adler Hellman interviews a woman, Josefina, who left the social experience of factory work, where she earned one and a half times minimum wages, to engage in domestic work where she earned four minimum wages—still not enough: "Right now I work six days a week, twelve hours a day, and when, for some reason, I have to get my hands on extra money, the only thing I can think of doing is to bring home laundry and wash and iron until two or three in the morning. But, at some point, even I have to go to sleep! . . . you can't sit around waiting for political parties or political leaders to rescue you, to change your life. You can only do that for yourself. And the only way you can do that is by working harder." The face of structural adjustment in Ecuador was an increased female participation rate in the labor force from 40 to 52 percent, until decimation of factory work forced them back into domestic service or street vendoring. In Bolivia, many rural women assumed responsibility for farms as partners, fathers, and sons migrated for jobs, while other rural women migrated to cities to take domestic work, joining urban women who also left home to find work, leaving their children to play in city streets. Across Africa and Latin America (other than the Mexican *maquiladoras*), Davis notes that deindustrialization, with male emigration, "compelled women to improvise new livelihoods as piece workers, liquor sellers, street vendors, lottery ticket sellers, hairdressers, sewing operators, cleaners, washers, ragpickers, nannies, and prostitutes."

Why should the "comparative advantage of women's disadvantage" replace the "social contract" as a premise for the new development model prescribed by the debt regime?   ☯

Sources: Benería (1992:97); Davis (2006:159); Dolan (2004); Hellman (1994:71–72); Kohl and Farthing (2006:82).

In Mexico, as part of the IMF loan rescheduling conditions in 1986, food subsidies for basic foods such as tortillas, bread, beans, and rehydrated milk were eliminated. Malnourishment grew. Minimum wages fell 50 percent between 1983 and 1989, and purchasing power fell to two-thirds of the 1970 level. The number of Mexicans in poverty rose from 32.1 to 41.3 million, matching the absolute increase in population size during 1981–1987. By 1990, the basic needs of 41 million Mexicans were unsatisfied, and 17 million lived in extreme poverty.[46] Meanwhile, manufacturing growth rates plummeted, from 1.9 in 1980–1982 to 0.1 in 1985–1988, leading to a considerable decline in formal employment opportunities.[47] Coupled with drastic cuts in social services, the reduction in manufacturing led to further deterioration of living standards. By 1987, 10 million people could not gain access to the health system, a situation that contributed to the "epidemiological polarization" among social classes and regions—such as the difference between the infant mortality rates of northern and southern Mexico, as well as between those of rural and urban areas and lower and upper classes.[48] With extensive state financial support, Mexico became a significant agro-exporter—by 1986, exporting to the United States more than $2 billion worth of fresh fruits, vegetables, and beef but also importing from that country $1.5 billion in farm products, largely basic grains and oil seeds. IMF conditions raised prices on staple foods, reducing the state's role in subsidizing food staples.[49]

In Africa, the severity of the debt burden meant that Tanzania, the Sudan, and Zambia were using more than 100 percent of their export earnings to service debt in 1983. In Zambia, the ratio of outstanding debt to gross national product (GNP) increased from 16 to 56 percent in 1985. African economies were particularly vulnerable to the fall in commodity prices during the 1980s, with individual export commodities counting for anything between 40 and 85 percent of export earnings. With falling commodity prices, an African coffee exporter had to produce 30 percent more coffee to pay for one imported tractor and then produce more coffee to pay for the oil to run it.[50]

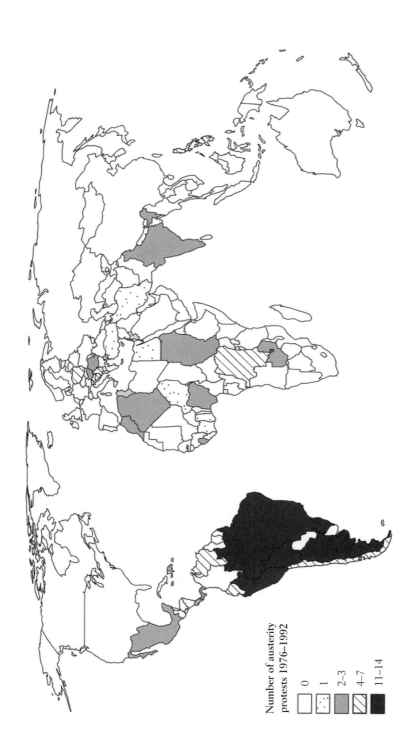

Number of austerity
protests 1976–1992

☐	0
⊡	1
▦ (gray)	2–3
▨ (hatched)	4–7
■ (black)	11–14

Figure 5.1   Locations of Riots Against Austerity Programs

IMF/World Bank adjustment policies in Africa reduced food subsidies and public services, leading to urban demonstrations and riots in Tanzania, Ghana, Zambia, Morocco, Egypt, Tunisia, and Sudan. In Zambia, for example, the price of cornmeal—a staple—rose 120 percent in the mid-1980s following adjustment. And since corn is a crop controlled by men, cultivation of corn was expanded at the expense of peanuts, a cash crop grown by women. School enrollments declined as skilled Africans migrated in droves. Between 1980 and 1986, average per capita income declined by 10 percent, and unemployment almost tripled.[51] In effect, all the "development" indicators, including infant mortality, took a downturn under the impact of adjustment policies. Oxfam reported in 1993 that World Bank adjustment programs in sub-Saharan Africa were largely responsible for reductions in public health spending and a 10 percent decline in primary school enrollment. In the late 1980s, UNICEF and the UN Commission for Africa reported that adjustment programs were largely the cause of reduced health, nutritional, and educational levels for tens of millions of children in Asia, Latin America, and Africa.[52]

CASE STUDY

IMF Riots—Citizens Versus Structural Adjustment

The so-called "IMF riots" swept across the Second and Third Worlds, expressing the demise of the development project. Between 1976 and 1992, some 146 riots occurred in 39 of the approximately 80 debtor countries, including Romania, Poland, Yugoslavia, and Hungary. These large-scale, often coordinated, urban uprisings protested the public austerity measures, the rioters often breaking into food banks. Walton and Seddon define these austerity protests as "large-scale collective actions including political demonstrations, general strikes, and riots . . . animated by grievances over state policies of economic liberalization implemented in response to the debt crisis and market reforms urged by international agencies."

The rioters contested the unequal distribution of the means of livelihood, targeting policies that eroded the social contract. Collapsing social entitlements included a range of subsidized services to members of hyper-urbanized environments, including food, health care, education, transportation, and housing. Riots sought to restore basic mechanisms of social reproduction. They also targeted the IMF as the source of policies undermining national public capacity, and therefore, popular sovereignty. Björn Beckman claimed that the logic of the structural adjustment program was to "further weaken the motivation of the state to respond to the popular demands that have been built into the process of postcolonial state formation."

Given the profound transition underway across the structurally adjusted Third World, should this series of protests be understood as being about more than shrinking material resources—such as shrinking democratic space, or even the demise of the promise of development?   🌍

Sources: Beckman (1992:97); Kagarlitsky (1995:217); Walton and Seddon (1994).

During the "lost decade" of the 1980s, the poorer regions of the world economy lost considerable ground. From 1978 to 1992, more than 70 countries of the former Third World undertook 566 stabilization and structural adjustment programs imposed by the IMF and the World Bank to control their debt.[53] All this restructuring did not necessarily resolve the debt crisis. In fact, the debtor countries collectively entered the 1990s with 61 percent more debt than they had held in 1982.[54] If we combine per capita GDP figures with changes in terms of trade and debt rescheduling, average per capita income is estimated to have fallen 15 percent in Latin America and 30 percent in Africa during the 1980s. But in South and East Asian countries, by contrast, per capita income rose. These states were more in step with the global economy, benefiting from the oil boom in the Middle East, the most rapidly growing market, to which they exported labor, receiving lucrative remittances in turn. The Asian states were relatively immune to the "lost decade" because the ratio of their debt service to exports was half that of the Latin American countries during the 1970s.[55]

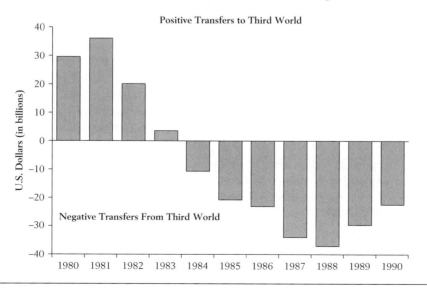

Figure 5.2   Net Transfers of Long-Term Loans to Third World States
Source: UN, *Human Development Report* (1997:64).

As a consequence of growing debt, many countries found themselves under greater scrutiny by global managers, in addition to surrendering greater amounts of their wealth to global agencies. The turning point was 1984. In that year, the direction of capital flows reversed—that is, the inflow of loan and investment capital into the former Third World was replaced by an *out-flow* in the form of debt repayment (see Figure 5.2). The (net) extraction of financial resources from the Third World during the 1980s exceeded $400 billion.[56] At the same time, massive bank debt had become public debt, the repayment of which now fell on the shoulders of the governments themselves, especially their more vulnerable citizens. The banks wrote off some debt, but they were protected from complete debt loss by the First World governments, whose central bankers had agreed in 1974 (with the Bank of International Settlements) to stand behind commercial bank loans, as lenders of last resort.[57]

The debt crisis exacerbated the demise of the Third World. It continued to lose collective political ground as debt management eroded national sovereignty, and it fractured into several zones, including a "Fourth World"— impoverished regions, especially in countries in sub-Saharan Africa. At the same time, the demise of Third World collective and national sovereignty was mirrored in the opening up of the Third World, now as the global South, to Northern-imposed disciplines, foreign investment, and unsustainable export production to defray debt.

Challenging the Development State

Debt regime procedures eroded national economic management and, by extension, the social contract development states had with their citizens. Keynesian (state interventionist) policies eroded through the 1970s in the First World as an emerging neo-liberal doctrine proposed "freeing markets from the state." Public expenditure fell, as trade and financial liberalization rose, enabling relocation of firms offshore, and undermining organized labor.

As neo-liberalism consolidated its orthodoxy in the 1980s, debt managers demanded a *shrinking* of states of the former Third World, through reductions in social spending and the **privatization** of state enterprises. As a condition of debt rescheduling, governments sold off their public assets. As a result, the average number of privatizations in this region of the world expanded tenfold across the decade. From 1986 to 1992, the proportion of World Bank SALs demanding privatization rose from 13 to 59 percent, and by 1992 more than 80 countries had privatized almost 7,000 public enterprises—mostly public services such as water, electricity, or telephones.[58]

Although there is no doubt that some development state elites had pursued excessive public financing, privatization accomplished two radical changes:

- It reduced public capacity in developmental planning and implementation, thereby privileging the corporate sector.
- It extended the reach of foreign ownership of assets in the global South— precisely the condition that governments had tried to overcome in the 1970s.

Between 1980 and 1992, the stock of *international* bank lending rose from 4 to 44 percent of the GDP of the countries of the Organisation for Economic Co-operation and Development.[59] Rather than losing the money they had loaned in such excessive amounts, banks earned vast profits on the order of 40 percent per annum on Third World investments alone.[60] Foreign investment in the Third World resumed between 1989 and 1992, increasing from $29 billion to $40 billion (especially in Mexico, China, Malaysia, Argentina, and Thailand).[61] The restructured global South was now quite profitable for private investment: wages were low, governments were not competing in the private capital markets, and an export boom in raw materials, manufactures, and foodstuffs was underway.

Through a case-by-case adjustment, the debt regime transformed the development project. Martin Khor, director of the Third World Network, saw structural adjustment as

a mechanism to shift the burden of economic mismanagement and financial mismanagement from the North to the South, and from the Southern elites to the Southern communities and people. Structural adjustment is also a policy to continue colonial trade and economic patterns developed during the colonial period, but which the Northern powers want to continue in the post-colonial period.[62]

Each measure either undermined the coherence, or commercialized the sovereignty, of national economies. Lowered wages reduced local purchasing power. Wage earners had to tighten their belts; as a result, the market for local goods contracted. Privatization of public enterprises reduced state capacity. They were no longer in a position to enter into joint ventures with private firms and lay plans for production priorities; rather, private firms appropriated formerly public functions (those that were profitable). Finally, export expansion often displaced local production systems. The case study of the Dominican Republic offers a parallel example of the challenge to state developmentalism under the conditions of the debt regime.

CASE STUDY

Turning the Dominican Republic Inside Out?

Ever since the Dominican Republic achieved independence from Spain in the nineteenth century, it has been a "sugar republic," with secondary exports of coffee, cocoa, and tobacco. In the 1980s, the contribution of these primary commodity exports to total export earnings fell from 58 to 33 percent. Under pressure from the IMF, the government responded with an *export-substitution strategy* to generate new export revenues to service its substantial foreign debt. This strategy fit with the 1980s U.S. Caribbean Basin Initiative (CBI) to promote foreign investment in agro-exports. Nontraditional exports included tropical root crops such as yams and taro; vegetables and horticultural crops such as peppers, tomatoes, green beans, and eggplants; and tropical fruits such as melons, pineapples, and avocados. Beef products were the most significant agro-industrial export.

Agricultural restructuring reversed government supports for basic food production, with the result that more than 50 percent of the Dominican household food basket was now imported. As elsewhere, domestic food production depended on state support, restriction of imports, subsidized credit and technical assistance for small producers, and stabilization of prices for the poorer classes. Credit for these social programs dried up following structural adjustment. Rice, heavily subsidized for low prices, was "liberalized" in 1988, undermining a national crop and creating greater reliance on rice imports.

Meanwhile, the government leased old sugar plantation lands to TNCs, such as Chiquita and Dole, for pineapple production. With plantations elsewhere—in Hawaii, Thailand, the Philippines, Guatemala, and Honduras—TNCs are able to negotiate favorable conditions from host governments. Laura Raynolds noted that "most of the roughly 2,000 workers in the new pineapple plantations are casual day laborers who are unprotected by national labor legislation. These workers, many of whom are women, have no job security and are paid less than even the subminimum wage. Labor unions have either been crushed outright or co-opted by the combined forces of the state and the transnational corporations."

If governments expand agro-industrial production to improve their participation in the world market, how can this new form of neoliberal development be equitable and sustainable?

Sources: Raynolds (1994:218, 231–232); Raynolds et al. (1993:1111).

State and Society Restructuring

During the debt regime, the World Bank established local agencies (parastatals) to administer its SAPs. Giving the market free rein is arguably a euphemism for allowing global actors (representatives of IFIs, banks, firms) a stronger hand in determining what should be produced, where, and for whom. Structural adjustment loans restructure national economies and redistribute power within the state. The latter involves privileging the central bank and trade and finance ministries over program-oriented ministries (social services, agriculture, education). This power shift removes resources from state agencies that support and regulate economic (e.g., ISI) and social sectors affecting the majority of the citizenry, especially the poorer classes. These resources are shifted to the agencies more directly connected to global enterprise: global economic criteria override national social criteria.

Perhaps the most dramatic example of state restructuring was that of Mexico. Between 1980 and 1991, Mexico negotiated 13 SALs with the World Bank and six agreements with the IMF. The Bank proposed an agricultural SAL in 1986 to assist in the elimination of tariffs on imported food, privatization of rural parastatal agencies, liberalization of trade and domestic food prices, "sound" public investment, and cutbacks in the agricultural ministry. These were the conditions of the loan. Rural social services gave way to agro-industrial priorities. In 1991, a follow-up SAL further liberalized food importing, privatized state-owned monopolies, and eliminated price guarantees on corn—a drastic step. Deteriorating social conditions forced the Bank to subsidize national Pronasol and Procampo programs, offering financial assistance to poor rural producers. Mexico experienced a decade of liberal reforms, mandated by the global managers and pursued by the government to maintain its creditworthiness—a dress rehearsal for NAFTA.[63]

In Africa, SAPs reveal a telling rethinking of the state's role in development. Initially, as presented in the World Bank's 1981 (Berg) report, the goal of "shrinking" the state was justified as a way to improve efficiency and reduce urban bias.[64] Structural adjustment programs directly challenged the political coalitions and goals of the national development state. At the same time, SAPs strengthened finance ministries in the policy-making process. Within African states, power moved from the development coalitions (urban planning, agriculture, education) to the financial group, managing a state's ability to obtain international credit. The report revealed a shift in Bank lending practices from assisting development concerns to tying aid to "comprehensive policy reform."[65]

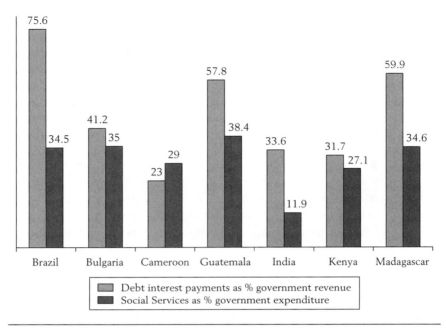

Figure 5.3   Government Spending on Foreign Debt and Social Services
(Selected Countries, 1995)

Source: World Bank, *World Development Report,* 1998–1999.

Note: Social Services includes health, education, social security, welfare, housing, and community services.

The World Bank's premise for the policy shift was that development states were overbureaucratic and inefficient on one hand, and unresponsive to their citizenry on the other. In the Bank's sub-Saharan Africa report, it reinterpreted "shrinking" the state to mean a reorganization of state administration to encourage popular initiatives. Some of these observations were credible, confirmed by authoritarian government, corruption, and "hollow" development financing—such as Zaire President Mobutu's lavish global-set lifestyle and Côte d'Ivoire President Félix Houphouët-Boigny's construction in his home village of a larger-than-the-original replica of St. Peter's basilica in the Vatican. Nevertheless, the solutions proposed and imposed by the Bank substituted growing external control of these countries in the name of financial orthodoxy.[66] In its 1989 report titled *Sub-Saharan Africa: From Crisis to Sustainable Growth: A Long-Term Perspective Study,* the Bank advanced the idea of "political conditionality." It proposed "policy dialogue" with recipient states, leading to "consensus forming"—a sophisticated way of constructing political coalitions within the recipient state that embrace economic reforms proposed by the multilateral agencies.[67] One observer noted, "It has become an explicit target of the institutions, and the World Bank in particular, to shift the balance of power within governments towards those who expect to gain from the policy reforms encouraged by the institutions and/or those who are in any case more sympathetic towards such changes."[68]

This strategy is actually a way of remaking states through "institution building." It continues the original practice of Bank projects legitimizing the input of technical experts in national planning. The new practice deepens IFI involvement by organizing coalitions in the state committed to redefining the government's economic priorities, at the expense of accountability to the citizenry. Noting the revival of "trusteeship" in the 1990s, Jeffrey Sachs observed,

> Not unlike the days when the British Empire placed senior officials directly into the Egyptian and Ottoman finance ministries, the IMF is insinuated into the inner sanctums of nearly 75 developing-country governments around the world—countries with a combined population of some 1.4 billion. These governments rarely move without consulting the IMF staff, and when they do, they risk their lifelines to capital markets, foreign aid, and international respectability.[69]

When states become unaccountable, citizens may withdraw into a "shadow" economy and society, as illustrated in the Tanzanian case study.

CASE STUDY

Tanzanian Civil Society Absorbs Structural Adjustment

While structural adjustment is a standard prescription, its implementation varies across states, depending on government capacity and levels of social and political resistance from the citizenry. Resistance takes both formal and informal paths. Political democratization may be one outcome of urban grassroots resistance to their government's betrayal of the development alliance's social pact in implementing austerity measures. Another may involve depending on the "informal economy" as a survival strategy. This is the case in Tanzania, a country founded in President Nyerere's vision of a benevolent state anchored in rural villages practicing an African socialism of shared property, collective labor, and a social ethic derived from the traditional African family.

At the turn of the 1980s, the Tanzanian state, with an already weakened capacity to extract resources, initiated a policy of economic liberalization prior to a 1986 agreement with the IMF, which deepened economic distress. While public sector managers and the mass party organizations opposed structural adjustment, urban dwellers in general were surprisingly quiescent. Between 1974 and 1988, with real wages falling by 83 percent, Tanzanians intensified their income-generating activities "off the books"—with crop sales on parallel markets in the agricultural sector; sideline incomes for wage workers such as baking, carpentry, or tailoring; schoolchildren absenteeism so that children could work for family income; supplementary tutorials by school teachers; moonlighting physicians; and so forth. As Aili Maria Tripp remarks, austerity "was somewhat softened by the fact that more than 90 percent of household income was coming from informal businesses, primarily operated by women, children, and the elderly. By providing alternatives to the state's diminishing resource base, these strategies diverted demands that otherwise might have overwhelmed the state . . . In the end, little was demanded of a state that had placed itself at the center of the nation's development agenda and had established itself as the guarantor of society's welfare."

Does this kind of self-organizing activity offer us a glimpse of an alternative, sustainable conception of development, or is it simply an intensified form of feminized social reproduction? 🌍

Sources: Rist (1997:130–132); Tripp (1997:3–6, 13).

In summary, the debt regime reformulated the terms of economic management, relocating power within states, and from states in the former Third World to global agencies. World Bank and IMF programs of adjustment substituted for a true multilateral management of the debt crisis. These conditions imposed standard rather than locally tailored remedies on indebted states. Governments and business elites in the former Third World countries collaborated in this enterprise, often for the same reasons they had promoted development financing in previous decades: they are well placed to benefit from infusions of foreign capital, some of which is used for patronage. Meanwhile, the debt burden is borne disproportionately by the poor.

Summary

The demise of the Third World as a political bloc had political and economic origins. Politically, its subordination came about through the politics of containment, whereby Western intervention and military alliances secured client regimes in strategic world regions. Democracy was less important than showcasing development favoring a free enterprise model and "economic openness." As the NAM lost influence, the Third World regrouped to pressure the First World to reform the architecture of the international economy, via the unsuccessful NIEO bid. The defeat of this political initiative dovetailed with the economic differentiation among Third World countries.

Global financial organization mapped on to global production systems emerging via Third World export strategies. Offshore money markets redistributed private capital to governments as loans, and transnational corporations invested in export production. A frenzy of development initiatives ensued, as Third World states sought to emulate the NICs. Public investments complemented and underwrote private enterprise. When credit dried up in the 1980s, debt repayment schemes reversed both aid-for-development programs and TNC investment. Debt rescheduling concentrated financial power in the hands of the IFIs, and was conditioned on the privatization of state agencies and projects, as well as erosion of the social contract. This marked consolidation of "global governance," whereby lending institutions adopted a powerful trusteeship role in the debtor nations in the 1980s, a relationship founded in a growing faith in the authority of the market. In this sense, the debt crisis was a dress rehearsal for the globalization project.

Further Reading

Benería, Lourdes and Shelley Feldman, eds. *Unequal Burden: Economic Crises, Persistent Poverty, and Women's Work*. Boulder, CO: Westview Press, 1992.

George, Susan. *The Debt Boomerang: How Third World Debt Harms Us All*. Boulder, CO: Westview Press, 1992.

Gibbon, Peter, Yusuf Bangura, and Arve Ofstad. *Authoritarianism, Democracy and Adjustment: The Politics of Economic Reform in Africa*. Uppsala, Sweden: Nordiska Afrikainstitutet, 1992.

Woods, Ngaire. *The Globalizers: The IMF, the World Bank and Their Borrowers*. Ithaca, NY: Cornell University Press, 2006.

Select Websites

Bretton Woods Project (USA): www.brettonwoodsproject.org
Structural Adjustment Participatory Review International Network: www.saprin.org

PART III

The Globalization Project
(1980s–)

6

Instituting the
Globalization Project

The globalization project succeeded the development project—not because development is dead but because its coordinates have changed. Development, formerly a public project, has now been redefined as a private, global project. Why not just "globalization" (without the project)? Isn't globalization inevitable? Maybe so, but as a vehicle of development it is sobering to realize that, despite the promise of prosperity with "free markets," material benefits are largely confined to only about one-third of the world's population. The remainder toil in highly exploitative work settings, or struggle to survive on marginal lands or urban margins, as markets capture resources for the global minority that has purchasing power. To call it a project emphasizes the politics of globalization. Markets are neither natural nor free. They are institutional constructs, managed by powerful players, including international financial institutions, banks, corporations, states, and even non-governmental organizations (NGOs). The distinctiveness of the globalization project is that it has involved political intervention to overcome the limits of the development project.

As we saw in the previous chapter, economic nationalism came to be viewed as limiting development because it obstructed the transnational mobility of goods, money, and firms in the service of efficient (i.e., private) allocation of global resources. As early as 1971, at the inception of the (corporate-based) World Economic Forum, its first publication declared: "Nationalism is economically indefensible."[1] And so, with economic nationalism in decline, the development mantle has been assumed by powerful corporate players in the world market. Representing them are institutions such as the World Trade Organization (WTO) that seek to govern this new global project. The founding director-general of the WTO, Renato Ruggiero, expressed this when he observed in 2000,

> It is a new world. . . . The Cold War is over. Even more significant is the rise of the developing world as a major power in the international economy as a result of the shift to freer markets and open trade—an event that could rank with the industrial revolution in historical significance. All this is taking place against the backdrop of globalization—the linking together of countries at different levels of development by technology, information, and ideas, as well as by economics.

To be more explicit, the future of development lies with the world market, linked by the rules of neoclassical economic discourse. Ruggiero goes on to say,

> More than ever before, trade and the rules of the trading system intersect with a broad array of other policies and issues—from investment and competition policy to environmental, developmental, health, and labor standards. . . . If we want real coherence in global policymaking and a comprehensive international agenda, then coordination has to come from the top, and it must be driven by elected leaders . . . progress in resolving the challenge of the new century will hinge on our ability not just to build a coherent global architecture, but to build a political constituency for globalization. . . . Without the WTO, we will go back to a world of national barriers, protectionism, economic nationalism, and conflict.[2]

Thus the director-general of the WTO articulated the vision of the globalization project: the implementation of "market rule" via the restructuring of policies and standards across the nation-state system. Trade (two-thirds of which is controlled by TNCs) was to be privileged as the vehicle of development. Internationalist ideals stem from the view that trade brings peace. But does this axiom hold, and what kind of trade relationships do we mean? After more than two decades of trade liberalization, the world order is marked by war, terror, and various forms of fundamentalism (economic, religious, ethnic), responsible for an array of social exclusion and conflict.

The globalization project did not begin on any particular date, but it signifies a new way of thinking about development. Global management of capitalism emerged in the 1970s (with the G-7), and in the 1980s when the Bretton Woods institutions made explicit claims about *managing a global economy*, as the global managers implemented a debt regime.

The global managers include the Bretton Woods institutions, transnational corporate elites (arguably a global ruling class with an interest in facilitating market rule to privilege corporate rights), and governments restructured for market freedoms. Among these political and economic elites, a consensus emerged, redefining development in private terms emphasizing "trade not aid." Backed with the financial coercion of multilateral institutional debt management, it assumed the name of the **Washington Consensus**. Thus the globalization project was born.

As we shall see, the globalization project rests on unstable foundations, expressed in a growing array of alternatives articulated by mushrooming resistance movements as well as by disaffected members of the Washington Consensus. Here we focus on the institutional dimensions and tensions of the globalization project to illustrate the new global politics of development.

What Are the Elements of the Globalization Project?

The globalization project combines several strands:

- a (Washington-based) consensus among global managers/policymakers favoring market-based rather than state-managed development strategies;
- centralized management of global market rules by the G-7 states;
- implementation of these rules through multilateral agencies (World Bank, IMF, and WTO);
- concentration of market power in the hands of TNCs and financial power in TNBs;
- subjection of all states to economic disciplines (trade, financial), varying by geopolitical position, global currency hierarchy, debt load, resource endowments, and so forth;
- realization of global development via new class, gender, race, and ethnic inequalities; and
- resistance at all levels, from marginalized communities to state managers to factions even within multilateral institutions, contesting unbridled market rule.

The Globalization Project

Officially, globalization is considered a global development strategy—in World Bank terms, this means *successful participation in the world economy*. During the 1980s, the means to development was identified with liberalization—in particular, privatization of public functions and the "freeing" of markets for labor, money, goods, and services. U.S. President Reagan reiterated this theme in 1985: "America's economic success . . . can be repeated a hundred times in a hundred nations. Many countries in East Asia and the Pacific have few resources other than the enterprise of their own people. But through free markets they've soared ahead of centralized economies."[3] While Reagan's statement was historically inaccurate (the NICs combined strong states with protectionism), nevertheless this neoliberal ideology served to guide structural adjustment policies as the precursors of the globalization project.

The export orientation of the East Asian NICs thus was idealized to legitimize market rule across the world. In fact, the Reagan administration turned the free market ideal *against* the economic nationalism of Japan and the Asian NICs to open their markets. Meanwhile, the United States led a parallel attempt to build a free market global consensus—focusing on breaking down the resistance of the Soviet empire (the Second World) to market capitalism. This was central to the emerging globalization project.

CASE STUDY

Incorporating the Second World Into the Globalization Project

The restructuring of the Second World marked its demise, with the Cold War ending in 1989. This set the stage for the globalization project, realizable only in a unilateral (versus a bipolar) world order.

In 1986, Hungary, Romania, the former Yugoslavia, and Poland were subject to IMF supervision of their economies. Most of these states had started borrowing from Western financial institutions during the 1970s, often to pay for basic consumer items demanded by their increasingly restive civilian populations. By 1986, Soviet President Mikhail Gorbachev was formulating plans for *perestroika* (restructuring) in exchange for membership in the Bretton Woods institutions.

Earlier, in 1982, the IMF had tendered an austerity plan in Hungary on the condition that centrally planned production be replaced by "market-responsive" and "financially disciplined" enterprises, along with reductions in subsidies of food, transportation, heating fuel, and housing. These subsidies were the foundation of the well-established basic *economic* rights of the socialist systems. During the 1980s, small-scale state enterprises were privatized, and workers were now earning piece rates determined not by the work performed (a normal union contract) but by the profit rate of the enterprise. Social equality was being redefined along Western lines as the equality of "private opportunity." But former public officials in the Second World had the lock on opportunity, enriching themselves and their relatives as public property was privatized. Joyce Kolko remarked, "There was growing resentment in the general population at the rising prices, falling living standards, and the new rich."

By the early 1990s, Eastern European per capita income levels resembled those of the former Third World. The per capita incomes of Poland and Mexico were about the same, as were those of Hungary and Brazil. Because Eastern European populations have higher levels of education and stable population growth rates, they differ from former Third World societies. In far-eastern Russia, South Korean companies outsourced garment production to beat quotas on apparel imports into the United States under the Multi-Fiber Agreement. Just 440 miles from Seoul, where average hourly apparel labor costs were $2.69 in 1998, Vladivostok labor cost only 56 cents an hour—some of that labor being Chinese! Because Chinese workers are used to 12-hour days and two days off a month, Korean employers have used Chinese labor to pressure desperate Russian seamstresses and cutters into accepting sweatshop working conditions.

The incorporation of Eastern Europe into the project of globalization reveals a deep compromise of citizens' basic needs in the name of the market. Did the precipitous decline in Russian living standards, with an explosion of organized crime and AIDS, portend development under globalization?

Sources: Kagarlitsky (1995); Kolko (1988:278–96); Working (1999:D1, 23).

With the advent of the globalization project, development has not disappeared; rather, its meaning has changed and become more problematic. Global elites have reframed development as the deepening of markets, as resource allocators. As governments privilege markets, they are likely to disadvantage citizens who are vulnerable to, or unable to participate or compete in, markets. Far from being a "flat world," the global market has quite selective criteria, favoring mobile corporations (and jobs) over relatively immobile populations. Governments face a constant dilemma of balancing the quite unequal needs of their citizens with the competitive volatility of investment and trade relations (to which they are beholden via their national accounts and currency value). Freeing of markets has an elegant ring until it threatens public systems of social reproduction, rendering large segments of national populations vulnerable to shrinking social securities and insecure employment. The globalization project involves political choices to (re)define the bearings and future of states and their civic responsibilities. If competing in the world market requires policies reducing public expenditure that may reduce safeguards and standards of employment, health care, and education, then globalization is a decision, not an inevitability.

The choices implicit in the globalization project call forth different interpretations of the purpose of development—whether it is governed by economic efficiency or social justice, corporate or social welfare, resource exploitation or ecological sustainability, centralized political-economic power or participatory economic democracy, or market versus human values. We are witnessing a massive tug-of-war across the world between proponents of these various positions. The tug-of-war has simplified into two camps, symbolized by the annual meetings of the **World Economic Forum** (representing officialdom: the global political-economic managers and corporate elite) and the **World Social Forum** (representing global justice movements against the dominant corporate model). A key source of tension concerns the relatively new concept of governance, which overrides and reformulates government.

Global Governance

In the shift from development to globalization projects, governments face a world order in which global institutions have assumed a more powerful governing role. This role is by no means absolute, and it requires compliance from the states themselves. The question of compliance is central, as there are two ways of guaranteeing compliance: consensus and coercion:

- Consensus works where governments and citizens accept the legitimacy of neo-classical economic theory: that market rule is neutral and efficient.
- Coercion is necessary where liberalization is questioned or resisted.

Ultimately, the most effective way of guaranteeing compliance is to institutionalize market rule, where individual governmental functions are recomposed as global governance functions and enforced through multilateral protocols. Indeed, at the first ministerial meeting of the WTO in December 1996, Director-General Ruggiero remarked that preparing a global investment treaty was similar to "writing the constitution of a single global economy." Here we examine how **global governance** has evolved.

The governance mechanisms of today were anticipated in World Bank loan policy changes in the midst of the debt crisis. Traditionally, the Bank focused on *project* loans for public infrastructure in Third World states.

Project loans continue into the present, but in the 1980s the Bank shifted its emphasis from project to *policy* loans. It linked loans to policies that pursued market-oriented economic growth strategies, especially the structural adjustment loan (SAL). In 1983, World Bank President Clausen remarked, "The fundamental philosophy of our institution is to help countries diversify their exports . . . and to have an export orientation."[4] The priority had shifted to stabilizing global financial relations and opening up southern economies to accelerated resource extraction, rather than funding national projects.

By the 1990s, global debt management was firmly institutionalized in the World Bank and the IMF. As these institutions were ultimately beholden to the so-called Group of 7 (G-7) "northern" powers, the newly formed South Commission (an organ of the global South) made a provocative declaration in 1990:

> What is abundantly clear is that the North has used the plight of developing countries to strengthen its dominance and its influence over the development paths of the South. . . . While adjustment is pressed on them, countries in the North with massive payments imbalances are immune from any pressure to adjust, and free to follow policies that deepen the South's difficulties. The most powerful countries in the North have become a *de facto* board of management for the world economy, protecting their interests and imposing their will on the South. The governments of the South are then left to face the wrath, even the violence, of their own people, whose standards of living are being depressed for the sake of preserving the present patterns of operation of the world economy.[5]

While identifying global governance, perhaps narrowly, with the North–South power relation, the South Commission's declaration draws attention to a new dimension in development discourse: the priority given to managing the world economy as a *singular entity*. In other words, the World Bank/IMF partnership in structurally adjusting particular states is a method of governing and an attempt to resolve the instability in a deregulated global money market. Ongoing management of global financial relations has become a practical necessity to stabilize economies and open or "denationalize" them in the process.

 CASE STUDY

Mexican Sovereignty Exposed—From Above and Below

Mexico's admission into the Organisation for Economic Co-operation and Development (OECD) via its participation in NAFTA precipitated the 1994 *Zapatista* uprising in Chiapas, a region of intensive resource extraction by foreign companies. Protesting President Salinas's decision, *Zapatista* spokesperson Subcomandante Marcos claimed it was a "death sentence for indigenous peoples." The *Zapatistas* declared, "When we rose up against a national government, we found that it did not exist. In reality we were up against great financial capital, against speculation and investment, which makes all decisions in Mexico, as well as in Europe, Asia, Africa, Oceania, the Americas—everywhere." Having questioned Mexican sovereignty, the uprising unsettled regional financial markets. The *Zapatistas* suggested that NAFTA was a confidence trick of the globalization project:

> At the end of 1994 the economic farce with which Salinas had deceived the Nation and the international economy exploded. The nation of money called the grand gentlemen of power and arrogance to dinner, and they did not hesitate in betraying the soil and sky in which they prospered with Mexican blood. The economic crisis awoke Mexicans from the sweet and stupifying dream of entry into the first world.

The Mexican *peso* lost 30 percent of its value in December 1994, generating a negative "tequila effect" throughout Latin American financial markets. International financiers hastily assembled a financial loan package of $18 billion to stabilize the *peso*. The United States committed over $9 billion, while the European Central Banks provided $5 billion. Canada also contributed $1 billion, and a dozen global banks, including Citibank, added a $3 billion line of credit. Finally, the IMF was called in to lend both money *and* its stamp of approval to restore investor confidence in the Mexican economy. U.S. President Clinton remarked in 1995, "Mexico is sort of a bellwether for the rest of Latin America and developing countries throughout the world." Confidence in NAFTA was also at stake.

If the Mexican bailout was to stabilize the global economy and legitimize the globalization project, the question remains why Chiapas has been occupied by the Mexican federal army ever since. What is it about the globalization project that makes it value foreign investment over minority rights?

Sources: Bradsher (1995:D6); Starr (2000).

Global circuits (of debt, money, investment, and pension funds) are so embedded in national economies (and vice versa) that stabilizing these destabilizing financial relations now dominates national policy making. In this way, the new forms of global governance seek, simultaneously, to ensure open economies and the institutional mechanisms to manage the volatile side effects—evidenced in domino-like financial crises. While adopted by countries (variably), governance protocols favoring open markets reflect requirements of, or conditions favored by, the **global managers**—officials of the international financial institutions (IMF, World Bank), G-7 political elites, executives of TNCs, and global bankers. Indebted states restructure their political-economic priorities to obtain creditworthiness in the eyes of the global financial community. An agro-export priority, which may negatively affect national food security, nonetheless conforms to the requirements of sound financial policy. It may enhance foreign exchange earnings for a time, but it reorients agriculture to supplying foreign consumers. Thus global governance essentially deepens global market relations within states.

Internalizing global governance involves two significant (and related) changes in power relations:

- Debt rescheduling conditions actively reorganize the structure and priorities of states and societies.
- Reorganization is unrepresentative, as global bureaucrats, responding to financial signals rather than citizen scrutiny, often decide how states should conduct their economic affairs.

The first change has involved deploying loan conditions to establish a set of norms and disciplines to reward those countries complying with the policies of the Washington Consensus, and to penalize those not complying. An UNCTAD analyst noted that the reframing of development was expressed in a shift to "ahistorical performance assessment," grouping countries as "success stories" or "failures," depending on their willingness to adopt policy reforms, and remain accountable to the norms of global governance.[6]

The second consequence of the governance revolution has been an expanding "trusteeship" role for the multilateral agencies. This procedure illustrates the reach of global regulatory mechanisms in framing national policy making, compromising national sovereignty. Under these conditions, the World Bank, now the principal development (financing) agency, has played a definite governing role. It "dictate[s] legal and institutional change through its lending process" and, since its 1989 report, it now asserts that evaluating governance in debtor countries is within its jurisdiction[7]—in spite of the fact that citizens do not elect the World Bank, nor the IMF, nor have they formally consented to the protocols through which the WTO governs development, broadly termed "liberalization."

Liberalization and the Reformulation of Development

The globalization project arose via the dismantling of the development project, through liberalization. Debtor governments that shrank the state, opened the economy, and adopted austerity measures were rewarded by the debt managers with credit released in tranches (staggered portions) to ensure their continuing compliance with loan conditions. Liberalization *down-grades* the social goals of national development, while *upgrading* participation in the world economy (tariff reduction, export promotion, financial deregulation, relaxation of foreign investment rules). Together, these policies reformulated development as a global project—implemented through liberalized states incorporated into a world market constructed by transnational banks and firms, informatics, and multilateral institutions dedicated to a vision of corporate globalization. While liberalization privileges a corporate development model, its proponents claim it facilitates capital transfer, competition, and trade expansion as methods of increasing economic growth and general well-being. As suggested in the following case study of Chile, liberalization is also realized through new forms of social inequality.

CASE STUDY

Chile—The Original Model of Economic Liberalization

Chile is perhaps the founding model of economic liberalization. A military coup in 1973 eliminated the democratically elected socialist president Salvador Allende, implementing detention, torture, and execution of thousands of Chileans as part of an eight-year period of debilitating authoritarian rule. General Augusto Pinochet pursued a radical free market reform, otherwise known as "shock treatment," masterminded by economists trained at the University of Chicago, a center of neoclassical economics. Over the next two decades, 600 of the country's state enterprises were sold; foreign investment expanded into strategic sectors such as steel, telecommunications, and airlines; trade protection dwindled; and the dependence of the Chilean gross domestic product (GDP) on trade grew from 35 percent in 1970 to 57.4 percent in 1990. In other words, *Chile was structurally adjusted before structural adjustment became fashionable.* Sergio Bitar, Allende's minister of mining, remarked that privatization was "the greatest diversion of public funds that has occurred in our history, without the consultation of public opinion or accountability to a congress."

Chile was one of the most democratic of Latin American nations prior to the assault on its parliamentary and civil institutions. Debt restructuring in the 1980s increased social polarization. The share of national income of the richest 10 percent of the people rose from 35 percent to 47 percent, while that of the poorest half of the population declined from 20 percent to 17 percent. Social spending continued to fall, wages were frozen, and the *peso* was seriously devalued. Deindustrialization set in, unemployment levels rose to between 20 and 30 percent, and real wages suffered a 20 percent reduction. Meanwhile, an export boom occurred, retiring debt and earning the Chilean experiment a reputation as a miracle. U.S. President Bush declared in Chile in 1990, "You deserve your reputation as an economic model for other countries in the region and in the world. Your commitment to market-based solutions inspires the hemisphere."

By 1990, about 40 percent of the 13 million Chilean people were impoverished in a country once known for its substantial middle class. The pursuit of global efficiency had weakened the domestic fabric of social security and local production. In consequence, a sustained grassroots movement, centered in the *poblaciones* (slums) and active from the mid-1970s, succeeded in regaining elections in 1988, when Pinochet was defeated. Since then, Chile has privatized its health and social security system—again modeling the new "market state," now informing U.S. domestic policy. With privatization, the working poor disproportionately subsidized the health needs of the 2 million poorest Chileans, and pensions declined (sharpened by the informalization of the workforce). In 2006, a new, socialist president, Michelle Bachelet (whose father was tortured and killed during Pinochet's regime), was elected on a platform of restoring a more equitable social security system.

Why is it that military rule, the rundown of public goods, disregard for human rights, and new forms of social polarization all conditioned the Chilean anticipation of the project of globalization? 🌐

Sources: Bello (1994:42, 44–45, 59); Collins and Lear (1996:157, 162); George (1988:131–132); Schneider, quoted in Chomsky (1994:184); Schneider (1995:3, 194, 201).

Liberalization involves restructuring domestic economies to expand markets. Theoretical justification for the strategy of market opening derives from nineteenth century English political economist David Ricardo's concept of **comparative advantage**—linking economic growth to optimizing trading advantage through economic specialization, reflecting a nation's relative resource endowments. The theorem stated that when countries exchange their most competitive products on the world market, national and international economic efficiency results.[8] This theorem contradicts the development project's ideal of a series of integrated national economies, affirming the globalization project's focus on the global economy as the unit of development. But the theorem did not allow for capital mobility, which today is central to the construction of a (corporate-based) comparative advantage. Even here, "capital mobility" is often leveraged by export credit agencies (ECAs), whose loans to Southern countries help finance and guarantee foreign investment by Northern corporations. The British ECA's goal is to "help exporters of UK goods and services to win business and UK firms to invest overseas by providing guarantees, insurance and reinsurance against loss."[9] The U.S. ECA favors AT&T, Bechtel, Boeing, General Electric, and McDonnell Douglas. During the 1990s, development loans from ECAs averaged about twice the amount of the world's total development assistance.

Until the 1970s, "comparative advantage" represented a minority strand of economic thought, being out of step with social history since labor and citizen movements demanded social entitlements and protection from unregulated markets, especially after the Great Depression of the 1930s. As wage and social program costs ate into profits, a corporate countermovement resuscitated neoclassical market theory, relegating Keynesian ideas of state intervention and public investment to the background. The political form of neoclassical economic theory, **neoliberalism**, took universal shape in welfare reform/reversal, in wage erosion, in relaxing trade controls, and in privatization schemes. The resulting globalization project matured in the wake of the collapse of state socialism in the Soviet empire and the ending of the Cold War in 1990. Symbolically, this represented the new global reach of neoliberal capitalism.

CASE STUDY

Minidragon Singapore Constructs Comparative Advantage

Singapore is an exceptional city-state, highly dependent on foreign investment. Ruled by a paternalistic People's Action Party (PAP) since gaining independence from Britain in 1959 and its 1965 expulsion from the Malaysian federation, it is known as one of the Pacific Asian "minidragons." Its NIC status depended on centralized planning, and a corporatist political system that silenced political opposition, turned labor unions into agents of the state, and elaborated a social discipline based on Confucian ethics of loyalty.

In 1985 a government economic committee recommended a new strategy to liberalize the economy. Beginning with Singapore Airlines, the government privatized its substantial public sector, fostering local enterprise and high-tech foreign investment. The recent technological upgrading in financial services and manufacturing is part of a strategy to position Singapore as the source of specialized exports (including producer services such as computer technologies) to the fastest growing region of the world economy, the Asian Pacific region, developing high-value and "clean" agro-technology parks. Current critic of neoliberal globalization, ex-IBM Senior VP Ralph Gomory, singles out Singapore as paradigmatic of Asian countries (now China and India) upgrading from shirts and shoes, and capturing high-tech jobs from the United States by luring American companies with the promise of lower wage costs, tax breaks, and subsidies, reducing U.S. high-value exports and high-wage jobs, and driving up its trade deficits.

Expressing new doubts in *Global Trade and Conflicting National Interests* (2000), economists Gomory and William Baumol ask: if free trade is such a win–win scenario, why has America been losing?   🌐

Sources: Deyo (1991); Greider (2007); Ufkes (1995).

The doctrine of comparative advantage legitimizes the relationships between liberalization's downward pressure on social rights and its export regime. It is evident in the enlargement of the global labor force at the base of ubiquitous supply chains (foodstuffs, manufactures, services), and in the deepening of natural resource extraction. Where the latter threatens habitats, displaced peasants, fisherfolk, and forest dwellers join the swelling pool of labor, some of whom find work in export production. This doctrine, represented as the new development strategy for countries as they find their world market niche, is more appropriately understood as a *global development* device, where local and global firms mobilize cheap land and labor for export production to provision distant consumers, thus: "millions of acres once used to feed poor families in poor countries are now used to grow kiwis, asparagus, strawberries, and baby carrots for upper-middle-class consumers who can now eat what was once the fare of kings—365 days a year."[10]

Resource extraction is pegged to a development standard of "high mass consumption," an expanding consumer class, and its "insatiable appetite for energy, private automobiles, building materials, household appliances, and other resource-intensive commodities." Between 1950 and 1999, for example, private automobile ownership grew from about 53 million to an estimated 520 million cars, and the average American home has expanded in size by one-third since 1970.[11]

Under these circumstances, fueled by "freeing" markets to supply relatively cheap resources, commercial extraction of natural resources has intensified globally, threatening environments and resource regeneration. The close correlation between debt, export liberalization, and high rates of deforestation, as depicted in Figure 6.1, is well known.[12] In Chile, timber exports doubled in the 1980s, reaching beyond industrial plantations to the logging of natural forests. Chile's export boom overexploited the country's natural resources beyond their ability to regenerate.[13] In Ghana, the World Bank's African *model* of structural adjustment, exports of mining, fishing, and timber products were accelerated to close the widening gap between cocoa exports and severely declining world prices of cocoa. From 1983 to 1988, timber exports increased from $16 million to $99 million, reducing Ghana's tropical forest to 25 percent of its original size.[14] The NGO Development GAP (Group for Alternative Policies) reported that deforestation,

> threatens household and national food security now and in the future. Seventy-five percent of Ghanaians depend on wild game to supplement their diet. Stripping the forest has led to sharp increases in malnutrition and disease. For women, the food, fuel, and medicines that they harvest from the forest provide critical resources, especially in the face of decreased food production, lower wages, and other economic shocks that threaten food security.[15]

After 70 countries underwent structural adjustment, the resulting glut of exports produced the lowest commodity prices seen on the world market since the 1930s. For example, in West Africa between 1986 and 1989, cocoa producers expanded their exports by 25 percent, only to suffer a 33 percent price fall on the world market. The NGO Oxfam named this syndrome the "export-led collapse."[16] Between 1990 and 2000, the world coffee industry doubled in value to $60 billion, with 60 producer countries—but farmers received half as much as in 1990. Across the world today, 20 million households produce coffee, but the overproduction has brought the price of beans to a 30-year low. For a $2.70 cup of coffee, farmers receive on average 2.3 cents, while the transnationals (such as Proctor & Gamble, Philip Morris, and Nestlé) receive around $1.33.[17] The point is that debt management via export expansion has deepened the model of *global* development, as Southern resources in particular have been opened up or developed to service the global consumer class.

Exporting to earn foreign exchange involves three dynamics: selling domestic resources (cheapened by the global export regime) to firms supplying global markets and delivering the revenues to multilateral lenders as debt repayment; recreating "resource bondage," associated with the colonial division of labor; and depleting and undermining the sustainability of natural resources that provide subsistence security to the poor ("the commons") and, in the case of forests, threaten the wellbeing of the planet. Central to the concept of the commons is the hydrological cycle, upon which natural and human systems depend, and which is threatened by such development operations as the diversion of water resources via intensively irrigated agro-export production, the destruction of water catchments by mining operations, and the appropriation of water by eucalyptus plantations replacing natural forests.

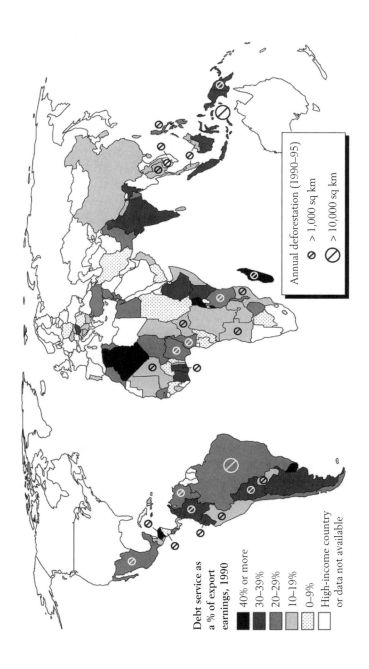

Figure 6.1   Debt and Deforestation

Sources: Thomas et al. (1994); World Bank, *World Development Report* (1998–1999).

Depletion of the Brazilian Amazon forest has intensified recently, under the Avanca Brasil, a $40 billion state-supported project to open the Amazon for its timber and farmland, and service debt from the foreign exchange proceeds. Cargill, the global agribusiness, has the contract to build a new port terminal in the Amazon delta, to connect the huge Mato Grosso soy fields with the insatiable appetite of the ballooning middle class of China, which entered the twenty-first century as the world's largest importer of soy oil, meal, and beans. The Brazilian government has introduced a deforestation licensing system in the Mato Grosso state, but neighboring states of Para and Rondonia remain even more frontier-like in yielding the forest to loggers, sawmill operators, cattle ranchers, and speculators expecting to profit from the continuation of Brazil's export boom.[18] Illegal roads, or *viscinais* (over 105,000 miles), cross indigenous territories, ecological reserves, defying government regulations and facilitating illegal logging. Para state includes the largest of these, the Trans-Iriri, and, despite government claims of slowing deforestation, satellite images have shown an increase of 50 percent between 2005 and 2007. Loggers cut secondary paths from the Trans-Iriri highway, eventually replacing rainforest with cattle ranches, which contract with European supermarkets.[19]

As a development strategy, export reliance is problematic, especially where primary commodity prices remain low (especially compared to higher value manufactured goods and services)—and *The Economist* declared in 1999 that commodity prices were at an all-time low for the previous century and a half. Export reliance is compounded by biotechnical substitution. For example, many prepared foods and drinks now substitute high-fructose corn syrup for sugar, resulting in a collapse of the world sugar market as sugar imports decline. As a result, producers in Brazil, India, the Philippines, Thailand, and several African and Caribbean countries lost markets just at the time when their debt servicing demanded increased exports.[20]

Contrary to neoclassical theory, export reliance often puts regions in the global South at a *comparative disadvantage*. Liberalization substitutes reliance on the world market for self-reliance as the organizing principle of development. The flow of credit to debt-stressed nations typically depends on renunciation of national development norms, including public investment, protection of local producers, labor forces, communities, environments, and social entitlements. All of these norms are viewed as impediments to the market, which is why the globalization project begins with market liberalization as the path to "efficiency." Scaling back public capacity transformed nation-states into market states concerned with improving global economic activity. It is not surprising, therefore, that during the 1990s, private foreign investment became the main source of supply of capital to the global South, growing by more than five times.[21]

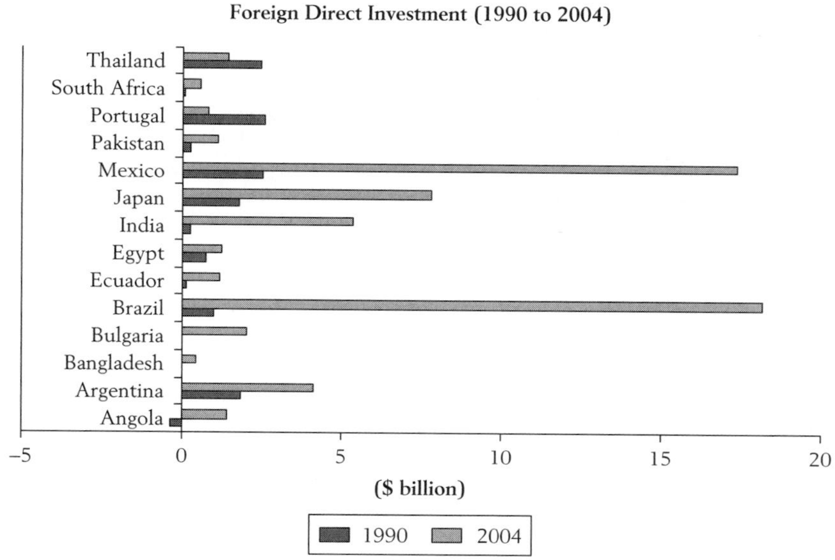

Foreign Direct Investment (1990 to 2004)

Figure 6.2   Select Private Foreign Direct Investment Flows in the 1990s

Source: http://devdata.worldbank.org/wdi2006/contents/Section6.htm, *World Development Indicators 2006*

The globalization project includes an explicit vision of global order, quite distinct from that of the era of the development project:

- In the development project era, the slogan was "Learn from, and catch up with, the West." Now, under comparative advantage, the slogan is "Find your niche in the global marketplace."
- While the development project held out *replication* as the key to national development, the project of globalization presents *specialization* as the path to economic prosperity.

But specialization in monoculture, or the global assembly line, does not alter the reality that the mechanisms of specialization—wage cutting, foreign investment concessions, privatization, and reduction of social entitlements—are repeated everywhere, intensifying market competition. Short-term efficiencies are sought at the long-term expense of the social contract and the environment. In theory, this may produce greater productivity, but at the cost of considerable and irreversible economic and social marginalization, impoverishment, environmental stress, and displacement.

GATT and the Making of a Free Trade Regime

The debt regime elevated the Bretton Woods institutions to a governance role, targeting the global South. From 1986 to 1994, the *whole world* became the target of the Uruguay Round of the General Agreement on Trade and Tariffs (GATT). The Uruguay Round was to establish a set of new and binding rules concerning free trade, freedom of investment, and protection of intellectual property rights. Once formulated, these rules framed the WTO. Agricultural trade was central to the Uruguay Round's challenge to economic nationalism.

The United States engineered the creation of the GATT in 1948 as an alternative to the International Trade Organization (which included provisions from the UN Declaration of Human Rights concerning full employment, working conditions, and social security).[22] Through GATT, trade expansion was *delinked from the social contract.* From 1948 through 1980, GATT reduced tariff rates on trade in manufactured goods by more than 75 percent.[23] Agriculture was excluded from the GATT. In the 1980s, at a time of recession and declining industrial leadership, the United States initiated the Uruguay Round, with the aim of liberalizing agriculture and services (banking, insurance, telecommunications), in which the North held a competitive advantage. Northern pressure and the promise of open markets for southern products, including agricultural goods, won acceptance from the South.[24]

The liberalization movement was supported by an activist lobby of "free trader" agro-exporting states (the Cairns Group), TNCs like IBM and American Express, and agribusinesses such as Cargill, Ralston-Purina, General Mills, Continental Grain, RJR Nabisco, and ConAgra, looking to reduce trade barriers, domestic price supports, and supply-management policies restricting demand for farm inputs such as fertilizer and chemicals. Corporations produce and sell farm products across the world—they take advantage of seasonal variation and dietary variation and engage in redundant "food swaps." Alternatively, family farmers are spatially fixed and depend on national farm policy—input and price subsidies, farm credit, risk insurance, and import controls—for their economic viability.

Given competitive dumping of surplus foods by the United States and the EC, depressing agricultural prices by 39 percent (1975–1989),[25] GATT proposed an "urgent need to bring more discipline and predictability to world agricultural trade."[26] Southern farm sectors were adversely affected by dumping, deepening food import dependency, especially in sub-Saharan Africa. However, while liberalization was expected to stabilize markets, it has not stabilized farming in the global South, since markets are controlled by huge agribusiness corporations, which dictate prices at the expense of family farmers. Legitimizing this power, the United States challenged GATT's Article XI food security provisions, arguing for comparative advantage:

> The U.S. has always maintained that self-sufficiency and food security are not one and the same. Food security—the ability to acquire the food you need when you need it—is best provided through a smooth-functioning world market. . . .[27]

Globally managed "food security" depends on a contradictory complex of conditions: trade liberalization; highly subsidized northern "granaries;" and corporately managed food circuits. From the global South, this is perceived as promoting "recolonization"[28]—despite support from agro-exporting NACs such as Malaysia (palm oil), the Philippines (coconut oil), and Thailand (rice), even as their domestic producers are swamped by imports displacing staple foods.

In short, the making of a free trade regime reconstructed "food security" as a market relation, privileging and protecting corporate agriculture and placing small farmers at a comparative disadvantage. Food security would now be "governed" through the market by corporate, rather than social, criteria.

The World Trade Organization

The singular achievement of the GATT Uruguay Round was the creation of the **World Trade Organization (WTO)** on January 1, 1995. The WTO, with 150 voting members (January 2007), assumes unprecedented power to enforce GATT provisions. It is unprecedented because, as discussed below, the WTO is arguably less about trade rule consistency than about governing member states via liberalization. *Free trade* is a misnomer for the reach of WTO rules. In combination, they challenge national democratic processes, removing decision making to nontransparent tribunals located in Geneva, Switzerland, using "market logic" to override individual government policy where it interferes with "free trade."

Unlike the GATT (a trade treaty only), the WTO has independent jurisdiction like the United Nations. That is, it has the power to enforce its rulings on member states, and these include rulings going beyond simply cross-border trade into the realm of "trade-related" issues. This means setting rules regarding the movement of goods, money, and productive facilities across borders—rules that restrict countries from enacting legislation or policies discriminating against such movement. WTO rules, in advancing trade freedoms, privilege corporate rights to compete internationally. This means ensuring that TNCs receive treatment equal to that received by domestic firms and reducing or removing local restrictions (e.g., labor, health, environmental laws) on trade and investment that might interfere with corporate competitiveness in the global marketplace. The WTO staff are unelected bureaucrats and proceedings are secret, denying citizen participation in making and evaluating policy. In its confidential bureaucratic guise, such global governance, framed by the discourse of neo-classical economic theory, subordinates the sovereignty of the nation-state, the historic site of the social contract and democracy. In 1994, World Bank economist Herman Daly warned: establishing rules to override national governments' capacity to regulate commerce "is to wound fatally the major unit of community capable of carrying out any policies for the common good."[29]

The WTO has an *integrated dispute settlement* mechanism. If a state is perceived to be distorting trade obligations in one area, such as curbing investments in timber cutting to protect a forest, it can be disciplined through the application of sanctions against another area of economic activity, like some of its manufactured exports. Member states can lodge complaints through the WTO, whose decision holds automatically unless every member of the WTO votes to reverse it. Should states refuse to comply, the WTO can authorize the plaintiff to take unilateral action. The ambit of the dispute settlement mechanism is wide, covering trade, investment, services, and intellectual property. That is, in seeking to "harmonize" trade relationships, the WTO sponsors the diluting of national sovereignty in economic and social policy. Martin Khor, director of the Third World Network, suggests that, in claiming to reduce "trade-distorting" measures, the WTO becomes "development-distorting."[30] The very *threat* of such challenges has already had the effect also of diluting national laws protecting human and environmental health.

The WTO, in enforcing market freedoms, *depoliticizes* their profound social impact. Thus the 1996 Singapore Ministerial Declaration invites objection to labor rights laws: "We reject the use of labor standards for protectionist purposes, and agree that the comparative advantage of countries, particularly low wage developing countries, must in no way be put into question."[31] And, as the outgoing director-general of GATT, Peter Sutherland, declared in 1994, "Governments should interfere in the conduct of trade as little as possible."[32] This implies a *general* challenge to national laws and regulations regarding the environment, health, preferential trade relations, social subsidies, labor legislation, and so on. While the challenge does not eliminate all laws, it seeks to *harmonize* regulation internationally, lowering the ceiling on democratic initiatives within the national polity.[33] As we shall see, the goal of depoliticizing the economy can backfire, and this explains in large part the mushrooming global social justice movement.

In this sense, although implementation is uneven, the WTO expresses the essence of the globalization project. That is, global managers assume extraordinary powers to govern the web of global economic relations lying across nation-states, privileging corporate over democratic rights. We now examine four of the principal and mutually reinforcing protocols of the WTO: the Agreement on Agriculture (AoA), Trade-Related Investment Measures (TRIMs), Trade-Related Aspects of Intellectual Property Rights (TRIPs), and the General Agreement on Trade in Services (GATS).

The Agreement on Agriculture (AoA)

The 1995 Agreement on Agriculture advocated universal reductions in trade protection, farm subsidies, and government intervention. Many Southern farmers have been unable to recover the cost of their production in the face of a 30 percent or more collapse of world prices for farm goods in the first half-decade since the AoA was instituted.[34] Hypocritically, countries with the capacity to pay (U.S. and European states) retained subsidies, at the expense of much larger Southern farm populations, threatened daily with the dumping of cheap farm commodities.

With liberalization, farmers everywhere are under pressure to compete by selling cheap. Corporate farmers survive by subsidized "scale economy." In the mid-1990s, 80 percent of farm subsidies in the OECD countries concentrated on the largest 20 percent of (corporate) farms, rendering small farmers increasingly vulnerable to a deregulated (and increasingly privately managed) global market for agricultural products. Between 1998 and 1999, UK farm income fell by about 75 percent, driving 20,000 farmers out of business, and U.S. farm income declined by almost 50 percent between 1996 and 1999. In the global South, conservative estimates are that between 20 and 30 million people have lost their land from the impact of AoA trade liberalization, including 1.75 million rural Mexicans.[35]

CASE STUDY

Global Comparative Disadvantage—The End of
Farming as We Know It?

A recent report from Public Citizen's *Global Trade Watch* documents a common process of elimination of small farmers across the whole North American region as the legacy of NAFTA. While about 2 million Mexican *campesinos* have lost their maize farms to cheap and heavily subsidized corn exports from the North, U.S. farmers are also faced with an intensification of competitive imports from Mexico and Canada, replacing crops grown in the United States, such as fruit, vegetables, and other labor-intensive food-stuffs. Since 1994, some 33,000 U.S. farms with under $100,000 annual income have disappeared (six times the decline for 1988–1993). In Mexico, half of the rural population earns less than $1.40 a day (insufficient to feed themselves), with about 500 people leaving the countryside daily.

Policy changes such as these enhance agribusiness power. Public Citizen notes with respect to U.S. policy,

> Proponents of the legislation contended it would make farming more efficient and responsive to market forces; in reality it essentially handed the production of food to agribusiness. . . . Congress has had to appropriate emergency farm supports—in massive farm bailout bills—every year since the legislation went into effect.

But 56 percent of U.S. emergency taxpayer assistance went to the largest 10 percent of the farms. Meanwhile, agribusiness restructured, with input indus-tries and output industries consolidating alliances to "encircle farmers and consumers in a web . . . from selling seeds and bioengineering animal varieties to producing the pesticides, fertilizers, veterinary pharmaceuticals and feed to grow them to transporting, slaughtering, processing, and packaging the final 'product.'" Once NAFTA opened Mexico to 100 percent foreign investor rights, Pillsbury's Green Giant subsidiary relocated its frozen food processing from California to Mexico to access cheap wages, minimal food safety stan-dards, and zero tariffs on re-export to the United States. Cargill purchased a beef and chicken plant in Saltillo, and Cargill de Mexico invested nearly $200 million in vegetable oil refining and soybean processing in Tula. Anticipating continent-wide liberalization; Tyson Foods has operations in Mexico, Brazil, Argentina, and Venezuela; ConAgra processes oilseed in Argentina; Archer Daniels Midland crushes and refines oilseed, mills corn and flour, and bio-engineers feeds in Mexico, Central America, and South America; and Wal-Mart is in Mexico, Argentina, and Brazil. Public Citizen remarks,

> Multinational agribusinesses were positioned uniquely to take advantage of trade rules that force countries to accept agricultural imports regardless of their domestic supplies. The companies utilized their foreign holdings as export platforms to sell imported agriculture goods in the United States, and by thus increasing supply put negative pressures on U.S. agriculture prices.

When liberal policy and northern subsidies enable corporations to *construct* comparative advantages, rendering family/peasant farming "inefficient" and redundant, how can "market-based allocation" retain credibility in context of the dispossession of peasant cultures, enlarging the "planet of slums," and growing food insecurity? 🌍

Sources: Davis (2006); Jordan and Sullivan (2003:33); Public Citizen (2001:ii–iv, 10, 13, 16, 19–21).

Liberalization is evidently less about freeing trade than about consolidating a corporate food regime.[36] Through the AoA, the WTO institutionalized the private form of food security. Under the AoA, states no longer have the right to self-sufficiency as a national strategy. Rather, the minimum market access rule guarantees the "right to export" (therefore the requirement to import), even under conditions of subsidized exports. "Food security," then, is not food self-reliance but rather food import dependency for a large minority of southern states—those adversely affected by world market dumping of northern food surpluses. By the mid-1990s, half of the foreign exchange of the 88 low-income food deficit countries went to food imports.[37] Food-dependent states' food bills grew, on average, 20 percent between 1994 and 1999, despite record low prices. Meanwhile, northern states continue farm support (a practice that has paralyzed WTO Ministerials in the twenty-first century).

In the absence of public capacity in the South, unprotected farmers are at a comparative disadvantage. In 2000, Oxfam asked, "How can a farmer earning US$230 a year (average per capita income in LDCs [least developed countries]) compete with a farmer who enjoys a subsidy of US$20,000 a year (average subsidy in OECD countries)?"[38] In India, Devinder Sharma observes, "Whereas for small farmers the subsidies have been withdrawn, there is a lot of support now for agribusiness industry. . . . The result is that the good area under staple foods is now shifting to export crops, so we'll have to import staple food."[39] In the 1980s, 90 percent of agricultural research expenditures in Latin America went to food crop research, switching to 80 percent focused on export crops during the 1990s.[40] Forty percent of Kenya's children work on plantations, which export pineapple, coffee, tea, and sugar. While these foodstuffs supply European markets, 4 million Kenyans face starvation.[41] This is one common face of development via the globalization project.

Trade-Related Investment Measures (TRIMs)

TRIMs arose within the context of the GATT Uruguay Round, in an attempt to reduce "performance requirements" imposed on foreign investment by host governments. Such requirements might include expecting a TNC to invest locally, hire locally, buy locally, and transfer technology as a quid pro quo for investment access.[42] The WTO uses TRIMs to manage the cross-border movement of goods and services production, especially—as the WTO website explains—since trade is closely linked with investment via "the fact that one-third of the $6.1 trillion total for world trade in goods and services in 1995 was trade within companies—for example between subsidiaries in different countries or between a subsidiary and its headquarters." The point of TRIMs is to secure investor rights at the expense of domestic development measures. As one proponent argues, "The multinational corporate community would then be able to rationalize their regional and global sourcing strategies on the basis of productivity, quality, and cost considerations in place of the political dictates that now disrupt their operations."[43]

CASE STUDY

Evolving Corporate Property Rights

TRIMs laid the foundations for corporate property rights, allowing foreign investors to challenge a government for imposing "performance requirements." NAFTA and the Free Trade Agreement for the Americas (FTAA) initiative deepen corporate property rights by allowing expanded investor rights to be enforced privately through secret trade tribunals. Under NAFTA's Chapter 11, corporations can bypass domestic courts and directly sue governments when municipal, state, or national legislation threatens their profits. Thus the U.S. Metalclad Corporation successfully sued Mexico over environmental protection. The municipality of Guadalacazar (San Luís Potosí state) had refused a construction permit to Metalclad to develop a toxic waste landfill in an ecologically protected zone. The company had secured a permit from the federal and state governments, but the municipal government stood firm, as it had with a Mexican owner of the site, and was required to compensate Metalclad to the tune of $16.6 million. Because of these extended rights in regional trade agreements, there is mounting pressure for a new WTO agreement that would extend TRIMs to allow corporations to sue governments for restriction of profits.

International law regards only states as "subjects," and corporations (and individuals) as "objects," accountable to states, the historic site and source of sovereignty. As corporations have become more powerful, while they continue to operate under the international law radar in terms of accountability, the new "trade" agreements appear to be empowering them as "subjects" with rights to hold states accountable to their profitability requirements.

Why would states sign on to protocols that subvert their sovereign power and ability to represent their citizens? 🌐

Sources: Cutler (2001); McBride (2006); Wallach and Woodall (2004:270).

The argument in favor of TRIMs is they reduce domestic content requirements that misallocate local resources, raise costs, penalize competitive investment, and burden consumers, in addition to slowing technological adoption, reducing quality, and retarding management practices.[44] In other words, the role of TRIMs is to enhance conditions for transnational investment by reducing the friction of local regulations. Greater freedom for investors under TRIMs is justified by evidence of "higher-than-average wages and benefits, advanced technology, and sophisticated managerial and marketing techniques," as well as a stronger "integration effect" with the local economy. It is exemplified in the Mexican auto industry, where parent firms invested in local supply firms for self-interest and not because of local content requirements, resulting in the creation of globally competitive Mexican auto part suppliers. Also, in the Malaysian semiconductor industry, an indigenous machine tool firm matured from supplying parts to foreign investors to supplying high-precision computer-numeric tools and factory automation equipment to international and domestic markets.[45] But the "integration effect" favors integration the other way: of local producers into the world market, rather than foreign investors integrating into a program of domestic industrialization.

The TRIMs protocol includes reducing the escalating cost and beggar-thy-neighbor practice of "locational incentive packages"—where countries compete for business through concessions. In a commissioned OECD study (1994), the "Irish model" emerged as a paradigmatic case—where Ireland used incentives (grants of 60 percent of fixed assets, 100 percent of training costs, free building sites and rent subsidies in industrial parks, and extremely low tax rates) to attract more than 1,000 TNCs, generating nearly 100,000 jobs: more than 50 percent of Irish industrial output and 75 percent of manufactured exports.[46] In the 1990s, Ireland emerged as a prosperous export platform for the European market (building on a period of labor disorganization via deindustrialization). This model was copied by Mexico and Brazil *vis-à-vis* the North American and global markets.

Remember, Shannon, Ireland was the site of the first export processing zone (EPZ) in 1958. While TRIMs may attempt to regulate export platform concessions to preserve the principle of comparative advantage, in challenging domestic requirements on foreign investment, TRIMs encourage EPZs, whose sole domestic link is labor, minus its civil rights. As we have seen, cheap, disorganized labor is the one "comparative advantage" many governments in the global South have to offer (sanctioned by the World Bank in its 1995 *World Development Report*).

Trade-Related Aspects of Intellectual Property Rights (TRIPs)

The WTO website defines **intellectual property rights** as "rights given to persons over the creations of their minds. They usually give the creator an exclusive right over the use of his/her creation for a certain period of time." The TRIPs protocol was defined by a coalition of 12 major U.S. corporations, a Japanese federation of business organizations, and the agency for European business and industry. Based on a synthesis of European and U.S. patent laws, intellectual property rights protection is to be administered by the WTO. Advocates claim that it simplifies the protection of property rights across national borders and protects and promotes innovation for everyone by guaranteeing profits from technological developments, such as computer software, biotechnological products and processes, and pharmaceuticals. But critics contest this corporate definition of intellectual rights, arguing that biodiverse and generic knowledges should remain available to human kind as a global "commons."[47]

At the turn of the twenty-first century, when a scientist from Abbott Laboratories isolated a frog secretion to develop a painkiller, the Ecuadorian government demanded compensation on behalf of Ecuador and the Amazonian Indians, who use the chemical as poison on their hunting arrows. It did so under the terms of the 1992 Convention on Biological Diversity, which confirms national sovereignty over genetic resources, affirming the principle that nations are entitled to "fair and equitable sharing of the benefits." Many commercial drugs these days derive from chemicals found in tropical flora and fauna. The Northern lifestyle is directly connected to the extraction of these sorts of resources, such as drugs from the rosy periwinkle of Madagascar to fight childhood leukemia and testicular cancer; Brazzein, a powerful sweetener from a West African berry; biopesticides from the Indian neem tree; and human cell lines to identify genes causing illnesses such as Huntington's disease and cystic fibrosis.[48]

It seems rational that the world's biodiversity—such as the frog secretion—should service humankind. This is why so much attention is being paid to preserving the tropical rainforests, for example, given their rich biological variety. At issue is the question of control of resources, and the relationship between Northern lifestyle and the rights of indigenous peoples in the developing nations, mostly in the global South.

The global South contains 90 percent of global biological wealth, and scientists and corporations of the North hold 97 percent of all patents. Patents on biological wealth give patent holders exclusive control over use of the genetic materials. Corporations have often patented genetic material obtained from a Southern country without payment or obligation, turned it into a commodity such as a medicine, and then charging a fee for use of the genetic resource in local production or high prices for the commodity—even to the country where the material originated, often over centuries. Critics view this appropriation of genetic material by foreigners as **biopiracy**. A London-based NGO, ActionAid, defines biopiracy as

> the granting of patents on plant varieties or individual genes, proteins and gene sequences from plants in the South by commercial and industrial interests. This privatisation of living organisms often involves companies taking indigenous plant varieties from developing countries and using these species for the extraction of genes, or genetically modifying . . . existing plants.[49]

In this sense, TRIPs are another weapon in the WTO corporate property rights arsenal. Biopiracy need not be limited to plant varieties. Attempts have been made to acquire human and other animal genetic material, as well as nonplant microbiological material. The entire living world is very much up for grabs in this particular vision of commodifying natural endowments and resources. TRIPs grew out of an attempt to stem intellectual property pirating of Western products (watches, CDs, etc.) in the global South but, ironically, it now appears to sanction a reverse biological form of piracy on a disproportionate scale, threatening livelihood, rather than commodity rights. About 1.4 billion people in the global South depend primarily on farm-saved seeds and on crop genetic diversity as the basis of cultural and ecological sustainability. Farmers express concern that if firms can patent traditional seed stock, planting of traditional crops may be liable for patent infringement.[50] This concern arises because firms such as I.C. Industries and Pioneer Hi-bred sought licensing rights to use a gene from an African cowpea. When inserted into crops such as corn and soybeans, the gene increases pest resistance. As the Rural Advancement Foundation International (RAFI, now ETC) asked, "The question is, who are the inventors? [The scientists] who isolated the gene? Or West African farmers who identified the value of the plant holding the gene and then developed and protected it?"[51] In valuing techno-scientific over indigenous knowledge, an intellectual property regime (IPR) regime creates an unequal relation—endangering farmers' rights to plant their crops and threatening to expropriate genetic resources developed by peasants, forest dwellers, and local communities over centuries of cultural experimentation. The IPR regime privileges governments and corporations as legal entities and disempowers villagers by disavowing their indigenous knowledge rights.[52]

The TRIPs protocol establishes uniform standards, globally, for intellectual property rights protection, allowing exclusion of plants and animals from patent laws but insisting on intellectual property rights for "inventors" of micro-organisms, microbiological processes and products, and plant varieties, which must be either patentable or subject to an effective *sui generis* system, which states interpret to mean plant variety protection. The latter stems from the 1992 Convention on Biological Diversity (CBD), which confirmed national sovereignty over genetic resources and affirmed that nations are entitled to "fair and equitable sharing of the benefits." The CBD is a commitment to conserve biological diversity, recognizing traditional knowledges and obliging member states to conserve knowledge for biological wealth. In addition, it empowers states to enact national laws to protect biodiversity. However, how states interpret that right and obligation is part of the controversy.[53]

The significance of the *sui generis* system for plants lies in its potential for alternative formulations, recognizing and securing collective rights for agricultural and medicinal plant biodiversity. A *sui generis* system premised on collective rights to biodiversity would recognize diverse cultural knowledges and practices. The *sui generis* principle was affirmed in the case of the Texas-based company RiceTec, Inc., which sells "Kasmati" rice and "Texmati" rice, claiming rights to basmati rice. In June 2000, under popular pressure, the Indian government successfully challenged four of the 20 claims for this patent on the grounds that the grain, as well as the seeds and plants producing the grain, is the product of centuries of indigenous breeding and cultivation.[54]

CASE STUDY

Big Pharma and the Question of Intellectual Property Rights

Perhaps the most visible controversy over IPRs has centered on the question of generic antiretroviral drugs to treat HIV/AIDS patients, of whom there are over 40 million worldwide. Brazil produced generic versions prior to the TRIPs agreement in 1996, sidestepping royalties to the pharmaceutical companies, and reducing the price by 80 percent. The government saves about $250 million a year on the drugs, and also on hospital care for untreated patients. Government labs, researching the composition of Pharma drugs to produce lower cost generics locally, were threatened with a WTO dispute. UNCHR and WHO intervention on the grounds of human rights secured an outcome with the Health Ministry negotiating price reductions of over 50 percent with the drug companies.

Meanwhile, South Africa's Treatment Action Campaign (TAC), spearheading the struggle for affordable medicine for HIV-related illnesses (joined by *Médecins Sans Frontières* and Oxfam), helped to shame 39 pharmaceutical transnational corporations (TNCs) into settling a suit they brought against the South African government to stop it purchasing generic drugs from third parties (like Brazil).

The typical antiretroviral AIDS drug cocktail costs U.S.$10,000–$15,000—beyond the reach of a large proportion of HIV carriers in the global South. Large countries, such as India, Egypt, Thailand, Argentina, and Brazil, manufacture cheap generic drugs (around $600) to reduce public health costs, becoming targets for challenges by Big Pharma, citing infringements of the TRIPs protocol's protection of patent rights. A loophole, allowing countries to manufacture or import generic drugs for national health emergencies, challenged for several years by the companies and the United States, was ratified by the WTO in August 2003. Meanwhile, GlaxoSmithKline, brand sensitive, became the first company to sell AIDS drugs at cost in the global South.

Not only have commercial drugs been developed largely with public funding and then patented by firms that spend twice as much on marketing as on research and development, but Africa, which has 80 percent of the world's AIDS patients, comprises just 1 percent of the market for the big four: Merck, Pfizer, GlaxoSmithKline, and Eli Lilly. Their average profit margins, over 30 percent, are among the highest in the world. Only 10 percent of the annual global health research budget targets diseases such as malaria, tuberculosis, and HIV/AIDS, which account for 90 percent of global health problems, while profitable health problems (e.g., obesity) gain most attention. Under these circumstances, the push is on to break Big Pharma's monopoly. In January 2007, Sunil Shaunak, professor of infectious diseases at Imperial College, London, and a colleague, modified the molecular structure of patented drugs for infectious diseases, producing "ethical pharmaceuticals" with the potential, via patents, to dramatically reduce costs. Five months later, the Clinton Foundation brokered a discount on costly second-line generic AIDS drugs, and a deal for more user-friendly first-line drugs—buying them from Indian manufacturers, with the potential to bargain for lower prices with American companies with branded antiretroviral drugs, and possibly to embolden imitation of Brazil and Thailand in overriding patents.

In times of health crises—or indeed at any time—should intellectual property rights be used to subordinate public rights to corporate rights?   🌏

Sources: Altman (2002:A12); Ayittey (2002); Becker (2003:14); Booth (1998); Boseley (2007); Central Intelligence Agency (2000); De Waal (2002:23); Dugger (2007:6); Elliott (2001:12); Flynn (2002); Gevisser (2001:5–6); *Guardian Weekly* (November 21–27, 2000:14);   Le Carre (2001:13–13); Medecins Sans Frontieres website, www.msf.org; Perlez (2001:A12); Stuart (2003:21).

General Agreement on Trade in Services (GATS)

Services, unlike goods, are defined as "anything you can not drop on your foot."[55] They include public and financial services. The 1994 GATS regime opened markets for trade in services by establishing the rights to corporate "presence" in member countries for the delivery of a service in the areas of finance, telecommunications, and transport. "GATS 2000" is a fundamentally more far-reaching protocol to compel governments to provide unlimited market access to foreign service providers, without regard for social and environmental impacts of the service activities.[56] As Tony Clarke notes, GATS 2000 involves the following:

- Imposing severe constraints on the government's ability to protect environmental, health, consumer, and other public interest standards. A "necessity test" requires government proof that regulations on service provision are the "least trade restrictive," parallel with WTO rules on trade in goods.
- Restricting government funding of public works, municipal services, and social programs. Using WTO "national treatment" protocols on government procurement and subsidies, it would impede the role of government funds for public services, making them equally available to foreign-based private service corporations.
- The guaranteed access of private service corporations to domestic markets in all sectors, including health, education, and water, is accelerated by permitting commercial presence in GATS member countries.
- "Every service imaginable is on the table, including a wide range of public services in sectors that affect the environment, culture, energy and natural resources, plus drinking water, health care, K–12 education, post-secondary education, and social security; along with transportation services, postal delivery, prisons, libraries, and a variety of municipal services."
- Finally, access provisions are more profound, applying to most government measures affecting "trade-in-services," such as labor laws, consumer protection, subsidies, grants, licensing standards and qualifications, market access restrictions, economic needs tests, and local content provisions.

In other words, GATS threatens to replace the social contract between state and citizen with a private contract between corporation and consumer. The democratic claims of the citizen-state (expressed in municipal contracts for construction, sewage, garbage disposal, sanitation, tourism, and water services) would yield to the private capacities of the consumer-citizen, at the expense of the public interest and its development expressions. In this proposal, we see the elimination of all vestiges of the development state and its replacement by corporate services globally.

Who Is Behind GATS 2000, and Who Stands to Gain?

The GATS 2000 agenda was drawn up by a powerful transnational coalition of corporate service providers, including the following:

• **U.S. Coalition of Service Industries (USCSI)**—composed of electronic entertainment and telecommunication giants AOL Time-Warner, AT&T, and IBM; energy and water enterprises such as Enron and Vivendi Universal; financial empires such as Citigroup, Bank of America, and J. P. Morgan Chase; investment houses such as Goldman Sachs and General Electric Financial; health insurance corporations such as the Chubb Group; management and consultant corporations such as KPMG and Pricewaterhouse Coopers; and express delivery services such as United Parcel and Federal Express;

• **European Services Forum**—composed of 47 corporations, including financial giants Barclays PLC and Commerzbank AG; telecommunications: British Telecom, Telefonica, and Deutsche TelekomAG; water: Suez-Lyonnaise des Eaux; health insurance companies the AXA Group and CGU plus Norwich Union; financial consultants Arthur Andersen Consulting; publishing and entertainment giant Bertelsmann; and brand-name empires such as Daimler-Chrysler Services and Marks and Spencer PLC;

• **Japan Services Network**—under the leadership of the CEO of Mitsubishi.

Since the late 1980s, on the heels of debt regime-mandated privatization, trade in services tripled to 25 percent of world trade. As Figure 6.3 shows, the global North dominates international trade in services. The Bush administration predicted in 2002 that the elimination of barriers to services would create $1.8 trillion in new global commerce annually, with $450 billion earned by U.S. firms.

Sources: Clarke (2001); Phillips (2002); Watkins (2002:21).

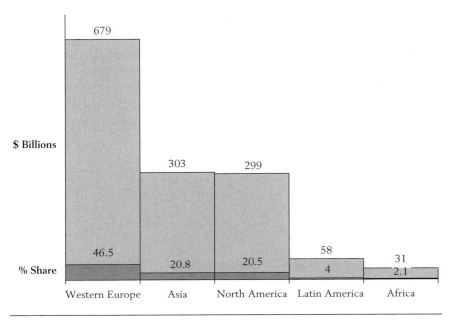

Figure 6.3   World Exports of Commercial Services by Region, 2001

Source: International Trade Statistics, WTO (2001).

The strategy used by the proponents of GATS 2000 is, to term it appealingly, a *trade agreement*, and it demands openness to "cross-border" provision of services (by TNCs) as a condition for opening EU and U.S. markets in garments, textiles, and agricultural products.[57] Oxfam's Kevin Watkins notes that this is a replay of the Uruguay Round, when the global North offered to open its markets in return for protection of TNC patents (which cost the global South $40 billion in increased technology costs), and suggests that, while the game has changed, the rules are the same: "The West buys your bananas and shirts if you give its banks and insurance companies unrestricted access to your markets."[58] GATS advocates argue that the conversion of public entities into privately owned, profit-making concerns eliminates bureaucratic inefficiency and government debt, providing superior services on a user-pays basis. A World Development Monitor report cautions against foreign control of services—citing the liberalization of financial banking services in Aotearoa/New Zealand, where affordable financial services and low-cost loans disappeared, leading the government to propose the public establishment of a new bank, the People's Bank.[59]

CASE STUDY

Water, Water, Everywhere? Unless It's a Commodity . . .

When a service is commodified, it becomes the property of only those who can afford to buy it. Its availability on the market for some makes it scarce for others. In Vellore, India, Coca-Cola's bottling plant has mined water from surrounding borewells, parching the lands of more than 2,000 people residing near the plant and contaminating remaining water, exacerbating women's water-fetching (Coke has since joined with Rotary to ensure potable water for schools in the region). Globalize this, backed up by GATS, and a market-induced water shortage threatens.

If oil wars marked the end of the twentieth century, water wars will define the twenty-first century, according to a World Bank vice president. While 90 percent of wastewater in the global South is still discharged into rivers and streams, the looming water crisis has two sources: the skewing of water use priorities (e.g., agribusiness vs. small farmers; export processing zones vs. citizen needs; urban flush toilets vs. equitable distribution of safe drinking water); and pressures to privatize water.

Water is understood to be the last infrastructure frontier for private investors. Only 5 percent of water services are in private hands, and expansion opportunities are estimated at a trillion dollars. Water privatization is dominated by two French TNCs: Vivendi SA and Suez Lyonnaise des Eaux. Other TNCs involved include Bechtel, Enron, and General Electric. The GATS protocol favors privatization of this public good, and implementation is anticipated by a provision in NAFTA forbidding a country from discriminating in favor of its own firms in the commercial use of its water resources. Meanwhile, the IMF and the World Bank demand privatization of water services as a funding condition.

A case in point is Ghana, where an IMF loan tranche in 2002 was only released on condition that the government required "full cost recovery" in all public utilities, including water. Vivendi, Suez, and Saur of France and Biwater of Britain use this condition to cherry-pick lucrative contracts, leaving sewerage, sanitation, urban poor, and rural water provision for local authorities and communities. While the national budget is downsized to save money for loan repayment, a public service disappears, and water prices go through the roof. One community member exclaimed, "The rain does not fall only on the roofs of Vivendi, Suez, Saur and Biwater, neither does it fall only on the roofs of the World Bank and the IMF; it falls on everyone's roof. Why are they so greedy?" Partly because of such stories, change of heart by governments, and for reasons of risk, water companies are withdrawing from ventures in poor countries.

Maude Barlow distinguished between *water trading* and *water sharing*: "In a commercially traded water exchange, those who really need the water would be least likely to receive it. . . . Importing water for only those who could afford it would reduce the urgency and political pressure to find real, sustainable and equitable solutions to water problems in water-scarce countries." She suggests that "with current technologies and methods available today, a conservative estimate is that agriculture could cut its water demands by close to 50 percent, industry by 50 to 90 percent, and cities by one-third without sacrificing economic output or quality of life. What is missing is political will and vision."

Should the availability and distribution of a basic and precious resource such as water or food be governed by market forces, which tend to favor only those with purchasing power and compromise human rights?   🌐

Sources: www.corpwatchindia.org/issues/PID.jsp?articleid=1603; Amenga-Etego (2003:20–21); Barlow (1999:2, 7, 14, 18, 27, 33, 38); Godrej (2003:12); Vidal (2003:24).

Regional Free Trade Agreements (FTAs)

Regional free trade agreements represent the advance guard of the WTO regime. These are agreements among neighboring countries to reform trade and investment rules governing their economic intercourse. Free trade agreements include the North American FTA (NAFTA: including Canada, the United States, and Mexico), the Union of South American Nations (Unasul), the Greater Arab Free Trade Area (GAFTA: including Jordan, Bahrain, UAE, Tunisia, S. Arabia, Syria, Iraq, Oman, Qatar, Kuwait, Lebanon, Libya, Egypt, Morocco, Sudan, Yemen, and Palestine), and the South African Development Community (SADC: including Angola, Botswana, Lesotho, Malawi, Mozambique, Namibia, South Africa, Swaziland, Zambia, and Zimbabwe).

The megaregions are **NAFTA,** centered on the United States; the **European Union (EU),** centered on Germany; and the **Asian-Pacific Economic Cooperation (APEC),** centered on Japan. They are considered megaregions because they produce about two-thirds of world manufacturing output and three-quarters of world exports. In fact, the market represented by the "triad" countries belonging to these three megaregions consists of more than 600 million middle-class consumers "whose academic backgrounds, income levels both discretionary and nondiscretionary, life-style, use of leisure time, and aspirations are quite similar."[60]

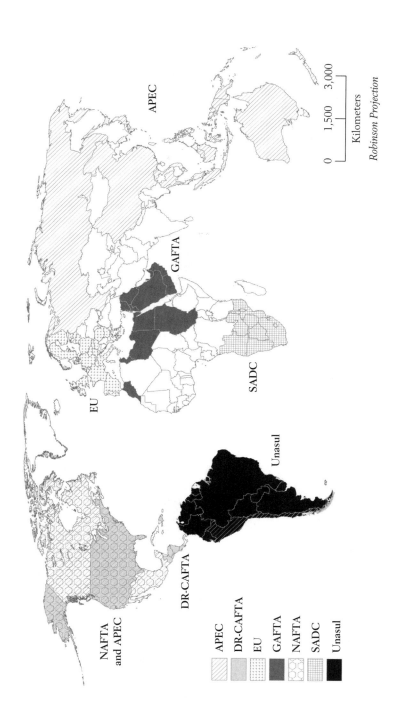

APEC

GAFTA

EU

SADC

Unasul

NAFTA
and APEC

DR-CAFTA

APEC
DR-CAFTA
EU
GAFTA
NAFTA
SADC
Unasul

Kilometers

0   1,500   3,000

Robinson Projection

Figure 6.4   Major Free Trade Zones

The Region-State Versus the Nation-State in the Borderless World

Japanese economist Kenichi Ohmae depicts the global economy as a "borderless world," rendering states "powerless." He argues that the "region-state" (e.g., the San Diego/Tijuana zone; the growth triangle of Singapore, Johore of southern Malaysia, and the Riau Islands of Indonesia; and the South China region, linking Taiwan, Hong Kong, and the Chinese province of Guandong) is the natural economic zone in a borderless world: "Because of the pressures operating on them, the predictable focus of nation states is on mechanisms for propping up troubled industries," whereas "region states . . . are economic not political units, and they are anything but local in focus. They may lie within the borders of an established nation state, but they are such powerful engines of development because their primary orientation is toward—and their primary linkage is with—the global economy. They are, in fact, its most reliable ports of entry." In theory, Ohmae's perspective describes the purest form of "flow governance," where the region-state ignores legitimacy issues faced by states, individually or collectively in free trade agreements, in coauthoring or authoring market rule. But in practice, states do coordinate such zones and manage the populations and social conditions included in and exploited by the zones—as demonstrated by Aihwa Ong's discussion of Malaysia's "graduated sovereignty," through which the state differentially manages a "state-transnational network" for global corporations, and labor relations for ethnic Chinese, Indians, and immigrants from neighboring states.

Sources: Ohmae (1990:80, 89, 99); Ong (2000).

Regionalist groupings subscribe to the principles of global free trade, implementing them among neighboring states. NAFTA was economically logical, if not sensible, for Canada and Mexico, which conduct 70 percent of their trade with the United States.[61] As regional integration occurs, states elsewhere respond with local regional groupings, anticipating the possible exclusion of their exports from other trading blocs. In this sense, regionalism is a defensive strategy. Thus the three megaregions formed in defensive relation to one another, where the European Union's creation of a single currency and common market, termed *Fortress Europe*, deepened integration in the Asia-Pacific region and the Americas.[62]

Regionalism embodies tensions around sovereignty associated with the globalization project. The bureaucratic secrecy of the European Union's 1991 Treaty of Maastricht, for example, was challenged in the European Court of Justice, lawyers for the European Council of Ministers responding, "There is no principle of community law which gives citizens the right to EU documents."[63] A monetary union to create a single currency, the euro, generated further tensions, deferring the question of a social charter (labor protections) by focusing on financial disciplines and dismantling the "social market" in order "to build Europe à l'americaine."[64] Conflict over privatization is endemic in Europe, with Norway and Sweden leading the way by retaining and strengthening public services, and Spain experiencing a spread of "participatory budgeting" in cities such as Cordoba, Seville, Getafe, and Albacete.

Meanwhile, in the Americas, states negotiating the **Central American Free Trade Agreement (CAFTA)** with the United States are facing more stringent conditions than embodied in the WTO, where countries with incomes less than $1,000 per capita (Nicaragua) at least receive special and differential treatment. Similarly with NAFTA (but not the WTO), the CAFTA allows corporations the right to sue governments for regulations that jeopardize profits (such as protecting labor rights and environmental standards).

CASE STUDY

NAFTA—Regional Economic Success, Social Failure?

NAFTA, founded in 1994, regulates flows of goods, services, and capital between the three member nations (Canada, the United States, and Mexico) according to the open-door provisions of the WTO. National and local regulations regarding health, labor, and environmental standards are subordinated to market rule and managed by unelected bureaucrats.

NAFTA formalized a decade-long structural adjustment of Mexico. Opposition presidential candidate Cuauhtémoc Cárdenas argued in run-up debates that, "Exploitation of cheap labor, energy, and raw materials, technological dependency, and lax environmental protection should not be the premises upon which Mexico establishes links with the United States, Canada, and the world economy." As exports shifted from oil to manufactured goods, 85 percent of which moved north, the government secured this export relation with further wage cuts (60 percent decline since 1976) in return for the end of U.S. protectionism. In 1995, Mexican hourly labor costs were 9 percent of those in the United States. Low wages, and large-scale displacement of maize farmers by corn imports from the United States, generate streams of Mexicans across the U.S. border.

While trade volume has nearly tripled and the Mexican economy is now the world's ninth largest, Mexico's 50 percent rate of poverty has not changed since the early 1980s, even though the population grew from 70 to 100 million from 1980 to 2000. The professional and business middle class, formerly Mexico's shining achievement, is unstable and declining, while the richest 10 percent control 50 percent of Mexico's financial and real estate assets. Mexico is considered a paradox like Brazil where, despite its resources, wealth is so polarized.

Meanwhile, a "region-state" called the Plan Puebla de Panama (PPP), a vast infrastructure and cheap labor zone linking nine southern states of Mexico with Central America and Colombia, is under construction. From the Mexican government's viewpoint, the PPP is an attempt to colonize its southern fringes, discipline the Zapatista rebels, and revive the failed promise of NAFTA. As Tom Hayden argues, "Relocating the crisis-ridden *maquiladora* industry to southern Mexico, where wages are half those of the Mexican *maquilas* on the U.S. border, is a desperate effort to prevent the hemorrhage of jobs to China, where 'nimble Chinese hands,' in the words of the *Los Angeles Times,* sew and stitch for 40 cents an hour, only one-sixth of the Mexican wage."

How can this free trade agreement, framed by the market logic of extracting resources and profits from casualized labor, simultaneously be considered both a success and a failure? 🌐

Sources: Fenley (1991:41); Fidler and Bransten (1995); Hayden (2003); Jordan and Sullivan (2003); Moody (1999:133); Resource Center Bulletin (1993:2); Schwedel and Haley (1992:54–55); Thompson (2002a).

The Globalization Project, World Bank Style

Under the umbrella of global governance in the globalization project, the World Bank (and IMF) play a central role. Certainly 1980s structural adjustment policies (SAPs) preceded the universal adoption of liberalization policies through the WTO and its FTA cousins from the mid-1990s. But the international financial institutions (IFIs), recognizing the limitations of SAPs in rendering the poor even more vulnerable, were compelled to create a Social Emergency Fund (World Bank) and a new Compensatory and Contingency Financing Facility (IMF) in 1988 to target those who fell through the cracks. In the 1990s, the IFIs evolved global policies reformulated as "globalization with a human face," starting with the **Heavily Indebted Poor Countries (HIPC) Initiative** of 1996, to provide exceptional assistance to countries with unsustainable debt burdens. Zambia, for example, had a net transfer of $335 million in debt repayment, which was equivalent to government spending on health and education.[65] The IFIs' goal was to stave off a legitimacy crisis by elaborating "governance" mechanisms that continue to this day as poverty reduction remains unfulfilled. And legitimacy is crucial, since both institutions depend increasingly on loan repayment by borrowing countries to bankroll their operations, as northern countries have significantly reduced their contributions.

Securing legitimacy involved "democratizing" SAPs, with the goal of encouraging countries and non-governmental organizations to take "owner-ship" of policy formation and implementation—as outlined in the Bank's Comprehensive Development Framework of 1997–98. By 1999, an enhanced HIPC was created with African debtor states in mind, defining "conditional-ity" by a broad, participatory poverty reduction strategy.[66] The Bank Director spoke of a "civil society revolution," basing development on "inclusion and participation, bringing together civil society, local competition, NGOs, the private sector, and the poor themselves . . . in order to foster trust and sus-tainability."[67] In this context, the Bank commissioned a "Voices of the Poor" project: 60,000 poor women and men in 50 countries expressed deep dissat-isfaction with government corruption, while celebrating the Bank. Participating researchers, who engaged in "participant observation" of the project, noted that poor voices were translated, institutionally, to build legit-imacy for the Bank.[68] While this exercise was underway, the hard truth was that, by 1999, HIPC-eligible country debt had quadrupled, from $59 to $205 billion, between 1996 and 1999, mobilizing activists in the North, in partic-ular the Jubilee 2000 organization, dedicated to debt forgiveness.[69]

Under these circumstances, the IFIs, still committed to debt repayment, repackaged neo-liberal policies in participatory rhetoric, and proceeded to incorporate NGO leaders into the Bank's networks. Unpopular SAPs were refashioned as "partnerships," with states required to author their own development plans, subject to IFI approval, on which loans, debt reschedul-ing, and debt forgiveness can be made. These plans, known as **Poverty Reduction Strategy Papers** (**PRSPs**) are compiled as "performances:" "to meet the charge that imposing conditions is undemocratic, the IFIs now insist that other stakeholders, such as NGOs, churches, unions, and busi-ness, rather than just governments, are involved in writing the plans."[70] The PRSPs are a form of crisis management, with deepening global inequality and social unrest, and these participatory governance mechanisms mark a new evolutionary stage in IFI management of the global South. The Bank's initial Bretton Woods focus on *project* loans for public infrastructure shifted to *policy* loans geared to structural adjustment in the global South during the 1980s, as market reforms redefined IFI development philosophy. Now PRSPs focus on new *process* conditions.[71]

The World Bank and the IMF characterized the PRSP program in 2002 as "a new approach to the challenge of reducing poverty in low-income countries based on country-owned poverty reduction strategies."[72] The new procedures, in holding states accountable for poverty reduction, embed public priorities in private relationships—in effect fashioning "governance states."[73] Here, private commercial law adopted as public policy at the national level, embraces WTO prescriptions for countries to "trade themselves out of poverty." At the global level, the project of poverty reduction, paralleling the 2000 **Millennium Development Goals (MDGs)**, entails policy coordination between the WTO, the IMF and the World Bank.[74]

Global governance has thus evolved into coordination through a process privileging international NGOs with access to information and resources, enabling them to leverage initiatives within states. Thus World Vision International and Médicins sans Frontières are pervasive in Africa today, organizing local schools and clinics in lieu of failed states, respectively.[75] As Oxfam, for example, observes: "PRSPs offer Oxfam and other NGOs major opportunities to influence policy and practice at local, national, and international levels, both at the formulation and implementation stage."[76] In this way, participation displaces existing political institutions, reconfiguring reform coalitions inside and outside states, which can constrain other civil society groups as well as the state itself.[77] The privatization of states is also shaped by Transnational Policy Networks (TPNs)—in Africa through the African Policy Institutes Forum, created by the Bank to serve as professional training program centers, and serving as sites for preparation of PRSPs.[78] Privatization no longer means simply selling off public assets, but integrating segments of states into TPNs that operate as global market intermediaries—especially the IFIs and the international NGO community, acting as "surrogate representative(s) of . . . civil society in the state–donor partnership."[79]

Promoting market access reconstructs the state–civil society relation by complementing (or compromising) the state's authority with the authority of "civil society," subjected to market governance mechanisms such as "budget monitoring" to secure conditionality, and establish "a surveillance architecture capable of disciplining democracy."[80]

Promoting market access also includes incorporating the poor. Within the terms of neoliberalism, since governments are deemed no longer directly responsible for the poor, responsibility falls on the poor themselves. Most PRSPs, despite emphasizing pro-poor growth, exclude policies to redistribute wealth and promote equality.[81] In the twenty-first century world, the poor are viewed as "inhabiting a series of local places across the globe that, marked by the label 'social exclusion,' lie outside of normal civil society. Their route back into the amorphous space of inclusion that the rest of us inhabit is through the willing and active transformation of themselves to conform to the disciplines of the market, since it is that which they are ultimately rejoining."[82]

The policy of the IFIs has been to stimulate such "resubjectification" with micro-credit initiatives. Part of the renewal of the legitimacy of the development establishment (canonized by the awarding of the 2006 Nobel Peace Prize to Grameen Bank founder, Muhammad Yunus), has involved extending microloans through NGO intermediaries to informal slum-dwellers. The rationale is that microlending will redirect existing survival networks, celebrated by the Bank as "social capital," into entrepreneurial activities.[83] Thousands of microfinance institutions in over 100 countries currently serve about 25 million.[84] Arguably, the outcome is to stabilize the informal world of the poor at the same time as they are subject to the new disciplines of credit relations, and the IFIs gain much-needed legitimacy for reaching out to the "Fourth World."

Summary

The development project incubated a new direction in the world capitalist order, which hatched during the 1980s debt crisis. The new direction was the globalization project, an alternative way of organizing economic growth corresponding to the growing scale and power of the transnational banks and corporations. The increasing volume of economic exchanges and the greater mobility of money and firms required forms of regulation beyond the reach of the nation-state but embedded within the system of nation-states. The WTO represents one such form of regulation.

The new global regulatory system subordinated states' social protections to liberalization. Overall, despite differences among states, they became surrogate managers of the global economy (or "market states"). These tendencies are replicated in regional free trade agreements, which express goals similar to those of the globalization project by locking in the open-door provisions of the neoliberal doctrine.

The standardized prescriptions for liberalization reorganize regions and locales: from the removal of Mexican *campesinos* from long-held public lands to the rapid dismantling of public ownership of the economies of Eastern Europe to the proliferation of export processing zones and agro-export platforms. Many of these mushrooming export sites suffer the instability of flexible strategies of "footloose" firms, as they pick and choose their way among global sourcing sites. Social protections decline as communities lose their resource bases (declining social subsidies, dwindling forests) or their employment bases (as firms downsize or move offshore).

Under these conditions, globalization is everything but universalist in its consequences. It assigns communities, regions, and nation-states new niches or specialized roles (including marginalization) in the global economy. The development project proposed social integration through national economic growth under individual state supervision and according to a social contract between government and citizenry. Alternatively, the globalization project offers new forms of authority and discipline according to the laws of the market. Whether these forms of authority and discipline are based in global institutions such as the World Trade Organization, the World Bank and the IMF, or in national institutions managing the global marketplace within their territories, together they perform the governance functions of the globalization project.

Further Reading

Mgbeoji, Ikechi. *Global Biopiracy: Patents, Plants, and Indigenous Knowledge.* Ithaca, NY: Cornell University Press, 2006.
Payne, Anthony. *The Global Politics of Unequal Development.* New York: Palgrave Macmillan, 2005.
Rosset, Peter M. *Food is Different: Why We Must Get the WTO Out of Agriculture.* Halifax, NS: Fernwood, 2006.
Soederberg, Susanne. *Global Governance in Question: Empire, Class and the New Common Sense in Managing North–South Relations.* London: Pluto, 2006.
Wallach, Lori and Patrick Woodall, eds. *Whose Trade Organization? A Comprehensive Guide to the WTO.* London: New Press, 2004.

Select Websites

International Forum on Globalization (USA): www.ifg.org
Millennium Development Goals (MDGs): www.un.org/millenniumgoals
Public Citizen Global Trade Watch (USA): www.citizen.org/trade
UN Capital Development Fund: www.uncdf.org
World Health Organization (WHO): www.who.int/en
World Trade Organization (WTO): www.wto.org

7

The Globalization
Project in Practice

The globalization project is about market integration, legitimacy management, and resistance. At the turn of the twenty-first century, the United Nations reported that the richest 20 percent of the world's population enjoyed 30 times the income of the poorest 20 percent in 1960, but by 1997 the difference was of the order of 74.[1] The exacerbation of global inequality via market integration made legitimacy management a priority for the development establishment in order to justify staying the course with liberalization and the corporate agenda. Food riots, poverty stabilization schemes, and a dramatic uprising in the Chiapas province of southern Mexico underscored the 1994 statement by the Inter-American Development Bank on the eve of the World Trade Organization (WTO)'s formation: "The resumption of economic growth has been bought at a very high social price, which includes poverty, increased unemployment, and income inequality, and this is leading to social problems."[2] Five years later, the WTO Seattle Ministerial (1999) registered a threshold in global "anti-globalization" protest, as a variety of justice movements from across the world blocked the proceedings, giving voice to a widespread discontent with the neo-liberal model of global development. The following year, the United Nations offered the world "globalization with a human face" in the Millennium Development Goals, dedicated to addressing the key challenges of the new century: extreme poverty, pandemic disease, environmental damage, gender inequality, and Southern debt.

And all this occurred during an explosion of the "fast world," driven by the internet boom, corporate mergers, and healthy looking national accounts, as rates of foreign investment and trade ballooned.

The globalization project has two faces: the face of unprecedented prosperity for a minority of the world's investors and consumers; and the face of poverty, displacement, job and food insecurity, health crises (AIDS), and a widening band of informal activity (over 1 billion slum-dwellers) as people make do in lieu of stable jobs, government supports, and sustainable habitats. This will be the subject matter of this chapter.

Here, we consider some of the characteristic practices of globalization as a project. These are: outsourcing; displacement; informalization; and recolonization. They provide the stimulus to the global justice movements examined in Chapter 8.

Outsourcing

Outsourcing involves the relocation of goods and services production as a cost-reduction strategy and a means to increase operational flexibility of an organization. It is symptomatic of two related processes: "deregulation" and the hypermobility of capital, and the transformation of employment—often in the form of casualization. The latter includes accessing "informal" labor, discussed in a separate section. Under neoliberalism, in addition to corporate outsourcing, governments outsource service contracts to reduce public expenditure and/or privilege the private sector. GATS and IFIs promote this kind of outsourcing, often with the effect of transferring monopoly power over the management of utilities to corporations, and outsourcing "governance" functions to NGOs.

Thus a 1998 World Bank loan to the Dominican Republic, requiring privatization of its power sector, passed the generation and distribution of electricity to Enron, among other companies. Following rate increases between 51 and 100 percent, citizens refused to pay, and the state stepped in to subsidize the price increases, at additional cost to taxpayers of $5 million a month. With payments in arrears, Enron's subsidiary induced blackouts (including schools and hospitals), leading to deepening protests, eight deaths, and a massive sell off by the Dominican government of its remaining power assets at almost a $1 billion discount.[3] Similarly, when the South African government outsourced Telkom, the state telephone company, in 2003, it completed the privatization of this essential service, which already had increased tariffs for poor households while slashing rates for rich families and firms, and cut 80 percent of new land lines because of the inability of poor subscribers to pay.[4]

And in 2001, Philippines President Arroyo broke up and outsourced the state-owned National Power Corporation, following threats from the IMF and the Asian Development Bank to withhold credits worth nearly $1 billion. Here, "legislation, which privatizes the state distribution system, does not privatize the associated debt. Filipino taxpayers will continue to shoulder the burden."[5]

Meanwhile, in health care, the World Bank has maintained a policy that public sector inefficiencies hinder service delivery, and made loans to outsource public health to private managed care initiatives. In Latin America, TNCs such as Aetna, CIGNA, the American International Group (AIG), and Prudential have invested heavily in Argentina, Chile, Brazil, and now Ecuador. There are three characteristic effects of neoliberal policy:

- Access to health care for the poor shrinks while investments grow—"between 1996 and 1999, revenues of multinational health care corporations grew much faster in Latin America than in the United States."
- Outsourcing and cutbacks in public sector budgets reduce preventative programs, allowing banished diseases such as cholera, dengue fever, and typhus to reemerge as epidemics.
- As has happened in a dozen states in the United States, after profiting through the privatization of public health care systems, managed care organizations and health insurance companies move on when profit margins fall.[6]

CASE STUDY

Embedded Outsourcing—"Strategic Localization" in the Philippines

Challenging the homogenizing imagery of globalization, Steven McKay shows how corporate outsourcing of high-tech electronics production is not only about accessing cheap labor. It is also about local labor relations shaping global industry. In this case, the Philippine state combines with firms (such as Intel, Texas Instruments, Philips, Toshiba, and Hitachi) to access locally specific and flexible labor forces necessary to the distinctive demands of technology-intensive assembly and test manufacturing of semiconductors and computer hard disk drives. As McKay observes, the state has "transformed its export processing zone program from an emphasis on deregulated public zones to attract simply manufacturing assemblers in the 1970s to a model of reregulated, privatized, high-tech enclaves that appeal to the multinational manufacturers of the twenty-first century." Much like Aihwa Ong's observations on how the Malaysian and Indonesian states create "graduated sovereignty" via new, ethnoracialized technology enclaves privileging transnational corporate citizenship, McKay notes how such enclaves enable firms to develop particular work regimes that depend on manipulating local labor markets in gendered recruitment practices, union avoidance policies, and dispersal of worker housing, to manufacture loyalty and work incentives. Just as Carla Freeman notes (below) that workers in informatics compare their new job identities favorably with alternatives in agriculture, the informal sector, service, or garment industries, so one of McKay's interviewees observed, "If I weren't working now, I'd still be in school or staying home, selling fish balls. Or doing laundry or selling barbequed bananas." Another noted, "Compared with [a nearby food processing plant] its nicer [here] because they're all contractuals there. There are more benefits [here] too . . . the pay is a lot if there's OT." Still another said, "I'm not satisfied with the wages. Still, I prefer to stay because it's really difficult to look for a job now, especially because I'm not a college graduate. If I didn't have this job, I'd be in the hills, farming." Regularizing, rather than casualizing, high-tech jobs, McKay notes that firms "invest in particular places and strategically localize elements of their work regimes in order to lower production costs, and/or better secure labor control and worker commitment."

From a wider lens, "strategic localization" fits within a regional division of labor, where design and manufacturing technologies concentrate in Japan, South Korea, and Taiwan, followed by intermediate production in Singapore, Malaysia, and Thailand, and the labor-abundant sites in China, India, Indonesia, and Vietnam. While the Philippines straddles the latter two categories, China is simultaneously moving aggressively into design and engineering. From this angle, outsourcing patterns are as much regionally subdivided (with labor forces progressively "defeminized" up the hierarchy), as they are embedded socially and politically in local production relations.

When states privatize, they outsource public services. How does this differ from host states privatizing their sovereignty by providing TNCs with access to potential gender and ethno-racial divisions among their citizen-subjects as embedded forms of global outsourcing?

Sources: McKay (2006:13–14, 39, 130, 170, 188–189, 197, 217); Ong (2000).

Corporate outsourcing has become virtually synonymous with globalization. We have seen how the "world factory" emerged on a foundation of the NIDL, as a forerunner of the era of global integration. This pattern, amplified by TRIMs, is now consolidated as the "**global division of labor,**" extending to high and low paid services and perishable agricultural commodities. Diane Perrons states that the global division of labor "leads to factories, call centers, and packing plants being created in poorer countries and regions, but further links consisting of people moving in search of work and a better life have emerged on an unprecedented scale."[7] We address the latter part of this dynamic under "Displacement" below. But outsourcing of production has depended on the deepening of information and communication technologies (ICTs), especially microprocessing power, and developments in fiber optics—for example, "e-mailing a 40 page document from Chile to Kenya costs less than 10 cents, faxing it about $10 and sending it by courier $50." In 2001, "more information was sent over a single cable in a second than over the entire Internet in a month in 1997."[8] This compression of space by time enhances the ability of firms to manage far-flung and fragmented outsourcing operations—coordinating movement of components through the supply chain, and of foods shipped across seasonal and time zones.

On top of a steady movement offshore of manufacturing jobs from the 1970s, service jobs began migrating from North to South in the 1990s. For instance, between 1996 and 2000, U.S. corporate outsourcing grew from $100 billion to $345 billion, concentrating in call centers, graphic design, computer programming, and accountancy.[9] Many new jobs in the Caribbean, for example, are data processing positions that large U.S. insurance, health industry, magazine subscription renewal, consumer credit, and retailing firms have shifted offshore at a lower cost. Swissair, British Airways, and Lufthansa relocated much of their reservations operation to Indian subcontractors in Bangalore, where "the staff are well educated at English-speaking universities yet cost only a fraction of what their counterparts are paid in the North." Swissair claims, "We can hire three Indians for the price of one Swiss." The relocation of revenue accounts preparation saved 8 million francs and 120 jobs in Zurich. Eastern Europe has become an increasingly competitive site for labor-intensive computer programming, as well as "virtual sweatshops" where Romanians provide computer gaming services for wealthy Western players.[10] The Delhi telecomputing firm Selectronic receives doctors' dictation from a U.S. toll-free number, transcribing and transmitting transcriptions as texts to an American HMO, while America Online employs 600 Filipinos to answer over 10,000 technical and billing inquiries per day, mainly from the United States (80 percent of AOL's customer e-mail)—paying its customer-service representatives a daily rate equivalent to an hour's pay for an unskilled American worker. With outsourcing upgrades in India into product R&D, financial analysis and handling insurance claims and payrolls, call center employee wages have increased by 50 percent, providing an opportunity for the Philippines, where call center jobs rose 100 percent over five years to 200,000 in late 2006.[11] IT services (now at 8 percent of GDP) have been expanding in India at a rate of between 30 and 60 percent every year, with new frontiers of "virtual services" beyond customer-service centers beckoning to TNCs—"health care, where a scan may be carried out in one country, processed in another, and sent to a third for another opinion before being sent back home again, is one example."[12] The economics profession may be another mobile "virtual service." Thomas Friedman refers to this as the "democratization of technology," a conceptual forerunner of his "flat world," implying that technological capability enables the South to participate on a leveled global playing field.

CASE STUDY

High Heels and High Tech in Global Barbados

In an innovative study of "pink-collar" work and identities in the Caribbean, Carla Freeman explores how an Afro-Caribbean workforce has embraced the global division of labor in the informatics industry. Disadvantaged by Mexico's stranglehold on trade preferences with North America, the export-oriented countries of Barbados, Jamaica, and Trinidad offer their English-speaking tradition to the outsourcers.

Barbados, with a literacy rate of 98 percent and a reputation for order and polite service, turned itself into a haven for offshore information-based data-processing work, globally sourced by subsidiaries of British and U.S. telecommunication corporations:

> On a typical shift . . . between about fifty and one hundred Barbadian women sit in partitioned computer cubicles of a given production floor from 7:30 in the morning until 3:30 in the afternoon, taking a half-hour break for lunch and sometimes a fifteen-minute stretch in between. Their keystrokes per hour are monitored electronically as they enter data from airline ticket stubs, consumer warranty cards, or the text of a potboiler novel for top U.S. airlines, appliance houses, and publishers. In each case, the surveillance of the computer, the watchful eye of supervisors, and the implementation of double-keying techniques are all aspects of the production process integral to the companies' guarantee of 99 percent accuracy rates.

While such work is deskilled and clearly gendered, Freeman found that, despite better pay in the canefields, these women find these "pink-collar" jobs attractive because of the identification with office work and informatics technology, because the Barbados Development Plan—development via information-based exports—includes guarantees of basic employment benefits, such as maternity and sick leave and three weeks of paid vacation, and because differentiation from field and factory work through dress codes and associated consumption styles enables them to "experience class as gendered Afro-Caribbean subjects within a distinctly feminized arena."

How should we understand the distinction between the discourse of global capitalism as an objective "economic" order with income hierarchies, and its actual realization through cultural filters, where the development subject—such as these Barbadian women, for instance—involves a complex local combination of global class and gender relations?

Source: Freeman (2000:23–48, 65).

India, in particular, is blessed with an English-speaking tradition and, like parts of the Caribbean, South Africa, Pakistan, and the Philippines, language has become a comparative advantage for this kind of service outsourcing. At the Delhi call center Spectramind, in addition to a two-hour seminar on the royal family, one set of "recruits receive a 20-hour crash course in British culture. They watch videos of British soap operas to accustom them to regional accents. They learn about Yorkshire pudding. And they are taught about Britain's unfailingly miserable climate." Another set of recruits, exposed to American TV shows and sporting slang, are "trained in the nuances of baseball, and Blue 'Tennessee Titans' pennants fly above their desks."[13] Following liberalization in 1991, foreign corporations established Indian subsidiaries to outsource jobs in IT, financial services, business processes, pharmaceuticals, and automotive components, generating thousands of new jobs, and annual rates of growth twice those in the North. The ruling right-wing Bharatiya Janata Party (BJP), noting (inflated) numbers of 100 million rescued from poverty, a tripling of cell phones in the early years of the twenty-first century, and a message that India was "moving slowly but steadily towards becoming a global power," proclaimed a "Shining India" campaign, as Bangalore, Hyderabad, Delhi, and Mumbai displayed their new-found wealth as emerging "global cities."[14] While one-third of Bangalore's population are slum-dwellers, half "lack piped water, much less cappuccino, and there are more ragpickers and street children (90,000) than software geeks (about 60,000)."[15] The bubble was burst in the 2004 elections, when "unshining India" voted the BJP out of office. Not only are two-thirds of the populace (230 million) still residing in publicly neglected and deteriorating rural habitats, but the IT sector generates less than 2 percent of national income, employs 1 million in an economy where 8 million join the labor force annually,[16] and, as Praful Bidwai noted at the Mumbai World Social Forum, "There are other distressing figures that tell Indian reality better: appalling stagnation in health, nutrition, and education indicators."[17] In other words, outsourcing generates clusters of prosperity networked more often across national borders than within them. The 2004 election confirmed a deep contradiction between the global seduction of technology and export parks, and addressing national inequalities.

In addition to ICTs and TRIMs, debt is also a driver of outsourcing opportunities. Access to cheaper land and labor in the South is often created through coercion—whether displacement of farmers by artificially cheapened imports of food, or government "eminent domain" claims. India is building on experiments already underway in Andhra Pradesh state, such as Vision 2020, to consolidate agro-industrial estates—"farmed on a contract basis for corporations using genetically-modified seeds to produce agro-exports of vegetables and flowers, and requiring the displacement of upwards of 20 million small farmers."[18] In 2006, the Indian government planned a Special Economic Zone on the site of 45 villages, one-third of the size of nearby metropolitan Mumbai for export production: "forcibly acquiring land at a pittance and handing it over to [Reliance Industries] to sell to businesses in the SEZ. It will be a satellite city in a prime location—close to the major highways, ports, and the site for the new international airport."[19]

Rural land appropriation for outsourcing industries is routine in China where, in Dongguan City (Reebok and Nike shoes), local farmers now live off factory rents, while tens of thousands of migrants from the hinterland swell the workforce, with Korean or Taiwanese managers.[20] Datang, a rice farming village in the late 1970s, with a cottage industry in socks, now produces nine billion socks annually: "Signs of Datang's rise as a socks capital are everywhere. The center of town is filled with a huge government-financed marketplace for socks. The rice paddies have given ways to rows of paved streets lined with cookie-cutter factories. Banners promoting socks are draped across buildings."[21] Renamed "Socks City," Datang is one of many new coastal cities: southeast is Shenzhou, the world's necktie capital; west is Sweater City and Kids' Clothing City; and to the south, in the low-rent district, is Underwear City.[22] In one of these cities, *China Blue* (2006) was filmed in a blue jeans factory—portraying reliance on labor of teenage girls fresh from the rural hinterland. With an ethnographic approach, the film documents how pressures to cut costs are passed down from the English buyer, through the factory owner, to his vulnerable workforce, who are also forced to work shifts lasting sometimes more than 40 hours to meet "just in time" orders. Buyers, under pressure to ensure ethical brands, send inspectors who focus on product quality and turn a blind eye to the duplicate time cards and employee coaching organized by factory owners. Global assembly work typically intensifies gender and ethnic inequalities, often generating powerlessness among adolescents, and intergenerational tensions as young people are at once seduced by, and excluded from, symbols of modernity associated with off-farm work.[23]

The "ecology" of outsourcing includes social stratification. For example, the global supermarket revolution centralizes food processing and retailing via continuing pressure on small or independent producers.[24] Thus, in the Amazon, meat purchasing from small ranchers by local slaughterhouses has been replaced by large commercial ranchers producing directly for supermarkets that service the Brazilian and global market. European supermarkets dominate the beef export market with extensive cattle ranching, and Europe and the Middle East account for 75 percent of Brazil's beef exports. Transnational firms such as Ahold, Carrefour, and Wal-Mart comprise 70–80 percent of the top five supermarket chains in Latin America, centralizing procurement from farmers across the region (and their own processing plants) and, together with Nestlé and Quaker, supplying regional consumer markets throughout the Mercosur trading bloc. In Guatemala, where supermarkets control 35 percent of food retailing, "their sudden appearance has brought unanticipated and daunting challenges to millions of struggling, small farmers," lacking binding contractual agreements, rewarded only if they consistently meet new quality standards, and facing declining prices as they constitute a virtually unlimited source for retailers.[25]

"Standards" are critical to the outsourcing revolution. WTO regulation of trade relations is complemented by extensive private regulation of production standards, regarding quality, safety, packaging, and convenience. The new "audit culture" generates certification schemes such as EurepGAP, an association of European supermarket chains concerned with regulating quality, safety, environment, and labor standards surpassing publicly required standards.[26] But certification often *follows* health crises—thus, in May 2007, hundreds of deaths were reported in the United States, Panama, and Australia from a "toxic pipeline" whereby diethylene glycol, an industrial solvent substituted as a counterfeit syrup in various medicines (cough syrup, fever medication, injectable drugs, toothpaste), was found to originate in "chemical country" near the Yangtze Delta—"showing how China's safety regulations have lagged behind its growing role as low-cost supplier to the world."[27] Risk management encourages production consolidation—UK supermarkets are doing this to reduce their exposure to risk by expanding control over production and distribution.[28] In Kenya, where about 90 percent of horticulture is destined for Europe (especially the United Kingdom), the shift from smallholder-contract production to centralized employment on farms and in packhouses in the mid-1990s has in turn transformed farming women into a migrant labor force, as a household survival strategy.[29] Likewise, in Brazil's

Sao Francisco Valley, "new agricultural districts" exporting mangoes, grapes, tomatoes, and acerola must meet specific quality controls and design, as well as setting parameters for labor and environmental conditions.[30] A successful producer comments that

> the market had changed and was demanding quality. We had to change too; more qualified people, new technologies at harvest and after harvest; packing houses, cooling chambers, packaging and wrapping papers. . . . We had to travel, to hire external experts, and to develop new systems of cutting and irrigation. There were changes in labor control and in the ways fertilization, pulverization and timing were done; the introduction of computer programming was also new.[31]

Displacement

In the shadow of globalization lurks a rising dilemma: the casualization of labor and the redundancy of people. Despite, and perhaps because of, an expanding global economy, numbers of unemployed (including hard-to-count long-term unemployed) in the global North have risen from 10 to almost 50 million between 1973 and the early twenty-first century.[32] This is the dilemma of structural unemployment, where automation and/or outsourcing of work sheds stable jobs and where redundant workers cease rotating into new jobs. It is matched across the world by other forms of displacement, including SAP-mandated dismantling of ISI sectors, forced resettlement by infrastructural projects (e.g., 1.9 million peasants will be resettled in China's Three Gorges Dam project),[3] civil wars, and the destabilization of rural communities by market forces (dumping of cheap food, corporatization of agriculture, and decline of farm subsidies). From 1996 to 2001, 40 percent of state-owned industrial enterprises disappeared, displacing 36 million workers—mainly female. At the turn of the twenty-first century, one billion workers (one-third of the world's labor force, mainly Southern) were either unemployed or underemployed.[33]

Displacement begins with depeasantization, a process synonymous with modernity. Ruling and trading classes have always viewed the peasantry as expendable, and the development narrative sustains the unsustainable assumption that peasants are redundant in the modern world. It is uncontestable that agriculture is the main source of food and income for the majority of the world's poor. While about 3.8 billion people directly depend on the agricultural sector, more than half of the south's population is agrarian, rising to 85 percent in some of the poorest countries. The FAO notes,

"Agriculture is also of great social, cultural, and environmental significance for rural communities. It tends to be particularly important for women, who have the main responsibilities for feeding their families and are estimated to produce 60–80% of food grown in most developing countries."[34] In particular, agro-ecological farming, sustained by seed-swap networks, maintains a deeper array of biodiversity than chemical-dependent monocultures, with more trees, crop diversity, and natural predators to control pests and disease. Long-term food security depends on diversity of crop species, in contrast to industrial agriculture's dependence on 15 crop species for 90 percent of its food calories. Researchers find that, contrary to conventional assumptions, adoption of organic and agro-ecological approaches produces higher yields, in part because the goal is *optimizing* sustainable yields, rather than *maximizing* output via soil exhaustion.[35] Despite compelling evidence that smallholder agriculture can anchor agro-ecological methods and be the most effective form of rural poverty alleviation, the subordination of agriculture everywhere to corporate farming and retailing is steadily driving peasants into an exploding global slum.

As we saw in Chapter 6, neoliberal food security means privileging food importing over local farming for many southern states. Grain trader Cargill's chairman observed, "There is a mistaken belief that the greatest agricultural need in the developing world is to develop the capacity to grow food for local consumption. This is misguided. Countries should produce what they produce best—and trade."[36] But as the transnational peasant coalition Via Campesina notes, "the massive movement of food around the world is forcing the increased movement of people."[37] In Mexico, not only have almost 2 million *campesinos* lost their farms under the NAFTA corn import regime, but tortilla prices have risen 380 percent. The government recently reported that over 1 million children (one in eight) are chronically malnourished. IRC Americas program director Laura Carlsen asks, "Did economic integration in agriculture enable the nation to import cheap food and solve hunger?"[38] Under the WTO's Agreement on Agriculture, decoupling of (Northern) subsidies from prices removes the price floor, establishing a *low* "world price" for agricultural commodities, and favoring traders and processors in the global food industry at the expense of farmers everywhere. At the 1999 WTO Ministerial in Seattle, a Honduran farmer observed, "Today, we cannot sell our own farm products on the markets because of . . . imports . . . of cheap food produce from Europe, Canada, and the U.S. . . . Free trade is for multinationals; it is not for the small peasant farmers."[39]

Liberalization policies are rooted in IMF-World Bank structural adjustment measures, which have routinely required "free markets" in grain—for example, in formerly self-sufficient countries like Malawi, Zimbabwe, Kenya, Rwanda, and Somalia. Somalia's pastoral economy was decimated by a structural adjustment program of duty-free imports of subsidized beef and dairy products from the European Union.[40] In India, following a decade of neoliberalism, the Ministry of Agriculture stated in 2000, "The growth in agriculture has slackened during the 1990s. Agriculture has become a relatively unrewarding profession due to an unfavorable price regime and low value addition, causing abandoning of farming and migration from rural areas."[41] Corporate seed prices have inflated tenfold, and cheap food imports have undercut local farmers and processors. Meanwhile, agro-exports of affluent commodities such as farmed shrimp, flowers, and meat, in the name of food security, increase human insecurities. In sub-Saharan Africa, the official "famine" threshold has been crossed for 15 million people. SAPs contribute to this by promoting export agriculture and replacing state marketing boards with private buyers. The attraction of foreign exchange and profit discriminate against small producers. In Zambia, those living below the poverty line rose from 69 to 86 percent between 1996 and 2001. Across Lesotho, Malawi, Mozambique, Swaziland, Zambia, and Zimbabwe, 51 percent of the population live below national poverty lines. The neoliberal paradox is that "free" markets exclude and/or starve populations dispossessed by their implementation.[42]

CASE STUDY

Corporate Philanthropy and the Return of the Green Revolution

A recent joint venture between the Rockefeller and Gates Foundations, the *Alliance for a Green Revolution in Africa (AGRA)*—pitched, in participatory terms, as an improvement on the top-down methods of the original Green Revolution—has been met by considerable skepticism. The issue is relatively simple: while GR technology improves yields, poor villagers do not have the cash to buy the food. Sophia Murphy, of the U.S. Institute for Agriculture and Trade Policy, noted that the GR, "ignored the issue of market power: the companies who sell the inputs, and buy, process, distribute, and retail the food produced were vastly more powerful than the farmers and in turn, extracted much of the economic benefit." Further, as reported by the NGO Food First, "In both Mexico and India, studies revealed that the Green Revolution's expensive seed, fertilizer, pesticide, and irrigation programs favor a minority of well-to-do farmers. The Green Revolution ends up indebting the smallholder majority, many of whom are pushed into landlessness and poverty. According to the Indian government, between 1993 and 2003, over 100,000 bankrupt Indian farmers committed suicide." Other effects of GR technology are degradation of tropical agro-ecosystems, loss of agro-biodiversity on which smallholder livelihoods depend, expansion of the "chemical treadmill," and the marginalization of successful agro-ecological and non-corporate approaches to agricultural development. Arguably, land reform and stable markets are more sustainable than technologies of displacement, especially in an era of rising oil and fertilizer prices.

If small farmers are a key source of food for the world's working poor, why displace them with policies that convert food into a commodity to be purchased by the global minority with purchasing power, given the "planet of slums" problem? 🌐

Sources: Davis (2006); Food First (2006:1–2); Murphy (2006); Patel (2007).

Global economic integration intensifies displacement as the global economy stratifies populations across, rather than simply within, national borders. With provocative imagery, Jacques Attali, former president of the European Bank for Reconstruction and Development, distinguishes *rich nomads* ("consumer-citizens of the privileged regions") from *poor nomads* ("boat people on a planetary scale"):

> In restless despair, the hopeless masses of the periphery will witness the spectacle of another hemisphere's growth. Particularly in those regions of the South that are geographically contiguous and culturally linked to the North—places such as Mexico, Central America, or North Africa—millions of people will be tempted and enraged by the constant stimulation of wants that can't be satisfied. . . . With no future of their own in an age of air travel and telecommunications, the terminally impoverished will look for one in the North. . . . The movement of peoples has already begun; only the scale will grow: Turks in Berlin, Moroccans in Madrid, Indians in London, Mexicans in Los Angeles, Puerto Ricans and Haitians in New York, Vietnamese in Hong Kong.[43]

Such fears, founded in latent stereotypes, underlie the concern of the global managers and many Northern consumer-citizens to stem the tide of global labor migration, and fears of associations with terrorism. Consequences range from the spread of "gated communities" and the Hummer to a rollback of civil rights in the global North.

A cursory glance at the newspapers in the global North confirms a broad anxiety about the ethnic composition of the underground global labor force, often manifested in outbreaks of racist violence toward "guest workers." This attitude has spread in Europe, where as many as 3 million "illegal" migrants (from Eastern Europe, Turkey, Central Asia, China, and Francophone West Africa) work in restaurants, construction, and farming—they "enjoy none of the workers' rights and protections or social benefits of the state . . . are paid less than the legal wage, and are often paid late, with no legal recourse." Advocates argue that legalizing the status of the *"sans papiers"* would reduce xenophobia.[44] The guest worker phenomenon is not unique to the twenty-first century, and the cycles of attraction and expulsion mirror economic cycles in host countries. For example, in 2002, facing an economic downturn, the Malaysian government expelled 400,000 Indonesian workers, who returned home to join the 40 million unemployed.[45]

In the global North, continuing immigration is in the interests of firms needing cheap labor and of privileged people needing servants. The *displacement of love* via the feminization and export of care workers from the South to care for children of working women in the North has been termed the "global heart transplant," and linked to the "care drain" from the South via "chains of love," whereby migrant women work as "global nannies" at considerable emotional cost to their own children, who in turn are cared for by relatives or teenage girls at home.[46]

Migrant Labor in the Global Economy: Economic and Environmental Refugees

In the early twenty-first century, as many as 175 million people were estimated to be living as expatriate laborers around the world. Asian women are the fastest growing group of foreign workers, increasing by about 1 million each year. Environmental migration is increasingly significant, with reports that 1 billion people could be displaced by climate change by 2050. Current sources include:

- 135 million people whose land is being desertified;
- 900 million of the world's poorest, existing on less than a dollar a day and living in areas vulnerable to soil erosion, droughts, desertification, and floods;
- 200 million people facing rising sea levels due to climate change;
- 50 million people in famine-vulnerable areas subject to climate change; and
- 550 million people already suffering from chronic water shortage.

Sources: Baird (2002:10); Boyd (1998:17); Perrons (2005:211); Vidal (2007).

Labor: The New Export

The mobility rights for capital guaranteed by neoliberalism do not extend to labor. Nevertheless, labor increasingly circulates, seeking employment opportunities—whether "legal," "illegal," or slave/bonded labor. Migration is not new to this century. The separation of people from the land is etched into the making of the modern world. Colonialism propelled migrations of free and unfree people. Between 1810 and 1921, 34 million people, mainly Europeans, emigrated to the United States alone. The difference today, perhaps, is in the feminization of global migration: 75 percent of refugees and displaced persons are women and children.[47]

During the 1980s, spurred by debt regime restructurings, there was an internal migration in the former Third World of between 300 and 400 million people.[48] This pool of labor has contributed to global migration from overburdened cities to Northern regions as migrants seek to earn money for families back home. Roughly 100 million kinfolk depend on remittances of the global labor force. In the 1990s, for example, two-thirds of Turkey's trade deficit was financed by remittances from Turks working abroad. In 2001, Bangladeshi workers in Southeast Asia or the Middle East sent home $2 billion, the second largest source of foreign exchange after garment exports. Mexico, a nation of 100 million, earns more than $9 billion a year in remittances—almost as much as India, which has a population of 1 billion. And Latin America and the Caribbean received $25 billion in 2002 from remittances which, along with foreign direct investment, now represent a more important source of finance than private lending there.[49]

The influx of foreign exchange not only supplies much-needed hard currency but, in an era of structural adjustment and privatization, remittance money supplements or subsidizes public ventures. Thus, in Indonesian villages, remittances finance schools, roads, and housing in lieu of public funding. Migrants recently invested $6 million in new roads, schools, churches, water systems, and parks in Zacatecas, Mexico and President Fox commented, "The families that receive the money use it to buy shoes or beans, clothes, or books for their children. Now we want to channel part of that money for production for projects that generate jobs," matching, peso for peso, money remitted by migrant workers for public works projects in their home communities.[50]

Spurred by debt, labor export has become a significant foreign currency earner: Filipino overseas earnings are estimated to amount to $5.7 billion, for example. About 6 million Filipinos—increasingly from rural areas—work overseas in 130 countries as contract workers (seamen, carpenters, masons, mechanics, or maids).[51] The government of the Philippines includes labor in its export-led development strategy.[52] In addition to products, labor is exported—mainly to the oil-rich Middle East, where contractors organize the ebb and flow of foreign labor. One contractor, Northwest Placement, a privately run recruiting agency, receives 5,000 pesos ($181)—the maximum allowed by the Labor Department—from Filipino applicants on assurance of a job; this covers the costs of a medical check, visas, and government clearance fees. Not surprisingly, there are also plenty of unlicensed agencies operating.[53]

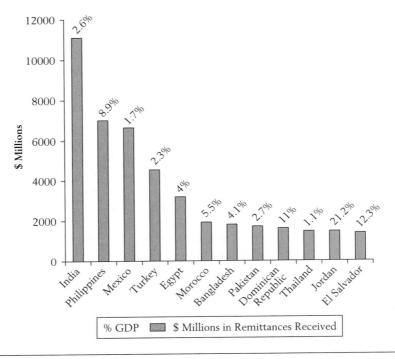

Figure 7.1   Top 12 Developing Country Receivers of Remittances, 1999

Sources: International Monetary Fund (2001); World Bank (2000a).

CASE STUDY

Trafficking in Women—The Global Sex Trade Versus Human Rights

Human trafficking is the fastest growing form of bonded labor in today's global market, and the leading human rights violation. It is estimated that between 700,000 and 2 million women and children are trafficked annually, and that there are about 10 million trafficked people working at risk. After drug smuggling and gun running, human trafficking is the third largest illegal trade (with an annual profit of about $6 billion). Child trafficking dwarfs the trans-Atlantic slave trade at its peak, by a magnitude of 10. Some destinations are farming, restaurant labor, domestic servitude, fishing, mail-order brides, market stall labor, shop work, and the sex trade.

Human rights exploitation of trafficked people, who lack legal status and language skills, is easy and widespread. Since 1990, about 30 million women and children have been trafficked for prostitution and sweatshop labor. The rise in trafficking is directly related to the feminization of global poverty and the use of the internet as a sex forum.

In Thailand, female emigration took off in the 1980s, as the East Asian boom disrupted cultural traditions and family livelihoods. Young women flooded into Bangkok from the Thai countryside, looking for income to remit to their villages, many ending up in Europe, the United States, Japan, South-East Asia, Australia, South Africa, or the Arabian Gulf in the burgeoning sex industry by deceit or by choice (being a relatively high-income trade open to uneducated women). Thai sex tourism contributed to the demand for Thai women overseas. Research in northern Thailand has shown that about 28 percent of household income was remitted by absent daughters. A common motive is relieving poverty and debt, and often parents sell their daughters for a cash advance to be paid off by work in the global sex industry. Alternatively, individual women pay an agent's fee of around $500. From then on, women are devoid of rights: working as bonded labor; subject to arrest for illicit work and illegal residence; lacking rights to medical or social services overseas; forced to sell sex; at high risk of contracting HIV; and targets of racial discrimination and public humiliation if arrested.

Action against trafficking is hampered by collusion between source families and agents; by the lifestyle of the women, trapped by underground employers; and by governments interested in suppressing information to avoid adverse publicity.

How can global human rights agencies address the trafficking tragedy when governments are reluctant to intervene for fear of loss of foreign exchange or tourist dollars? 🌐

Sources: Pyle (2001); Skrobanek et al. (1997:13–31, 68, 103); "Slavery in the 21st Century" (2001:18); Worden (2001).

International labor circulation combines formal policies with decidedly informal working conditions. Migrant workers routinely lack human rights. Workers in the Gulf states, for example, are indentured, with no civic rights, no choice of alternative jobs, and no recourse against poor employment conditions and low wages—which are determined by the income levels of the country of origin. Migrant workers must surrender their passports on arrival; they reportedly work 12 to 16 hours a day, seven days a week. Governments in the migrant workers' home countries in Asia, dependent on foreign currency earnings, are reportedly resigned to the exploitation of their nationals. International labor union organizations have been ineffectual, especially as Middle Eastern states have united to suppress discussion in international forums of working conditions inside their countries.[54]

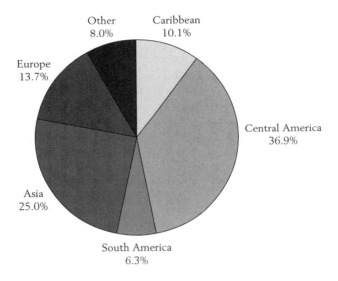

Figure 7.2.   The Foreign-Born Population in the United States, 2003

Source: U.S. Census Bureau, *Current Population Survey, 2003 Annual Social and Economic Supplement*, www.census.gov/prod/2004pubs/p20-551.pdf.

Labor comes from all over the world into the United States, as shown in Figure 7.2. The scale is such that immigrants retain their cultural and linguistic traditions rather than assimilate: "the old American 'melting pot' is now cooking a variegated stew, each of whose ingredients maintains a singular taste."[55] Increasingly, minority cultures form identifiable "transnational communities" in their new work sites, sustaining regular contact with sending countries and other migrant communities through electronic communication and remitting income to families left behind. The juxtaposition of distinct cultures in countries to which labor migrates creates a *multicultural* effect—not necessarily benign, as a New York City Labor Department Official noted: "In the underground economies of the ethnic enclaves of Vietnamese, Cuban, Dominican, Central American, and Chinese, it is a case of immigrants exploiting immigrants."[56] Neoliberal restructuring has amplified "ethnicism," including "nativism," in a backlash against immigration related to rising economic uncertainties. Ironically, NAFTA promised that rising levels of Mexican employment and wages would reduce "illegal" immigration into the United States. While factory jobs expanded by 1 million in the 1990s, by 2007 they had shrunk to roughly the same level at the inception of NAFTA in 1994, and Mexican wages were down 14 percent. Meanwhile 500 of Mexico's 3,700 *maquilas* have shut, with a loss of 300,000 jobs mostly in textiles and electronics, and mostly to China; and millions of *campesinos* have been displaced by corn imports and withdrawal of rural credit. American debates about "illegals" routinely ignore this context, blaming individuals, not structured policies.[57]

CASE STUDY

Multiculturalism and Its Contradictions

In France, the question of multiculturalism has been tested recently with the growing presence of the more than 3.5 million Muslims living in that country. Muslims comprise a quarter of the total immigrant population (mostly from European countries). Their presence stems from a French policy to import large numbers of North African men for factory and construction work from the 1960s through 1974, after which families were allowed to join the men. Arab and African immigrants and their French-born children form an increasingly distinct suburban underclass in French society. A principal of a Parisian school with a large immigrant population remarked, "In the 1970s and 1980s, we promoted multiculturalism. We had a day of couscous, a day of paella, it was '*vive la difference*' much of the time. Now the pendulum is going the other way."

France has more than 1,000 *banlieues sensibles* ("sink estates") in which immigrants from a variety of cultures are crowded into high-rise, rundown ghettos—built originally in the 1960s and 1970s to house immigrant workers. Unemployment among 20- to 29-year-olds of North African origin runs at about 40 percent, compared with 10 percent for youths of French origin. Street crime and social protest fan French fears, contributing to the 2007 election of French President Sarkozy, who called protesting immigrant youth "scum." Yasser Amri, a successful graduate of one of the largest council estates, claimed, "It's the end of the republican ideal. The French republic deals with citizens, not individuals. But here, people aren't citizens. They don't know what they are. Not Algerian, or Moroccan or West African, but not French citizens either. They're unrecognized, unremembered, and unrepresented. No wonder they rebel."

Why is it that representations of globalization use images of a homogeneous global market culture, rather than revealing the cultural tensions arising from the inequalities through which the project of globalization is realized?

Sources: Henley (2003:3); Henley and Vasagar (2003:3); Riding (1993).

The conditions in which labor circulation has intensified have made multiculturalism a fragile ideal. Labor export arrangements deny rights and representation to migrant workforces, and deteriorating economies and communities in global-economic centers spark exclusionist politics that scapegoat cultural minorities. Development project ideals informed a politics of inclusion, rooted in broad-based class movements and political coalitions more committed to assimilation and the redistribution of resources. Under neoliberalism, inclusion is threatened by separatist politics. The "race to the bottom" is not just about wage erosion, it is also about tensions around difference.

Informalization

The globalization project is Janus-faced. It exaggerates the market culture at the same time as it intensifies its opposite—a growing culture of informal, or marginal, activity. This culture involves people working on the fringes of the market, performing casual and unregulated (often outsourced) labor, working in cooperative arrangements, street vending, or pursuing what are deemed illegal economic activities. Those who are bypassed or marginalized by development often form a culture parallel to the market culture. The question of whether informal culture is a real alternative or simply an unrecognized or impoverished margin of the formal culture depends on the context. For example, revival of subsistence farming may improve living standards over working as a rural laborer or existing on the urban fringe, as long as land is available. Marginalization is closely associated with forms of displacement—for example, cycles of expansion and contraction of formal economic activity, or the concentration of resources in fewer corporate hands, generates **informalization**.

Informalization is a politico-cultural process. With the rise of market societies, the boundaries of the formal economy were identified and regulated by the state for tax purposes, but they have always been incomplete and fluid, often by design and certainly by custom. An army of servants and housecleaners, for example, routinely works "off the books." Casual labor has always accompanied small-scale enterprise and even large-scale harvesting operations where labor use is cyclical. Also, a substantial portion of labor performed across the world every day is unpaid labor—such as housework and family farm labor.

Distinguishing between a formal economy with its legal/moral connotations, and an informal sector with its illegal or immoral connotations, is either artificial or political. We make the distinction here as it reveals the limits of official, formal development strategy, and identifies alternative, informal livelihood strategies—often intimately connected and mutually conditioning. Economists and governments make the distinction because national accounting measures legal cash transactions. By ignoring informal activity, development policy discounts and marginalizes substantial mechanisms of social reproduction, on which the formal "productive economy" depends. The consequences of this artificial distinction illuminate the crisis of structural adjustment, spotlighting the gendered foundations of material life. To illustrate, Bharati Sadasivam notes that the language of SAPs focuses

overwhelmingly on the "productive economy," on making profits and covering costs. In the process, it takes for granted the "reproductive economy," which meets needs and sustains human beings. Macro models of mainstream economics assume that the process of reproduction and the maintenance of human resources will continue regardless of the way resources are reallocated. These models conceal the large contribution to the economy provided by the production and maintenance of the labor supply through childbirth and childcare, shopping, cooking, and housework. Economic reforms such as structural adjustment policies that call for cutbacks in state services and the free play of market forces fail to consider how such changes affect the relation between the "productive economy" and the "reproductive economy." Because the latter is sustained by unpaid nonmarket work mostly undertaken by women, macroeconomics also assumes an unlimited supply of female labor. It expects this labor to adjust to and compensate for any changes in the "reproductive economy" brought about by macroeconomic policy measures such as withdrawals in state subsidies and services as well as rises in prices and taxes.[58]

The "informal economy" comprises two related domains: forms of social reproduction complementing production (as above); and informal "productive" activity off the books. For example, one of the world's largest slums, Dharavi, has an "informal" output of $1.25 billion a year, largely from the work of 250,000 people recycling the discarded waste of Mumbai's 16 million citizens. Before celebrating such ingenious microentrepreneurship among Dharavi's 1 million slumdwellers, note that most "workshops are constructed illegally on government land, power is routinely stolen and commercial licenses are rarely sought. There is just one lavatory for every 1,500 residents, not a single public hospital, and only a dozen municipal schools. Throughout the slum chicken and mutton stalls dump viscera into open drains thick with human and industrial waste; cholera, typhoid, and malaria are common. Taps run dry most of the time."[59]

Slumdwellers now comprise *a third* of the global urban population, and almost 50 percent of the population of the global South. UN-HABITAT estimates that the world's highest percentages of slumdwellers are in Ethiopia (99.4 percent of the urban population), Chad (99.4 percent), Afghanistan (98.5 percent), and Nepal (92 percent). Mumbai is the global slumdweller capital, with 10–12 million, Mexico City and Dhaka (9–10 million each), and then Lagos, Cairo, Karachi, Kinshasa-Brazzaville, São Paulo, Shanghai, and Delhi (6–8 million each).[60]

In effect, neoliberal development and the generation of a "planet of slums" go together. Of course, these *peri-urban* communities, as they are known, have been expanding throughout the twentieth century, as the world's urban population surpassed that of the countryside in 2006.

> Cities have absorbed nearly two-thirds of the global population explosion since 1950, and are currently growing by a million babies and migrants each week. . . . The global countryside, meanwhile has reached its maximum population and will begin to shrink after 2020. As a result, cities will account for virtually all future world population growth, which is expected to peak at about 10 billion in 2050. Ninety-five percent of this final buildout of humanity will occur in the urban areas of developing countries. . . . Indeed, the combined urban population of China, India, and Brazil already roughly equals that of Europe and North America.[61]

With global integration, the lines are drawn even more clearly, on a larger scale, and possibly more rapidly. There are professional and managerial classes—the Fast World elite—who participate in global circuits (involved with products, money, electronic communications, high-speed transport) linking enclaves of producers/consumers across state borders. Many of these people increasingly live and work within corporate domains, linked to the commercial and recreational centers, in turn delinked from national domains.[62] And there are those whom these circuits bypass or indeed displace.

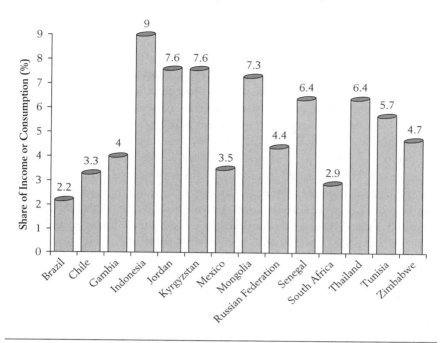

Figure 7.3   Income of the Poorest 20 Percent of Populations of Selected Countries, 1994–1999

Source: World Bank, World Development Indicators, 2002.

These are the redundant labor forces, the structurally unemployed, the marginals, who live in shantytowns and urban ghettos or circulate the world.

Informalization involves two related *processes:* the casualization of labor via corporate restructuring and the development of new forms of individual and collective livelihood strategies. The distinctive feature of corporate globalization is the active informalization of labor cascading across the world, as it is flexible, cheap, and depresses wages everywhere. Beginning with EPZs, labor has been progressively *dis*organized via weakening and dismantling of labor regulations, in cycles of competition including first-generation labor forces as depeasantization has proceeded. ILO estimates (2002) show some variation in the percentage of informalization of non-agricultural employment: 48 percent in North Africa, 51 in Latin America, 65 in Asia, and 72 in sub-Saharan Africa. Following the 1997 Asian financial crisis, South Korea's informal labor force of almost 7 million exceeded its 6.15 million full-time workers, and South Africa's informal labor sector reached 1.8 million by 2001, one-third of the workforce.[63]

Central to this global process has been the informalization of Chinese labor, with the state lifting its ban on rural migration, and also disbanding state-owned enterprises. Given the draconian agricultural tax system in China, and an urban/rural differential greater than anywhere else, between 1996 and 2000 over 176 million peasants migrated to cities, despite lacking the social benefits extended to urban residents, finding work mainly in newly zoned export factories and costing foreign corporations one-third the wage of city-born workers, itself a fraction of Northern wage costs. During this migration, the female percentage of informal workers rose from 45 to over 65 percent.[64] This feminized informal labor force (as in *China Blue*) is highly exploitable. Sociologist Li Quiang's study of Beijing migrants (2002) revealed that one quarter were unpaid, almost two-thirds worked over ten hours a day, with a sizeable percentage working over 16 hours a day (over and above rush order episodes), and health care was non-existent.[65]

Meanwhile, in export agriculture from the global South, millions of women, comprising between 50 and 90 percent of workers employed in producing, processing, and retailing high-value horticultural crops (roses, apples, snowpeas, green beans, and avocados) experience "informalization." TNCs organize these global supply chains, using their market power to pass business costs and risk on to suppliers, who in turn displace these on to their workforce. The ILO reports that rights violations of agricultural workers are "legion," and that women suffer weak labor rights, casualization, low wages, long hours, lax health and safety practices, gender stereotyping, and sexual harassment. Human rights violations of informal agricultural labor extend to child labor—for example, in 2003–04, almost 83,000 children worked on cotton seed farms in India's Andhra Pradesh state, some supplying subsidiaries of TNCs such as Advanta, Bayer, Monsanto, Syngenta, and Unilever. NGOs report that many are under 10 years old, 85 percent are girls, and many are migrants from low castes, sold into debt bondage to pay off family loans: the "children's job is usually to cross-pollinate cotton flowers by hand for up to 13 hours a day; in the process they are exposed to toxic pesticides . . . and complain of headaches, nausea, and convulsions."[66]

The other face of informalization is the expanding range of activities of production and social reproduction occurring in the "shadow economy," comprising over 50 percent of the population of the global South. Commercial agriculture and habitat degradation routinely expel peasants and laborers from rural livelihoods; they migrate to urban centers where, as they hear on the radio and through migrant networks, jobs and amenities are available. Thus, as Hernando de Soto, a libertarian critic of development and urban bias, observes,

Quite simply, Peru's legal institutions had been developed over the years to meet the needs and bolster the privileges of certain dominant groups in the cities and to isolate the peasants geographically in rural areas. As long as this system worked, the implicit legal discrimination was not apparent. Once the peasants settled in the cities, however, the law began to lose social relevance. The migrants discovered that their numbers were considerable . . . that they were excluded from the facilities and benefits offered by the law . . . that they must compete not only against people but also against the system. Thus it was, that in order to survive, the migrants became informals.[67]

This representation of "informalization" dovetails with official, neoliberal narratives framing "social exclusion" in supply-side terms—namely, that the informal is the "anti-economy," marginality is a personal deficit, and the solution is through individual responsibility. Constructed in this way, marginality is not considered the responsibility of either the state or the economy, and "the route through which 'the excluded' are to better themselves is increasingly confined to local and community-based projects organized outside of and instead of state-funded and supported welfare systems."[68] While such spatial and normative distinction serves to isolate responsibility, it obscures the dynamic culture of the rapidly proliferating informal sector.

However, Kalpana Sharma's *Rediscovering Dharavi* (the Mumbai slum) observes,

- It is a story of ingenuity and enterprise; it is a story of survival without subsidies or welfare; it is a story that illustrates how limited is the term "slum" to describe a place that produces everything from suitcases to leather goods, Indian sweets, papads, and gold jewelry.
- Every square inch of Dharavi is being used for some productive activity. This is "enterprise" personified, an island of free enterprise not assisted or restricted by the state, or any law. It brandishes its illegality. Child labor, hazardous industries, adulteration, recycling, popular products from cold drinks to toothpaste produced in Dharavi—it is all there for anyone to see. . . .
- The atmosphere in Dharavi, even on a holiday, is like being on a treadmill. Everyone is busy, doing something. . . .
- If you want to eat the best *gulab jamuns* in town, buy the best *chiki*, acquire an export quality leather handbag, order World Health Organization (WHO) certified sutures for surgery, see the latest design in ready-made garments being manufactured for export, get a new suitcase or an old one repaired, taste food from the north and the south, see traditional south Indian gold jewelry—there are few better places in all of Mumbai than Dharavi.[69]

While such positive accounts restore perspective on life in "informal" areas, slumdwellers face recurring violence through demolition of their shacks. Gayatri Menon's research on Dharavi notes: "Crafting a home on a public thoroughfare is an exceptionally precarious and creative production that involves a desperate attempt to obtain invisibility while always being on display. For pavement dwellers, evidence of their presence in public spaces, and the absence of a private space to which they may retreat, is their vulnerability."[70] Reframing the notion of "invisibility," Fantu Cheru represents the active withdrawal of African peasants from a failing formal economy, including paying taxes, as a "silent revolution:" "the resuscitation of rural co-operatives, traditional caravan trade across borders, catering services and other activities that had once fallen into disuse, depriving the state of the revenue that traditionally financed its anti-people and anti-peasant development policies."[71] Here, exit is a strategic solution for producers and workers consistently bypassed by state policies. Serge LaTouche views the informal as

> comprehensive strategies of response to the challenges that life poses for displaced and uprooted populations in peri-urban areas. These are people torn between lost tradition and impossible modernity. The sphere of the informal has, incontestably, a major economic significance. It is characterized by a neo-artisanal activity that generates a lot of employment and produces incomes comparable to those of the modern sector.[72]

CASE STUDY

Informalization Versus the African State— The Other Side of "Globalization"

Aili Mari Tripp views the burgeoning informal sector across Africa as a form of resistance. Viewing informalization as more than a passive outcome of state or corporate restructuring, she focuses on the creative ways in which Africans have responded to the failure of development states, exacerbated by more than a decade of structural adjustment. Urban farming has proliferated in the absence of food subsidies, such that 68 percent of families in Dar es Salaam, Tanzania grow their own vegetables and raise livestock. Noncompliance with the state has generated new institutional resources in Tanzania:

> Hometown development associations became visible in the late 1980s as urban dwellers sought to provide assistance to the rural towns from which they originated. They used these associations to build schools, orphanages, libraries, roads, and clinics; to establish projects to conserve the environment; to provide solar electricity and water; to disburse soft loans to women's groups engaged in business; and to raise funds for flood relief and other such causes. These new

associations resemble the early, ethnically based welfare and burial societies that formed in Dar es Salaam in the early 1900s to help new migrants adjust to city life, except that their focus today is to assist people in their rural towns and villages.

In addition to these new resources, traditional resources such as midwifery and craftwork are revived, often undertaken by women. And new activities—from street vending, pastry selling, and hairbraiding to exporting seaweed—have sprung up. In some cases, informal businesses have become so successful in monetary terms that they have moved into the formal sector (e.g., in flour milling, dry cleaning, and prawn farming). The phenomenon of informalization combines individual enterprise as well as "moral economy," where community interests, rather than markets, define the values shaping economic activity. In Tanzania, the significance of informalization led to the 1991 Zanzibar Declaration, which acknowledged the legitimacy and social necessity of informal activities, outside of official corruption.

Is it possible to view informalization as one of today's problems to which there is no modern solution? 🌍

Sources: O'Meara (1999:34); Santos (2002); Tripp (1997:13, 127, 188).

The "lost decade" intensified pressures to consolidate new livelihood strategies in already overburdened cities. Among Mexico's urban poor, collective pooling of resources to acquire land, shelter, and basic public services (water, electricity) was one widespread strategy for establishing networks among friends and neighbors to build their own cheap housing.[73] In 1992, Mexican intellectual Gustavo Esteva observed of the culture of the "new commons:"

> Peasants and grassroots groups in the cities are now sharing with people forced to leave the economic center the ten thousand tricks they have learned to limit the economy, to mock the economic creed, or to refunctionalize and reformulate modern technology. The "crisis" of the 1980s removed from the payroll people already educated in dependency on incomes and the market people lacking the social setting enabling them to survive by themselves. Now the margins are coping with the difficult task of relocating these people. The process poses great challenges and tensions for everyone, but it also offers a creative opportunity for regeneration.[74]

This culture, embedded in dense social networks among informals, has emerged as a new "safety valve" for the development establishment. An expanding sector of socially excluded people became embarrassing to the agents of structural adjustment, since traditional/collective forms of mutual aid and livelihood strategies among informals were considered modern anachronisms, destined to disappear with development. To address this legitimacy crisis, and stabilize the poor (through the market, beyond the state), the culture of informality, serving as a survival mechanism for the poor, was redefined by the World Bank as an economic resource, referred to as **social capital**, to be targeted by microlending. While microcredit has had some success in supporting low-income women, research in Nepal shows that it can also reinforce gender hierarchies, where women's work burden intensifies and husbands gain control of their business income—which means individual empowerment needs to be complemented with transformations in gender relations.[75]

Illustrating how informality is spatially segregated under neoliberalism, Julia Elyachar's *Markets of Dispossession* details how the Bank proceeded to channel grant funds through Cairo banks, converted to interest-bearing microloans to be disbursed by enterprising NGOs to the poor. With dubious success, this new form of "empowerment debt" seeks to stimulate microenterprise via adoption of an individualist neoliberal subjectivity by the poor as they gain access to credit as a "human right" (the language of the Grameen Bank). For Elyachar, the social/relational value of the culture of informality is converted/reduced to economic value, with disciplinary consequences:

> With community networks conceptualized as social capital, NGOs became a vantage point from which outsiders could gain access to the value that those social networks produce. NGOs could potentially tap the vaunted trust and mutual respect of social networks for capitalist firms. This potential was most nicely illustrated when the Grameen Bank of Bangladesh, the grandfather of the microlending phenomenon, signed a contract with the multinational agricultural firm Monsanto (which has been at the center of debates about genetically engineered foods). Monsanto wanted to use the microloan credit networks of Grameen Bank to distribute its seeds, collect payments, and discipline those peasants who tried to store their seeds for reproduction rather than buying Monsanto's genetically engineered, self-destructing variety. As this incident made clear, NGOs and their microlending networks based on "community trust" can become "low-cost Pinkertons" enforcing financial discipline, just as much as SAPs have enforced discipline on a macro scale.[76]

On top of the privations of structural adjustment, microcredit schemes also deplete mutual aid networks essential to survival of the poorest: women and children. Mercedes de la Rocha warns that, in Mexico, "persistent poverty over two decades has effectively brought the poor to their knees," and an NGO worker in Haiti claims the "tradition of mutual giving that allowed us to help each other and survive—this is all being lost."[77] Under these conditions, regions of informality become anomic, deepening human exploitation such as child prostitution and organ selling, Chennai (India) having become world renowned for its "kidney farms."[78]

According to UN-HABITAT, slum populations now expand annually by 25 million. Consequently, countries like India are developing secondary cities to absorb informals—as India's chief economic planner, Montek Singh Ahluwalia, observes: "One hundred million people are moving to cities in the next 10 years, and it's important that these 100 million are absorbed into second-tier cities instead of showing up in Delhi or Mumbai."[79] *Planet of Slums* author Mike Davis notes that, with "high-tech border enforcement blocking large-scale migration to the rich countries, only the slum remains as a fully franchised solution to the problem of warehousing this century's surplus humanity."[80]

Global Recolonization

The globalization project is realized through quite selective mechanisms of accumulation, dispossession, and neglect. Neglect includes the incapacity of debt-stressed governments to support communities that do not contribute to accumulation. Poorer states, with borrowed funds earmarked to promote exports to service debt, are unable to subsidize sectors and communities on the margins. In sub-Saharan Africa, total debt servicing amounts to four times the amount spent on health and education.[81] A Commission for Africa report, in 2005, noted that "African universities were in a 'state of crisis' and were failing to produce the professionals desperately needed to develop the poorest continent."[82] Vulnerable regions have no real channels of representation, especially in Africa, where the nation-state has always been an arbitrary and "uncomfortable fit." There, postcolonial states, overly centralized and militarized, have generally served as instruments of wealth extraction—a condition exacerbated by neoliberal policies weakening civic institutions. The latter are replaced by unrepresentative networks of NGOs (the new "civil society"), managing the outsourcing of "governance" (and seasoned civil servants) with privately funded projects, leaving behind low-paid government workers, "with the inevitable consequences of corruption and an explosion of 'parallel businesses.'"[83] In turn, the formal democratization of African states, coinciding with severe SAPs, has shifted responsibility on to electorates themselves for state failures associated with policies imposed by unelected international financiers. James Ferguson observes that African global marginalization stems from the condition where "capital 'hops' over 'unusable Africa,' alighting in mineral-rich enclaves that are starkly disconnected from their national societies." Ferguson continues, "it is worth asking whether Africa's combination of privately secured mineral-extraction enclaves and weakly governed humanitarian hinterlands might constitute not a lamentably immature form of globalization, but a quite 'advanced' and sophisticated mutation of it."[84] The model, restoring a colonial division of labor at the expense of coherent national institutions and societies, represents a form of recolonization.

The contrast between Zambia's formerly paternalistic copper mining industry—with extensive social investment in housing, schools, hospitals, social workers, and sports clubs, and contemporary oil mining in Angola—is instructive. Whereas the former industry shed its social amenities under the glare of neoliberal reforms, the Angolan oil industry was private from the start, where "nearly all of the production occurs offshore . . . and very little of the oil wealth even enters the wider society. In spite of some 25 years of booming oil production, Angolans today are among the most desperately poor people on the planet."[85] The dominant model emerging across the African oil states, similar to that of Angola, is characterized by "enclaved mineral-rich patches efficiently exploited by flexible private firms, with security provided on an 'as needed' basis by specialized corporations while the elite cliques who are nominal holders of sovereignty certify the industry's legality and international legitimacy in exchange for a piece of the action."[86] John LeCarré's 2006 novel *The Mission Song* fictionalizes this pattern.

Whether we view the African condition as a "scar on the conscience of the world" (ex-UK Prime Minister Tony Blair), or as "the African tragedy,"[87] its deepening world-economic marginalization expresses the selectivity of neoliberal development. "Marginalization" is an ambiguous term: given that sub-Saharan Africa's foreign trade accounted for 52.7 percent of GDP in 2003, compared with a global average of 41.5 percent, one might argue that Southern countries' "wealth is inversely proportional to their integration."[88] The 20 lowest-ranked countries in a UNDP (2004) ranking of "human poverty" (economic and wellbeing measures) are in Africa, which accounts for 39 of the 50 lowest-ranked countries. Between 1975 and 1999, regional per capital GNP of sub-Saharan Africa fell from 17.6 to 10.5 percent of the world average, and health, mortality, and adult-literacy levels declined at comparable rates.[89] Africa has been described as a "lost continent," where the daily caloric intake is below that of Mexico or China by a third or more, and "340 million people, or half the population, live on less than US$1 per day. . . . Only 58 percent of the population have access to safe water."[90] The FAO reports that one in three people in sub-Saharan Africa are hungry. Child mortality below age five is 174 in 1,000, compared with a world average of 89 in 1,000, and the survivors confront pneumonia, tuberculosis, malaria, and an exploding AIDS epidemic that is devastating lives and the continent's financial resources.[91] Worldwide, 36 million people are infected with HIV, 70 percent of them in sub-Saharan Africa (as shown in Figure 7.4). In South Africa, 20 percent of adults are infected, and in 2003 there were approximately 15 million orphans. Africa has lost 12 million people to AIDS, and is home to more than 60 percent of all people living with HIV.[92] African countries have submitted to structural adjustment programs over the past two decades, with comparatively little financial aid. The Heavily Indebted Poor Countries (HIPC) debt relief package, instituted by the IMF and the World Bank in 1996, targeted 40-odd countries, 32 of which are African. Conditionality included demonstrating six years of prudent fiscal management. At the turn of the twenty-first century, the failure of this initiative to spur growth or relieve poverty led to the Bank admitting failure in making Africa's foreign debt "sustainable" to the G-8 countries, shortening the six-year demonstration, requiring that aid be spent on education and health (although without the ability to ensure compliance).[93]

Even so, Africa's repayments now exceed its receipts. The augmentation of the HIPC initiative in 2005 reinforced its neoliberal conditionalities of

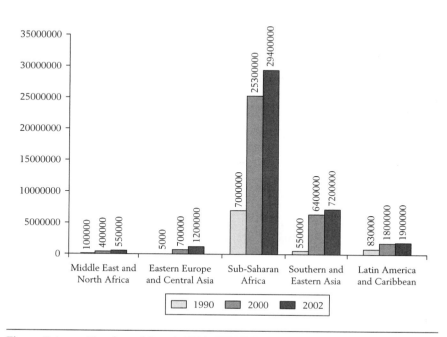

Figure 7.4   Number of People With HIV/AIDS, 1990–2002

Sources: www.avrt.org; www.unicef.org/sowc02/g32.htm (2002).

macroeconomic austerity and privatization of services, despite acknowledgment by the Bank that the objectives of financial liberalization were not met, as billions of dollars a year flow offshore into private accounts. Recall that almost 50 sub-Saharan African states are represented by two directors at the Bretton Woods institutions, while eight northern states enjoy a director each, and the United States, with more than 15 percent of the votes, retains veto power.[94]

Meanwhile, in response to complaints by African politicians that large multilateral aid flowed quickly into Asia following the 1997 financial crisis, the IMF and World Bank admitted that their assistance to Asia reflected that region's greater significance to the global financial system.[95] The World Bank's 1997 Development Report, *The State in a Changing World*, spotlighted the decay of the African state, despite IFI contribution to this outcome through "bad state/good market" policies leading to neglect of education, erosion of infrastructure and institutional capacity, and rising unemployment.

The **New Partnership for African Development (NEPAD)**, an African initiative agreed to by the G-8 (although without the follow-up of promised aid), continues this policy, urging African leaders to promote "democracy and human rights in their respective countries . . . [while simultaneously] instituting transparent legal and regulatory frameworks for financial markets."[96] Capital flight from every African country to open up its financial markets is endemic. "Africa's continued poverty ('marginalization') is a direct outcome of excess globalization, not of insufficient globalization, because of the drain from ever declining prices of raw materials (Africa's main exports), crippling debt repayments and profit repatriation to transnational corporations."[97] Nevertheless, foreshadowing the formation of the **African Union** in 2002, chaired by South African President Thabo Mbeki, NEPAD continues to promote neoliberal economic policies, offering Africa to the corporate global elite in a poverty alleviation strategy:

> The continued marginalization of Africa from the globalization process and the social exclusion of the vast majority of its peoples constitute a serious threat to global stability. . . . We readily admit that globalization is a product of scientific and technological advances, many of which have been market-driven. . . . The locomotive for these major advances is the highly industrialized nations.[98]

NEPAD commits African states to "good governance," from liberalization to peer review of human rights abuses and corruption, as a condition for Northern financial support. Citing the failure of African states to condemn the excesses of the Mugabe government of Zimbabwe, Muna Ndulo argues that, since Africa will be not able to deliver on the governance or peer review issues, "Western countries have a perfect excuse now for not delivering on NEPAD."[99]

Arguably, under the neoliberal mantle, Africa is designated as an "extractive resource," via an agenda of recolonization. This function is embodied in three sets of forces: the historic structuring of the postcolonial African state; the restructuring of African states via "global governance"; and the resource grab as the energy crisis dovetails with China's rising demand for world resources to sustain its explosive growth.

While urban bias was common across the Third World, it was amplified in Africa by state patronage systems constructed during colonialism on the basis of artificial tribal hierarchies.[100] The African one-party state arose out of the difficulties in securing power in and administering nation-states with artificial political boundaries. Such bifurcated power, between the centralized modern state and a "tribal authority which dispensed customary law to those living within the territory of the tribe," conditioned the current failure of African states, where neoliberalism overlays and enlarges often despotic (and ethnically based) regimes.[101] This structure of power has facilitated the exploitation of rural areas by urban elites, enriched by foreign investment in resource extraction. For example, Kinshasa, the capital of Zaire (the Congo), a "giant spider at the hub of a subcontinental web, acted as an 'overwhelming suction pump' absorbing all attainable rural resources as well as whatever might be milked from foreign donors and investors."[102]

Governance reform framed the World Bank's influential 1989 report, *Sub-Saharan Africa: From Crisis to Sustainable Growth*: "Africa needs not just less government but better government—government that concentrates its efforts less on direct [economic] interventions and more on enabling others to be productive."[103] Liberalization targeted the one-party state, demanding democratization of African states, with the goal of releasing entrepreneurial forces in states and societies, and opening up to foreign investment and trade.

CASE STUDY

Ethnic Politics, Resources, and the Recolonization of Nigeria

Nigeria, with more than 250 ethnic groups, has three dominant groups: the Hausa-Fulani, the Yoruba, and the Ibo, with quite distinct political practices. The Hausa-Fulani in the north have roots in autocratic, bureaucratic, and hierarchical precolonial states; the Yoruba in the west have a tradition of loose confederation among centralized kingdoms where monarchs were elected by, and shared power with, a council of chiefs; and the Ibo in the south practiced decentralized and egalitarian forms of social organization.

National unity is routinely compromised by ethnically driven politics, with interethnic competition heightened by resource scarcities.

Related to these fracture lines is an elemental division of Nigeria into a Muslim north and a Christian south, exacerbated by the exploitation of the south's oil resources by the north, where oil rents have financed a string of corrupt generals since Nigeria's independence in 1960. Per capita income is now one-quarter of what it was in the 1980s. The generals have not reinvested profits in the Niger Delta (population of 7 million) to pre-empt secession of the south, like the Biafran secession in 1967. In an internationally condemned incident in 1995, Nigerian writer Ken Saro-Wiwa was executed by the regime when he protested southern underdevelopment, linking it to exploitation by the northern-dominated government and foreign oil interests, and demanding compensation for the region and his Ogoni people.

Mobil, Shell, Texaco, Chevron, and other Western oil companies extract oil from the Delta—for example, Chevron's worldwide revenues of $30.6 billion in 1998 matched Nigeria's GNP of $30.7 billion in 1997 (one of Africa's biggest). Meanwhile, between 1970 and 2000, extreme poverty among Nigerians grew from 19 million (36 percent) to 90 million (70 percent). Mobil, Shell, and Chevron now play a *de facto* government role in the absence of state investment. Local movements demanding compensation have managed to involve these firms in financing basic community development needs such as running water, electricity, hospitals, and roads. But the oil companies' social "license to operate" enables an industry to extract profits from price rises justified by political instability, and the representation of Africa as the new frontier of terrorism.

All modern states embody historic tensions between formal secularism and historical layering of race and ethnic political relations, which are exacerbated by the impact of globalization. Why should African states be any different?

Sources: Cohen (1998:A1); Onishi (1998:A1, A6; 1999:20–29); Sandbrook (1995:93–94); Zalik (2004); Zalik and Watts (2006).

Governance reforms enable the "resource grab" in Africa, where natural resource exports accounted for almost 80 percent of exports in 2000, compared with 31 percent for the global South and 16 percent for the North. UNCTAD noted in 2003 that 12 African countries depended on a single export commodity: crude petroleum (Angola 92 percent, Congo 57, Gabon 70, Nigeria 96, and Equatorial Guinea 91), copper (Zambia 52 percent), diamonds (Botswana 91 percent), coffee (Burundi 76 percent, Ethiopia 62, Uganda 83), tobacco (Malawi 59 percent), and uranium (Niger 59 percent).[104]

The following year, UNCTAD recorded foreign direct investment in Africa at $15 billion ($2 billion in 1986), noting that most new investment is in mineral extraction, especially in Angola, Equatorial Guinea, Nigeria, and Sudan, and in deepwater oilfields off the West African coast—from which 25 percent of North American oil imports will come by 2015.[105]

In an era of Chinese ascendancy, the resource grab intensifies. Once self-sufficient in oil (1990), China was the second largest importer of oil after the United States by 2003, accounting for 40 percent of rising demand for oil in 2001–05.[106] One-third of its oil is African. The Chinese National Petroleum Corporation (which overtook Shell in 2006 as the world's sixth largest oil company) and two other large Chinese oil firms operate in 17 African countries, including Sudan (Darfur notwithstanding), where a Chinese state-owned company owns 40 percent of the oil concession in the south (with 4,000 Chinese troops protecting Beijing's oil interests).[107] In 2006, China made a $1.4 billion deal to develop new oilfields in Angola, which became the largest supplier to China, ahead of Saudi Arabia. The deal includes China rebuilding Angola's railway and bridges, similar to oil contracts linked to rebuilding railways in Nigeria and Algeria.[108]

China's relation to Africa resembles colonization, but with a twenty-first century twist. Between 2001 and 2006, China's trade with Africa rose fivefold, to $50 billion, exceeding its trade with the EU, and positioning it as Africa's third largest trading partner. It has almost 700 state companies with investments in 800 joint projects in Africa.[109] The Council on Foreign Relations reported in 2006, "China is acquiring control of natural resource assets, out-bidding Western contractors on major infrastructural projects and providing soft loans and other incentives to bolster its competitive advantage."[110] That same year, exploiting a "South–South" rhetoric, China claimed its growing interests as a "strategic partnership with Africa, featuring political equality and mutual trust, economic win–win cooperation"—implying that China does not require governance reforms and anti-corruption initiatives as a condition for aid and trade, as do the IFIs, "which some see as a way to justify links with abusive regimes such as those in Zimbabwe and Sudan."[111] Meanwhile, China is educating thousands of African university students, and dispatching hundreds of advisers and doctors to Africa. At the second Syno-African Conference in 2003, China cancelled $10 billion of African debt, providing debt relief to 31 countries.[112]

In the wake of debilitating neoliberal reforms and endless debt servicing, and NEPAD, African countries now have access to a super-wealthy state not from the global North, and lacking its colonial baggage. Yet neocolonial relations obtain. South Africa, where 86 percent of clothing imports are Chinese, has lost 300,000 textile jobs since 2002. Since 2000, Nigeria lost 350,000 jobs directly and 1.5 million indirectly due to Chinese competition.[113] Cheap imports of Chinese manufactured goods are matched by Chinese investment in the sectors such as commercial aviation, agricultural machinery, urban transportation, and telecommunications.[114] Human Rights Watch claims Chinese policies in Africa (following the historic lead of the West) have "propped up some of the continent's worst human-rights abusers."[115] Exploitation of natural resources reproduces the pattern of "export of sustainability" begun under colonialism. China is known to import illegally cut timber from forests in Cameroon, the Congo, and Equatorial Guinea. Forest clearing increases vulnerability to erosion, river silting, flooding, landslides, and habitat loss. Gas flaring in oil regions adds to carbon emissions (Niger delta emissions match the annual emissions of Sweden). And concerns have been raised over "the environmental impact of various Chinese-run mining operations in Africa, including copper mines in Zambia and Congo, and titanium sands projects in ecologically sensitive parts of Mozambique, Kenya, Tanzania, and Madagascar."[116]

As the twenty-first century approached, sub-Saharan African states experienced destabilizing forces from within and without. From *within*, as economic conditions deteriorated with little relief from structural adjustment, democratizing trends spread, drawing inspiration from the collapse of the Eastern European one-party states and responding to governance pressures from the global managers. But in the context of declining economic opportunity, democratizing trends are complicated by internal conflict along protective ethnic lines. These lines often become the pretext for and the vehicle of civil wars and ethnicized struggles for control over national resources—as evidenced in the implosion of Rwanda and Somalia and the breakup of Ethiopia in the mid-1990s. With climate change exacerbating drought conditions, and scarcity of basic resources (as in the current Sudanese conflict, where the Arab-allied government conducts a genocidal policy against African farmers in Darfur, at a cost of 200,000 deaths and 2.5 million displaced), such struggles are likely to intensify, fueled by the arms merchants, and the exploitation of proxy groups by foreign interests with their eye on resources. The Chinese government rejects claims made by human rights activists that financial engagement with the Sudanese government prolongs the humanitarian crisis.[117] Michael Renner comments on the syndrome of the vicious cycle in the Sudan that,

> Oil exports have permitted the central government to carry on with the war against southern rebels. To keep paying for the war, the government must expand oil production, but this requires exploiting oil deposits deeper and deeper in rebel-held territory. To control oil-rich areas in southern Sudan, government forces are conducting a scorched earth campaign at terrible human cost. Oil finances the war; the war provides access to oil.[118]

From *without,* African states broke with their initial (Organization for African Unity) noninterference agreement, and a series of interventions has ensued, beginning with Uganda's involvement in the Rwandan conflict in 1994. Congo was the site of intervention from six neighboring states at the turn of the century, with President Kabila allied with Zimbabwe, Angola, Namibia, and Chad against eastern rebels supported by Uganda and Rwanda.[119] African boundaries have become more problematic as state sovereignty has dwindled: across the global South, "particularly in sub-Saharan Africa, government forces are in decay and private security organizations are on the rise, including forces loyal to regional warlords, citizens' self-defense groups, corporate-sponsored forces, foreign mercenaries, and criminal gangs. In fact, it is becoming more difficult to make clear-cut distinctions between legitimate and illegitimate, and between public and private, security forces."[120] One dramatic manifestation of the loss of political cohesion of some African states is an exploding refugee population, consisting of "international refugees" and "internally displaced persons," underlining civilian casualty in the militarization of the continent, which has deep roots linking the colonial era to an era of recolonization. The nineteenth century scramble for Africa, symbolized by the Berlin Conference of 1884, best known for violations of its agreements for an orderly division, is on again—with the United States expecting to obtain 25 percent of its oil imports from Africa as an alternative to the Persian Gulf, and France, Britain, India, and China competing for oil, gas, timber, bauxite, copper, diamonds, gold, and coltan.

Summary

The globalization project has many social and political consequences and implications for the future of the world. We have examined just four phenomena: outsourcing, displacement, informalization, and recolonization. None of these is unique to the global project. They have all appeared in previous eras but not on the scale found today. They are linked—indeed, they are mutually conditioning processes, being four dimensions of a single process of global restructuring affecting all countries, although with local variation.

The technological shedding of labor and the downsizing and stagnation produced by structural adjustment programs expands the informal sector. Indeed, the institution of wage labor is undergoing substantial change across the world. Not only is wage employment contracting, but wage labor is also displaying a *casualizing* trend, where jobs become part-time and impermanent. The strategies of flexibility embraced by firms contribute to this informalization as much as the growing surplus of populations displaced from their land and livelihood. Some observers see informalization as a counter-movement to the official economy and to state regulation—asserting a culture of the "new commons." Informalization of both stripes, withdrawal from corrupt, ineffectual, and/or predatory states, and marginalization by selective corporate "cherry-picking" of local resources, is endemic in Africa today, which perhaps illustrates that colonization is a permanent feature of a world system premised on accumulation. Our task is to specify how that works, and to understand that development evolves through different forms and relationships of inequality.

Further Reading

Caraway, Teri L. *Assembling Women: The Feminization of Global Manufacturing.* Ithaca, NY: Cornell University Press, 2007.

Davis, Mike. *Planet of Slums.* London: Verso, 2006.

Elyachar, Julia. *Markets of Dispossession: NGOs, Economic Development, and the State in Cairo.* Durham, NC: Duke University Press, 2005.

Ferguson, James. *Global Shadows: Africa in the Neoliberal World Order.* Durham, NC: Duke University Press, 2006.

Select Websites

China Labor Watch: www.chinalaborwatch.org
FoodFirst Information and Action Network: www.fian.org
Grameen Bank: www.grameen-info.org
International Labor Rights Forum: www.laborrights.org
International Labour Organization (ILO): www.ilo.org
Maquila Solidarity Network (Canada): www.maquilasolidarity.org
The Meatrix: www.themeatrix.com
Migrant Rights International (Switzerland): www.migrantwatch.org
TransAfrica Forum (USA): www.transafricaforum.org
Transparency International: www.transparency.org
Union Network International: www.union-network.org
United Nations High Commissioner for Refugees (UNHCR): www.unhcr.ch

PART IV

Rethinking Development

8

Global Development and Its Countermovements

The globalization project has been a relatively coherent perspective and has had a powerful set of states, agencies, and corporations working on its behalf (via the philosophy of neoliberalism). Nevertheless, its discourse and rules are always in contention *because* this project is realized through various inequalities. Like the development project, the globalization project is an attempt to fashion the world around a central principle (the market) through powerful political and financial institutions. Framed as a discourse of rights and freedom, the power of the organizing principle ultimately depends on the interpretation and effect of these ideals. Diane Perrons defines it thus: "Neo-liberalism is a powerful ideology and appeals to people's self-interest. It implies that free markets are somehow a natural and inevitable state of affairs in which individual endeavor will be rewarded and perhaps because of this the poor accept growing inequalities because they think they have a chance of becoming rich themselves as society appears to be freer and more open."[1]

Countermovements resist aspects of globalization. Further, they *shape* globalization by representing the material and discursive conditions targeted by global institutions for appropriation. Ethical consumption has not only become quite widespread today (e.g., fair trade, non-violent diamonds, non-sweatshop clothing), but brand-makers embrace it (if selectively—for example, Starbucks' single fair trade variety) as corporate responsibility. Corporations manage profitability by managing their image, in a public marketplace where human rights and environmental sustainability are politicized by countermovements. Image management may be just that, so contention continues, deepened by the emergence of alternative visions. Most governments feel the pressure to play by the new and emerging global rules, but their citizens do not always share their outlook. And where global restructuring weakens nation-states (by eroding their public welfare function, increasing social and regional polarization, and reducing state patronage systems), citizens have fresh opportunities to renew the political process. This chapter surveys some of these countermovements, exploring their origins and goals. Examining each movement offers a particular angle on the reformulation of development in the globalization project. Most countermovements converge as "global justice movements" (environmentalism, feminism, cosmopolitan activism, and food sovereignty), but some are conservative responses, such as the fundamentalist countermovement.

(1) Fundamentalism – counter movement

Fundamentalism usually expresses a desire to recover the simplicity and security of traditional codes of behavior. But it is never quite so simple. First, who decides what is traditional? There may be sacred texts, but they are open to interpretation. And fundamentalist movements are usually split by factional differences and power struggles. Second, what are the conditions under which fundamentalism comes to the fore? These conditions are likely to shape the leadership and the interpretation of tradition. In the United States of the twenty-first century, the broad-based fundamentalism espousing family values can be understood only in the context of a significant decline in the proportion of the population that is actually a part of the traditional nuclear family structure. Even then, the nuclear family is not exactly traditional; the extended family is the more traditional structure. What may be "traditional" is the age-old and unquestioned power of the family patriarch.

In uncertain times, constructing the fundamentals of what holds people together often moves to the front burner. People gravitate to fundamentalism for protection and security, and to make sense of the world around them and their places in it. We have seen a variant of this in the rising use of ethnic politics as competition for jobs grows while the economy shrinks. Nothing is absolute or definite about the content of fundamentalism or about the elevation of ethnic identity as a way of drawing boundaries between people. The interpretation of ethnicity is quite flexible and depends very much on the historical and social context in which people reconstruct ethnic divisions. Nevertheless, in an increasingly confused and unstable world, the *presumed* essentialism of ethnic identity either comforts people or allows them to identify scapegoats. In whatever form, fundamentalist politics has become a powerful weapon for mobilizing people as the stable political and class coalitions of the development era crumble.

In a post-2001 world, Northerners equate fundamentalism with activities by people of the Islamic faith. This in itself is a fundamentalist response as, by portraying Islam in monolithic and alien terms, it ignores the variety of Islamic orders, the relationship between fundamentalism and modernity, and the fact that other religious fundamentalisms (e.g., Christianity and Hinduism) have displayed an equal capacity for violence. The common assumption made about fundamentalism being antithetical to modernity is evident in easy depictions of a world divided into secular versus religious states, and materialist opportunism versus absolute values. As Tariq Ali points out, "For Islamists, none of the rulers of existing Muslim states today are 'true' Muslims. Not a single one. Hence the struggle to change the existing regimes and replace them with holy emirates. Some orthodox Jews regard the very existence of Israel as a disgrace."[2] During the 1990s, such easy depictions appeared via public intellectuals—notably Samuel Huntington's *Clash of Civilizations*, which depicted a world divided into eight cultures of religion but riven between the West (valuing "individualism, liberalism, constitutionalism, human rights, equality, liberty, the rule of law, democracy, free markets") and the Rest (epitomized by the most menacing: Islam and Confucianism).[3] However, this "clash" did not prevent the United States, in pursuing a form of imperial fundamentalism itself, from supporting the most hard-line Islamic fundamentalisms against communism or progressive/secular nationalism during the Cold War: the Muslim brotherhood against Egyptian president Nasser, the Sarekat-i-Islam against Indonesian president Sukarno, the Jamaat-e-Islami against Pakistan president Bhutto and, later, Osama bin Laden and the Taliban against the secular-communist president Najibullah of Afghanistan.[4]

The point is that fundamentalism and modernity are inextricably tied, and easy dichotomies misrepresent the complex relationship between them. And attacking the essentialism of fundamentalism with further essentialism (as dominant states tend to do) is questionable. At this time, a more constructive approach is to understand the appeal of fundamentalist constructions (by leaders and politicians) for people.

In the shadow of September 11, 2001, *The New York Times* reported the rise of Islam as a political force in Africa and "the stunning spread of hard-line Islamic law from one small Nigerian state in 1999 to a third of the country's 36 states today."[5] Rather than confirming the topical question asked by Americans in the post–September 11 era, "Why do they hate us?"— projecting deep-seated envy of the West on to the Muslim world—the report detailed the limits of Western modernity in Africa:

Islamic values have much in common with traditional African life: its emphasis on communal living, its clear roles for men and women, its tolerance of
polygamy. Christianity, Muslims argue, was alien to most Africans. . . . Other
Western values like democracy have been a disappointment here, often producing sham elections, continued misrule and deep poverty.[6]

An Anglican bishop noted, "For many Africans, it makes more sense to
reject America and Europe's secular values, a culture of selfishness and half-
naked women, by embracing Islam."[7] Under these circumstances, Muslims
supported the Hisbah organization's imposition of *Shariah* (Islamic law) in
Kano, Nigeria's largest Muslim city. The president of the Hisbah justified
this assertion of political Islam in terms that depend on engaging with
modernity and its contradictions:

It is the failure of every system we have known. We have had colonialism,
which was exploitative. We had a brief period of happiness after independence,
then the military came in, and everything has been going downward since then.
But before all this, we had a system that worked. We had *Shariah*. We are
Muslims. Why don't we return to ourselves?[8]

We should note how this leader not only constructs an absolute sense of
the Muslim identity but also validates it by referring to an imagined past in
which the justice system (which is harsh, particularly on women—but, to
defenders of Islamic justice, nothing like the death penalty in the West) is
believed to have worked. The construction of *Shariah* as a repository of previous traditions and justice, although fundamentalist, cannot be understood
outside of its encounter with modernity. As Olivier Roy has noted, "Islamism
is the *sharia* plus electricity." This is particularly so since the return to democratic elections in Nigeria in 1999 (after years of military rule) allowed
Islamic law to be reintroduced through the ballot box.[9] In other words,
modernity and fundamentalism are intertwined.

Development, whether based in oil wealth or not, fuels fundamentalist
opposition via overcrowded cities. In Egypt, a legitimacy crisis stemming
from economic stagnation and political corruption in the government has
emboldened Islamic fundamentalism. Its ranks have expanded among the
urban poor, partly because Islam offers community and basic services in the
midst of the disorder of huge, sprawling cities such as Cairo. In southern
Egypt's public schools, fundamentalist teachers reimpose the veil on girls
and revise schoolbooks to emphasize Islamic teachings. They argue that
secularization has suppressed Egypt's deep Islamic and Arab roots in the
pursuit of a communion with Western culture.[10] In Turkey, Istanbul's population has doubled every 15 years. When the modern Turkish Republic was

created in 1923, only 15 percent of its population of 13 million was urban. Now, two-thirds of Turkey's 60 million people live in urban areas. These city dwellers offer fertile ground for an Islamic revival challenging Kemalism, the ruthless, secular politics of development associated with the founder of the Turkish republic (1923), Kemal Ataturk.[11] In 2002, the Islamic party, the AKP, came to power, drawing on religious fervor in the heartland, where polygamy is practiced and female illiteracy is high, and from where young men with conservative values come to swell the ranks of the urban poor. The AKP has transformed this disenchantment into a political mandate for an Islamist revival that is at once modern and appeals to the European Union (as a source of investment and trade)—offering economic hope and a counterweight to fundamentalism.[12]

In the wake of the attacks on September 11, 2001, the Western press focused on likely correlations between economic deprivation and religious fundamentalism. A report filed from Pakistan touches a Western nerve by drawing attention to the demographic profile of Peshawar (common to southern cities), where young men crowd the streets, with 63 percent of the population younger than age 25. The reporter noted,

> Their anger is only loosely articulated, often because they are struggling to survive. . . . They live where globalization is not working or not working well enough. They believe, or can be led to believe, that America—or their pro-American government, if they live under one—is to blame for their misery. . . . Poor families do their best to send a son to school, but in the end they cannot manage. The son will get a backbreaking job of some sort, or . . . [enrol] at a *madrassah*, most of which offer free tuition, room, and board. And that's where they learn that it is honorable to blow yourself up amid a crowd of infidels and that the greatest glory in life is to die in a *jihad*.[13]

The shortcomings of this kind of representation of a close relation between fundamentalism and terrorism are that the tensions between political cultures in an unequal world do not resolve themselves in such a simplistic fashion. In fact, power lies in representation—whether it is the power of an imam to interpret the Koran or the power of powerful states and their publicist-journalists to identify those fundamentalisms they regard as threatening to their sense of world order. From the global South, the fundamentalism of neoliberal economics in structurally adjusting political economies, privatizing public goods, withdrawing subsidies, cutting wages, and patenting plant varieties is just as real and threatening to the stability of their communities and their sense of world order. Ultimately, the identification of which fundamentalisms lead to which kind of terror (stateless or state based) is a question of power relations.

Fundamentalist movements abroad in the world have two main features. First, they articulate the uncertainties and legitimacy deficit experienced through the limits of development and the increasing selectivity of globalization. Second, they often take the form of ethnonationalist resurgence against perceived threats to cultural integrity. The combination may involve contesting the "fundamentalisms" of globalization (financial, institutional, or imperial) and offering alternative ways of organizing social life—whether in defensive or aggressive terms. The point is that what gets represented as fundamentalism is usually one-sided, obscuring its political roots in modernity.

Environmentalism

Environmentalism as a countermovement involves questioning modern assumptions that nature and its bounty are infinite. It has two main strands. One derives from growing environmental awareness among Northern citizens, most recently inspired by the publication of Rachel Carson's book *Silent Spring* in 1962. This path-breaking work documented the disruption in the earth's ecosystems caused by agricultural chemicals. Its title refers to the absence of birdsongs in the spring. Carson's metaphor dramatized the dependence of life on sustainable ecological systems. It also emphasized the West's rationalized perception of nature as "external" to society. This perception encourages the belief that nature is an infinitely exploitable domain.[14]

A range of "green" movements has mushroomed throughout the North as the simple truths revealed by Carson's study have gained an audience. "Greens" typically challenge the assumptions and practices of unbridled economic growth, arguing for scaling back to a renewable economic system of resource use. One focus is agricultural sustainability—that is, reversing the environmental stress associated with capital- and chemical-intensive agriculture, linked to a fast-growing movement for organic food. A key goal is maintaining a natural aesthetic to complement the consumer lifestyle, the emphasis being on preserving human health and enhancing leisure activities.

The second strand of environmentalism involves Southern movements (known as the "environmentalism of the poor") to protect particular bioregions from environmentally damaging practices. Across the world, where rural populations produce 60 percent of their food, human communities depend greatly on the viability of regional ecologies for their livelihood. Such movements are therefore often distinguished by their attempts to protect existing cultural practices. In contrast to Northern environmentalism, seeking to regulate the environmental implications of the market, Southern environmentalism questions market forces. This is especially true where states and firms seek to "monetize" and harvest natural resources on which human communities depend.

Local communities have always challenged environmentally damaging practices where natural conservation is integral to local culture. Opposition has included eighteenth century English peasants protesting the enclosure of the commons; nineteenth century Native Americans resisting the takeover of their lands and the elimination of the buffalo; and Indians struggling against British colonial forestry practices.

In the late twentieth century, forest dwellers across the tropics grabbed the world's attention as they attempted to preserve tropical rainforests from extensive timber cutting. Logging and beef cattle pasturing in degraded forest areas intensified with the agro-export boom of the 1980s, amplifying Southern environmentalism. Demands for Northern-style environmental regulation gathered momentum to address environmental stresses from resource mining and river damming to the overuse of natural resources, resulting in desertification, excessive water salinity, and chemical contamination associated with the green revolution.

The common denominator of most environmental movements is a belief that natural resources are not infinitely renewable. The finiteness of nature has been a global preoccupation, from the neo-Malthusian specter of population growth overwhelming land supplies and the food grown on it to anxiety about the dwindling supplies of raw materials, such as fossil fuels and timber, that sustain modern economies.

Lately, however, this rather linear perspective has yielded to a more dynamic one that sees a serious threat to natural elements such as the atmosphere, climates, and biodiversity. Trees may be renewable through replanting schemes, but the atmospheric conditions that nurture them may not so easily be replenished. The world has moved to a new threshold of risk to its sustainability:

> It used to be feared that we would run out of non-renewable resources—things like oil, or gold. Yet these, it seems, are the ones we need worry least about. It is the renewables—the ones we thought would last forever—that are being destroyed at an accelerating rate. They are all living things, or dynamic parts of living ecosystems.[15]

Furthermore, the very survival of the human species is increasingly at risk as pollution and environmental degradation lead to public health epidemics. These include lead poisoning, new strains of cancer, cataracts from ozone destruction, immune suppression by ultraviolet radiation, and loss of genetic and biological resources for producing food and medicines.[16]

The mode of production of renewable resources undermines ecological sustainability. While a tree plantation may provide timber products, it cannot perform the regenerative function that natural systems perform because it is a monoculture reducing natural diversity. Robert Repetto, of the World Resources Institute, articulated the shortcomings of conventional economic notions of value:

> Under the current system of national accounting, a country could exhaust its mineral resources, cut down its forests, erode its soils, pollute its aquifers, and hunt its wildlife and fisheries to extinction, but measured income would not be affected as these assets disappeared . . . difference[s] in the treatment of natural resources and other tangible assets confuse the depletion of valuable assets with the generation of income. . . . The result can be illusory gains in income and permanent losses in wealth.[17]

As a consequence of the appreciation of "nature's services," a form of ecological accounting is emerging—for example, it has been estimated that the economic value of the world's ecosystem services is currently around $33 trillion a year, exceeding the global gross national product (GNP) of $25 trillion. Whether or not it is appropriate to value nature in this way, this trend is an antidote to traditional economics reasoning, which renders environmental impact invisible.[18]

The change in thinking has been stimulated from several quarters. In the first place, there are the **new social movements** (conceptualized in the following box), some of which are the subject of this chapter. Their appearance on the historical stage reflects a critique of capitalist developmentalism and a search for new forms of social and political action, and subjectivity.[19]

What Are the New Social Movements?

"New social movements," such as the greens, feminism, shackdwellers, food sovereignty, worker-owned cooperatives, participatory budgeting, food policy councils, self-housing associations, neighborhood assemblies, landless workers, and so on, share a criticism of the economism, centralism, and hierarchies of the development project. Gaining formal rights as abstract citizens in the state (the "old social movement" goal) is secondary to developing particular practices that question dominant values and power relations. Thus, as J. K. Gibson-Graham suggests: when unemployed workers in Argentina occupied abandoned factories during the 2001 financial crisis, they had to learn to transcend their individualist (wage-oriented) worker mentalities in order to construct "an economy and sociality of 'solidarity' as members of the unemployed workers' movement." Similarly, slumdwellers in the Alliance, in Mumbai, India, in dialogue with the Homeless People's Federation in South Africa, build community-managed savings schemes to construct their frugal (and continually threatened) material world, and use self-surveying and enumeration to produce a politics of visibility to affirm their presence by, as Gayatri Menon claims, "quietly encroaching upon and thereby transforming the political categories [e.g., "citizenship"] through which demolitions of the dwellings of the urban poor derive their legitimacy."

Sources: Gibson-Graham (2006:xxv, xxxv); Menon (2007).

The second indication of a change in thinking is a growing awareness of the limits of "spaceship earth." From the late 1960s, space photographs of planet Earth dramatized the biophysical finiteness of our world. The dangerous synergies arising from global economic intercourse and ecology were driven home by the Brundtland Commission's declaration in 1987: "The Earth is one but the world is not. We all depend on one biosphere for sustaining our lives."

Third, various grassroots movements focus attention on the growing conflict on the margins between local cultures and the global market. For example, the Kayapo Indians of the Amazon strengthened their demands by appealing to the global community regarding defense of their forest habitat from logging, cattle pasturing, and extraction of genetic resources. One response by the Brazilian government to this kind of demand was the creation of self-managing extractive reserves for native tribes and rubber tappers to protect them from encroaching ranchers and colonists. These reserves are relatively large areas of forestland set aside, with government protection, for extractive activities by forest dwellers.[20]

Finally, during the era of neoliberalism, the pressure on natural resources from the rural poor has intensified. This pressure stems from the long-term impoverishment of rural populations forced to overwork their land and fuel sources to eke out a subsistence. As land and forests were increasingly devoted to export production in the 1980s, millions of rural poor were pushed into occupying marginal tropical forest ecosystems. Environmental degradation, including deforestation, resulted. Environmental movements pursue "sustainable development"—emphasizing self-organizing development versus the dominant centralizing version. Resistance to the Narmada Dam is a case in point.

Since the 1980s, the Indian government has been implementing a huge dam project in the Narmada River valley, with assistance from the World Bank. This massive project involves 30 large and more than 3,000 medium and small dams on the Narmada River, expected eventually to displace more than 2 million people. In 1992, at the time of the Earth Summit, there was an embarrassing release of an independent review (the first ever) of the Bank's Sardar Sarovar dam project in India. Commissioned by the Bank president, the review claimed "gross delinquency" on the part of the Bank and the Indian government in both the engineering and the forcible resettlement of indigenous peoples. These revelations and the growing resistance movement, the Narmada Bachao Andolan (Movement to Save the Narmada), succeeded in forcing the Bank to withdraw its support for this project. Grassroots opponents to the dam argue that the resistance

> articulates . . . the critical legacy of Mahatma Gandhi . . . of the struggles all over the country that continue to challenge both the growing centralization and authoritarianism of the state and the extractive character of the dominant economic process—a process which not only erodes and destroys the subsistence economies of these areas, but also the diversity of their systems. . . . The movement is therefore representative of growing assertions of marginal populations for greater economic and political control over their lives.[21]

Sustainable Development

The concept of **sustainable development** gained currency as a result of the 1987 Brundtland report, titled *Our Common Future*. The report defined sustainable development as "meet[ing] the needs of the present without compromising the ability of future generations to meet their own needs."[22] How to achieve this remains a puzzle. The Brundtland Commission suggested steps such as conserving and enhancing natural resources, encouraging grassroots involvement in development, and adopting appropriate technologies (smaller scale, energy conserving). While acknowledging that "an additional person in an industrial country consumes far more and places far greater pressure on natural resources than an additional person in the Third World," the Commission nevertheless recommended continued emphasis on economic growth to reduce the pressure of the poor on the environment.[23]

The report did not resolve the interpretive debate over the root cause of environmental deterioration—whether the threat to our common future stems from poverty or from affluence:

- Those who argue the poverty cause consider the gravest stress on the environment to be impoverished masses pressing on resources. Population control and economic growth are the suggested solutions.
- Those who identify affluence as the problem believe that the gravest stress on the environment comes from global inequality and the consumption of resources to support affluent lifestyles.

Measures of this latter effect abound, one of the more provocative being the claim that each U.S. citizen contributes 60 times more to global warming than each Mexican and that a Canadian's contribution equals that of 190

Indonesians.[24] This perspective has generated former World Bank economist Herman E. Daly's "impossibility theorem:" that "a U.S. style high-resource consumption standard" is no longer appropriate for planetary sustainability.[25]

Earth Summits

The terms of this debate infused the 1992 United Nations Conference on Environment and Development (UNCED). Popularized as the Rio de Janeiro "Earth Summit," it was the largest diplomatic gathering ever held. The United Nations Environment Program (UNEP) organized the conference to review progress on the Brundtland report. Conference preparations resulted in a document, known as *Agenda 21*, detailing a global program for the twenty-first century and addressing all sides of the debate, which continued through the decade, to the rather low-key and ineffectual follow-up 2002 World Summit on Sustainability in Johannesburg.

The South, for instance, recognizes that the North has an interest in reducing carbon dioxide emissions and preserving biodiversity and the tropical rainforests for planetary survival. It agreed to participate in a global program in return for financial assistance, and called for massive investment by the North in sustainable development measures in the South, including health, sanitation, education, technical assistance, and conservation.[26]

However, UNCED detoured from the question of global inequities, stressing environmental protection to be a priority, but "without distorting international trade and investment."[27] The outcome was a shift in emphasis from the Brundtland report: privileging *global* management of the environment over local/national concerns; and maintaining the viability of the global economy rather than addressing deteriorating economic conditions in the South. The globalization project was alive and well.

During the 1990s, after destroying more than 50 percent of Southeast Asian forests, logging companies from Burma, Indonesia, Malaysia, the Philippines, New Guinea, and South Korea moved on to Amazonia. Brazil offered Amazonia as the logging frontier of the twenty-first century—allowing private interests to legally challenge indigenous land titles, building a huge transport infrastructure as a subsidy to private investment in Brazilian natural resources, implementing plans to resettle thousands of Brazilians under pressure from the Sem Terra landless workers' movement, and privatizing 39 of its national forests to attract foreign loggers. Meanwhile, under the terms of the IMF bailout of Indonesia in the 1997 crisis, that country's forests are open to foreign ownership, and the WTO has a national treatment code allowing foreign investors to claim the same rights as domestic ones, which threatens to institutionalize "cut-and-run" logging around the world.[28]

Managing the Global Commons

Environmental management is as old as the need for human communities to ensure material and cultural survival. *Global* environmental management seeks to preserve planetary resources, but there is not yet any resolution as to what end, nor as to the terms on which states will participate. Consider the Kyoto Protocol to limit carbon dioxide emissions. Following U.S. President Clinton's agreement in 1997 to sign, a congressman argued the protocol was "unfair because it exempts 77 percent of all countries from any obligations. China, India, Mexico, and Brazil, just to name a few, are completely unfettered by the Treaty—these countries already have the competitive advantages of cheap labor, lower production costs, and lower environmental, health, and safety standards. If President Clinton has his way, now these countries will be free to develop and pollute all they want, while the U.S. economy goes into a deep freeze."[29] If there ever was a deep freeze coming, it would be hastened by neoliberal policy encouraging corporate access to lax conditions overseas. Nevertheless, this reaction highlights the competitive and ethical dilemmas involved in coming to collective agreement on managing planetary resources—aside from the fact that Kyoto is only binding on countries responsible for just 19 percent of global emissions.[30]

Within the terms of the globalization project, it is not difficult to see that states, strapped for foreign exchange and sometimes required to undergo reform to earn foreign exchange, are beholden to corporations that want to exploit natural resources and/or secure control over their supply in the future. In many cases, local inhabitants—with NGO support—have led the charge to question the commercialization and degradation of environments to which they are historically and spiritually attached. Southern grassroots movements, in particular, regard global environmental managers and their powerful state allies as focused on managing the global environment to ensure the profitability of global economic activity. This includes regulating the use of planetary resources and global waste sinks such as forests, wetlands, and bodies of water. Instead of linking environmental concerns to issues of social justice and resource distribution, the new "global ecology" has converged on four priorities:

- reducing greenhouse gas emissions, mainly from automobiles and burning forests;
- protecting biodiversity, mainly in tropical forests;
- reducing pollution in international waters;
- curbing ozone-layer depletion.

The institutional fallout from UNCED strengthened global economic management. A **Global Environmental Facility (GEF)** was installed, geared to funding global ecology initiatives. The World Bank initiated the establishment of the GEF to channel monies into global environmental projects, especially in the four areas identified above; 50 percent of the projects approved in the GEF's first tranche were for biodiversity protection. In addition, UNCED, via the Food and Agricultural Organization (FAO), planned to zone Southern land for cash cropping with the assistance of national governments. Under this facility, subsistence farming would be allowed only where "natural resource limitations" or "environmental or socioeconomic constraints" prevent intensification. And where governments deem marginal land to be overpopulated, the inhabitants would be forced into transmigration or resettlement programs.[31]

The logic of this scenario is that of managing the "global commons" and viewing surplus populations and their relation to scarce natural resources as the immediate problem, rather than situating the problem of *surplus* population in a broader framework that recognizes extreme inequality of access to resources. In Brazil, for example, less than 1 percent of the population owns about 44 percent of the fertile agricultural land, and 32 million people are officially considered destitute. Structural adjustment policies, grain imports, and expansion of soy export production have dispossessed small peasants. Under conditions where Brazilian social ministries have lost power, landless peasants who do not join the Sem Terra (see below) or the mass migration to the towns or the frontier are incorporated into NGO-organized "poverty management" programs, constituting a cheap labor force for wealthy landowners.[32]

Global ecology, geared to environmental management on a large scale, has priorities for sustainability that often differ from those of the remaining local environmental managers. It is estimated that there are 200 to 300 million forest dwellers in South and South-East Asia, distinct from lowland communities dependent on irrigated agriculture. Some of these people have been given official group names assigning them a special—and usually second-class—status in their national society: India's "scheduled tribes" (*adivasis*), Thailand's "hill tribes," China's "minority nationalities," the Philippines' "cultural minorities," Indonesia's "isolated and alien peoples," Taiwan's "aboriginal tribes," and Malaysia's "aborigines." Challenging their national status and elevating their internationally common bonds, these groups have recently redefined themselves as "indigenous."[33]

Indigenous and tribal people around the world have had their rights to land and self-determination enshrined in the International Labor Organization Convention. Nevertheless, they are routinely viewed from afar as marginal. The World Bank, in adopting the term "indigenous" in its documents, stated in 1990, "The term indigenous covers indigenous, tribal, low caste, and ethnic minority groups. Despite their historical and cultural differences, they often have a limited capacity to participate in the national development process because of cultural barriers or low social and political status."[34]

Viewed through the development lens, this perspective carries a significant implication. On the one hand, it perpetuates the often unexamined assumption that these cultural minorities need guidance. On the other hand, it often subordinates minorities to national development initiatives, such as commercial logging or government forestry projects involving tree plantations. More often than not, indigenous peoples find themselves on the receiving end of large-scale resettlement programs justified by the belief that forest destruction is a consequence of their poverty.

The focus on poverty as the destroyer of forests guided the establishment of the Tropical Forest Action Plan (TFAP) in the 1980s by a global management group consisting of the World Bank, the Food and Agricultural Organization, the **United Nations Development Program**, and the World Resources Institute. TFAP was designed to pool funds to provide alternative fuel-wood sources, strengthen forestry and environmental institutions, conserve protected areas and watersheds, and promote social forestry. It became the "most ambitious environmental aid program ever conceived," and as such attracted requests for aid from 62 southern states looking for new, seemingly "green," sources of funds for extraction of forest products for export. TFAP projects were completed in Peru, Guyana, Cameroon, Ghana, Tanzania, Papua New Guinea, Nepal, Colombia, and the Philippines. Seeing their effects, however, and charging that the TFAP projects furthered deforestation through intervention and zoning, a *worldwide rainforest movement* mobilized sufficient criticism (including that of Britain's Prince Charles) that the TFAP initiative ended. Forestry loans, however, continued through the World Bank.[35]

CASE STUDY

Chico Mendes—Brazilian Environmentalist by Default

As the leader of Brazil's National Council of Rubber Tappers, Chico Mendes concerned himself with the safety of his tappers as ranchers tried to force them off their land. By the Catholic Church's reckoning, between 1964 and 1988, a total of 982 murders over land disputes in the Amazon occurred, largely by ranchers' hired guns. Under these circumstances, the Brazilian government obtained a forestry loan from the World Bank for "agro-ecological zoning" in the Brazilian Polonoroeste area of Rondônia and Mato Grosso to set aside land for farmers, extractive reserves for the rubber tappers (so they could supplement their tapping wages with sales of other forest products), and protected Indian reserves in addition to national parks, forest reserves, and other protected forest areas. The minorities affected were not consulted, even though Mendes lobbied the World Bank in Washington on behalf of the rubber tappers in 1988. He feared a repetition of the mistakes made in the 1980s, when Rondônia was occupied by impoverished settlers who burned the Amazonian jungle in vain hopes of farming, observing,

> We think that the extractive reserves included in Polonoroeste II only serve to lend the Government's project proposal to the World Bank an ecological tone—which has been very fashionable lately—in order to secure this huge loan. . . . What will be created will not be extractive reserves, but colonization settlements with the same mistakes that have led to the present disaster of Polonoroeste. In other words, a lot of money will be spent on infrastructures which do not mean anything to the peoples of the forest and the maintenance of which will not be sustainable.

Mendes was later murdered by a hired gun for his part in championing the rubber tappers' cause to secure their land. While he was a forest worker, he left an environmentalist's legacy in the idea of the extractive reserve, which is still taking root. At the very moment that the Rondônian Natural Resources Management Project loan was approved in 1992, the Brazilian land agency, the INCRA, "was proceeding with plans to settle some 50,000 new colonists a year in areas that were supposed to be set aside as protected forests and extractive reserves for rubber tappers under the Bank project."

Was the legacy of Chico Mendes the idea of extractive reserves or of the power of resisting the violence of development? 🌍

Sources: Rich (1994:167–69); Schemo (1998:A3).

Environmental Resistance Movements

In all these cases, there is a discernible pattern of collaboration between the multilateral financiers and governments concerned with securing territory and foreign exchange. Indigenous cultures, on the other hand, are typically marginalized. Indonesia's Forestry Department controls 74 percent of the national territory, and the minister for forestry claimed in 1989, "In Indonesia, the forest belongs to the state and not to the people. . . . They have no right of compensation" when their habitats fall to logging concessions.[36]

Under these conditions, "environmentalism of the poor" proliferates. It takes two forms: active resistance, which seeks to curb invasion of habitats by states and markets; and adaptation, which exemplifies the centuries-old practice of renewing habitats in the face of environmental deterioration. In the latter practice lie some answers to current problems.

One dramatic form of resistance was undertaken by the Chipko movement in the central Himalaya region of India. Renewing an ancient tradition of peasant resistance in 1973, the Chipko adopted a Gandhian strategy of non-violence, symbolized in tree-hugging protests led primarily by women against commercial logging. Similar protests spread across northern India in a move to protect forest habitats for tribal peoples. Emulating the Chipko practice of tree planting to restore forests and soils, the movement developed a "pluck-and-plant" tactic. Its members uprooted eucalyptus seedlings—the tree of choice in official social forestry, even though it does not provide shade and ravishes aquifers—and replaced them with indigenous species of trees that yield products useful to the locals. Success of these movements has been measured primarily in two ways: by withdrawal of Bank involvement and the redefinition of forestry management by the government; and by the flowering of new political associations, sometimes called "user groups," which are democratic and dedicated to reclaiming lands and redefining grassroots development.[37]

Environmental activism proliferates across the South. In Thailand, where the state promotes eucalyptus plantations that displace forest dwellers, there has been

> an explosion of rural activism. . . . Small farmers are standing up to assassination threats; weathering the contempt of bureaucrats; petitioning cabinet officials; arranging strategy meetings with other villagers; calling on reserves of political experience going back decades; marching; rallying; blocking roads; ripping out seedlings; chopping down eucalyptus trees; burning nurseries; planting fruit, rubber, and forest trees in order to demonstrate their own conservationist awareness. . . . Their message is simple. They want individual land rights. They want community rights to local forests which they will conserve themselves. They want a reconsideration of all existing eucalyptus projects. And they want the right to veto any commercial plantation scheme in their locality.[38]

CASE STUDY

Las Gaviotas—Tropical Sustainability

In the early 1970s, Paulo Lugari and collaborators (engineers, artists, students, Indians, and even street children) built a sustainable village in the remote plains of Colombia, 500 kilometers from the capital, Bogotá. Despite continuous violence within the country around the coca economy, Las Gaviotas has survived, supported by ingenious renewable energy technology (water systems, distillers, solar-powered cookers, windmills, and pumps), hydroponic farming, and a project of regenerating surrounding rainforest from the barren savannah soil. Knowing the savannah was once part of the Amazon forest, Lugari managed to inoculate Caribbean pine seedlings to take and perform the function of catalysts in providing shade, increasing soil moisture and promoting biodiversity. The regenerated forest yields drinking water, with valuable resins, oils, and fragrances from the forest supporting this experiment in self-sufficiency. The village supports 200 workers with piece rate wages and room, board, and medical care; 50 resident families, and some 500 children from the region, have accessed its school. Adults rotate among jobs in the village (construction, planting, gardening, and cooking). Aside from providing a haven from civil strife, social collaboration involves all in the project of sustainability. "The success of Las Gaviotas in sustainably supporting the community from the products of the regenerated rainforest has prompted new dreams of expanding the forest across the savannah, with both environmental and social benefits. . . . Plans to achieve this extraordinary environmental and social transformation, beginning with a tenfold expansion of the forest around Las Gaviotas," won government endorsement in 2004. Further plans for developing the carbon sequestration system, production of potable water, and ecotourism have obtained financial support from a Belgian socially responsible corporation, Zero Emissions Research and Initiatives (ZERI).

Can the marriage of grassroots environmentalism with "green capitalism" be sustainable, in both senses of the term?

Source: White and Mariño (2007:22).

As grassroots environmentalism mushrooms across the South, community control gains credibility by example. At the same time, the institutional aspects of technology transfer associated with the development project come under question. An ex-director of forestry at the Food and Agricultural Organization commented,

> Only very much later did it dawn on the development establishment that the very act of establishing new institutions often meant the weakening, even the destruction of existing indigenous institutions which ought to have served as the basis for sane and durable development: the family, the clans, the tribe, the village, sundry mutual aid organizations, peasant associations, rural trade unions, marketing and distribution systems and so on.[39]

Forest dwellers have *always* managed their environment. From the perspective of colonial rule and developers, these communities did not appear to be involved in management because their practices were alien to the specialized pursuit of commercial wealth characterizing Western ways beginning under colonialism. Local practices were therefore either suppressed or ignored.

Now, where colonial forestry practices erased local knowledge and eroded natural resources, recent grassroots mobilization, such as the Green Belt Movement in Kenya organized by women, has re-established intercropping to replenish soils and tree planting to sustain forests. Where development agencies and planners have attempted to impose irrigated cash cropping, such as in eastern Senegal, movements such as the Senegalese Federation of Sarakolle Villages have collectively resisted in the interests of sustainable peasant farming.[40]

CASE STUDY

Local Environmental Managers in Ghana

Hundreds of local communities have evolved new resource management practices as livelihood strategies, often with the aid of **nongovernmental organizations** (NGOs). A case in point is the revival of local environmental management in the Manya Krobo area of southeastern Ghana, in the wake of environmental deterioration visited on the forestland by cash cropping. British colonialism promoted the production of palm oil, followed by cocoa cultivation, for export. The displacement of forest cover by monocultural cocoa crops led to severe degradation of the soils. With cocoa prices falling in the second half of the twentieth century, local farmers shifted to growing cassava and corn for local food markets; they also cultivated oil palms and activated a local crafts industry (distilling) used for subsistence rather than for export. Forest restoration technologies, combined with food crops, have emerged as a viable adaptation. These restoration methods are based on the preservation of pioneer forest species rather than the fast-growing exotics (with purchasable technological packages) promoted by development agencies as fuel-wood supplies and short-term forest cover.

When a community is attempting to recover a stable livelihood, which includes developing technologies appropriate to retaining ecological balance, does that count as development?

Source: Amanor (1994:64).

The challenge for environmental movements in the South is twofold: to create alternatives to the capital- and energy-intensive forms of specialized agriculture and agro-forestry appropriate to the goal of restoring and sustaining local ecologies; and to build alternative models to the bureaucratic, top-down development plans that have typically subordinated natural resource use to commercial, rather than sustainable, social ends. Perhaps the fundamental challenge to Southern environmentalism is the perspective that has defined World Bank programming: "Promoting development is the best way to protect the environment."[41] The question is whether development, understood from the Bank's perspective, is a source of sustainability.

Feminism

The term *féminisme* first appeared in France in the 1880s, referring to a movement for women's rights. It reappeared in the 1970s as "second-wave feminism," in the midst of the women's liberation movement for gender equality, taking on multiple meanings for women in the Third World, women of color, lesbians, and working women.[42] With respect to development, feminism has served to transform our understanding of the meaning, and implications, of development as well as to institutionalize policy agendas committed to broad gender equality in a transformed concept of human development: "supporting the development of peoples' potential to lead creative, useful, and fulfilling lives."[43] Thus, in 1999, the Women's International Coalition for Economic Justice issued a Declaration for Economic Justice and Women's Empowerment, which demanded: "macro-policies designed to defend the rights of women and poor people and protect the environment, rather than expand growth, trade, and corporate profits exclusively. . . . Redefining economic efficiency to include measuring and valuing women's unpaid as well as paid work. Economic efficiency needs to be reoriented towards the effective realization of human development and human rights rather than growth, trade, and corporate profits."[44]

Embedded within this statement are three feminist threads that weave an alternative development agenda: valuing equality in productive work; valuing the work of social reproduction; and reorienting social values from economism to humanism. These threads have informed successive phases of feminist influence on development thinking—in particular, issues concerning economic justice in the workplace, social policy supporting unpaid labor, and identification of the threat to human sustainability embodied in the mutual reinforcement of patriarchy and the market system. Thus the Advocacy Guide to Women's World Demands, arising from the 2000 World March of Women, declared,

> We live in a world whose dominant economic system, neoliberal capitalism, is fundamentally inhuman. It is a system governed by unbridled competition that strives for privatization, liberalization, and deregulation. It is a system entirely

driven by the dictates of the market and where full enjoyment of basic human rights ranks below the laws of the marketplace. The result: the crushing social exclusion of large segments of the population, threatening world peace and the future of the planet. . . .

Neoliberalism and patriarchy feed off each other and reinforce each other in order to maintain the vast majority of women in a situation of cultural inferiority, social devaluation, economic marginalization, "invisibility" of their existence and labor, and the marketing and commercialization of their bodies. All these situations closely resemble apartheid.[45]

The trajectory of feminist influence on development began with the first UN World Conference on Women, held in Mexico City in 1975, focused on extending existing development programs to include women—especially regarding equality in employment and education, political participation, and health services. This movement was known as **Women in Development (WID)**, and framed the UN Decade for Women (1976–85). Since then, the movement has changed gears, shifting from remedies to alternatives,[46] or what Rounaq Jahan terms an "integrationist" to an "agenda-setting" approach, which challenges the existing development system of thought with a feminist perspective.[47] The goal includes involving women as decision makers concerned with empowering all women in their various life situations, and championing opposition to all forms of gender discrimination (e.g., gendered divisions of labor). This has come to be known as **Gender and Development (GAD)**, which refocuses on the different development priorities and needs of women and men without segregating gender issues into separate projects. The WID/GAD initiatives have focused on influencing development discourse and practice, especially through policy-making in the development agencies.

An important resource in this project has been the Convention on the Elimination of All Forms of Discrimination Against Women (CEDAW), adopted by the United Nations Assembly in 1979, Article 5 of which imposes the responsibility on states to transform customs, attitudes, and practices that discriminate against women. This convention was the culmination of 30 years' work by the UN Commission on the Status of Women, which has been instrumental in documenting discrimination against women.

Feminist Formulations

The WID position concerned redressing the absence of gender issues in development theory and practice, in particular "women's inequality of access to and participation in the definition of economic structures and policies and the productive process itself."[48] A powerful argument by Danish economist Esther

Boserup concerned women's role in food production, especially in sub-Saharan Africa, and how the introduction of productivity-enhancing technologies privileged males, dichotomizing agriculture between (male) commercial and (female) subsistence farming, downgrading women's status and, given development accounting's focus on cash-generating activity, essentially "invisibilizing" women's contribution. Boserup's claim for equity revalued women's work as equally requiring development resources and, as Jane Jaquette noted, since this concerned African women, "the claim that women should have more equal access to resources could not be dismissed as a 'Western' or 'feminist' import," despite questions raised about Boserup's premise that precolonial gender roles were equal.[49]

In the development debate, WID feminists identified problems and formulated remedies in the following ways:

- Women have always been *de facto* producers, but technological and vocational supports have been minimal because development focuses on male cash-earning activity. Planners should therefore recognize women's contributions, especially as food producers for rural households and even urban markets, where males labor when not migrating to the agro-export or cash crop sector.
- Women bear children, and a more robust understanding of development includes education, health care, family planning, and nutrition as social supports.
- Finally, since women perform unpaid household/farm labor in addition to any paid labor, development planners should pursue ameliorative measures. Findings reveal that where women can be incorporated into income-earning activities, a net benefit accrues to community welfare since male income is often dissipated in consumer/urban markets. Thus, in addition to claiming what women need from development, WID advocates what development needs from women.[50]

In contrast, GAD feminism has offered development remedies as follows:

- Since gender is socially constructed, it is important to address gender inequality not simply on the basis of who is doing what, and whether it is valued, but also by asking questions about how activities come to be valued, by whom, and in whose interest. The goal is to not simply identify women's discrimination, but also to understand the structuring of gender discrimination.
- Households are differentiated social units, with conflictive and/or cooperative gendered divisions of labor. Therefore it is important to understand the nature of relations between productive and reproductive work, to understand the impact of development on household relations and vice versa.
- By shifting the focus to gender relations, or roles, and making visible the work of social reproduction, GAD enables policy makers to see where it "pays" (in development/efficiency, rather than equity, terms) to deliver resources to women.

The WID/GAD project has served as a platform for reforming development initiatives, with the World Bank initiating WID projects in 1987, and shifting towards the GAD approach in the mid-1990s. WID projects were largely supplemental, and left unchallenged questions of differential access to services, resources and opportunities between women and men, and the social/development consequences. Since the 1995 Beijing Conference on Women, the Bank has attempted to "mainstream" gender issues, with variable results.[51]

Outside of what might be called "policy-feminism," feminist movements have proliferated into a matrix of "transnational feminist networks" (TFNs, see list of websites at end of chapter), working in national organizations, multilateral and intergovernmental organizations, and with local organizations to advocate for particular questions such as human rights, demilitarization, labor standards, and so on. Valentine Moghadam notes that, with ICTs, global communication allows these TFNs a fluid constituency and flexibility, which combines with non-hierarchical feminist principles and both formal and informal ways of operating. Some of these TFNs include:[52]

- DAWN (Development Alternatives with Women for a New Era): gender and economic justice, IFI policy, reproductive rights and health—especially for poor Southern women, redistribution of global wealth;
- WIDE (Women in Development Europe): enhanced European aid to ACP (African, Caribbean, and Pacific) countries, feminist alternatives to economic theory and development policies of the North, the IFIs, and the WTO;
- WEDO (Women's Environment and Development Organization): equal participation of women in policy making, formulation of alternative and sustainable solutions to global problems, democratization of the WTO;
- WLUML (Women Living Under Muslim Laws): promotes human rights of women in Muslim states, exposes fundamentalist and state collusion, implementation of CEDAW in all Muslim states;
- SIGI (Sisterhood Is Global Institute): human rights advocacy for women.

In keeping with the "new social movement" designation, DAWN, for example, argues that "women should not depend on government but develop autonomously through self-organization," and its manifesto spells out its humanistic vision:

Each person will have the opportunity to develop her or his full potential and creativity, and values of nurturance and solidarity will characterize human relationships. In such a world women's reproductive role will be redefined: men will be responsible for their sexual behavior, fertility and the well-being of both partners. Child care will be shared by men, women, and society as a whole. . . .[53]

The humanism evolved from an initial identification of "male bias" in social attitudes and thought, and in public policy, as laid out in Diane Elson's *Male Bias in the Development Process* (1991). Elson notes that structural adjustment policies assume an infinite capacity of women to perform the work of social reproduction, given austerity cutbacks in social services: "the hidden 'equilibrating factor' is the household's, and particularly women's ability to absorb the shocks of stabilization programs, through more work and 'making do' on limited incomes."[54] Male bias that ignores unpaid labor uses terms like "efficiency" so that streamlining costs for a public hospital, for example, achieves efficiency by "transferring costs from the productive to the reproductive economy," where women's additional and unpaid work in caring for convalescing patients at home compensates for the shortfall in hospital care."[55] And WIDE, for example, extended this to a general critique of the "free market" thesis, arguing that women must "reclaim the market in a global system where every part of life—even a person's kidney—is increasingly peddled as a commodity, and which sees people as consumers rather than citizens."[56]

Thus a feminist paradigm has emerged which is not simply about adding women to the equation. Rather, from the standpoint of women's experience, feminists have gained a unique perspective on the limits, silences, and violence of an economic model that accounts only for certain definitions of what constitutes "productive" work, via an unsustainable system of accounting that has no debit side (for what economists term "externalities"). It stems from the UN System of National Accounts, which records additions to Gross National Product, but not "costs" such as discrimination (in schooling, nutrition, employment), environmental degradation, the invisible work of social reproduction in the home, and so forth. As Marilyn Waring notes in *If Women Counted: A New Feminist Economics* (1988), economics serves as a "tool of people in power," insofar as value is imputed to a narrow band of cash-generating activity: women, assigned to the household, are discounted, and informals, indigenous peasants, nomads, and forest dwellers are marginalized or displaced as "unproductive," along with disregard for "nature's economy." Thus economic theory conditions the possibility of a predatory relationship towards women and nature through development practices. The conventional development paradigm, in positing a rationalist (Eurocentric) approach—including the liberal development subject—discounts diverse non-European knowledges governed by ecological and cultural practices, where stewardship of nature is integral to cultural renewal, rather than being a programmatic construction.[57]

Broadly, the feminist paradigm stresses that development is a relational, not a universal, process, and we should be aware of how our ideals shape assumptions about other societies and their needs. Concerns for the empowerment of women in Third World settings should refer to those circumstances, not to abstract ideals of individual emancipation. Consider the "feminization of global labor." As Jeffrey Sachs argues in *The End of Poverty* (2005), regarding the garment factory expansion in Bangladesh, "sweatshops are the first rung on the ladder out of extreme poverty," for the female workers who have "grown up in the countryside, extraordinarily poor, illiterate and unschooled, and vulnerable to chronic hunger and hardship in a domineering patriarchal society."[58] Far from an unproblematic gain for women, sweatshop jobs are constructed for women as repetitive, dead-end, and often debilitating, so that their introduction to the global economy is on unequal terms. Cynthia Enloe's research, guided by the question "what makes labor cheap?" argues that women are not simply acted on by globalization; rather, corporate strategies depend on local constructions of femininity.[59] And, while Asian women have experienced wage gains (until "defeminization" through industrial upgrading in the Asian regional division of labor), research on Mexican *maquiladoras* reveals a different experience, where wages stagnate.[60] As Lourdes Benería argues, for contextualization, "evaluation of the effects of employment for women needs to take into consideration what happens at the level of gender socialization and power relations."[61] As it happens, women's organizations in the *maquiladoras* have gone beyond traditional male concerns with wages—raising health, reproduction freedom, and environmental concerns, and challenging "the idea that what happens in the factory is separate from what happens in the community and that the company's responsibility does not extend beyond the factory gate."[62]

Women and the Environment

Where Southern grassroots movements entail protection of local resources and community, women typically play a defining role. This has always been so, but one consequence of colonialism is that this activity has become almost exclusively a women's preserve. As private property in land emerged, women's work tended to specialize in use of the commons for livestock grazing, firewood collection, game hunting, and seed gathering for medicinal purposes. These activities allowed women to supplement the incomes earned by men in the commercial sector. Women assumed a role as environmental managers, often forced to adapt to deteriorating conditions as commercial extractions increased over time.

The establishment of individual rights to property under colonialism typically privileged men. The result was to fragment social systems built on the complementarity of male and female work. Men's work became specialized: in national statistics, it is routinely counted as contributing to the commercial sector. Conversely, the specialization of women's labor as "non-income earning" work means women's work remains outside the commercial sector, leaving much of it invisible. The domain of invisible work includes maintaining the commons. It is not, however, sufficient to assume—as some eco-feminists do—that women constitute a "natural" constituency for environmental stewardship. Rather, women's relationship to nature is part of their labor of social reproduction: "women relate to natural resources as part of their livelihood strategies, which reflect multiple objectives, powerful wider political forces and, crucially, gender relations, i.e., social relations which systematically differentiate men and women in processes of production and reproduction."[63]

At the practical level, women engage in multifaceted activity. Across the world, women's organizations have mobilized to manage local resources, empower poor women and communities, and pressure governments and international agencies on behalf of women's rights. Countless activities of resource management undertaken by women form the basis of these practices. Perhaps most basic is the preservation of biodiversity in market and kitchen gardens. In Peru, the Aguarun Jivaro women nurture more than 100 varieties of manioc, the local staple root crop. Women have devised ingenious ways of household provisioning beside and within the cash-cropping systems managed by men. Hedgerows and wastelands become sites of local food crops.[64] Forest products (game, medicinal plants, condiments) are cultivated and harvested routinely by women. In rural Laos, more than 100 different forest products are collected chiefly by women for home use or sale. Women in Ghana process, distribute, and market game. Indian women anchor household income with an array of nontimber forest products amounting to 40 percent of total Forest Department revenues—as do Brazilian women in Acre, working by the side of the male rubber tappers.[65]

In Kenya, the Kikuyu women in Laikipia have formed 354 women's groups to help them coordinate community decisions about access to and use of resources. Groups vary in size from 20 to 100 neighbors, both squatters and peasants; members contribute cash, products, and/or labor to the group, which in turn distributes resources equally among them. The groups have been able to pool funds to purchase land and establish small enterprises for the members. One such group, the Mwenda-Niire, was formed among landless squatters on the margins of a large commercial estate. Twenty years later, through saving funds, by growing maize and potatoes among the owner's crops, and through political negotiation, the group purchased the 567 hectare farm, allowing 130 landless families to become farmers. Group dynamics continue through labor-sharing schemes, collective infrastructure projects, and collective marketing. Collective movements such as this go beyond remedying development failures. They restore women's access to resources removed from them under colonial and postcolonial developments.[66]

Women, Poverty, and Fertility

Women's resource management can be ingenious, but often poverty subverts their ingenuity. For example, where women have no secure rights to land, they are less able to engage in sustainable resource extraction. Environmental deterioration may follow. When we see women stripping forests and overworking fragile land, we are often seeing just the tip of the iceberg. Many of these women have been displaced from lands converted for export cropping, or they have lost common land on which to subsist.

Environmental damage stemming from poverty has fueled the debate surrounding population growth in the former Third World. Population control has typically been directed at women—ranging from female infanticide to forced sterilization (as in India) to family planning interventions by development agencies. In Peru, government agencies seized the initiative from women and NGOs, deploying a women's health program to perform 80 percent of sterilizations in a sterilization campaign to cut Peru's fertility rate almost in half since 1961.[67] Feminists entered this debate to protect women from such manipulation of their social and biological contributions.

Feminists advocate enabling women to take control of their fertility without targeting women as the source of the population problem. They oppose the "global gag" rule imposed by U.S. President Bush in 2001, disqualifying NGOs that provide or advocate legal abortion services from receiving U.S. funding. On a global scale, the current world population of almost 6 billion is expected to double by 2050, according to UN projections, unless more aggressive intervention occurs. Studies suggest that female education and health services reduce birthrates. The 1992 World Bank report pointed out that women without secondary education, on average, have seven children; if almost half these women receive secondary education, the average declines to three children per woman.[68]

In addition, recent evidence based on the results of contraceptive use in Bangladesh has been cited as superseding conventional theories of "demographic transition." Demographic theory extrapolates from the Western experience a pattern of demographic transition whereby birthrates decline significantly as economic growth proceeds. The threshold is the shift from preindustrial to industrial society, in which education and health technologies spread. This is expected to cause families to view children increasingly as an economic liability rather than as necessary hands in the household economy or as a response to high childhood mortality rates. Evidence from Bangladesh showed a 21 percent decline in fertility rates during the decade and a half (1975–1991) in which a national family planning program was in effect. The study's authors claimed that these findings "dispute the notion that 'development is the best contraceptive,'" adding that "contraceptives are the best contraceptive."[69]

Feminist groups argue that family planning and contraception need to be rooted in the broader context of women's rights. Presently, almost twice as many women as men are illiterate, and that difference is growing. Poor women with no education often do not understand their rights or contraceptive choices. The International Women's Health Coalition identified the Bangladesh Women's Health Coalition, serving 110,000 women at 10 clinics around the country, as a model for future UN planning. This group began in 1980, offering abortions. With suggestions from the women it served, the coalition has expanded into family planning, basic health care services, child immunizations, legal aid, and training in literacy and employment skills.[70]

The correlation between women's rights and low fertility rates has ample confirmation. In Tunisia, the 1956 Code of Individual Rights guaranteed women political equality, backed with family planning and other social programs that included free, legal abortions. Tunisia is a leader in Africa, with a population growth rate of only 1.9 percent. The director-general of Tunisia's National Office of Family and Population, Nebiha Gueddana, claims that successful family planning can occur in a Muslim society: "We have 30 years of experience with the equality of women and . . . none of it has come at the expense of family values."[71] And in Kerala, where the literacy rate for women is two and a half times the average for India and where the status of women has been high throughout the twentieth century relative to the rest of the country, land reforms and comprehensive social welfare programs were instrumental in achieving a 40 percent reduction in the fertility rate between 1960 and 1985, reducing the population growth rate to 1.8 percent in the 1980s.[72]

With supportive social conditions, fertility decisions by women can have both individual and social benefits. Fertility decisions by individual women usually occur within patriarchal settings—households or societies—as well as within definite livelihood situations. It is these conditions that women's groups have identified as necessary to the calculus in fertility decisions. Recently, population debates have incorporated elements of the feminist perspective, which emphasizes women's reproductive rights and health in the context of their need for secure livelihoods and political participation.[73] This view was embedded in the document from the 1994 UN Conference on Population and Development. Although contested by the Vatican and some Muslim nations (particularly Iran), the document states that women have the right to reproductive and sexual health, defined as "a state of complete physical, mental, and social wellbeing" in all matters relating to reproduction.[74]

Women's Rights

Feminism has clearly made an impact on the development agenda since the days of WID's inception. However, the improvement of women's material condition and social status across the world has not followed in step, even if the statistical reporting of women's work in subsistence production has improved.[75]

In 1989, at the end of a decade of structural adjustment, the United Nations made the following report in its World Survey on the Role of Women in Development:

> The bottom line shows that, despite economic progress measured in growth rates, at least for the majority of developing countries, economic progress for women has virtually stopped, social progress has slowed, and social well-being in many cases has deteriorated, and because of the importance of women's social and economic roles, the aspirations for them in current development strategies will not be met.[76]

Five years later, the United Nations' *Human Development Report 1994* found that, "despite advances in labor-force participation, education, and health, women still constitute about two-thirds of the world's illiterates, hold fewer than half of the jobs on the market and are paid half as much as men for work of equal value."[77] Even so, feminism has put its stamp on the reformulations of development; the UN 1994 report declared the following in response to the crisis in the former Third World:

> It requires a long, quiet process of sustainable human development . . . [a] development that not only generates economic growth but distributes its benefits equitably; that regenerates the environment rather than destroying it; that empowers people rather than marginalizing them. It is development that gives priority to the poor, enlarging their choices and opportunities and providing for their participation in decisions that affect their lives. It is development that is pro-people, pro-nature, pro-jobs, and pro-women.[78]

The 1995 UN Conference on Women in Beijing produced a Platform for Action, emphasizing re-evaluation of the notion that progress is measured by economic growth, refocusing on gender disadvantages via notions of justice, equality, human rights, and capabilities.[79] In 2005, UNESCO sponsored a decadal anniversary "stock-taking" of the condition of women, including proposals for measuring women's empowerment (a timely complement to

CEDAW). The core of this report was twofold: first, that the Millennium Development Goals, in producing gender-neutral development indicators (other than primary education), remained silent regarding women's unpaid care work, reproductive and sexual rights, subjection to violence, and empowerment needs (for example, emphasizing secondary school opportunities which in turn would increase marriage age, reduce fertility, improve employment prospects, and reduce child malnutrition); and second, that in developing empowerment measures, "it is as important to determine women's participation and rights *across* social groups as it is to understand women's access and rights in relation to men's access and rights."[80]

The question of women's rights also concerns how different cultures regulate women's private lifestyles. In Muslim cultures, with considerable variation, women's rights remain subordinated to Islamic law or, as Muslim feminists claim, to male interpretation of the Koran. In Morocco, for example, women require the permission of male relatives to marry, name their children, or work. Sisters inherit half as much as brothers, and male coercion in marriage is customary. Islamic women's groups across the Muslim world are mobilizing against what they term *Muslim apartheid,* in addition to working to eliminate "honor killings" of daughters/sisters who have sex outside of marriage. In the Mediterranean region, rapid urbanization has produced more educated and professional women who focus on changing secular laws to make an end run around Islamic law.[81] Different methodologies have emerged to assist the balancing of women's international rights with the question of cultural relativism (respecting cultural difference). They include the "principled approach," in which human rights trump state religious laws; a "balanced approach," which juxtaposes gender rights and religious freedoms to clarify boundary claims; and the "world-traveller approach," emphasizing cultural sensitivity.[82]

Finally, in an earlier evaluation of the Beijing Conference, the Women's Environment and Development Organization reported that 70 percent of 187 national governments had laid plans to improve women's rights, 66 countries have offices for women's affairs, and 34 of these have legislative input. Pressure from local and international women's organizations since the Beijing conference, in countries as different as Mexico, Germany, New Zealand, and China, has made some gains, such as instituting laws against domestic violence.[83] But the 2005 UNESCO report noted that much is yet to be accomplished across the world—for example, just 15.6 percent of elected parliamentarians are women; women account for two-thirds of illiteracy; nowhere do women earn the same as men—the wage gap (on average 50–80 percent) is especially wide in the private sector; only two of the 49 presidents of the UN General Assembly have been women; and violence against women continues.[84]

Cosmopolitan Activism

Perhaps the litmus test of the globalization project is that, as global integration intensifies, the currents of cosmopolitan activism deepen. Class or ethnic-based communities, regions, and networks mobilize to challenge and provide alternatives to the global order. Such challenges occur at or across different scales. Cosmopolitan activism recognizes that environmental issues are simultaneously labor issues and that women's issues are not just confined to fertility, reproduction, and women's work but also include housing, credit, and health—where each of these dimensions of development is gendered in a project realized through multiscale patriarchal structures.

Cosmopolitan activism includes cooperatives that reorganize a community around democratic values and restoring local ecological balance. Indigenous movements may assert their cultural rights to regional territories. The fair trade movements may organize transnational networks to revalue producers and what is produced in relation to social justice concerns shared with distant consumers. These multilayered initiatives contribute to new thinking about governance: from the idea of "subsidiarity" (locating decision making at the lowest possible level) to David Held's related call for a **"cosmopolitan project"**[85] to Wolfgang Sachs's notion of **"cosmopolitan localism,"** based in the valuing of diversity as a universal right:

> Today, more than ever, universalism is under siege. To be sure, the victorious march of science, state, and market has not come to a stop, but the enthusiasm of the onlookers is flagging. . . . The globe is not any longer imagined as a homogeneous space where contrasts ought to be levelled out, but as a discontinuous space where differences flourish in a multiplicity of places.[86]

Cosmopolitan activism questions the assumption of uniformity in the global development project and assert the need to respect alternative cultural traditions as a matter of respect and global survival. They represent different initiatives to preserve or assert human and democratic rights within broader settings, whether a world community or individual national or subnational arenas. This is the spirit behind the concept of "cosmopolitan democracy."[87]

CASE STUDY

Andean Counterdevelopment or "Cultural Affirmation"

Cosmopolitan localism takes a variety of forms. One form is a dialogical method of privileging the local worldview, including an evaluation of modern Western knowledge from the local standpoint. This means learning to value local culture and developing a contextualized understanding of foreign knowledges so that they do not assume some universal truth and inevitability, as claimed by Western knowledge and its officialdom. In this sense, modernity is understood as a peculiarly Western cosmology arising from European culture and history, which includes universalist claims legitimizing imperial expansion across the world. In the Peruvian Andes, indigenous writers and activists formed an NGO in 1987 called PRATEC (Proyecto Andino de Tecnologias Campesinas), which is concerned with recovering and implementing traditional Andean peasant culture and technologies via education of would-be rural developers. PRATEC links the Andean cosmology to its particular history and local ecology. It does not see itself as a political movement but rather as a form of cultural politics dedicated to revaluing Andean culture and affirming local diversity over abstract homogenizing knowledges associated with modernity. One PRATEC peasant explained, "We have great faith in what nature transmits to us. These indicators are neither the result of the science of humans, nor the invention of people with great experience. Rather, it is the voice of nature itself which announces to us the manner in which we must plant our crops." Andean peasants grow and know some 1,500 varieties of quinoa, 330 of kaniwa, 228 of tarwi, 3,500 of potatoes, 610 of oca (another tuber), and so on. A core founding member of PRATEC explained that "to decolonize ourselves is to break with the global enterprise of development." In the context of the collapse of Peru's formal economy, the delegitimization of government development initiatives, and environmental deterioration, PRATEC is one alternative, rooted in indigenous ecology and a participatory culture that puts the particularity of the Western project in perspective.

Is it possible to question development as a particularization of Western power, and yet incorporate some "universals" (reason, rights, etc.), as Anna Tsing suggests—as "engaged universals [which] travel across difference and are charged and changed by their travels?"

Sources: Apffel-Marglin (1997); Tsing (2004:8).

The most potent example of cosmopolitan activism was the peasant revolt in Mexico's southern state of Chiapas, a region in which small peasant farms are surrounded by huge cattle ranches and coffee plantations. About a third of the unresolved land reforms in the Mexican agrarian reform department, going back more than half a century, are in Chiapas. The government's solution over the years has been to allow landless *campesinos* to colonize the Lacandon jungle and produce subsistence crops, coffee, and cattle. During

the 1980s, coffee, cattle, and corn prices all fell, and *campesinos* were pro-
hibited from logging—even though timber companies continued the practice.[88] The revolt had these deepening class inequalities as its foundation. But
the source of the inequalities transcended the region.

On New Year's Day, 1994, hundreds of impoverished peasants rose up
against what they perceived to be the Mexican state's continued violation of
local rights. Not coincidentally, the revolt fell on the day NAFTA was implemented. To the Chiapas rebels, NAFTA symbolized the undermining of the
revolutionary heritage in the Mexican Constitution of 1917, by which communal lands were protected from alienation. In 1992, under the pretext of
structural adjustment policies and the promise of NAFTA, the Mexican
government opened these lands for sale to Mexican and foreign agribusinesses. In addition, NAFTA included a provision to deregulate commodity
markets—especially the market for corn, the staple peasant food.

The Chiapas revolt illustrates cosmopolitan localism well because it
linked the struggle for local rights to a political and historical context. That
is, the *Zapatistas* (as the rebels call themselves, after Mexican revolutionary
Emilio Zapata) perceive the Mexican state as the chief agent of exploitation
of the region's cultural and natural wealth. In one of many communiqués
aimed at the global community, Subcomandante Marcos, the *Zapatista*
spokesperson, characterized the Chiapas condition as follows:

> Oil, electric energy, cattle, money, coffee, bananas, honey, corn, cocoa, tobacco,
> sugar, soy, melons, sorghum, mamey, mangos, tamarind, avocados, and
> Chiapan blood flow out through a thousand and one fangs sunk into the neck
> of Southeastern Mexico. Billions of tons of natural resources go through
> Mexican ports, railway stations, airports, and road systems to various desti-
> nations: the United States, Canada, Holland, Germany, Italy, Japan—but all
> with the same destiny: to feed the empire. . . . The jungle is opened with
> machetes, wielded by the same *campesinos* whose land has been taken away
> by the insatiable beast. . . . Poor people cannot cut down trees, but the oil com-
> pany, more and more in the hands of foreigners, can. . . . Why does the federal
> government take the question of national politics off the proposed agenda of
> the dialogue for peace? Are the indigenous Chiapan people, only Mexican
> enough to be exploited, but not Mexican enough to be allowed an opinion on
> national politics? . . . What kind of citizens are the indigenous people of
> Chiapas? "Citizens in formation?"[89]

In these communiqués, the Ejército Zapatista de Liberación Nacional
(EZLN) movement addresses processes of both decline and renewal in
Mexican civil society. The process of decline refers to the dismantling of the
communal tradition of the Mexican national state symbolized in the infamous

reform of Article 27 of the Constitution. The article now privileges private (foreign) investment in land over the traditional rights of *campesinos* to petition for land redistribution within the *ejido* (Indian community land held in common) framework. The *Zapatistas* argue that this reform, in conjunction with NAFTA liberalization, undermines the Mexican smallholder and the basic grains sector. The *Zapatistas* understand that the U.S. "comparative advantage" in corn production (6.9 U.S. tons versus 1.7 Mexican tons per hectare, including infrastructural disparities) seriously threatens Mexican maize producers, especially because, under NAFTA, the Mexican government has agreed to phase out guaranteed prices for staples such as maize and beans.[90] With an estimated 200 percent rise in corn imports under NAFTA's full implementation by 2008, more than two-thirds of Mexican maize production has been threatened, with almost two million *campesinos* displaced by heavily subsidized corn imports from the United States.[91]

Renewal involves the "citizenship" demands by the Chiapas movement—meaning the need for free and fair elections in Chiapas (and elsewhere in Mexico), adequate political representation of *campesino* interests (as against those of Chiapas planters and ranchers), and the elimination of violence and authoritarianism in local government. The EZLN's demands included a formal challenge to a centuries-old pattern of *caciquismo* (local strongman tradition) in which federal government initiatives have routinely been thwarted by local political and economic interests.[92]

The renewal side also includes the demonstration effect of the Chiapas revolt because communities throughout Mexico have since mobilized around similar demands—especially because local communities face common pressures, such as market reforms. In challenging local patronage politics, the *Zapatistas* elevated demands nationally for inclusion of *campesino* organizations in political decisions regarding rural reforms, including equity demands for small farmers as well as farm workers. They also advanced the cause of local and/or indigenous development projects that sustain regional ecologies and cultures.[93]

What is distinctive about the Chiapas rebellion is the *texture* of its political action. Timed to coincide with the implementation of NAFTA, it wove together a powerful and symbolic critique of the politics of globalization. This critique had two goals. First, it opposed the involvement of national elites and governments in implementing neoliberal economic reforms on a global or regional scale—reforms that undo the institutionalized social entitlements associated with political liberalism. Second, it asserted a new agenda of renewal involving a politics of rights that goes beyond individual or property rights to human, and therefore community, rights. The push for regional autonomy challenged local class inequalities and demanded the empowerment of *campesino* communities. It also asserted the associative political style of the EZLN, composed of a coalition of *campesino* and women's organizations. Within the *Zapatista* movement, women have questioned the premise of official indigenous state policies that dichotomizes modernity and tradition, insisting on "the right to hold to distinct cultural traditions while at the same time changing aspects of those traditions that oppress or exclude them."[94] This involves blending the formal demand for territorial and resource autonomy with the substantive demand for women's rights to political, physical, economic, social, and cultural autonomy.

The *Zapatista* program rejects integration into outside development projects, outlining a plan for land restoration, abolition of peasant debts, and reparations to be paid to the Indians of Chiapas by those who have exploited their human and natural resources. Self-determination involves the development of new organizational forms of cooperation among different groups in the region. These have evolved over time into a "fabric of cooperation" woven among the various threads of local groupings. They substitute fluid organizational patterns for the bureaucratic organizational forms associated with modernist politics—such as political parties, trade unions, and hierarchical state structures.[95] In these senses, whether the *Zapatistas* survive the Mexican army's continuing siege of Chiapas and the current move to undercut the rebels with a regional investment and trade corridor (the Plan Pueblo de Panama—tapping into a low-cost pool of displaced labor that can compete in the "race-to-the-bottom" dynamic spearheaded by China), the movement they have quickened will intensify the unresolved tension between global governance and political representation.

CASE STUDY

The New Labor Cosmopolitanism—Social Movement Unionism

One consequence of the globalization project is labor union decline, as well as the casualization of labor associated with the restructuring of work and corporate downsizing, as firms and states pursue efficiency in the global economy. Another is the relocation of union activities from the global North to the newly industrialized countries (NICs). A new labor internationalism is emerging to present a solid front to footloose firms that divide national labor forces and to states that sign the free trade agreements (FTAs), weakening labor benefits.

The new labor internationalism was a key part of the political debate surrounding NAFTA. Led by the rank and file, organized labor joined a national political coalition of consumers, environmentalists, and others in opposing the implementation of NAFTA, arguing that, since Mexican unions were organs of the state which maintained a low minimum wage, NAFTA could not protect U.S. labor from unfair competition.

Subsequently, cross-border unionism to protect labor on either side has taken off. The stranglehold of the Mexican government on union organization frayed, evidenced by the formation of an independent union, the Authentic Labor Front, which formed an alliance with the U.S. United Electrical Workers, Teamsters, Steel Workers, and four other U.S. and Canadian unions in the early 1990s. The American Federation of Labor and Congress of Industrial Organizations (AFL-CIO) has since sought alliances with independent Mexican unions, including calling for independent labor organizing in the *maquiladoras*. On December 12, 1997, following a long struggle, the Korean-owned Han Young plant in Tijuana agreed to the formation of an independent union among its *maquila* factory workers, a 30 percent pay raise, and reinstatement of fired activists.

On International Women's Day (March 8) in 2002, the International Confederation of Free Trade Unions launched a three-year campaign, targeting female workers in export processing zones (EPZs) as well in the informal sector, realizing that in the latter there is a growing segment of future membership.

This development mirrors movements elsewhere in the global South, where independent unions respond to global integration. For instance, the Transnationals Information Exchange (TIE) forged networks of labor organization across the world, targeting the production of the "world car," and formed the Cocoa-Chocolate Network, based on the global commodity chain, whereby TIE linked European industrial workers with Asian and Latin American plantation workers and peasants, linking chocolate factories to the cacao bean fields. TIE practiced **social movement unionism**, connecting casualized labor across national boundaries, organizing regionalized networks of labor, and addressing issues of racism and immigrant workers. It evolved a flexible, decentralized structure that mirrors the age of lean production, empowering labor and its activists across the networks. Such social movement unionism is spreading in middle-income states such as Brazil, South Africa, Taiwan, and South Korea, where unions spearhead broad coalitions demanding democratization of political systems, linking economic rights (working conditions) with political rights (independent organization) and social rights (restoration of the social contract and responsiveness to social justice concerns). Their employment in globally competitive industries often lends them a strategic power through the strike.

If labor organizes transnationally, what cosmopolitan institutional mechanisms, beyond the nation-state, does it need to protect and sustain its rights to secure employment, fair wages, and just working conditions?   🌐

Sources: Beneria (1995:48); Brecher and Costello (1994:153–154); Calvo (1997); Dillon (1997, 1998); Moody (1999:255–262); Ross and Trachte (1990); Rowling (2001:24); Seidman (1994); Silver (2003).

Food Sovereignty Movements

At the turn of the twenty-first century, 850 million people (mostly in the global South) remain food insecure—that is, unable to meet their daily energy requirements. Meanwhile, six corporations handle 85 percent of the world grain trade, and integrated, centralized control of the food chain (from gene to supermarket shelf) intensifies. In the name of globalization, this northern model (including risks associated with factory farming and food scares) is exported as the solution to food insecurity, displacing Northern and Southern farmers. Canadian farmer Nettie Wiebe remarks, "The difficulty for us, as farming people, is that we are rooted in the places where we live and grow our food. The other side, the corporate world, is globally mobile."[96]

Resistances to the global conception of food security are mushrooming—framed by the alternative conception of **food sovereignty**. This means not just protecting local farming but revitalizing democratic, cultural, and ecological processes at the subnational level. The several million-strong farmers' transnational movement, La Vía Campesina, asserts that "farmers' rights are eminently collective" and "should therefore be considered as a different legal framework from those of private property." Vía Campesina, formed in 1992, unites 143 local and regional chapters of landless peasants, family farmers, agricultural workers, rural women, and indigenous communities across Africa, Europe, Asia, and North, Central, and South America, in 53 countries.[97] It claims that "biodiversity has as a fundamental base the recognition of human diversity, the acceptance that we are different and that every people and each individual has the freedom to think and to be. Seen in this way, biodiversity is not only flora, fauna, earth, water, and ecosystems; it is also cultures, systems of production, human and economic relations, forms of government; in essence it is freedom."[98]

Food sovereignty, in this vision, is "the right of peoples, communities, and countries to define their own agricultural, labor, fishing, food and land policies which are ecologically, socially, economically, and culturally appropriate to their unique circumstances."[99] Vía Campesina argues that food should not come under the WTO regime: food production plays a unique social role and should not be subordinated to market dictates. Food self-reliance comes first, followed by trade. The movement would subordinate trade relations to the question of access to land, credit, and fair prices, set politically via the rules of fair trade to be negotiated in the United Nations Conference on Trade and Development (UNCTAD), with active participation of farmers in building democratic definitions of agricultural and food policies. While the consumer movement (e.g., the 60,000 towns and villages of the European slow food movement) has discovered that "eating has become a political act," Vía Campesina adds, "Producing quality products for our own people has also become a political act . . . this touches our very identities as citizens of this world."[100] Access to land is a first step, and Vía Campesina declares,

> Access to the land by peasants has to be understood as a guarantee for survival and the valorization of their culture, the autonomy of their communities and a new vision of the preservation of natural resources for humanity and future generations. Land is a good of nature that needs to be used for the welfare of all. Land is not, and cannot be, a marketable good that can be obtained in whatever quantity by those that have the financial means.[101]

Perhaps the most significant chapter of Vía Campesina is the Brazilian land-less-workers' movement, the Movimento dos Trabalhadores Rurais Sem Terra (MST). Over two decades, the MST has settled almost half a million families on millions of acres of land seized by takeovers of unworked land. The stimulus has been a Brazilian development model of structural adjustment, in a context where 1 percent of landowners own (but do not necessarily cultivate) 50 percent of the land, leaving 4.8 million families landless. While Brazil's extensive system of agricultural subsidies was withdrawn, the Organisation for Economic Co-operation and Development (OECD) member states' agricultural subsidies continued at over US$300 billion a year. As the MST website notes, "From 1985 to 1996, according to the agrarian census, 942,000 farms disappeared, 96% of which were smaller than one hundred hectares. From that total, 400 thousand establishments went bankrupt in the first two years of the Cardoso government, 1995–96." Between 1985 and 1996, rural unemployment rose by 5.5 million, and between 1995 and 1999, a rural exodus of 4 million Brazilians occurred. While in the 1980s, Brazil imported roughly US$1 million worth of wheat, apples, and products not produced in Brazil, from "1995 to 1999, this annual average leapt to 6.8 billion dollars, with the importation of many products cultivable . . . in Brazil."[102]

The landless workers' movement draws legitimacy for its land occupations from the Brazilian constitution, which sanctions confiscation of uncultivated private property: "It is incumbent upon the Republic to expropriate for social interest, for purposes of agrarian reform, rural property, which is not performing its social function."[103] The MST is organized in 23 states of Brazil, and while dispossessed farmers comprise 60 percent of its membership, it also includes unemployed workers and disillusioned civil servants.

Land seizures—under the slogan of "Occupy! Resist! Produce!"—lead to the formation of cooperatives, which involve social mobilization "transforming the economic struggle into a political and ideological struggle."[104] Democratic decision-making develops cooperative relations among workers and alternative patterns of land use, financed by socializing a portion of settlement income. Participatory budgeting allocates funds for repairs, soil improvement, cattle feeding, computers, housing, teachers' salaries, child care, mobilization, and so on. Fundamental to this social project is Paulo Freire's dictum that "a settlement, precisely because it is a production unit, should also be a whole pedagogic unit."[105] Education starts from children's daily perspective, building on the learner's direct experience and communicating the inherent value of rural life. This differs from the productivism of the corporate economic model, including its disregard for rural wellbeing, farmer knowledges, and farmer rights.[106] João Pedro Stedile, president of the MST, observes,

> Under the objective economic conditions, our proposal for land reform has to avoid the oversimplification of classical capitalist land reform, which merely divides up large landholdings and encourages their productive use. We are convinced that nowadays it is necessary to reorganize agriculture on a different social base, democratize access to capital, democratize the agro-industrial process (something just as important as landownership), and democratize access to know-how, that is, to formal education.[107]

The MST's 1,600 government-recognized settlements include medical clinics and training centers for health care workers and 1,200 public schools employing an estimated 3,800 teachers serving about 150,000 children at any one time. A UNESCO grant enables adult literacy classes for 25,000, and the MST sponsors technical classes and teacher training. MST cooperative enterprises generate $50 million annually, producing jobs for thousands of members and (increasingly organic) foodstuffs and clothing for local, national, and global consumption. The priority given to producing staple foods for low-income consumers (rather than foods for affluent consumers in cities and abroad) led to a 2003 agreement with the Lula government for the direct purchase of settlement produce for the national Zero Hunger campaign.

As one commentator notes,

These collective enterprises show why the MST is considered a leader in the international **fair trade** movement. The movement is supplying a real, workable alternative to corporate globalization, putting community values and environmental stewardship before profit-making. MST co-ops offer a glimpse of what environmentally sustainable and socially just commerce would look like.[108]

CASE STUDY

The Case for Fair Trade

The idea of fair trade paralleled the intensification of global integration, with aid agencies sponsoring links between craftspeople from the global South and Northern consumers with a taste for "ethnic" products. Fair trade has now blossomed as a method of transcending abuses in the free trade system and rendering more visible the conditions of production of globally traded commodities to establish just prices, environmentally sound practices, healthy consumption, and direct understanding between producers and consumers of their respective needs.

Fair trade exchanges have an annual market value of $400 million, and the market for fair trade products (organic products such as coffee, bananas, cocoa, honey, tea, and orange juice—representing about 60 percent of the fair trade market, alongside organic cotton jeans and an array of handicrafts) expands at between 10 and 25 percent a year. Three fair trade labels— Transfair, Max Havelaar, and Fairtrade Mark—broke into European markets in the late 1980s and are now united under the Fairtrade Labelling Organizations International (FLO), an umbrella NGO that harmonizes different standards and organizes a single fair trade market (in the absence of national regulations). FLO aims to "raise awareness among consumers of the negative effects on producers of international trade so that they exercise their purchasing power positively." Laura Raynolds notes that certification of fair trade practices requires "democratically organized associations of small growers or plantations where workers are fully represented by independent democratic unions or other groups . . . [and] labor conditions . . . uphold basic ILO conventions (including rights to association, freedom from discrimination, prohibition of child and forced labor, minimum social conditions, and rights to safe and healthy work conditions)." Above-world market prices are guaranteed. In Costa Rica, for instance, a cooperative, Coopetrabasur, achieved Fairtrade registration to supply bananas, eliminating herbicide use, reducing chemical fertilizers, building democratic union procedures, raising wages, and establishing a "social premium" set aside for community projects such as housing improvement, electrification, and environmental monitoring.

Daniel Jaffee notes that fair trade embodies a "fundamental paradox" in utilizing the "mechanisms of the very markets that have generated . . . injustices." Thus TNCs such as Starbucks offer a fair trade variety, in the new phase of "green capitalism." The question is whether fair trade will remain a parallel movement only, encouraging at the most and primarily offering a fair outlet for dependent tropical producers, or whether it can mobilize public education and consumer purchasing power to democratize the global market.   🌐

Sources: Jaffee (2007:1) Ransom (2001b); Raynolds (2000:298, 301, 306); J. Smith (2002:40–41).

Summary

We have toured a few of the world's hot spots in this chapter, noting the particular forms social movements take in responding to the failures of developmentalism and the further disorganizing impact of corporate globalization. Responses range from withdrawal into alternative projects (e.g., women's cooperatives, recovery of noncapitalist agro-ecological practices) to attempts to reframe development as a question of rights and social protections (such as the feminist movement, social environmentalism, local autonomy rebellions, and right-wing fundamentalism). All these responses express the uncertainties of social arrangements under globalizing tendencies. Many express a fundamental desire to break out of the homogenizing and disempowering dynamics of the globalization project and to establish a sustainable form of social life based on new forms of associative politics.

Other forms of resistance to the globalization project include mushrooming consumer advocacy. One broad consumer movement has been the United Students Against Sweatshops (USAS), formed in 1998 after several years of campus organizing against the link between U.S. universities and offshore sweatshops producing logo-emblazoned clothing. Approximately 160 colleges support an anti-sweatshop code proposed by the Collegiate Licensing Company, which purchases apparel from the manufacturers. Continuing contention about the stringency of the code has led to building occupations and mass meetings at a number of campuses, including Duke, Wisconsin, Georgetown, Stanford, and Cornell. Nike responded by raising wages for its workers in Indonesia. In related human rights areas, consumer movements have successfully focused attention on child labor stitching soccer balls in Pakistan, although monitoring remains incomplete.

In sum, the road to the political future has several forks. Across the world, countermovements are forming in regional cereal banks in Zimbabwe, ecological campaigns by women's groups in West Bengal, *campesino* credit unions in Mexico, the emergence of solidarity networks among labor forces, food safety campaigns in Europe, and the defense of forest dwellers throughout the tropics. How effectively these movements will interconnect politically—at the national, regional, and global levels (through proliferating Social Forums)—is an open question. Another question concerns how these movements will negotiate with existing states over the terms of local and/or cultural sustenance. Potentially, the new movements breathe new life into politics. They transcend the centralizing thrust of the development states of the postwar era and present models for the recovery of democratic forms of social organization at different scales, as well as the extension of the meaning of civil society. Many communities left behind by the development and globalization projects look to NGOs, rather than to states or international agencies, to represent them and meet their needs. At a time of official legitimacy deficit, when NGOs take the initiative in guiding grassroots development activities, there is a question about the representativeness and accountability of NGOs themselves.

As the new century unfolds, it is clear that the assumptions and content of the global development project are in question from global justice movements, and even from the boardrooms of TNCs and development agencies, and the corridors of state power. In the following and concluding chapter, we examine how our future and the future of development are shaping up.

Further Reading

Baviskar, Amita. *In the Belly of the River: Tribal Conflicts Over the Development in the Narmada Valley*. New York: Oxford University Press, 2005.

Desmarais, Annette Aurélie. *La Vía Campesina. Globalization and the Power of Peasants*. Halifax, NS: Fernwood, 2007.

George, Susan. *Another World Is Possible If. . . .* London: Verso, 2004.

Jackson, Cecile and Ruth Pearson, eds. *Feminist Visions of Development: Gender Analysis and Policy*. New York: Routledge, 1998.

Martinez-Alier, Joan. *The Environmentalism of the Poor: A Study of Ecological Conflicts and Valuation*. London: Edward Elgar, 2002.

Raynolds, Laura T., Douglas Murray and John Wilkinson, eds. *Fair Trade: The Challenges of Transforming Globalization*. Abingdon, UK: Routledge, 2007.

Starr, Amory. *Naming the Enemy: Anti-Corporate Movements Confront Globalization*. London: Zed Books, 2000.

Select Websites

Amnesty International: www.amnesty.org
Behind the Label (USA): www.behindthelabel.org
Corporate Watch (USA): www.corpwatch.org
Development Alternatives with Women for a New Era (DAWN): www.dawnnet.org
Equal Exchange: www.equalexchange.com
Erosion, Technology, and Concentration: www.etcgroup.org
Fairtrade Labelling Organizations International (FLO), Germany: www.fairtrade.net
Focus on the Global South, Thailand: www.focusweb.org
Food First (USA): www.foodfirst.org
Friends of the Earth International (Netherlands): www.foei.org
Genetic Resources Action International (GRAIN): www.grain.org
Global Environment Facility (USA): www.gefweb.org
Global Exchange (USA): www.globalexchange.org
Greenpeace International, Netherlands: www.greenpeace.org/international/
International Forum on Globalization (USA): www.ifg.org
Jubilee South: www.jubileesouth.org
Médecins Sans Frontières: www.msf.org
Oxfam International (UK): www.oxfam.org
Public Citizen Global Trade Watch (USA): www.citizen.org/trade
Rainforest Action Network (USA): www.ran.org
Survival International (UK: tribal peoples' rights): www.survival-international.org
Sweatshop Watch (USA): www.sweatshopwatch.org
Third World Network (Malaysia): www.twnside.org.sg
Transnational Institute (Netherlands): www.tni.org
United Nations Development Fund for Women (UNIFEM): www.unifem.org
United Students Against Sweatshops (USA): www.studentsagainstsweatshops.org
Via Campesina (Honduras): www.viacampesina.org

9

Development for What?

Development has always been a handmaiden to power, which is another way of saying development is realized through inequality. This does not mean that there has been no positive movement in basic development indicators (literacy, health, standard of living, innovation), or that such movement will not continue. But this is by no means a foregone conclusion, given the continuing impoverishment of, among other places, large parts of Africa and the complications of climate change. One of the few places where poverty reduction has occurred over the last 15 years has been China, where the state has managed the market.

Some say that development as an ideal has lost its credibility, given recent reports from the United Nations that more than 100 countries have experienced declining living standards over the past two decades.[1] Others say development has been redefined in the age of globalization and that the "trickle down" of wealth now depends not on individual national policies but on the dynamism and prosperity of the global economy, as well as the ability of populations to find their niche in this process. Still others say that development (culminating in an "age of high mass consumption") can no longer be realized because of "planetary overload" or because of the rapid polarization of wealth/poverty or power/marginalization in a global market system. However, it is important to understand the historic function of development, as a way to interpret and identify future trends.

Development as Rule

Development is ultimately about the accomplishment of power, through projects of rule. From the colonial, through the development, to the globalization

273

project, the ruling powers in each historical moment constructed a *rationale* for their rule, whether it was "civilization," "development," or "globalization." Each motif projected a mission of enabling the improvement of humankind through colonization, nationalism, or the market, via a universal matching principle: racial superiority, collective self-determination, or the self-maximizing individual. The accomplishment of rule in each moment depended on the construction of "subjects," "citizens," or "consumers." Each social category served as the ideal vehicle, and product, of development.

In representing the changing constructions of "development" across time like this, note that accomplishing these ideals is never straightforward. Colonized peoples were quite capable of making claims in the master language, for rights as citizens, rather than remaining as subjects. They appropriated the master's discourse of rights to fuel their movements for self-determination. Colonialism became historically illegitimate. But global power relations did not disappear; they transmuted. Self-determination was channeled through the now universal nation-state, and its ideal of citizenship. "Development" became the new project of rule, through which the First World defined the Third World as undeveloped and therefore a target of opportunity. U.S. President Truman's inaugural address in 1948 declared:

Only by helping the least fortunate of its members to help themselves can the human family achieve the decent, satisfying life that is the right of all people. Democracy alone can supply the vitalizing force to stir the peoples of the world into triumphant action, not only against their human oppressors, but also against their ancient enemies—hunger, misery, and despair. . . . Slowly but surely we are weaving a world fabric of international and growing prosperity.[2]

Within this world fabric, states assumed the development mantle, but within a closely managed and militarized Cold War security system. Under these conditions, development served to legitimize state elaboration of rule over their citizen-subjects. The premise of the UN System of National Accounts, privileging monetary relations and therefore those who turn money into capital, informed the development narrative. States brokered schemes of foreign aid and investment, partnering the private sector and interpreting citizenship as participation in a process of accumulation geared to maximizing GNP. The reach of the state was accomplished through forms of "internal colonialism" which sought to transform peasants, nomads, and forest dwellers from backward subjects into modern citizens.

To illustrate, consider the plan of Indonesia's Department of Social Affairs (DEPSOS) to continue the Dutch colonial project of resettling people from the hinterlands to areas accessible to the state. By 1994, this project had resettled 160,000 people, with a million more to go. The preamble of this project states that "the government has an obligation to ensure that all its citizens have the opportunity to participate in, and contribute to, development and it should therefore make a special effort to reach out to those who, through accidents of history or geography, have been excluded from this process."[3] This sentiment is strikingly parallel to President Truman's benevolent vision of bringing everyone into the "family fold." In doing so, development agencies and states must define the "family" and the "fold:" the former is the citizen-subject, and the latter is development, with disciplinary connotations. That is, development serves to justify the exercise of power by its agents (states, development institutions, businesses), which construct knowledge about subjects of development through programs of classification ("primitives," "the poor," the "Third World," the "excluded") in order to govern them. Governance has been the *raison d'être* of states since their inception, and development provides a historic legitimizing framework as benevolent rule according to technical criteria in the pursuit of prosperity.

Returning to Indonesia, Tania Li notes that critics view the resettlement project as destructive to indigenous cultures, relocating people to impoverished "camps" from ancestral habitats, rapidly transformed into logging, mining or plantation regions. Defenders argue this is modernization, and that people volunteer to be labeled "primitives," for which they are rewarded materially with housing, food and land, and who are the critics to judge? Li's point is simply that "so long as primitives exist—in the specter of the urban imagination and in the pages of program documents—they enable 'the state' to make the statements about the necessity for development and rule contained in the program logic."[4] In other words, development as rule depends on reproducing classifications that renew the legitimacy of the development enterprise. This process began in the era of decolonization, when the non-European world was classified as impoverished, with "ancient enemies—hunger, misery, and despair" (in Truman's words) needing the full attention of an international development project.[5]

Classifying colonials and ex-colonials in this way *conflated* three conditions: frugality (subsistence lifestyle), destitution (when frugality is deprived of its foundations in community ties to land, forest, and water), and scarcity (modernized poverty within the cash/commodity economy).[6] Arguably, Western "modernized poverty" was projected on to a largely frugal world (albeit in transition). This is not to say that addressing the destitution and poverty generated by colonialism was not a fundamental need and right, but that the means provided legitimacy for a project formulated to secure the

Western path, and therefore Western power, in the world. It is also not to say that the recipients, or subjects, of the development project did not necessarily want development of this kind. It is important to ask why, and under what conditions, development has had (and continues to have) so much appeal beyond the legitimizing role for its powerful agents? Li notes that the settlers recruited by Depsos already displayed the attributes expected at the end of the resettlement process—namely, knowledge of permanent agriculture, identification with modern health and education systems, capacity for rational thinking, and loyalty to the nation. In other words, the designation of "primitives" is an *external* label, with the success of the program inscribed in its recruitment process. While this is not always the case, the point is that institutionalized participation, now the dominant mantra of the development establishment, must be understood in context in order to establish how (not whether) development is accomplished.

Thus David Mosse's ethnography of a recent British-funded project of low-cost inputs to improve farming livelihoods in western India notes that development policy coherence is accomplished by enrolling different interests to participate in a given project, because it means jobs or contacts with powerful locals, "effectively turning participation into a commodity." Positive feedback from participants regarding the success of the participatory model confirms institutional legitimacy, regardless of the project outcomes.[7] Analogously, Amita Baviskar's research on a watershed project in central India shows how people participate in, legitimize, and contest development projects, and how participation is filtered through unequal relations of access to resources, rights, and power.[8] And Rebecca Klenk's research on women's identification with development in northern India's Uttar Pradesh state shows how participants in development initiatives "may simultaneously accommodate *and* contest the ways in which the gendered discourses of development locate them as marginal, 'problematic' subjects of an 'underdeveloped' nation-state." In other words, rural women not only did not identify directly as "backward;" they made strategic use of and reformulated the category of "development" to claim their own subjectivity.[9] As suggested in the previous chapter, this is akin to the food sovereignty movements that reformulate what it means to be "peasants" in the twenty-first century, representing their political struggles in the conventional terms of "sovereignty," even as they reformulate it as a form of self-determination at *sub-national* scales, in the name of "agrarian citizenship" (which in turn transforms the meaning of citizenship and modernity).[10]

While the accomplishment of development as a project of rule is at best circuitous, it nevertheless depends on systems of meaning that frame success and failure. Ironically, success and failure may be mutually reinforcing. As Mosse's work demonstrates, the construction of participation ensures success, even if the project is a failure in other terms. Shifting scale from "local" to "global," insofar as the development, or globalization, projects depend on overcoming poverty for their success, project legitimacy also depends on the "existence" of poverty. The question is how it is defined. If poverty is defined in such a way as to naturalize it as an *original* condition (rather than a social outcome), then it serves as a target of development opportunity. Arguably, Southern poverty has been regarded in such a way ever since forms of destitution created by colonialism merged with frugality in an undifferentiated image of an impoverished "Third World." The Earth Institute's Jeffery Sachs, for instance, recently naturalized poverty as an original condition, from which some of us have evolved:

> The move from universal poverty to varying degrees of prosperity has happened rapidly in the span of human history. Two hundred years ago the idea that we could potentially achieve the end of extreme poverty would have been unimaginable. Just about everybody was poor, with the exception of a very small minority of rulers and large landowners.[11]

And, naturalizing the "have/have-not" division, in 2000 World Bank president James Wolfensohn said, "We have yet to solve old problems—above all that of the yawning gulf between the haves and the have-nots of the world."[12] The point is, if development is realized through inequality—the most dramatic expression of which is undoubtedly the reproduction of the "planet of slums" phenomenon by the relentless displacement of the world's peasantries via a WTO regime dedicated to corporate agriculture—then its success (abundant commercial food) is simultaneously its failure (a billion slumdwellers).

More to the point, the reproduction of "surplus populations" may be understood as a failure within the development establishment, but it also renews the development mandate, and the legitimacy of the development institutions.[13] The 2000 Millennium Development Challenge and its unlikely goal of halving global poverty by 2015 exemplify this. Paul Cammack argues that the Bank's anti-poverty crusade, set in the context of a cumulative decade of *World Development Reports*, reveals a double-edged strategy of incorporating the world's poorest into the workforce, but as a reserve army of labor "that will enforce the disciplines of capitalist labor-markets across the greater part of humanity."[14] However, this is not just about cause and effect, because institutional legitimacy is renewed by creating *new approaches* to development. Thus, in the late 1990s, the World Bank transformed itself into a global development "knowledge bank," operating via the web-based Global Development Gateway. This is geared to coordinating a Global Development Network for sharing, brokering, and managing "knowledge resources," galvanizing a civil force of NGOs and corporate foundations to replace shrinking public capacities with flexible forms of development "governance," and constituting some of its data through the "Voices of the Poor" project.[15] And in 2002, President George W. Bush established the Millennium Challenge Account, by which his administration proposed to substitute grants for existing loans to Southern states complying with neoliberal forms of governance (privatization, liberalization, transparency).[16] Perhaps the definitive new solution to "old problems" has been the microfinance revolution.

The Microfinance Revolution

Microfinance embodies the neoliberal philosophy of devolving responsibility for development to the individual, as self-maximizer. To the extent that it sustains the "bad state/good market" principle, it is consistent with the ideology of the globalization project at large. To the extent that it enlists the NGO community in dispensing and monitoring credit and its repayment, it simultaneously empowers and disciplines its recipients—an ideal form of development as rule. And to the extent that it valorizes the poor as consumers of credit, it not only confirms the notion of "development as consumption" (the latest vehicle and product of development), but also it realizes the claim of 2006 Nobel Prize-winning Grameen Bank founder Muhammad Yunus that "credit is a fundamental human right." In short, the microfinance revolution serves to convert the social networks/culture of the poor into an economic value, to be incorporated into the privatized political economy of the twenty-first century.

Whatever the criterion of success—empowerment of marginalized women, stabilization of the poor, extension of frontiers of bank profits, reduction of the informal economy, expansion of microenterprise, enhancement of World Bank legitimacy, NGO-ization of development or new development "rents"— the fundamental significance is the manner in which this relationship renews a reductionist trope of "development as poverty alleviation" through the appropriation of alternative values and visions of social life. Referring to microcredit relations as "markets of dispossession," Julia Elyachar shows that "indigenous forms of production, markets, and sociability are transformed into resources for reproducing dominant forms of power."[17] Replacing social networks of survival with "empowerment debt" has proven to be a double-edged sword, incorporating "informals" successfully into credit relations that may create both new microenterprises and/or new individual dependencies (infused with class/gender inequalities), the loans often being used to meet daily consumption needs.[18] Where classifying informal practices as "poverty" (for reduction via "empowerment debt") disempowers informal cultural networks, the development establishment renews its legitimacy and power to perform development on a "human scale."

The story of the microfinance revolution is about managing the discursive agenda of development (as a project of rule). Since power is a relationship, appropriating opposition is the optimal strategy. Thus in 2000, when World Bank president Wolfensohn promoted development as, "globalization with a human face. Globalization that is inclusive. Globalization that promotes social equity and works for the poor," he described the Bank's operational decentralization, including co-option of its grassroots opponents:

> This vision . . . rejects top-down development devised behind closed doors in Washington (or even in national capitals in member countries). It is holistic and comprehensive, taking account of the interrelationships among the different elements of development strategies. It is based on inclusion and participation, bringing together civil society, local competition, NGOs, the private sector and the poor themselves. Bringing them together in order to foster trust and sustainability. . . . [19]

The Ethics of Empowerment

Taking advantage of ethical claims is a form of empowerment—potentially of claimants on both sides, to the extent that critics can embed ethical claims in institutional compromises, even if those institutions secure disproportionate power. At another remove, there is now a power struggle to define the discursive (and therefore policy) agenda regarding the climate change emergency, critical to the future of the global development agenda. As noted in Chapter 1, 2006 was a turning point, with the publication of the UK Stern Report, arguing the cost of a preventative strategy now of reducing carbon emissions was dwarfed by the cost of climate change impact in the future. But the cost has become a corporate opportunity, through the discursive appeal of "emissions trading," currently regarded as the obvious market solution. This purported solution did not materialize out of thin air, so to speak — liberal/philanthropic corporate leaders espousing "green responsibility" mobilized, beginning in the late 1990s with the creation of the U.S. Pew Center for Climate Change, chaired by Theodore Roosevelt IV, grandson of the Progressive Era and conservation president, and managing director of Lehman Brothers investment banking firm. Following the 2000 World Economic Forum meeting, which declared "climate change is the greatest threat facing the world," corporate leaders (from firms like Dupont, BP, Shell, Suncor, Alcan, Ontario Power, and French aluminum manufacturer

Pechiney) joined with U.S. advocacy group Environmental Defense to form the Partnership for Climate Action, announcing, "The primary purpose of the Partnership is to champion market-based mechanisms as a means of achieving early and credible action on reducing greenhouse gas emissions that is efficient and cost-effective." In 2004, Goldman Sachs established its Center for Environmental Markets, announcing that it would "aggressively seek market-making and investment opportunities in environmental markets," and "that the management of risks and opportunities arising from climate change and its regulation will be particularly significant and will garner increasing attention from capital market participants."[20]

The practice of marketing emissions has been institutionalized in the EU's Emissions Trading Scheme (2005), whereby carbon dioxide emissions permits have been assigned, free of charge, to European corporations. Noting that "the polluter was paid," and that, for example, the British government then calculated power firms would earn a windfall profit of about £1 billion, George Monbiot concludes,

> The Emissions Trading Scheme is a classic act of enclosure. It has seized something which should belong to all of us—the right, within the system, to produce a certain amount of carbon dioxide—and given it to the corporations.[21]

Monbiot's solution is public management of the problem, including a carbon rationing system based on principles of fairness, recognizing existing (global) inequalities of responsibility for emissions.

When *Newsweek* noted in March 2007 that, "Wall Street is experiencing a climate change," recognizing that "the way to get the green is to go green," it captured the legacy of the globalization project—namely, a double movement of posing market solutions to modern problems, but responding to ethical/environmental movements with "green capitalism." As above, maintaining the legitimacy and power of the corporate market means appropriating criticism and reformulating the project. Thus, sensitive to ethical concerns, Starbucks in 2000 introduced its single fair trade coffee brand, and British Petroleum changed its name to Beyond Petroleum. The "ethical branding" dynamic has become sufficiently institutionalized in the corporate market, through certification schemes (codes of conduct, production guidelines and monitoring corporate and supply chain standards), that it has been termed the "**NGO-Industrial Complex**."[22] But where certification remains a private operation, it lacks complete effect, enforcement, and credibility, raising the question of how to regulate corporate behavior in the long-term public, and global-ecological, interest.[23] Thus British retailing giant Sainsbury's embraces corporate environmentalism, proclaiming corporate social responsibility is now key to business strategy, with competition via quality and environmental awareness displacing price competition among the supermarket giants.[24] But the greening of British food retailing intensifies "food miles," as the rising consumption of organic foods now means offshore sourcing from China. In the global economy, what is good for the land, its agricultural workers, and consumers may not be good for the climate—a central paradox of globalization. A solution—localization of food sources—is also being promoted in the United Kingdom by brand-sensitive retailers.

Legitimacy Crisis of the Globalization Project

The other central paradox of the globalization project is the legitimacy of its development promise, and therefore its political viability. In 2006, ex–World Bank chief economist Joseph Stiglitz warned of a new era of protectionist backlash because globalization has not reduced but deepened inequalities.[25] Public opposition to neoliberalism has been continuous, ranging from cascading IMF riots through challenges to free trade agreements to the global justice (or "anti-globalization") movements, culminating in the establishment of the World Social Forum in 2001. World Economic Forum anxieties (its 2001 theme was the growing illegitimacy of the globalization project) and the fracturing of the Washington Consensus confirm deep divisions among the "global managers." And the 1997 Asian financial crisis, which exposed—and deposed—General Suharto's Indonesian military regime in a social rebellion against cronyism and neoliberal austerity, called IMF policies into question. During the crisis, the IMF admitted it may have worsened the financial crisis because speculator fears (of the IMF withholding funds and of domestic social instability) undermined the value of the *rupiah*, spurring democratic opposition. Malaysia's defiance of multilateral capital liberalization policy, protecting it from the crisis, symbolized a retreat from the IMF that heightened an "arrears crisis" which emerged during the 1990s.[26] Focus on the Global South founder Walden Bello's claims:

> Knowing how the Fund precipitated and worsened the Asian financial crisis, more and more of the advanced development countries are refusing to borrow from it or are paying ahead of schedule, with some declaring their intention never to borrow again. These include Thailand, Indonesia, Brazil, and Argentina. Since the Fund's budget greatly depends on debt repayments from these big borrowers, this boycott is translating into what one expert describes as a "huge squeeze on the budget of the organization."[27]

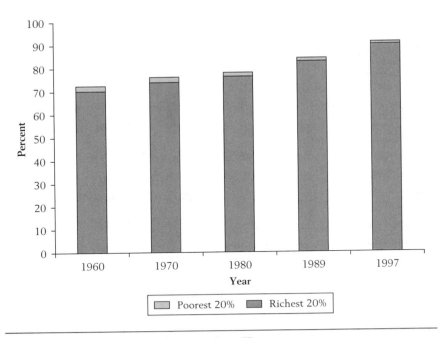

Figure 9.1   Share of Global Income Over Time

Source: Anderson and Cavanagh (2000).

Parallel to the resistance from states in the global South, the World Social Forum (WSF) has emerged to channel the politics of hundreds of global civil society. While the WSF slogan is "another world is possible," it views itself as a process, not an organization. Its Charter of Principles declares that it is a body "representing world civil society." It is not a "locus of power," as such; rather, it is a plural, diversified *network* that, "in a decentralized fashion, interrelates organizations and movements engaged in concrete action at levels from the local to the international to build another world . . . [and] encourages its participant organizations and movements to situate their actions as issues of planetary citizenship."[28] The WSF is a broad movement to re-embed markets socially. A spokesperson for the Living Democracy Movement, Vandana Shiva, claims,

> The philosophical and ethical bankruptcy of globalization was based on reducing every aspect of our lives to commodities and reducing our identities to [those] of mere consumers in the global marketplace. Our capacities as producers, our identity as members of communities, our role as custodians of our

natural and cultural heritage were all to disappear or be destroyed. Markets and consumerism expanded. Our capacity to give and share was to shrink. But the human spirit refuses to be subjugated by a world-view based on the dispensability of our humanity.[29]

The Latin Rebellion

The legitimacy crisis of neoliberal development has been most pronounced in Latin America, where a democratic revolution has swept the continent since the turn of the century. New presidents with social-democratic leanings have been elected in seven countries—Venezuela, Brazil, Argentina, Uruguay, Bolivia, Chile, and Ecuador—followed by the election of Sandinista leader Daniel Ortega in Nicaragua (Central America). More pragmatic and populist than ideological, these presidents share a social egalitarianism, drawing on the deepening frustration of poor and indigenous citizens with the deprivations of the globalization project.

After a quarter of a century of neoliberalism, three-quarters of Latin Americans remain poor, and social movements of women, labor, peasants, Indians, unemployed, and informals have mobilized against the privatization of basic resources (oil, gas, water) and public goods (hospitals, schools, transportation, pensions), low-wage labor, alienation of habitat, crippling foreign debt inherited from previous dictatorships, and the erosion of national sovereignty. Despite the difficulties of delinking from international financial structures, candidates from Mexico to Paraguay have positioned themselves electorally against the "free-market fundamentalism" of the Washington Consensus, and its proposal for a Free Trade Area of the Americas (FTAA). Controversial Venezuelan president Hugo Chávez, blessed (or cursed, as resource economists might say) with oil wealth, has poured billions of dollars into his "Bolivarian Revolution," expanding health care and education, subsidizing food and fuel, providing cash benefits for single mothers and low-interest loans for small businesses, and encouraging farm worker-owned cooperatives on ranches and sugar plantations seized by the state.[30] Venezuela's new constitution, passed by referendum and enacted in 2000, "guarantees all citizens the right to health and forbids the privatization of health services," representing the government's goal of remaking health care via social and participatory medicine. It invites Cuban doctors to treat, train, and dwell in working-class communities, which organize neighborhood local health committees to oversee clinic operations with government funds.[31] Integral to Chávez' "petro-populism," which is not anti-capitalist, is its social mobilization strategy:

To gain title to *barrio* homes built on squatted land, people must band together as neighbors and form land committees. Likewise, many public works require that people form cooperatives and then apply for a group contract. Cynics see these expanding networks of community organizations as nothing more than a clientelist electoral machine. Rank-and-file Chavistas call their movement "participatory democracy," and the revolution's intellectuals describe it as a long-term struggle against the cultural pathologies bred by all resource-rich economies—the famous "Dutch disease," in which the oil-rich state is expected to dole out services to a disorganized and unproductive population.[32]

To finance this revolution, Chávez instigated a new wave of "resource nationalism" in Latin America (parallel to Russian expropriation of foreign energy firms) in 2002, demanding that foreign oil companies enter into joint ventures, with the Venezuelan state holding at least 60 percent of the capital. Ecuador (expropriating Occidental Petroleum), Peru, and Bolivia followed, "where foreign companies, in particular the Brazilian Petrobras, accepted the nationalization of gas fields without a fight."[33] The drawback, at least in Venezuela, is that oil money has extended the "informal economy" into the state bureaucracy, where a parallel national development fund operates as an unaccountable source of patronage (Transparency International ranks Venezuela among the region's worst performers).[34] Nevertheless, the resource nationalism taps into a historic antipathy toward foreign control, with the populist dimension rooted deeply in indigenous suspicion of the "[European] white-settler elite that has dominated the continent for so many centuries."[35] Citing "looting by foreign companies," president Morales of Bolivia, Aymara Indian and former leader of the Bolivian *cocaleros*, declared, "This is just the start. Tomorrow or the day after it will be mining, then forestry and eventually all the natural resources for which our ancestors fought."[36]

While nationalist concerns drive electoral politics, the rebellion has a historic continental dimension. Drawing on the anti-colonial heritage of Simón Bolívar, (leader of nineteenth century independence movements in Venezuela, Colombia, Panama, Ecuador, Peru, and Bolivia), contemporary movements demand a second independence, from foreign corporations and banks, and U.S. military involvement across the continent. In 2004, at a meeting of the Americas' ministers of defense, 16 nations (led by Brazil) defeated a United States-backed Colombian proposal for an inter-American military force to intervene in any Latin American country—adding momentum to Venezuelan president Hugo Chávez's concept of a regional military bloc to defend national sovereignty against imperial intrusions. This was followed by the founding of the South American Community of Nations, akin to the EU, "without the corresponding wealth but with immense oil, water, mineral, and biodiversity resources. Together with the Caribbean Community (Caricom) and the Central American Common Market, this augured a possible alternative Latin American economic integration, with a single currency and independent of the United States."[37] A radical offshoot of this idea, hatched by Chávez and Cuban president Fidel Castro, is for an alternative regional economic bloc, named the Bolivarian Alternative for the Americas (ALBA), based on the concept of "cooperative advantage"—fostering mutual cultural and economic exchanges, such as cheap oil from Venezuela for Cuban doctors and teachers.

How these various initiatives evolve depends on the viability of the new governments—including strategic choices ranging from Venezuela's proposed "endogenous development" model, through Brazil and Argentina's neoliberalism with a human face, to the more radical grassroots experiments such as Brazil's "participatory budgeting" in cities such as Porto Alegre, and its landless-workers movement—and on the durability of the continental alliances. In addition to military and counter-intelligence pressure emanating from the United States (centered in the "drug war" in Colombia, where the Colombian military is financed by the United States to suppress coca production and protect the flow of oil from regions inhabited by the U'wa and other Indian populations), there is a geo-political struggle underway in the form of U.S. unilateral agreements (e.g., with Colombia and Peru) designed to undercut Latin regional alliances, and Chinese access to the continent's resources.[38]

The "Emerging Markets" of China and India

Alluding to a historical pendulum, Antoine van Agtmael in *The Emerging Markets Century* (2007) predicts that the Third World "will overtake the developed world by around 2030–35." He extrapolates from the powerhouse companies: Samsung of South Korea, Infosys of India, Haier of China, and Cemex of Mexico.[39] Whatever "overtaking" means, there is no doubt that the phenomenon of "Chindia" has the attention of the business community—whether as an investment opportunity or a threat to northern businesses or jobs. In the mid-1990s, one-third of U.S. jobs were estimated to be at risk due to the growing productivity of low-wage labor in China, India, Mexico, and Latin America.[40] By 2002, the UNDP noted the trends in GDP per capita: "China has moved from having one-twenty-first of the OECD average in 1975 to one-sixth in 2002 and India from one-fourteenth in 1980 to one-tenth today."[41]

In China, despite—and perhaps because of—its authoritarian socialist government, an economic revolution with global economic and ecological implications is underway. The average citizen now earns almost twice as much a year than the average Indian.[42] Factories spring up overnight in thousands of development zones, displacing rice paddies and farmlands, as foreign investors take advantage of relatively cheap unskilled labor provided by over a hundred million displaced peasants. China has been the final assembly station in commodity chains of TNCs, accounting for 60 percent of products manufactured in China.[43] Even though China controls 55 percent of the world market for laptop computers, and produces 30 percent of all flat-screen televisions and 20 percent of microprocessors, it essentially assembles components designed and made elsewhere, or uses copied designs.[44] The other 40 percent of manufactured products is constrained by the size of China's home market, given the historic low wage structure. But this model is in transition, as China faces a labor shortage. The reasons are complex, and include worker resistance to appalling conditions (reported on China Labor Watch's website), new lower-cost production sites in Vietnam, Bangladesh, and India, Chinese government investment in its hinterland as a policy shift in redistributing wealth regionally, and the legacy of China's historic "one child" policy.[45]

Meanwhile, in post-Shining India, "global manufacturers are already looking ahead to a serious demographic squeeze facing China. . . . India will have 116 million workers [aged 20 to 24 by 2020] to China's 94 million." While Indian infrastructure is still undeveloped (China invests seven times as much on roads, ports, electricity, and so on—though India is picking up the pace), the central government is pursuing an aggressive industrial park program in the "global/satellite cities" of Delhi, Mumbai, Kolkata, Hyderabad, and Chennai. TNCs like Renault-Nissan (joining forces with Mahindra & Mahindra of India), Ford, GM, Motorola, Hyundai and Posco of South Korea, and Mittal Steel of the Netherlands are transforming India from a service to a manufacturing center: manufactured exports to the United States are rising faster in percentage terms than those from China, and over two-thirds of foreign investment in the mid-2000s entered manufacturing.[46] India itself has emerged as the eleventh largest auto market in the world (China is the most dynamic), and local manufacturers such as Tata and Rajav compete with Renault to build low-cost models for the domestic market.[47] While two-thirds of Indians are still agrarian, India's rising middle class of some 300 million constitutes a sizeable consumer market. And this is symbolized by the supermarket revolution emerging in India. Hypercity, a Western-style supermarket opened in 2005 in the western suburbs of Mumbai, was India's first inroad into a retailing culture, 97 percent of which is located in small family-run shops. India held the global supermarkets at bay for a few years longer than China, which opened its doors in 2000 and now has half of the top 70 global retailers operating in its prosperous urban markets.[48] In late 2006, India's Reliance Industries

Limited opened its first wholly owned supermarket in Hyderabad, with the intention of beating Wal-Mart to the punch. But, for many Indians, this is not a cause for nationalist celebration: "at stake is the livelihood security of 12 million small shopkeepers, 40 million hawkers and at least 200 million (of the 600 million) small farmers".[49]

As a regional duo, China and India perhaps represent a counter-trend to the globalization project. While they have certainly positioned their labor forces in the global marketplace, they have not completely embraced neoliberal principles. During the 1997 Asian financial crisis, neither country melted, since they had capital and investment controls. China's currency is not freely convertible; the government still controls at least half of its industrial assets, and invests heavily in infrastructure, setting the pace for India.[50] Following the debacle of the neoliberal "Shining India" project in 2004, the new government refocused on an inclusive nationalism. While the West views the rise of China as a threat (in the short run to jobs, in the long run to geopolitical power), it is unclear what the future holds. In 2004, Beijing enunciated a New Security Concept eschewing hegemonism. At present, it is focused on securing resource supplies from various world regions. And, within Asia, these two powers are building a mutual relationship based in growing, and relatively equal, flows of capital and goods. China is India's second-largest trading partner.[51] More broadly, China is now central to regional integrating trends:

> In 2001, the Chinese authorities launched regional free trade areas with South and North East Asia, to be complete by 2010 . . . regional Asian trade with China has been growing far faster than Asian trade with the U.S. Japan's imports from China already exceed those from the U.S. and Japanese exports to China have been steadily rising. . . . These trends imply that we are seeing the first steps in the construction of a Chinese regional political economy.[52]

The nationalist turn in China and India is also a social and ecological imperative. Agrarian populations predominate in both countries, and rural unrest registers routinely. The rural backlash against neoliberalism was significant, if not decisive, in the 2004 elections on "Shining India." In 2007, the Indian central government suspended all land acquisition for establishing new SEZs and industrial parks pursuant to establishing a policy on rehabilitating displaced people. This followed pitched battles between the (communist) West Bengal government and peasants over plans to acquire 140,000 acres of land for SEZs to be developed by the Tata business group and Indonesia's Salim Group on the outskirts of Kolkata.[53] In China, land seizures by the government, in the name of development, generate ongoing rural resistance.

Meanwhile, intensive agriculture has accelerated. Chinese soils are deteriorating from reduced crop rotation, erosion, overfertilization, and the loss of organic content of soils once nourished by manure-based farming. More than 2,000 square kilometers of land turn to desert annually.[54] Millions of Chinese farmers have abandoned farming to circulate as a highly exploited reserve army of cheap labor, and analysts predict a global grain crisis, as China's food dependency grows.[55] In the book *Will the Boat Sink the Water? The Life of China's Peasants*, banned in China, the authors describe

> the vicious circle that ensnares the peasants of China, where unjust taxes and arbitrary actions—or total inaction—sometimes lead to extreme violence against the peasants. . . . In the last analysis the Triple Agri [*San-Nong*: the problem of agriculture, the problem of the rural areas, and the problem of the peasant] is nothing less than the problem of China. Not exclusively an agricultural issue or an economic one, it is the greatest problem facing the ruling party of China today. The problem is staring us in the face.[56]

In the face of these fundamental questions of stabilizing socioeconomic transformation on such a large scale, commentators note that a trend towards "social capitalism" is underway in China, which holds that "while capitalism is good, it must go hand-in-hand with social policy."[57] Analogous to Indian Prime Minister Singh's "Economic growth is not an end in itself. . . . [The direction] is equality and social justice," the forces shaping the future trajectories of China and India echo those in Latin America—suggesting that neoliberalism is in decline.[58]

A new conception of development is in the works, but hardly coherent. It will be driven by the "ecological climacteric," complicated in the meantime by unilateralist policies of the powerful states as they jockey to secure resources to sustain the current (questionable) identification of development with consumption.

The Ecological Climacteric

Development is at an important crossroads as the twenty-first century unfolds. Certainly, the top decile of the population of the global South has joined the world's affluent segment. But liberalization turns back the clock and intensifies the exploitation of Southern resources (including labor) to feed the insatiable appetites of a global consumer class, buoyed by easy credit from a deregulated financial system. Massive population displacements are accompanied by the elimination of staple foods for near-subsistence dwellers who constitute the majority of the world's population. This is capitalist development, but is it human development? And is it sustainable?

We face astounding problems as we deplete our physical environment. In the United States, 1 million acres disappear annually to urban-industrial development, and 2 million acres of farmland are lost annually to erosion, soil salinization, and flooding or soil saturation by intensive agriculture, which consumes groundwater 160 percent faster than it can be replenished. This encourages more offshore agriculture and food miles (but also relocalization of food markets). Meanwhile, the world has crossed the threshold to declining rates of agricultural productivity, 80 countries already experience serious water shortages, more than 1 billion people lack adequate access to clean water, and by 2025, two-thirds of the world's people will face water stress.[59]

Another cumulative scenario is the unpredictability associated with global environmental changes. The United Nations (UN) World Commission on Environment and Development has noted that "major, unintended changes are occurring in the atmosphere, in soils, in waters, among plants and animals, and in relationships among these. . . . The rate of change is outstripping the ability of scientific disciplines and our capabilities to assess and advise." These changes foretell threats to global public health arising from "planetary overload, entailing circumstances that are qualitatively different from the familiar, localized problem of environmental pollution"—threats such as immune suppression from ultraviolet radiation, indirect health consequences of climate change on food production and the spread of infections, and loss of biological and genetic resources for producing medicines.[60]

Global resources are disproportionately controlled and consumed by a small minority of the world's population, residing mainly in the First World. Northern nations account for 75 percent of the world's energy use and have produced two-thirds of the greenhouse gases altering the earth's climate. Since 1950, the world's population has consumed as many goods and services, and the U.S. population has used as many mineral resources as were consumed by all previous generations of people.[61] In short, the practice of development has brought us up sharply against growing environmental, resource, and health limits. It is too early to know whether humans are the ultimate "endangered species."

Under these conditions, a global "moral political-economy" is emerging under "hothouse conditions," so to speak. Claims for moral authority derive from constituents of "civil society" concerned with sustainability, including the trend towards "green capitalism." But reorganizing supply chains to

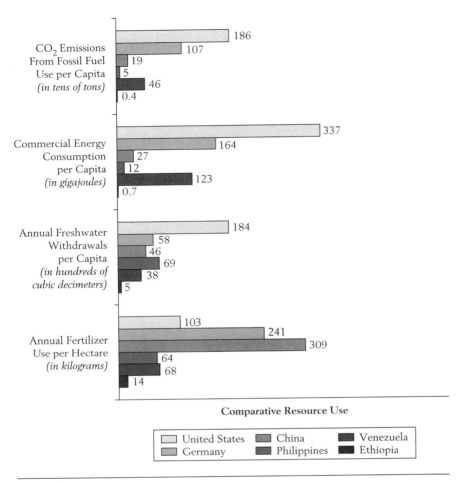

Figure 9.2   Resource Use in Selected Countries

Source: World Resource Institute (1998).

satisfy ethical and green concerns may not necessarily resolve social and ecological "externalities" on a global scale. Adjustments may not address the crisis of displacement, or growing food insecurity, without a coordinated reorientation of the global (food) system. Agrofuels is the new mantra, and Europe is already looking to Africa's land for its energy needs. Further, "High oil prices have also fueled the replacement of tropical forests with fields of grain and sugar cane. The most promising source of ethanol to fuel a new fleet of cleaner cars is Brazilian sugar cane, whose expanded production is pushing soy fields into the Amazon."[62] The same is true for palm oil which, once a food, is now replacing the rainforests of Indonesia and

Malaysia at an alarming rate (98 percent gone by 2022) as the new "green fuel."[63] Managing carbon reduction in this way reorients some agriculture to non-food crop production. In the South, in addition to failing to address (land) hunger, it has negative effects on the environment. Questions about the energy-intensive nature of agrofuel agriculture complicate this scenario.[64] How these contradictory developments may be resolved politically is an open question, but they are returning us to the centrality of ecology.

The "ecological climacteric" includes the social catastrophe of slumd-welling, related to the more general possibility of what archaeologists call "demographic collapse," precipitated by agro-industrialization.[65] New multi-lateral arrangements are necessary to address welfare and equity concerns across the world. Short-term cycles of redistribution of land and access to food might stabilize the conditions for basic social reproduction of the majority of the world's population. The path trodden by corporate agriculture, deepening food circuits, and offshore manufacturing subcontracting is inevitably inter-weaving social and environmental justice concerns—as populations lose more habitat and access to food and water, and are confronted with questions of health and labor rights. Intensified political mobilizations and relentless images and experiences of environmental and economic refugees may, in the short run, promote protectionism and ethnic nationalism, but in the longer run a collective survival ethic will be necessary to preserve human life on this planet. At present, world debate pivots on the adequacy of the market as a guardian of social and environmental sustainability. But this is a prelude to a broader, historical set of questions concerning the scale of human community and governance, as well as the basic contradiction between material affluence and survival of the human species. Development, once identified as "high mass consumption" within a framework of rule, has the opportunity now to adopt an ethical dimension, within a framework of necessity.

Further Reading

Economy, Elizabeth C. *The River Runs Black: The Environmental Challenge to China's Future*. Ithaca, NY: Cornell University Press, 2004.

Farmer, Paul. *Pathologies of Power: Health, Human Rights, and the New War on the Poor*. Berkeley: University of California Press, 2005.

Monbiot, George. *Heat: How to Stop the Planet Burning*. London: Allen Lane, 2006.

Pretty, Jules. *The Earth Only Endures: On Reconnecting With Nature and Our Place in It*. London: Earthscan, 2007.

Roberts, Timmons J. and Bradley C. Parks. *A Climate of Injustice: Global Inequality, North-South Politics, and Climate Policy*. Cambridge, MA: MIT Press, 2007.

Wallerstein, Immanuel. *The Decline of American Power*. New York: The New Press, 2003.

Notes

Chapter 1: Development and Globalization: Framing Issues

1. Crossette (1997).
2. Galeano (2000:25).
3. Norberg-Hodge (1992:95, 97– 98).
4. Roberts and Park (2007:9).
5. Monbiot (2006:15, 21).
6. Monbiot (2006:21).
7. Roberts and Parks (2007:9–10); Borger (2007:22).
8. Monbiot (2006:22).
9. Monbiot (2006:9).
10. Quoted in Yardley (2007:A9).
11. Yardley (2007:A9).
12. Monbiot (2006:51).
13. Ruggiero (1996).
14. Barlow (1999); Clarke (2001); Elyachar (2005); Hochschild (2003).
15. McMurtry (2002).
16. http://wikipedia.org/wiki/ Coltan.
17. Lang and Heasman (2004:240–41).
18. Lang and Heasman (2004:240).
19. Lang and Heasman (2004:241).
20. Radford (2005:12).
21. Hickman (2006:2).
22. Vidal (2006:13).
23. McMurtry (2002:221).
24. World Institute for Development Economics Research (2006).
25. Nancy Birdsall, quoted in David Rothkopf (2005).
26. Reardon and Timmer (2005:35–37).
27. Collins (1995).
28. Gupta (1998:309).
29. Cf, Barnet and Cavanagh (1994:383).
30. Rifkin (1992:147); French (2004:148).
31. Rohter (2003:3); Hall (2003).
32. Nepstad (2006).
33. Matthews (2006).
34. As Frances Moore Lappé pointed out in her *Diet for a Small Planet* a quarter of a century ago, the mass production of animal protein is an inefficient *and* inequitable use of world grain supplies, using seven times the amount of grain for livestock feed rather than human food.
35. Kimbrell (2002:16).
36. Millstone and Lang (2003:38).
37. Davis (2005:107–08).
38. World Institute for Development Economics Research (2006).
39. Hamilton (2003:24).
40. Hamilton (2003:28–30).
41. Gardner et al. (2004:18).
42. Brooks (2007:6).
43. Kennedy et al (2004:14).
44. Hamilton (2003:56–58).
45. Hamilton (2003:58–60).
46. Hamilton (2003:206).
47. LaTouche (2004:15).
48. *UNDP Human Development Report*, quoted in Rist (1997:9).
49. Quoted in Saul (2005:157).

Chapter 2: Instituting the Development Project

1. Cowan and Shenton (1996).
2. Mitchell (1991:68–75, 96).

3. Davidson (1992:83, 99–101).
4. Quoted in Rist (1997:58).
5. Bunker (1985).
6. Gupta (1998:309).
7. Friedmann (1999:39).
8. Bujra (1992:146).
9. Quoted in Stavrianos (1981:247).
10. Ali (2002:168).
11. Chirot (1977:124).
12. Davis (2001:26, 299, 315).
13. Davis (2001:327).
14. Davis (2001:328–29).
15. Davis (2001:332–35).
16. Wolf (1982:369, 377).
17. Mitchell (1991:175).
18. Cooper and Stoler (1997).
19. James (1963).
20. Memmi (1967:74).
21. Fanon (1967:254–55).
22. F. Cooper (1997:66–67).
23. Stavrianos (1981:624).
24. Quoted in Clarke and Barlow (1997:9).
25. Duncan (1996:120).
26. Adams (1993:2–3, 6–7).
27. Quoted in Esteva (1992:6).
28. Quoted in Davidson (1992:167).
29. Esteva (1992:7).
30. Rist (1997:79).
31. Ake (1996:36).
32. Cited in F. Cooper (1997:79).
33. Rostow (1960).
34. Sachs (1999:9).
35. Quoted in Hettne (1990:3).
36. Quoted in Dube (1988:16).
37. Bose (1997:153).
38. Lehman (1990:5–6).
39. Lehman (1990:5–6).
40. Kemp (1989:162–65).
41. Cardoso and Faletto (1979:129–31).

Chapter 3: The Development Project: International Relations

1. Block (1977:76–77).
2. Quoted in Brett (1985:106–07).
3. Quoted in Kolko (1988:17).
4. Wood (1986:38–61).
5. Magdoff (1969:124).
6. Rich (1994:72).
7. Woods (2006:207).
8. Rich (1994:58); George and Sabelli (1994:15).
9. Rich (1994:73).
10. Rich (1994:75).
11. Adams (1993:68–69).
12. Quoted in Magdoff (1969:54).
13. Magdoff (1969:124); Chirot (1977:164–65).
14. Quoted in Williams (1981:6–57).
15. Brett (1985:209); Wood (1986:73); Rist (1997:88).
16. Brett (1985:209); Wood (1986:73).
17. Adams (1993:73).
18. Rich (1994:84).
19. Harris (1987:28).
20. The term *newly industrializing countries* (NICs) was coined by the Organisation for Economic Co-operation and Development in 1979 and included four southern European countries: Spain, Portugal, Yugoslavia, and Greece. The common attributes of NICs were: rapid penetration of the world market with manufactured exports; a rising share of industrial employment; and an increase in real gross domestic product per capita relative to the First World. See Hoogvelt (1987:25).
21. Brett (1985:185–86).
22. Brett (1985:188).
23. Knox and Agnew (1994:347).
24. Hoogvelt (1987:64).
25. Knox and Agnew (1994:331). (Between 1975 and 1989, this group enlarged to include China, South Africa, Thailand, and Taiwan; Argentina dropped out.)
26. Martin and Schumann (1997:100–01).
27. Quoted in Brett (1985:188).
28. Harris (1987:102).
29. Grigg (1993:251).
30. Revel and Riboud (1986:43–44).
31. Grigg (1993:243–44); Bradley and Carter (1989:104). Self-sufficiency measures do not necessarily reveal the state of nutrition in a country or region, as a country—for example, Japan—may have a low self-sufficiency because its population eats an affluent diet, which depends on imports.
32. Friedmann (1982).

33. Quoted in Magdoff (1969:135).
34. Dudley and Sandilands (1975).
35. Friedmann (1990:20).
36. Perkins (1997).
37. Quoted in George (1977:170).
38. Friedmann (1990:20);
H. Friedmann (1992:373).
39. McMichael and Raynolds (1994:322). The terms *peasant foods* and *wage foods* are from de Janvry (1981).
40. Segelken (1995:5).
41. Quoted in Briscoe (2002:182–83).
42. Rifkin (1992:229–30).
43. Wessel (1983:158).
44. Berlan (1991:126–27); see also Dixon (2002).
45. Kimbrell (2002:16).
46. Burbach and Flynn (1980:66); George (1977:171).
47. Quoted in George (1977:171–72).
48. H. Friedmann (1992:377).
49. Gupta (1998:53, 58–59).
50. Kloppenburg (1988:xiv).
51. Gupta (1998:54); Busch and Lacy (1983).
52. Gupta (1998:54–56).
53. Patnaik (2003:13).
54. Quoted in Gupta (1998:50).
55. Quoted in Patel (2007:146–47).
56. Cleaver (1977:17); Walker (2004:185).
57. Cleaver (1977:28).
58. Vandana Shiva, quoted in Newman (2006:2).
59. Quoted in Gupta (1998:4).
60. Shiva (1997:50–51); Barndt (2002:38–39).
61. Newman (2006:1).
62. Dalrymple (1985:1069); Andrae and Beckman (1985); Raikes (1988).
63. George (1977:174–75).
64. Griffin (1974); Pearse (1980); Byres (1981); Sanderson (1986a); Dhanagare (1988); Raikes (1988); Llambi (1990).
65. Lipton (1977).
66. McMichael and Kim (1994); Araghi (1995).
67. Grigg (1993:103–04, 185); Araghi (1995).
68. DeereLeon (2001:332).
69. Rich (1994:95, 155).
70. Rich (1994:91, 97); Feder (1983:222).
71. Davis (2006).

Chapter 4: Globalizing National Economy

1. Arrighi (1994:68).
2. Gereffi (1989).
3. Cf. Evans (1995).
4. Cf. Barndt (2002).
5. Hoogvelt (1987:26–31). At the same time, as a consequence of import-substitution industrialization and the buoyancy of the export-oriented industrialization strategy in the 1970s, the composition of imports mainly from the First World moved from manufactured consumer goods to capital goods.
6. Landsberg (1979:52, 54).
7. See Gereffi (1994).
8. Quoted in Baird and McCaughan (1979:130).
9. Baird and McCaughan (1979:130–32); Bernard (1996). For an excellent and detailed study of the *maquiladora* industry, see Sklair (1989).
10. French (2000:83–85).
11. Henderson (1991:3).
12. Barnet and Cavanagh (1994:300); Dicken (1998:131); Ellwood (2001:68).
13. Fuentes and Ehrenreich (1983).
14. Fuentes and Ehrenreich (1983).
15. Elson and Pearson (1981:91).
16. On the gendered restructuring of the world labor force, see Mies (1991); Benería and Feldman (1992).
17. Perrons (2005:100); Baird and McCaughan (1979); *Instituto Nacional de Estadistica Geografia d informatica* (2004).
18. Perrons (2005:100).
19. Baird and McCaughan (1979:135–36).
20. Grossman (1979).
21. Baird and McCaughan (1979:135).
22. Hobsbawm (1992:56); Araghi (1999).
23. Davis (2006).
24. *Pacific Basin Reports* (August 1973:171).

25. Fröbel, Heinrichs, and Kreye (1979:34–36).
26. Henderson (1991:54).
27. Korzeniewicz (1994:261).
28. Henderson (1991).
29. *The Economist* (June 3, 1995:59); "Slavery in the 21st Century" (2001:8).
30. Moody (1999:183, 188).
31. Lang and Hines (1993:24); Holusha (1996).
32. Woodall (1994:24); Martin and Schumann (1997:100–01).
33. Milbank (1994:A1, A6).
34. Cited in Lewin (1995:A5).
35. *The Nation* (November 8, 1993:3).
36. Sanderson (1986b); Raynolds et al. (1993); Raynolds (1994).
37. DeWalt (1985).
38. Sanderson (1986b).
39. Friedland (1994).
40. Friedmann (1991).
41. P. McMichael (1993a).
42. Watts (1994:52–53).
43. Goss et al. (2000).
44. *The Economist* (June 3, 1995:59).
45. Schoenberger (1994:59).
46. Quoted in Appelbaum and Gereffi (1994:54).
47. Daly and Logan (1989:13); Schoenberger (1994:59–61); Chossudovsky (1997:87–88); Herbert (1996).
48. Templin (1994:A10); Meredith (1997).
49. Crook (1993:16).
50. Hayden (2003).
51. Uchitelle (1994:D2); Barboza (1999).

Chapter 5: Demise of the Third World

1. Hoogvelt (1987:58).
2. Berger (2004).
3. Pilger (2002:25).
4. Pilger (2002:28).
5. Pilger (2002:26–39).
6. Quoted in Magdoff (1969:53).
7. Berger (2004).
8. George (1988:6).
9. Amin (1997:28).
10. Quoted in Wood (1986:197).
11. Quoted in Adams (1993:123).
12. Hoogvelt (1987:80–87).
13. Rist (1997:152–53).
14. Schaeffer (1997:49); Helleiner (1996:171–75).
15. Hoogvelt (1987:87–95).
16. Strange (1994:112).
17. Crook (1992:10).
18. Helleiner (1996:111–19).
19. Strange (1994:107).
20. Quoted in Brecher and Costello (1994:30).
21. *The New Internationalist* (August 1993:18); Kolko (1988:24).
22. *Debt Crisis Network* (1986:25).
23. Kolko (1988:26).
24. Roodman (2001:21).
25. George (1988:33).
26. Lissakers (1993:66).
27. Roodman (2001:26).
28. Lissakers (1993:59).
29. Lissakers (1993:56).
30. Lissakers (1993:69–73).
31. Wood (1986:247, 253, 255); Evans (1979).
32. George (1988:6).
33. Walton and Seddon (1994:13–14).
34. George (1988:28–29).
35. Lissakers (1993:67).
36. A. Singh (1992:141).
37. A. Singh (1992:144).
38. George (1988:60).
39. Quoted in Roodman (2001:30).
40. Economic Commission for Latin America and the Caribbean (1989:123).
41. Barkin (1990:104–05).
42. Quoted in Helleiner (1996:177).
43. George (1988:41, 49).
44. Quoted in Roodman (2001:35).
45. Kohl and Farthing (2006:62, 72); Graham (1994); Beneria (2003:55).
46. de la Rocha (1994:270–71).
47. Barkin (1990:101, 103).
48. de la Rocha (1994:270–71).
49. George (1988:139, 143).
50. Cheru (1989:24, 27–28, 41–42).
51. Cheru (1989:24, 27–28, 41–42); Redding (2000).
52. Rich (1994:186–87).
53. A. Singh (1992:138–39, 147–48).
54. Bello et al. (1994).
55. George (1992:xvi).
56. George (1992:97).

57. Cox (1987:301).
58. Calculated from Crook (1993:16); Avery (1994:95); Hoogvelt (1997:138).
59. George (1988:97).
60. Crook (1992:9).
61. Crook (1993:16).
62. Arrighi (1990); Khor, quoted in Danaher and Yunus (1994:28).
63. Salinger and Dethier (1989); McMichael and Myhre (1991); Myhre (1994); Barry (1995:36, 43–44, 144).
64. Bangura and Gibbon (1992:19); World Bank (1981).
65. Gibbon (1992:137); Bernstein (1990:17).
66. Beckman (1992:99).
67. Gibbon (1992:141).
68. Stephany Griffith-Jones, quoted in Crook (1991:19).
69. Sachs (1998:17).

Chapter 6: Instituting the Globalization Project

1. Quoted in Saul (2005:209).
2. Ruggiero (2000:xiii, xv).
3. Quoted in Bello et al. (1994:72).
4. Kolko (1988:271–72).
5. The South Centre (1993:13).
6. Gore (2000).
7. Cahn (1993:161, 163); Rich (1994); Corbridge (1993:127).
8. Ricardo (1951).
9. Noreena Hertz, quoted in Collins (2007:179).
10. Barnet and Cavanagh (1994:236).
11. Klare (2002:14–17).
12. George (1992:11).
13. Nash (1994:C4): Bello et al. (1994:59).
14. Rich (1994:188).
15. Quoted in Bello et al. (1994:63).
16. Rich (1994:188).
17. Denny (2002:6).
18. Rohter (2002:A9); Vidal (2001:20).
19. Phillips (2007).
20. Hathaway (1987:40–41); World Bank (2000:14, 25).
21. Black (2002:62).
22. Clarke and Barlow (1997:12–13).
23. McMichael (1993b).

24. Adams (1993:196–197).
25. Middleton et al. (1993:127–129).
26. Quoted in Watkins (1991:44).
27. Quoted in Ritchie (1993:n. 25).
28. See Raghavan (1990).
29. Wallach and Sforza (1999:x).
30. Quoted in Ransom (2001a:27).
31. Quoted in Wallach and Woodall (2004:219).
32. Quoted in Wallach and Sforza (1999:x).
33. Tabb (2000:9).
34. Ritchie (1999).
35. Lehman and Krebs (1996); Gorelick (2000:28–30); Madeley (2000:75); Carlsen (2003).
36. McMichael (2005).
37. LeQuesne (1997).
38. Quoted in Bailey (2000); Murphy (1999:3).
39. Quoted in Madeley (2000:79).
40. Madeley (2000:54–55).
41. Salmon (2001:22).
42. Clarke and Barlow (1997:21).
43. Quoted in Schott (2000:237).
44. Moran (2000:235).
45. Moran (2000:224–26).
46. Moran (2000:231–32).
47. Dawkins (2000).
48. Tuxill (1999).
49. ActionAid (2000:2).
50. Madden and Madeley (1993:17).
51. Quoted in Weissman (1991:337).
52. Greenfield (1999).
53. Pollack (1999).
54. Juhasz (2002).
55. Clarke (2001).
56. Clarke (2001).
57. Wallach (2003).
58. Watkins (2002:21).
59. Juhasz (2002).
60. Ohmae (1985:xvi–xvii).
61. Baer (1991:132).
62. Baer (1991:146).
63. Goldsmith (1994:66, 67, 77).
64. Moody (1999:125–26, 181).
65. Woods (2006:164).
66. Woods (2006:168).
67. Wolfensohn (2000).
68. Narayan et al. (2002); Rademacher and Patel (2002).
69. Woods (2006:168).
70. Fraser (2005:317).

71. Fraser (2005:318).
72. Quoted in Weber (2004:197).
73. Harrison (2004).
74. Weber (2004:197).
75. Ferguson (2006:102–3).
76. Quoted in Fraser (2005:336).
77. Fraser (2005:319); Woods (2006:171).
78. Goldman (2005:229–30).
79. Abrahamsen (2004:186).
80. Fraser (2005:332).
81. Abrahamsen (2004:185).
82. Cameron and Palan (2004:148).
83. Elyachar (2005).
84. See www.uncdf.org.

Chapter 7: The Globalization Project in Practice

1. United Nations Development Program (1997).
2. Quoted in Saul (2005:157).
3. Wallach and Woodall (2004:113–14).
4. Bond (2006:82–83).
5. Diokno-Pascual (2003).
6. Iriart and Waitzkin (2004).
7. Perrons (2005:89).
8. Perrons (2005:169).
9. Robinson (2004:18).
10. Woodall (1994:24); Martin and Schumann (1997:100–01); Thompson (2005).
11. Friedman (2000:52); Greenlees (2006).
12. Caulkin (2007).
13. Harding (2001:23).
14. Tripathi (2004); Leader (2004); Müller and Patel (2004).
15. Davis (2006:172).
16. Watkins (2006).
17. Leader (2004).
18. Ainger (2003:25–26).
19. Bunsha (2006).
20. Chan (1996).
21. Barboza (2004:C3).
22. Eyferth and Vermeer (2003).
23. Green (2003).
24. Reardon et al. (2003).
25. Dugger (2004).
26. Busch and Bain (2004).
27. Bogdanich and Hooker (2007).
28. Dolan and Humphrey (2000:167).
29. Dolan (2004).
30. Marsden (2003:30, 57).
31. Marsden (2003:56).
32. Saul (2005:146).
33. Davis (2006:169, 199).
34. ActionAid (2005:11).
35. Parrott and Marsden (2002:5, 62).
36. Quoted in Lynas (2001).
37. Vía Campesina (2000).
38. Carlsen (2006).
39. Quoted in Madeley (2000:81).
40. Chossudovsky (2003).
41. Paringaux (2001:4).
42. LeQuesne (1997); Murphy (1999:3); Lappé et al. (1998:8–11); Patel and Delwiche (2002a:2); Waldman (2002:3).
43. Attali (1991:5, 14).
44. Richburg (2002:29).
45. Perlez (2002:10).
46. Hochschild (2003).
47. Enzenburger (1994:112); www.unfpa.org/modules/factsheets/emergencies_overview .htm.
48. Montalbano (1991:H7); Graw (1999); Ride (1998:9).
49. Montalbano (1991:F1); Sengupta (2002:3); Thompson (2002b:A3); World Bank Press Release No:2003/266/S.
50. Thompson (2002b:A3); Perlez (2002:10); *The Economist* (February 23, 2002:42).
51. Tan (1991a).
52. Ball (1990).
53. Tan (1991b).
54. MacShane (1991).
55. Andreas (1994:52).
56. Quoted in Perrons (2005:220).
57. Dawson (2006:135); Uchitelle (2007).
58. Sadasivam (1997:636).
59. McDougall (2007).
60. Davis (2006:23); Vidal (2004:18).
61. Davis (2006:1–2).
62. Reich (1991:42).
63. Boyd (2006:491, 495, 497).

64. Harvey (2005:127). Boyd (2006:493–94).
65. Chen and Wu (2006:205).
66. ActionAid (2004:35–36, 40).
67. de Soto (1990:11).
68. Cameron and Palan (2004:147–51).
69. Sharma (2000:78–79).
70. Menon (2007).
71. Cheru (1989:8, 19).
72. LaTouche (1993:130).
73. de la Rocha (1994).
74. Esteva (1992:21).
75. Rankin (2001:32).
76. Elyachar (2005:188–89).
77. Quoted in Davis (2006:184).
78. Davis (2006:190).
79. Giridharadas (2007:3).
80. Davis (2006:200–01).
81. Lang and Hines (1993:84); Hoogvelt (1997:129).
82. Polgreen (2007:4).
83. Ferguson (2006:38–39); Swift (2002:120–21).
84. Ferguson (2006:41, 12, 101).
85. Ferguson (2006:198–99).
86. Ferguson (2006:204).
87. Blair quoted in Ferguson (2006:2); Arrighi (2002).
88. Berthelot (2005:10).
89. Arrighi (2002:5).
90. Quoted in Patel (2002b).
91. Crossette (1998c:1).
92. Gevisser (2001:5–6); Perlez (2001:A1); Altman (2002:A12); Ayittey (2002).
93. Hawkins (1998:I); *The Economist* (June 26, 1999:23–25).
94. Bond (2006:39, 42, 51, 106).
95. French (1997:A3).
96. Patel (2002b).
97. Bond (2002).
98. Quoted in Bond (2002).
99. Ndulo (2002:9).
100. Davidson (1992:206, 257).
101. Bond (2001:53); Mamdani (2003).
102. Mamdani (1996:17–20).
103. World Bank (1989:5).
104. Bond (2006:58).
105. Ferguson (2006:194).
106. Harvey (2005:139); Watts (2005–06:36).

107. Elliott (2007:23).
108. McGreal (2006–07:6).
109. McGreal (2006–07:6); Muchena (2006:23).
110. Quoted in Muchena (2006:23).
111. McGreal (2006–07:6).
112. Muchena (2006–07:24).
113. Bond (2006:60).
114. Muchena (2006–07:24–25).
115. Quoted in Elliott (2007:23).
116. Bond (2006:74); Turner (2007).
117. Bodeen (2007:8A).
118. Renner (2002:10).
119. Fisher and Onishi (1999:A1, A9); French (1997:A1).
120. Renner (2002:18).

Chapter 8: Global Development and Its Countermovements

1. Perrons (2005:276).
2. Ali (2002:256).
3. Huntington (1993).
4. Ali (2002:275).
5. Onishi (2001:A14).
6. Onishi (2001:A14).
7. Quoted in Onishi (2001:A14).
8. Onishi (2001:A14).
9. Roy (1998:52); Smith (2002:30).
10. Ibrahim (1994:A1, A10).
11. Cowell (1994:A14).
12. Woollacott (2002:14).
13. Maass (2001:50).
14. A. J. McMichael (1993:51); Carson (1962).
15. Harrison (1993:54).
16. See A. J. McMichael (1993).
17. Quoted in Abramovitz (1999:12).
18. Abramovitz (1999:18–19).
19. Amin et al. (1990).
20. Stewart (1994:108–09).
21. Kothari and Parajuli (1993:233).
22. Quoted in Rich (1994:197).
23. Quoted in Middleton et al. (1993:19).
24. Agarwal and Nurain, cited in Rich (1994:262).
25. Quoted in J. Friedmann (1992:123).

26. Rich (1994:244–45).
27. Middleton et al. (1993:25).
28. Tautz (1997); Menotti (1998:352–362; 1999:181).
29. Quoted in Roberts and Bradley (2007:11).
30. Roberts and Bradley (2007:219).
31. Hildyard (1993:32–34).
32. Chossudovsky (1997:187–88).
33. Colchester (1994:71–72).
34. Quoted in Colchester (1994:72).
35. Rich (1994:160–165).
36. Quoted in Colchester (1994:78).
37. Colchester (1994:83, 88).
38. Lohmann (1993:10).
39. Quoted in Colchester (1994:89).
40. Rau (1991:156–157, 160).
41. Quoted in George and Sabelli (1994:170).
42. Van der Gaag (2004:15).
43. Gita Sen, quoted in Moghadam (2005a:103).
44. Quoted Moghadam (2005a:73).
45. Quoted in Moghadam (2005a:75–76).
46. Harcourt (1994:4).
47. Jahan (1995:13).
48. Razavi and Miller (1995:3).
49. Quoted in Razavi and Miller (1995:10).
50. Razavi and Miller (1995).
51. Sadasivam (1997:647–8).
52. Moghadam (2005a:14–17, 95).
53. Quoted in Moghadam (2005a:108).
54. Elson (1993:241).
55. Sadasivam (1997:636).
56. Quoted in Moghadam (2005a:112).
57. Harcourt (1994).
58. Sachs (2005:11–12).
59. Enloe (2004:59–60).
60. Fussell (2000).
61. Benería (2003:126).
62. Collins (2003:164–165).
63. Jackson (1993:1949).
64. Rocheleau (1991).
65. Abramovitz (1994:201).
66. Wacker (1994:135–139).
67. Boyd (1998).
68. "Battle of the Bulge" (1994:25).
69. Robey et al., quoted in Stevens (1994:A8).
70. Chira (1994:A12).
71. Quoted in Crossette (1994:A8).
72. Bello (1992–93:5).
73. Sen (1994:221).
74. Quoted in Hedges (1994:A10).
75. Benería (1992).
76. Quoted in Jahan (1995:77).
77. Quoted in Jahan (1995:109).
78. Quoted in Jahan (1995:109).
79. Walby (2005:371).
80. Moghadam et al. (2005b:401), emphasis added.
81. Simons (1999:A1, A6); Moghadam (1993).
82. Coomaraswamy (2001).
83. Crossette (1998a:A14).
84. Moghadam (2005b:203).
85. Held (1995).
86. Sachs (1992a:112).
87. Held (1995).
88. Fox (1994).
89. Communiqués No. 1, 22, quoted in AVA 42, 31 (1994:1).
90. Harvey (1994:14).
91. Mittal (1998:101); Carlsen (2003).
92. Hernández (1994:51); Harvey (1994:20).
93. Harvey (1994:36–37); Fox (1994:18).
94. Eber (1999:16).
95. Cleaver (1994:154–155); Swords (2007).
96. "Food and Farming" (2003:20); Ainger (2003:10–11) (Wiebe quote).
97. Desmarais (2007:6–17).
98. http://ns.rds.org.hn/via/theme.bio diversity.htm.
99. Quoted in Ainger (2003:11).
100. http://ns.rds.org.hn/via (Seattle Declaration, December 3, 1999).
101. http://ns.rds.org.hn/via/ themeagrarian.htm.
102. www.mstbrazil.org/Economic Model.html.
103. Article 184, quoted in Lappé and Lappé (2002:70).
104. Flavio de Almeida and Sanchez (2000).
105. Quoted in Dias Martins (2000).
106. Lappé and Lappé (2002:86–87).
107. Quoted in Orlanda Pinnasi et al. (2000).
108. Mark (2001).

Chapter 9: Development for What?

1. United Nations Development Report (1997).
2. Quoted in Saldaña-Portillo (2003:24) [emphasis added]
3. Li (1999:300).
4. Li (1999:305).
5. Escobar (1995).
6. Sachs (1992b).
7. Mosse (2004:649–50, 662).
8. Baviskar (2005).
9. Klenk (1999:61, 76).
10. Wittman (2005).
11. Sachs (2005:26).
12. Wolfensohn (2000).
13. DaCosta and McMichael (2007).
14. Cammack (2002:125).
15. Plehwe (2007); see also Goldman (2005); Narayan el al. (2002).
16. Soederberg (2006).
17. Elyachar (2005:29).
18. Menon (2001); Rankin (2001); Elyachar (2005)
19. Wolfensohn (2000).
20. Noble (2007).
21. Monbiot (2006:46).
22. Gereffi et al. (2001).
23. Seidman (2005).
24. Finch (2006:2).
25. The Observer, September 10 2006.
26. Woods (2006:165).
27. New Internationalist (2007:10).
28. World Social Forum (2003:355–57).
29. Shiva (2003:115).
30. Eviatar (2006:5).
31. Maybarduk (2004).
32. Parenti (2005:17).
33. Séréni (2007:12).
34. Paranagua (2007:27).
35. Gott (2006:33).
36. Glaister (2006:1).
37. Cockroft (2005).
38. Cockroft (2005); Renner (2002:38); Burbach (2006:6).
39. Kotkin (2007:4).
40. Uchitelle (1993); Chase (1995:16).
41. Perrons (2005:37).
42. Bradsher (2002:A1, A8).
43. Bobin (2006:17).
44. Bulard (2006:6).
45. Barboza (2006:1); Rocca (2007:10); Harvey (2005:148–149).
46. Bradsher (2006).
47. Gow (2007).
48. Ramesh (2006).
49. Sharma (2007).
50. Saul (2005:205).
51. Saul (2005:209).
52. Golub (2003:10).
53. Bidwai (2007).
54. Brown (2001:19).
55. Tyler (1994:D8); Brown (1994:19).
56. Chen and Wu (2006:ix, xi).
57. Rocca (2007:10).
58. Quoted in Saul (2005:206).
59. Barlow (1999); United Nations Environment Program (2002).
60. A. J. McMichael (1993:336).
61. Durning (1993:14–15).
62. Nepstad (2006).
63. MacKinnon (2007).
64. Lynas (2001).
65. Friedmann (2006); da Silva (2007).

References

Abramovitz, Janet N. 1994. "Biodiversity and Gender Issues." In *Feminist Perspectives on Sustainable Development,* edited by Wendy Harcourt. London: Zed.
———. 1999. "Nature's Hidden Economy." *World Watch* 11(1): 10–19.
Abrahamsen, Rita. 2004. "Review Essay: Poverty Reduction or Adjustment by Another Name?" *Review of African Political Economy* 99: 184–87.
ActionAid. 2000. "Crops and Robbers: Biopiracy and the Patenting of Staple Food Crops." Retrieved from www.actionaid.org.
———. 2004. *Power Hungry: Six Reasons to Regulate Global Food Corporations.* Johannesburg: ActionAid International.
Adams, Nassau A. 1993. *Worlds Apart: The North–South Divide and the International System.* London: Zed.
Agarwal, Bina. 1988. "Patriarchy and the 'Modernising State': An Introduction." In *Structures of Patriarchy: The State, the Community and the Household,* edited by Bina Agarwal. London: Zed.
Ainger, Katherine. 2003. "The New Peasants' Revolt." *New Internationalist* 353 (January/February): 9–13.
Ake, Claude. 1996. *Democracy and Development in Africa.* Washington, DC: Brookings Institute.
Ali, Tariq. 2002. *The Clash of Fundamentalisms: Crusades, Jihads, and Modernity.* London: Verso.
Alperovitz, Gar. 2003. "Tax the Plutocrats!" *The Nation,* January 27: 15–18.
Amanor, Kojo. 1994. "Ecological Knowledge and the Regional Economy: Environmental Management in the Asesewa District of Ghana." In *Development & Environment: Sustaining People and Nature,* edited by Dharam Ghai. Oxford, UK: Blackwell.
Amenga-Etego, Rudolf. 2003. "Stalling the Big Steal." *New Internationalist* 354: 20–21.
Amin, Samir. 1997. *Capitalism in the Age of Globalization.* London: Zed.
Amin, Samir, Giovanni Arrighi, Andre Gunder Frank, and Immanuel Wallerstein. 1990. *Transforming the Revolution: Social Movements and the World System.* New York: Monthly Review Press.
Anderson, Sarah and John Cavanagh, with Thea Lee. 2000. *Field Guide to the Global Economy.* New York: New Press.
Andrae, Gunilla and Björn Beckman. 1985. *The Wheat Trap.* London: Zed.
Andreas, Peter. 1994. "The Making of Amerexico." *World Policy Journal,* Summer: 45–56.
Apffel-Marglin, Frédérique. 1997. "Counter-Development in the Andes." *The Ecologist* 27(6): 221–24.
Apffel-Marglin, Frédérique and Suzanne L. Simon. 1994. "Feminist Orientalism and Development." In *Feminist Perspectives on Sustainable Development,* ed. Wendy Harcourt. London: Zed.
Appelbaum, Richard P. and Gary Gereffi. 1994. "Power and Profits in the Apparel Commodity Chain." In *Global Production: The Apparel Industry in the Pacific Rim,* edited by Edna

Bonacich, Lucie Cheng, Norma Chinchilla, Nora Hamilton, and Paul Ong. Philadelphia: Temple University Press.

Araghi, Farshad. 1995. "Global Depeasantization, 1945–1990." *The Sociological Quarterly* 36(2): 337–68.

——. 1999. "The Great Global Enclosure of Our Times: Peasants and the Agrarian Question at the End of the Twentieth Century." In *Hungry for Profit: The Agribusiness Threat to Farmers, Food, and the Environment,* edited by Fred Magdoff, John Bellamy Foster, and Frederick H. Buttel. New York: Monthly Review Press.

Arrighi, Giovanni. 1990. "The Developmentalist Illusion: A Reconceptualization of the Semiperiphery." In *Semiperipheral States in the World Economy,* edited by William G. Martin. Westport, CT: Greenwood.

——. 1994. *The Long Twentieth Century: Money, Power, and the Origins of Our Times.* London: Verso.

——. 2002. "The African Crisis," *New Left Review,* 15: 5–38.

Athreya, Venkatesh B., Göran Djurfeldt, and Staffan Lindberg. 1990. *Barriers Broken: Production Relations and Agrarian Change in Tamil Nadu.* Newbury Park, CA: Sage.

Attali, Jacques. 1991. *Millennium: Winners and Losers in the Coming World Order.* New York: Times Books.

Avery, Natalie. 1994. "Stealing from the State." In *50 Years is Enough: The Case Against the World Bank and the IMF,* edited by Kevin Danaher and Muhammad Yunus. Boston: South End.

Ayittey, George. 2002. "AIDS Scourge Saps Africa's Vitality." *The Financial Gazette,* April 18. Available at www.fingaz.co.zw.

Ayres, Ed. 1996. "The Shadow Economy." *WorldWatch* 9(4): 10–23.

Bacon, Kenneth M. 1994. "Politics Could Doom a New Currency Plan." *Wall Street Journal,* May 9: A1.

Baer, M. Delal. 1991. "North American Free Trade." *Foreign Affairs* 70(4): 132–49.

Bailey, Mark. 2000. "Agricultural Trade and the Livelihoods of Small Farmers." Oxfam GB Discussion Paper No. 3/00, Oxfam, GB Policy Department Oxford, UK. Retrieved from www.oxfam.org.uk/policy/papers/agricultural_trade/agric.htm.

Baird, Peter and Ed McCaughan. 1979. *Beyond the Border: Mexico & the U.S. Today.* New York: North American Congress on Latin America.

Instituto Nacional de Estadistica Geografia Informatica. 2004. Available at: www.inegi.gob.mx/inegi/default.asp.

Baird, Vanessa. 2002. "Fear Eats the Soul." *New Internationalist,* October: 9–12.

Ball, Rochelle. 1990. "The Process of International Contract Labor Migration from the Philippines: The Case of Filipino Nurses." PhD dissertation, Department of Geography, University of Sydney, Australia.

Bangura, Yusuf and Peter Gibbon. 1992. "Adjustment, Authoritarianism and Democracy in Sub-Saharan Africa: An Introduction to Some Conceptual and Empirical Issues." In *Authoritarianism, Democracy and Adjustment: The Politics of Economic Reform in Africa,* edited by Peter Gibbon, Yusuf Bangura, and Arve Ofstad. Uppsala, Sweden: Nordiska Afrikainstitutet.

Barboza, David. 1999. "Pluralism Under Golden Arches." *The New York Times,* February 12: D1, D7.

——. 2004. "In Roaring China, Sweaters are West of Socks City," *The New York Times,* December 24: C1, C3.

——. 2006. "Labor Shortage in China May Lead to Trade Shift," *The New York Times,* April 3: 1.

Barkin, David. 1990. *Distorted Development: Mexico in the World Economy.* Boulder, CO: Westview.

Barlow, Maude. 1999. *Blue Gold.* San Francisco: International Forum on Globalization.

Barndt, Deborah. 1997. "Bio/cultural Diversity and Equity in Post-NAFTA Mexico (or: Tomasita Comes North While Big Mac Goes South)." In *Global Justice, Global Democracy*, edited by Jay Drydyk and Peter Penz. Winnipeg/Halifax: Fernwood.

———. 2002. *Tangled Routes: Women, Work, and Globalization on the Tomato Trail.* New York: Rowman & Littlefield.

Barnet, Richard J. and John Cavanagh. 1994. *Global Dreams: Imperial Corporations and the New World Order.* New York: Touchstone.

Barry, Tom. 1995. *Zapata's Revenge: Free Trade and the Farm Crisis in Mexico.* Boston: South End.

"Battle of the Bulge." 1994. *The Economist,* September 3: 25.

Baviskar, Amita. 2005. "The Dream Machine: The Model Development Project and the Remaking of the State." In *Waterscapes: The Cultural Politics of a Natural Resource,* edited by Amita Baviskar. New Delhi: Oxford University Press.

Beams, Nick. 1999. "UN Figures Show: International Production System Developing." Retrieved from www.wsws.org/articles/1999/Oct1999/un-009.html.

Becker, Elizabeth. 2003. "U.S. Unilateralism Worries Trade Officials." *The New York Times,* March 17: 5.

———. 2003. "Poor Nations Can Purchase Cheap Drugs Under Accord." *The New York Times,* August 31: 14.

Beckman, Björn. 1992. "Empowerment or Repression? The World Bank and the Politics of African Adjustment." In *Authoritarianism, Democracy and Adjustment: The Politics of Economic Reform in Africa,* edited by Peter Gibbon, Yusuf Bangura, and Arve Ofstad. Uppsala, Sweden: Nordiska Afrikainstitutet.

Bello, Walden. 1992–1993. "Population and the Environment." *Food First Action Alert,* Winter, p. 5.

———. 1998. "Addicted to Capital: The Ten-Year High and Present-Day Withdrawal Trauma of Southeast Asia's Economies." In *FOCUS on the Global South.* Bangkok: Chulalongkorn University.

Bello, Walden, with Shea Cunningham and Bill Rau. 1994. *Dark Victory: The United States, Structural Adjustment and Global Poverty.* London: Pluto Press, with Food First and Transnational Institute.

Benería, Lourdes. 1992. "Accounting for Women's Work: The Progress of Two Decades." *World Development* 20(11): 1547–60.

———. 1995. "Response: The Dynamics of Globalization" (Scholarly Controversy: Global Flows of Labor and Capital). *International Labor and Working-Class History* 47: 45–52.

———. 2003. *Gender, Development, and Globalization: Economics as if All People Mattered.* New York: Routledge.

Benería, Lourdes and Shelley Feldman, eds. 1992. *Unequal Burden: Economic Crises, Persistent Poverty, and Women's Work.* Boulder, CO: Westview.

Berger, Mark. 2004. "After the Third World? History, Destiny and the Fate of Third Worldism." *Third World Quarterly* 25(1): 1–47.

Berger, Mark T. and Mark Beeson. 1998. "Lineages of Liberalism and Miracles of Modernisation: The World Bank, the East Asian Trajectory and the International Development Debate." *Third World Quarterly* 19(3): 487–504.

Berlan, Jean-Pierre. 1991. "The Historical Roots of the Present Agricultural Crisis." In *Towards a New Political Economy of Agriculture,* edited by W. Friedland, L. Busch, F. Buttel, and A. Rudy. Boulder, CO: Westview.

Bernard, Mitchell. 1996. "Beyond the Local–Global Divide in the Formation of the Eastern Asian Region." *New Political Economy* 1(3): 335–53.

———. 1999. "East Asia's Tumbling Dominoes: Financial Crises and the Myth of the Regional Model." In *Global Capitalism versus Democracy: Socialist Register 1999,* edited by Leo Panitch and Colin Leys. London: Merlin.

Bernstein, Henry. 1990. "Agricultural 'Modernization' and the Era of Structural Adjustment: Observations on Sub-Saharan Africa." *Journal of Peasant Studies* 18(1): 3–35.

Berthelot, Jacques. 2005. "The WTO: Food for Thought?" *Le Monde diplomatique*, December: 10–11.

Bidwai, Praful. 2007. "India: Special Economic Zones on the Backburner." *Inter Press Service*, February 12. Available at www.ips.org.

Bienefeld, Manfred. 2000. "Structural Adjustment: Debt Collection Device or Development Policy?" *Review*, 23(4): 533–82.

Black, Maggie. 2002. *The No-Nonsense Guide to International Development*. London: Verso.

Block, Fred L. 1977. *The Origins of International Economic Disorder: A Study of United States International Monetary Policy from World War II to the Present*. Berkeley: University of California Press.

Blustein, Paul. 2002. "Arab Economies Lie at the Root of Unrest." *Guardian Weekly*, February 14–20: 37.

Bobin, Frédéric. 2006. "Mutually Assured Dependence," *Guardian Weekly*, July 14–20: 17.

Bodeen, Christopher. 2007. "China: Economic Engagement Can Resolve Darfur Crisis." *Ithaca Journal*, May 16: 8A.

Bogdanich, Walt and Jake Hooker. 2007. "From China to Panama: A Trail of Poisoned Medicine." *New York Times*, May 6: 1, 24–25.

Bonacich, Edna and David V. Waller. 1994. "The Role of U.S. Apparel Manufacturers in the Globalization of the Industry in the Pacific Rim." In *Global Production: The Apparel Industry in the Pacific Rim*, edited by Edna Bonacich, Lucie Cheng, Norma Chinchilla, Nora Hamilton, and Paul Ong. Philadelphia: Temple University Press.

Bond, Patrick. 2001. "Radical Rhetoric and the Working Class during Zimbabwean Nationalism's Dying Days." *Journal of World-Systems Research* 7(1): 52–89.

———. 2002. "NEPAD." Retrieved from www.ifg.org/analysis/un/wssd/bondZnet.htm.

———. 2006. *Looting Africa. The Economics of Exploitation*. Pietermaritzburg: University of Kwa-Zulu Natal Press.

Bookman, Jay. 2002. "The President's Real Goal in Iraq." Retrieved from http://globalresearch.ca/articles/B0021A.html.

Booth, Karen. 1998. "National Mother, Global Whore, and Transnational Femocrats: The Politics of AIDS and the Construction of Women at the World Health Organization." *Feminist Studies* 24(1): 115–39.

Borger, Julian. 2007. "Scorched Earth Policy." *Guardian Weekly*, May 18: 21–23.

Borosage, Robert L. 1999. "The Global Turning." *The Nation*, July 19: 19–22.

Borthwick, Mark. 1992. *Pacific Century: The Emergence of Modern Pacific Asia*. Boulder, CO: Westview.

Bose, Sugata. 1997. "Instruments and Idioms of Colonial and National Development: India's Historical Experience in Comparative Perspective." In *International Development and the Social Sciences*, edited by Frederick Cooper and Randall Packard. Berkeley, CA: University of California Press.

Boseley, Sarah. 2007. "Scientists Find Way to Bring Cheap Drugs to Poor Nations." *Guardian Weekly*, January 5–11: 1.

Boyd, Rosalind. 2006. "Labour's Response to the Informalization of Work in the Current Restructuring of Global Capitalism: China, South Korea and South Africa." *Canadian Journal of Development Studies* 27(4): 487–502.

Boyd, Stephanie. 1998. "Secrets and Lies." *The New Internationalist* 303: 16–17.

Bradley, P. N. and S. E. Carter. 1989. "Food Production and Distribution—and Hunger." In *A World in Crisis? Geographical Perspectives*, edited by R. J. Johnston and P. J. Taylor. Oxford, UK: Blackwell.

Bradsher, Keith. 1995. "White House Moves to Increase Aid to Mexico." *The New York Times*, January 12: D6.

————. 2002. "India Slips Far Behind China, Once Its Closest Rival." *The New York Times*, November 29: A1, A8.

————. 2006. "A Younger India is Flexing Its Industrial Brawn." *The New York Times*, September 1: 1, C4.

Brandt Commission (Independent Commission on International Development Issues). 1983. *Common Crisis: North, South & Cooperation for World Recovery*. London: Pan.

Brecher, Jeremy and Tim Costello. 1994. *Global Village or Global Pillage? Economic Reconstruction from the Bottom Up*. Boston: South End.

Brecher, Jeremy, Tim Costello, and Brendan Smith. 2000. *Globalization From Below: The Power of Solidarity*. Cambridge, MA: South End.

Brett, E. A. 1985. *The World Economy Since the War: The Politics of Uneven Development*. London: Macmillan.

Briscoe, Mark. 2002. "Water: The Untapped Resource." In *The Fatal Harvest Reader: The Tragedy of Industrial Agriculture*, edited by Andrew Kimball. Washington: Island Press.

Brooks, Libby. 2007. "It's Not Enough to Say We Should Listen to Children." *Guardian Weekly*, February 23–March 1: 6.

Brown, Lester R. 1994. "Who Will Feed China?" *World Watch* 7(5): 10–19.

————. 1995. "China's Food Problem: The Massive Imports Begin." *World Watch* 8(5): 38.

————. 2001. "Bad Tidings on the Wind for Chinese." *Guardian Weekly*, June 7–13: 19.

Brown, Michael Barratt. 1993. *Fair Trade*. London: Zed.

Bruno, Kenny. 1998. "Monsanto's Failing PR Strategy." *The Ecologist* 28(5): 287–93.

Buckley, Stephen. 2001. "Brazil's Poor Learn to Help Themselves." *Guardian Weekly*, February 8–14: 27.

Bujra, Janet. 1992. "Diversity in Pre-Capitalist Societies." In *Poverty and Development in the 1990s*, edited by Tim Allen and Allan Thomas. Oxford, UK: Oxford University Press.

Bulard, Martine. 2006. "China Breaks the Iron Rice Bowl." *Guardian Weekly*, January: 6.

Bunker, Stephen. 1985. *Underdeveloping the Amazon: Extraction, Unequal Exchange and the Failure of the Modern State*. Urbana, IL: University of Illinois Press.

Bunker, Stephen G. and Paul S. Ciccantell. 2005. *Globalization and the Race for Resources*. Baltimore: Johns Hopkins University Press.

Bunsha, D. 2006. "Rural Resistance." *Frontline* 23(20), October: 1.

Burbach, Roger. 2006. "Bolivia Breaks Free of US Reins." *Guardian Weekly*, May 12–18: 6.

Burbach, Roger and Patricia Flynn. 1980. *Agribusiness in the Americas*. New York: Monthly Review Press.

Busch, Lawrence and William B. Lacy. 1983. *Science, Agriculture, and the Politics of Research*. Boulder, CO: Westview.

Busch, L. and C. Bain. 2004. "New! Improved? The Transformation of the Global Agrifood System." *Rural Sociology* 69(3): 321–46.

Buttel, Frederick H. 1992. "Environmentalization: Origins, Processes, and Implications for Rural Social Change." *Rural Sociology* 57(1): 1–28.

Byres, Terry J. 1981. "The New Technology, Class Formation and Class Action in the Indian Countryside." *Journal of Peasant Studies* 8(4): 405–54.

Cahn, Jonathan. 1993. "Challenging the New Imperial Authority: The World Bank and the Democratization of Development." *Harvard Human Rights Journal* 6: 159–94.

Calvo, Dana. 1997. "Tijuana Workers Win Labor Battle." Retrieved from tw-list@essential.org.

Canak, William L. 1989. "Debt, Austerity, and Latin America in the New International Division of Labor." In *Lost Promises: Debt, Austerity, and Development in Latin America*, edited by William L. Canak. Boulder, CO: Westview.

Cameron, Angus and Ronen Palan. 2004. *The Imagined Economies of Globalization*. London: Sage.

Cammack, Paul. 2002. "Attacking the Global Poor." *New Left Review* 13: 125–34.

Capell, Kerry. 2007. "GlaxoSmithKline: Getting AIDS Drugs to More Sick People." *Business Week*, January 29. Available at: www.businessweek.com/mag.

Cardoso, Fernando H. and Enzo Faletto. 1979. *Dependency and Development in Latin America.* Berkeley: University of California Press.

Carlsen, Laura. 2003. "The Mexican Farmers' Movement: Exposing the Myths of Free Trade." *Americas Program Policy Report.* Silver City (NM): Interhemispheric Resource Center. Available at www.americaspolicy.org.

———. 2006. "The World Needs its Small Farmers," *Americas Updater* 4: 16. Available at http://americas.irc-online.org/updater/3633.

Carson, Rachel. 1962. *Silent Spring.* Boston: Houghton Mifflin.

Castells, Manuel. 1998. *End of Millennium.* Oxford, UK: Blackwell.

Caulkin, Simon. 2007. "If Everything Can Be Outsourced, What is Left?" *Observer,* April 1.

Central Intelligence Agency. 2000. "The Global Infectious Disease Threat and Its Implications for the United States." Retrieved from www.cia.gov/cia/publications/nie/report/nie99-17d.html

Chan, Anita. 1996. "Boot Camp at the Shoe Factory." *Guardian Weekly,* November 17: 20–21.

Chase, Edward T. 1995. "Down and Out in London, Paris, and New York." *The Bookpress (Ithaca),* March: 16.

Chase-Dunn, Christopher. 1998. *Global Formation: Structures of the World-Economy.* Boulder, CO: Rowman & Littlefield.

Chatterjee, Partha. 2001. *Nationalist Thought and the Colonial World.* Minneapolis, MN: University of Minnesota Press.

Chen, Guidi and Wu Chuntao. 2006. *Will the Boat Sink the Water? The Life of China's Peasants.* New York: Public Affairs.

Cheru, Fantu. 1989. *The Silent Revolution in Africa: Debt, Development and Democracy.* London: Zed.

Chira, Susan. 1994. "Women Campaign for New Plan to Curb the World's Population." *The New York Times,* April 13: A12.

Chirot, Daniel. 1977. *Social Change in the Twentieth Century.* New York: Harcourt Brace Jovanovich.

Chomsky, Noam. 1994. *World Orders Old and New.* New York: Columbia University Press.

Chossudovsky, Michel. 1997. *The Globalisation of Poverty: Impacts of IMF and World Bank Reforms.* Penang: Third World Network.

———. 2003. *The Globalisation of Poverty and the New World Order.* Shanty Bay, ON: Global Outlook.

Chung, Youg-Il. 1990. "The Agricultural Foundation for Korean Industrial Development." In *The Economic Development of Japan and Korea,* edited by Chung Lee and Ippei Yamazawa. New York: Praeger.

Clarke, T. and M. Barlow. 1997. *MAI: The Multilateral Agreement on Investment and the Threat to Canadian Sovereignty.* Toronto: Stoddart.

Clarke, Tony. 2001. "Serving Up the Commons." *Multinational Monitor* 22(4). Retrieved from www.essential.org/monitor/mm2001/01april/corp2.html.

Cleaver, Harry. 1977. "Food, Famine and the International Crisis." *Zerowork* 2: 7–70.

———. 1994. "The Chiapas Uprising." *Studies in Political Economy* 44: 141–57.

Coates, Barry. 2001. "Big Business at Your Service." *Guardian Weekly,* March 15–21: 28.

Cockroft, James D. 2005. "Winds of Change and Internationalism from Latin America." January 14. Available at www.jamescockroft.com/?q=node/76.

———. 2005. "Latin America's Challenges to Imperialism." *LiP Magazine,* Summer: 60–62. Available at: www.jamescockroft.com/?q=node/91.

Cohen, Benjamin J. 1998. *The Geography of Money.* Ithaca, NY: Cornell University Press.

Cohen, Roger. 1998. "High Claims in Spill Betray Depth of Nigerian Poverty." *The New York Times,* September 20: A1, A6.

———. 1999. "Shiny, Prosperous 'Euroland' Has Some Cracks in Façade." *The New York Times,* January 3: A1, A6.

Colchester, Marcus. 1994. "Sustaining the Forests: The Community-Based Approach in South and Southeast Asia." In *Development & Environment: Sustaining People and Nature,* edited by Dharam Ghai. Oxford, UK: Blackwell.

Collins, Elizabeth Fuller. 2007. *Indonesia Betrayed: How Development Fails.* Honolulu: University of Hawaii Press.

Collins, Jane. 1995. "Gender and Cheap Labor in Agriculture." In *Food and Agrarian Orders in the World-Economy,* edited by Philip McMichael. Westport, CT: Praeger.

———. 2003. *Threads. Gender, Labor, and Power in the Global Apparel Industry.* Chicago: University of Chicago Press.

Collins, Joseph and John Lear. 1996. *Chile's Free Market Miracle: A Second Look.* Oakland, CA: Food First Books.

Coomaraswamy, Radhika. 2001. "Different But Free: Cultural Relativism and Women's Rights as Human Rights." In *Religious Fundamentalisms and the Human Rights of Women,* edited by Courtney W. Howland. New York: Palgrave.

Cooper, Frederick. 1997. "Modernizing Bureaucrats, Backward Africans, and the Development Concept." In *International Development and the Social Sciences,* edited by Frederick Cooper and Randall Packard. Berkeley: University of California Press.

Cooper, Frederick and Ann Laura Stoler, eds. 1997. *Tensions of Empire: Colonial Cultures in a Bourgeois World.* Berkeley, CA: University of California Press.

Cooper, Helene and Thomas Kuhn. 1998. "Much of Europe Eases Its Rigid Labor Laws and Temps Proliferate." *Wall Street Journal,* June 4: A1, A5.

Cooper, Marc. 1999. "No Sweat." *The Nation,* June 7: 11–14.

Corbridge, Stuart. 1993. "Ethics in Development Studies: The Example of Debt." In *Beyond the Impasse: New Directions in Development Theory,* edited by Frans J. Schuurman. London: Zed.

Cowan, M. P. and R. W. Shenton. 1996. *Doctrines of Development.* London: Routledge Kegan Paul.

Cowell, Alan. 1994. "Muslim Party Threatens Turk's Secular Heritage." *The New York Times,* November 30: A14.

Cox, Robert W. 1987. *Production, Power, and World Order: Social Forces in the Making of History.* New York: Columbia University Press.

Crook, Clive. 1991. "Sisters in the Wood: A Survey of the IMF and the World Bank." *The Economist,* Special Supplement, October 12: 5–48.

———. 1992. "Fear of Finance: A Survey of the World Economy." *The Economist,* Special Supplement, September 19: 5–48.

———. 1993. "New Ways to Grow: A Survey of World Finance." *The Economist,* Special Supplement, September 25: 3–22.

Crossette, Barbara. 1994. "A Third-World Effort on Family Planning." *The New York Times,* September 7, A8.

———. 1995. "Talks in Denmark Redefine 'Foreign Aid' in Post-Cold War Era." *The New York Times,* March 10: A5.

———. 1997. "Kofi Annan's Astonishing Facts!" In *Human Development Report 1997.* New York: United Nations Development Program.

———. 1998a. "Women See Key Gains since Talks in Beijing." *The New York Times,* March 8: A14.

———. 1998b. "A Uganda Tribe Fights Genital Cutting." *The New York Times,* July 16: A8.

———. 1998c. "Where the Hunger Season is Part of Life." *The New York Times,* Week in Review, August 16: 1, 5.

Cumings, Bruce. 1987. "The Origin and Development of the Northeast Asian Political Economy: Industrial Sectors, Product Cycles, and Political Consequences." In *The Political Economy of the New Asian Industrialism,* edited by Frederic C. Deyo. Ithaca, NY: Cornell University Press.

Da Costa, Dia and Philip McMichael. 2007. "The Poverty of the Global Order." *Globalizations*, 4(4): 593–607.

Dalrymple, D. 1985. "The Development and Adoption of High-Yielding Varieties of Wheat and Rice in Developing Countries." *American Journal of Agricultural Economics* 67: 1067–73.

Daly, M. T. and M. I. Logan. 1989. *The Brittle Rim: Finance, Business and the Pacific Region*. Ringwood, Australia: Penguin.

Danaher, Kevin and Muhammad Yunus, eds. 1994. *50 Years is Enough: The Case against the World Bank and the International Monetary Fund*. Boston: South End.

Darnton, John. 1994a. "In Poor, Decolonized Africa, Bankers are New Overlords." *The New York Times*, June 20: A1.

———. 1994b. "Africa Tries Democracy, Finding Hope and Peril." *The New York Times*, June 21: A9.

da Silva, Anna. 2007. "Calling the Shots: Global Networks of Trade in Vaccines." Paper presented to Hegemonic Transitions and the State conference, Simon Fraser University, Vancouver. February 23–24.

Davidson, Basil. 1992. *The Black Man's Burden: Africa and the Curse of the Nation-State*. New York: Times Books.

Davis, Mike. 2001. *Late Victorian Holocausts: El Nino Famines and the Making of the Third World*. London: Verso.

———. 2005. *The Monster at Our Door. The Global Threat of Avian Flu*. New York & London: The New Press.

———. 2006. *Planet of Slums*. London: Verso.

Dawkins, Karen. 1999. "Agricultural Prices and Trade Policy: Evaluating and Correcting the Uruguay Round Agreement on Agriculture." Paper submitted to UNCTAD/NGLS Consultation with NGOs, December 12–14, Geneva.

Dawkins, Kristin. 2000. "Battle Royale of the 21st Century." *Seedling* 17(1): 2–8.

Dawson, Alexander S. 2006. *Third World Dreams. Mexico Since 1989*. Nova Scotia: Fernwood.

de Castro, Josué. 1969. " Introduction: Not One Latin America." In *Latin American Radicalism*, edited by Irving Louis Horowitz, Josué de Castro, and John Gerassi. New York: Vintage.

Deere, Carmen Diana and Magdalena León. 2001. *Empowering Women: Land and Property Rights in Latin America*. Pittsburgh: University of Pittsburgh Press.

de Janvry, Alain. 1981. *The Agrarian Question and Reformism in Latin America*. Baltimore: Johns Hopkins University Press.

de la Rocha, Mercedes Gonzaléz. 1994. *The Resources of Poverty: Women and Survival in a Mexican City*. Cambridge, MA: Blackwell.

de Soto, Hernando. 1990. *The Other Path: The Invisible Revolution in the Third World*. New York: Harper & Row.

Denny, Charlotte. 2002. "Poor Always the Losers in Trade Game." *Guardian Weekly: Earth*, August: 6.

Denny, Charlotte and Larry Elliott. 2002. "Millions More Must Survive on $1 a Day." *Guardian Weekly*, June 25–July 3: 14.

Desmarais, Annette Aurélie. 2007. *La Vía Campesina: Globalization and the Power of Peasants*. Halifax, NS: Fernwood.

Devraj, Ranjit. 2001. "Room at the Top." *New Internationalist* 334 (May): 17.

De Waal, Alex. 2002. "What AIDS Means in a Famine." *The New York Times*, November 19: 25.

DeWalt, Billie. 1985. "Mexico's Second Green Revolution: Food for Feed." *Mexican Studies/Estudios Mexicanos* 1: 29–60.

Deyo, Frederic C. 1991. "Singapore: Developmental Paternalism." In *Mini-Dragons: Fragile Economic Miracles in the Pacific*, edited by Steven M. Goldstein. Boulder, CO: Westview.

Dhanagare, D. N. 1988. "The Green Revolution and Social Inequalities in Rural India." *Bulletin of Concerned Asian Scholars* 20(2): 2–13.

Dias Martins, Monica. 2000. "The MST Challenge to Neoliberalism." *Latin American Perspectives* 27(5): 33–45.

Dicken, Peter. 1998. *Global Shift: Transforming the World Economy*. New York: Guilford.

Dickinson, Torry D. and Robert K. Schaeffer. 2001. *Fast Forward: Work, Gender, and Protest in a Changing World*. Lanham, MD: Rowman & Littlefield.

Diokno-Pascual, Maitet. 2003. "Power Splurge." *New Internationalist* 355, April: 25.

Dillon, Sam. 1997. "After 4 Years of NAFTA, Labor is Forging Cross-Border Ties." *The New York Times*, December 20: A1, A7.

———. 1998. "U.S. Labor Leader Seeks Union Support in Mexico." *The New York Times*, January 23: A3.

Dixon, Jane. 2002. *The Changing Chicken: Chooks, Cooks, and Culinary Culture*. Sydney, Australia: UNSW Press.

Dolan, C. S. 2004. "On Farm and Packhouse: Employment at the Bottom of a Global Value Chain." *Rural Sociology* 69(1): 99–126.

Dolan, C. and J. Humphrey. 2000. "Governance and Trade in Fresh Vegetables: The Impact of UK Supermarkets on the African Horticulture Industry." *Journal of Development Studies* 37: 147–76.

Dube, S. C. 1988. *Modernization and Development—the Search for Alternative Paradigms*. London: Zed.

Dudley, Leonard and Roger Sandilands. 1975. "The Side Effects of Foreign Aid: The Case of Public Law 480, Wheat in Colombia." *Economic Development and Cultural Change* 23(2): 325–36.

Dugger, Celia W. 2004. "Supermarket Giants Crush Central American Farmers." *The New York Times*, December 28: A1, A10.

———. 2007. "Clinton Foundation Announces a Bargain on Generic AIDS Drugs." *The New York Times*, May 9: 6.

Duncan, Colin. 1996. *The Centrality of Agriculture. Between Humankind and the Rest of Nature*, Montreal & Kingston: McGill-Queen's University Press.

Durning, Alan Thein. 1993. "Supporting Indigenous Peoples." In *State of the World*, edited by Lester Brown. New York: Norton.

Dwyer, Michael. 1998. "IMF Starts to Query Its Own Ideology." *The Australian Financial Review*, November 30: 4.

Eber, Christine E. 1999. "Seeking Our Own Food: Indigenous Women's Power and Autonomy in San Pedro Chenalhó, Chiapas (1980–1998)." *Latin American Perspectives* 26(3): 6–36.

Economic Commission for Latin America and the Caribbean (ECLAC). 1989. *Transnational Bank Behaviour and the International Debt Crisis*. Santiago, Chile: ECLAC/UN Center on Transnational Corporations.

Edwards, Beatrice. 2003. "IDB Plan to Sell the Public Sector. The Cure or the Ill?" *NACLA* 36(4): 13–19.

Elliott, Larry. 2001. "Evil Triumphs in a Disease-Ridden World." *Guardian Weekly*, February 14–21: 12.

Elliott, Michael. 2007. "The Chinese Century." *Time*, January 22: 19–27.

Ellwood, Wayne. 1993. "Multinationals and the Subversion of Sovereignty." *New Internationalist* 246: 4–7.

———. 2001. *The No-Nonsense Guide to Globalization*. Oxford, UK: New Internationalist.

Elson, Diane, ed. 1991. *Male Bias in the Development Process*. Manchester: Manchester University Press.

———. 1993. "Gender-Aware Analysis and Development Economics." *Journal of International Development* 5(2): 237–47.

Elson, Diane and Ruth Pearson. 1981. "Nimble Fingers Make Cheap Workers: An Analysis of Women's Employment in Third World Export Manufacturing," *Feminist Review* 7: 87–101.

Elyachar, Julia. 2005. *Markets of Dispossession: NGOs, Economic Development, and the State in Cairo*. Durham, NC: Duke University Press.

Enloe, Cynthia. 2004. *The Curious Feminist: Searching for Women in a New Age of Empire*. Berkeley: University of California Press.

Enzenburger, Hans Magnus. 1994. *Civil Wars: From L.A. to Bosnia*. New York: New Press.

Erlanger, Steven. 1998. "Suharto Fostered Rapid Economic Growth, and Staggering Graft." *The New York Times*, May 22: A9.

Escobar, Arturo. 1995. *Encountering Development: The Making and Unmaking of the Third World*. Princeton, NJ: Princeton University Press.

Esteva, Gustavo. 1992. "Development." In *The Development Dictionary*, edited by Wolfgang Sachs. London: Zed.

Evans, Peter. 1979. *Dependent Development*. Princeton, NJ: Princeton University Press.

———. 1995. *Embedded Autonomy: States and Industrial Transformation*. Princeton, NJ: Princeton University Press.

Eviatar, Daphne. 2006. "Latin Left Turn." *The Nation*, December 25: 5–6.

Eyferth, J., P. Ho, and E. B. Vermeer. 2003. "Introduction: The Opening Up of China's Countryside." *The Journal of Peasant Studies* 30(3–4): 1–17.

Faison, Seth. 1997. "Detours Behind It: The Giant Follows Asian's Growth Path." *The New York Times*, March 4: A1, D4.

Fanon, Frantz. 1967. *The Wretched of the Earth*. Harmondsworth, UK: Penguin.

Farthing, Linda and Ben Kohl. 2001. "Bolivia's New Wave of Protest." *NACLA Report on the Americas* 34(5): 8–11.

Feder, Ernst. 1983. *Perverse Development*. Quezon City, Philippines: Foundation for Nationalist Studies.

Fenley, Lindajoy. 1991. "Promoting the Pacific Rim." *Business Mexico*, June: 41.

Ferguson, James. 2006. *Global Shadows: Africa in the Neoliberal World Order*. Durham, NC: Duke University Press.

Fernandez Kelly, Patricia. 1983. *For We are Sold, I and My People: Women and Industry in Mexico's Frontier*. Albany, NY: SUNY Press.

Fickling, David. 2003. "Rag-Trade Slaves Face Misery in America's Pacific Outpost." *Guardian Weekly*, March 20–26: 5.

Fidler, Stephen and Lisa Bransten. 1995. "Mexican Sell-Offs to Help Solve the Debt Crisis." *Financial Times*, August 1: 1.

Finch, J. 2006. "Sainsbury's Scores with Recovery Based on Quality Food." *The Guardian*, November 16: 21.

Fisher, Ian and Norimitsu Onishi. 1999. "Congo's Struggle May Unleash Broad Strife to Redraw Africa." *The New York Times*, January 12: A1, A9.

Flavio de Almeida, Lucio and Felix Ruiz Sanchez. 2000. "The Landless Workers' Movement and Social Struggles against Neoliberalism." *Latin American Perspectives* 22(5): 11–32.

Fraser, Alistair. 2005. "Poverty Reduction Strategy Papers: Now Who Calls the Shots?" *Review of African Political Economy*, 104/5: 317–40.

Friedman, Thomas. 2000. *The Lexus and the Olive Tree: Understanding Globalization*. New York: Anchor.

Flynn, Matthew. 2002. "Cocktails and Carnival." *New Internationalist* 346: 16–17.

"Food and Farming: The Facts." 2003. *New Internationalist* 353: 20–21.

Fox, Jonathan. 1994. "The Challenge of Democracy: Rebellion as Catalyst." *Akwe:kon* 11(2): 13–19.

Frantz, Douglas. 2002. "Turkey, Well Along Road to Secularism, Fears Detour to Islamism." *The New York Times*, January 8: A8.

Frasca, Tim. 2002. "The Sacking of Argentina." *The Nation*, May 6: 26–30.

Freeman, Carla. 2000. *High Tech and High Heels in the Global Economy: Women, Work, and Pink-Collar Identities in the Caribbean*. Durham, NC: Duke University Press.

"Free Trade: The Ifs, Ands, and Buts." 1993. *Resource Center Bulletin*, July: 31–32.

French, Hilary. 2000. *Vanishing Borders: Protecting the Planet in the Age of Globalization*. New York: Norton.

———. 2004. "Linking Globalization, Consumption, and Governance." In *State of the World, 2004: The Consumer Society*, edited by Linda Starke. Washington, DC: The World Watch Institute.

French, Howard W. 1997. "A Century Later, Letting Africans Draw Their Own Map." *The New York Times*, November 23: A1, A3.

Fried, Stephanie. 2003. "Writing for Their Lives: Bentian Dayak Authors and Indonesian Development Discourse." In *Forests, Coasts, and Seas: Culture and the Question of Rights to Southeast Asian Environmental Resources,* edited by C. Zerner. Durham, NC: Duke University Press.

Friedland, William H. 1994. "The Global Fresh Fruit and Vegetable System: An Industrial Organization Analysis." In *The Global Restructuring of Agro-Food Systems,* edited by Philip McMichael. Ithaca, NY: Cornell University Press.

Friedman, Thomas. 1999. "A Manifesto for the Fast World." *New York Times Magazine,* March 28. Retrieved from www.globalpolicy.org/nation/fried99.htm.

Friedmann, Harriet. 1982. "The Political Economy of Food: The Rise and Fall of the Postwar International Food Order." *American Journal of Sociology* 88S: 248–86.

———. 1990. "The Origins of Third World Food Dependence." In *The Food Question: Profits Versus People?* edited by Henry Bernstein, Ben Crow, Maureen Mackintosh, and Charlotte Martin. New York: Monthly Review Press.

———. 1991. "Changes in the International Division of Labor: Agri-Food Complexes and Export Agriculture." In *Towards a New Political Economy of Agriculture,* edited by William Friedland, Lawrence Busch, Frederick H. Buttel, and Alan P. Rudy. Boulder, CO: Westview.

———. 1992. "Distance and Durability: Shaky Foundations of the World Food Economy." *Third World Quarterly* 13(2): 371–83.

———. 1999. "Remaking 'Traditions': How We Eat, What We Eat, and the Changing Political Economy of Food." In *Women Working the NAFTA Food Chain,* edited by Deborah Barndt. Toronto: Second Story.

———. 2006. "Focusing on Agriculture." *Canadian Journal of Development Studies,* 27(4): 461–66.

Friedmann, John. 1992. *Empowerment: The Politics of Alternative Development.* Cambridge, UK: Blackwell.

Fröbel, Folker, Jürgen Heinrichs, and Otto Kreye. 1979. *The New International Division of Labor.* New York: Cambridge University Press.

Fuentes, Anna, and Barbara Ehrenreich. 1983. "The New Factory Girls." *Multinational Monitor* 4(8). Available at www.multinationalmonitor.org.

Fussell, M. E. 2000. "Making Labor Flexible: The Recomposition of Tijuana's *Maquiladora* Female Labor Force." *Feminist Economics* 6(3): 59–80.

Galeano, Eduardo. 2000. *Upside Down: A Primer for the Looking Glass World.* New York: Picador.

Gardner, Gary and Brian Halweil. 2000. "Underfed and Overfed: The Global Epidemic of Malnutrition." Worldwatch Paper No. 150, Washington, DC: Worldwatch Institute.

Gardner, Gary, Erik Assadourian, and Radhika Sarin. 2004. "The State of Consumption Today." *State of the World 2004.* Washington DC: Worldwatch Institute.

George, Susan. 1977. *How the Other Half Dies: The Real Reasons for World Hunger.* Montclair, NJ: Allenheld, Osmun and Co.

———. 1988. *A Fate Worse Than Debt: The World Financial Crisis and the Poor.* New York: Grove.

———. 1992. *The Debt Boomerang: How Third World Debt Harms Us All.* Boulder, CO: Westview.

George, Susan and Fabrizio Sabelli. 1994. *Faith and Credit: The World Bank's Secular Empire.* Boulder, CO: Westview.

Gereffi, Gary. 1989. "Rethinking Development Theory: Insights from East Asia and Latin America." *Sociological Forum* 4(4): 505–33.

———. 1994. "The Organization of Buyer-Driven Global Commodity Chains: How U.S. Retailers Shape Overseas Production Networks." In *Commodity Chains and Global Capitalism,* edited by Gary Gereffi and Miguel Korzeniewicz. Westport, CT: Praeger.

Gereffi, Gary, Ronie Garcia-Johnson, and Erika Sasser. 2001. "The NGO-Industrial Complex." *Foreign Policy,* July–August: 56–65.

Gevisser, Mark. 2001. "AIDS: The New Apartheid." *The Nation,* May 14: 5–6.

Gibbon, Peter. 1992. "Structural Adjustment and Pressures Toward Multipartyism in Sub-Saharan Africa." In *Authoritarianism, Democracy and Adjustment: The Politics of Economic Reform in Africa,* edited by Peter Gibbon, Yusuf Bangura, and Arve Ofstad. Uppsala, Sweden: Nordiska Afrikainstitutet.

Gibson-Graham, J. K. 2006. *A Postcapitalist Politics.* Minneapolis: University of Minnesota Press.

Gill, Stephen. 1992. "Economic Globalization and the Internationalization of Authority: Limits and Contradictions." *Geoforum* 23(3): 269–83.

Giridharadas, Anand 2007. "'Second Tier' City to Rise Fast under India's Urban Plan." *The New York Times,* May 13: 3.

Glaister, Dan. 2006. "How Morales Took on the Oil Giants." *Guardian Weekly,* May 12–18: 1.

Godrej, Dinyar. 2003. "Precious Fluid." *New Internationalist* 354: 9–12.

Golden, Tim. 1995. "Mexicans Find Dream Devalued." *The New York Times,* January 8: 5.

Goldman, Michael. 2005. *Imperial Nature. The World Bank and Struggles for Social Justice in the Age of Globalization.* New Haven: Yale University Press.

Goldsmith, James. 1994. *The Trap.* New York: Carroll & Graf.

Golub, Philip S. 2003. "China: The New Economic Giant." *Le Monde Diplomatique,* October: 10.

Gore, C. 2000. "The Rise and Fall of the Washington Consensus as a Paradigm for Developing Countries." *World Development* 28(5): 789–804.

Gorelick, Sherry. 2000. "Facing the Farm Crisis." *The Ecologist* 30(4): 28–32.

Goss, Jasper, David Burch, and Roy E. Rickson. 2000. "Agri-Food Restructuring and Third World Transnationals: Thailand, the CP Group and the Global Shrimp Industry." *World Development* 28(3): 513–30.

Gott, Richard. 2006. "Latin America is Preparing to Settle Accounts with Its White Settler Elite." *The Guardian,* November 15: 33.

Gow, David. 2007. "India Gets a Brand New Carmaker—As It Runs Out of Roads to Drive On." *The Guardian,* March 30: 8.

Gowan, Peter. 2003. "The American Campaign for Global Sovereignty." In *Fighting Identities: Socialist Register,* edited by Leo Panitch and Colin Leys. London: Merlin.

Graham, Carol. 1994. *Safety Nets, Politics, and the Poor: Transitions to Market Economies.* Washington DC: Brookings Institution.

GRAIN. 1998. "Biopiracy, TRIPs and the Patenting of Asia's Rice Bowl: A Collective NGO Situationer on IPRs and Rice." Retrieved from www.grain.org/publications/reports/rice/htm.

Graw, Stephen. 1999. "Overseas Labor Remittances: Spare Change or New Changes?" Paper presented at annual meeting of the Association for Asian Studies, April, Boston.

Green, L. 2003. "Notes on Mayan Youth and Rural Industrialization in Guatemala." *Critique of Anthropology* 23: 51–73.

Greenfield, Gerard. 1999. "The WTO, the World Food System, and the Politics of Harmonised Destruction." Retrieved from www.labournet.org/discuss/global/wto/html.

Greenlees, Donald. 2006. "Outsourcing Drifts to the Philippines after India Matures." *International Herald Tribune,* November 11: 1.

Greenpeace. 2006. "Eating Up the Amazon." Available at www.greenpeace.org.

Greider, William. 2001. "A New Giant Sucking Sound." *The Nation,* December 31: 22–24.

———. 2007. "The Establishment Rethinks Globalization." *The Nation,* April 30: 11–14.

Griffin, K. B. 1974. *The Political Economy of Agrarian Change: An Essay on the Green Revolution.* Cambridge, MA: Harvard University Press.

Grigg, David. 1993. *The World Food Problem.* Oxford, UK: Blackwell.

Grosfoguel, Ramon. 1996. "From Cepalismo to Neoliberalism: A World-Systems Approach to Conceptual Shifts in Latin America." *Review* 19: 131–54.

Grossman, Raquel. 1979. "Globalization, Commodity Chains and Fruit Exporting Regions in Chile." *Tijdschrift voor Economische en Sociale Geographie* 90(2): 211–25.

Gupta. Akhil. 1998. *Postcolonial Developments: Agriculture in the Making of Modern India.* Durham, NC: Duke University Press.

Hall, Derek. 2003. "The International Political Ecology of Industrial Shrimp Aquaculture and Industrial Plantation Forestry in Southeast Asia." *Journal of Southeast Asian Studies,* 34(2): 251–64.

Hall, Thomas D. 2002. "World-Systems Analysis and Globalization Directions for the Twenty First Century." In *Theoretical Directions in Political Sociology for the 21st Century,* vol. 2, edited by T. Buzzell. New York: Elsevier Science.

Hamilton, Clive. 2003. *Growth Fetish.* Sydney, Australia: Allen & Unwin.

Harcourt, Wendy. 1994. "Introduction." In *Feminist Perspectives on Sustainable Development,* edited by Wendy Harcourt. London: Zed.

Harding, Luke. 2001. "Delhi Calling." *Guardian Weekly,* March 15–21: 23.

Harper, Doug. 1994. "Auto Imports Jump in Mexico." *The New York Times,* July 7: D1.

Harris, Nigel. 1987. *The End of the Third World: Newly Industrializing Countries and the Decline of an Ideology.* Harmondsworth, UK: Penguin.

Harrison, Graham. 2004. *The World Bank and Africa: The Construction of Governance States.* London: Routledge.

Harrison, Paul. 1993. *The Third Revolution: Population, Environment and a Sustainable World.* Harmondsworth, UK: Penguin.

Harvey, David. 2005. *A Brief History of Neoliberalism.* Oxford, UK: Oxford University Press.

Harvey, Neil. 1994. *Rebellion in Chiapas: Rural Reforms, Campesino Radicalism, and the Limits to Salinismo.* San Diego: Center for U.S.–Mexican Studies.

Hathaway, Dale E. 1987. *Agriculture and the GATT: Rewriting the Rules.* Washington, DC: Institute for International Economics.

Hawkins, Tony. 1998. "At the Heart of Further Progress." *Financial Times,* June 2: I–VI.

Hayden, Tom. 2003. "Seeking a New Globalism in Chiapas." *The Nation,* April 7: 18–23.

Hedges, Chris. 1994. "Key Panel at Cairo Talks Agrees on Population Plan." *The New York Times,* September 13: A10.

Hedland, Stefan and Niclas Sundstrom. 1996. "The Russian Economy after Systemic Change." *Europe-Asia Studies* 48(6): 889.

Heffernan, William D. 1999. "Consolidation in the Food and Agriculture System." Report to the National Farmers Union. Retrieved February 5, 1999 from www.nfu.org/whstudy.html.

Heffernan, William D. and Douglas H. Constance. 1994. "Transnational Corporations and the Globalization of the Food System." In *From Columbus to ConAgra: The Globalization of Agriculture and Food,* edited by Alessandro Bonanno, Lawrence Busch, William Friedland, Lourdes Gouveia, and Enzo Mingione. Lawrence, KA: University Press of Kansas.

Held, David. 1995. *Democracy and the Global Order: From the Modern State to Cosmopolitan Governance.* Stanford, CA: Stanford University Press.

Helleiner, Eric. 1996. *States and the Reemergence of Global Finance: From Bretton Woods to the 1990s.* Ithaca, NY: Cornell University Press.

Hellman, Judith Adler. 1994. *Mexican Lives.* New York: Free Press.

Henderson, Jeffrey. 1991. *The Globalisation of High Technology Production.* London: Routledge & Kegan Paul.

Henley, Jon. 2003. "French Citizenship Ideal Dies in a High-Rise Hell." *Guardian Weekly,* January 16–22: 3.

Henley, Jon and Jeevan Vasagar. 2003. "Think Muslim, Drink Muslim, Says New Rival to Coke." *Guardian Weekly,* January 16–22: 3.

Herbert, Bob. 1996. "Nike's Pyramid Scheme." *The New York Times,* June 10: 33.

———. 1998. "At What Cost?" *The New York Times,* June 7: A15.

Hernández, Luis Navarro. 1994. "The Chiapas Uprising." In *Rebellion in Chiapas*, edited by Neil Harvey. San Diego: University of California—San Diego, Center for U.S.–Mexican Studies.

Hettne, Björn. 1990. *Development Theory and the Three Worlds*. White Plains, NY: Longman.

Hickman, Martin. 2006. "Earth's Ecological Debt Crisis." *The Independent*, October 9: 1–2.

Hightower, Jim. 2002. "How Wal-Mart is Remaking Our World." Pamphlet #7, Ithaca, NY.

Hildyard, Nicholas. 1993. "Foxes in Charge of Chickens." In *Global Ecology: A New Arena of Political Conflict*, edited by Wolfgang Sachs. London: Zed.

Hobsbawm, Eric J. 1992. "The Crisis of Today's Ideologies." *New Left Review* 192: 55–64.

Hochschild, Arlie Russell. 2003. "Love and Gold." In *Global Woman: Nannies, Maids, and Sex Workers in the New Economy*. New York: Metropolitan Books.

Holusha, John. 1996. "Squeezing the Textile Workers." *The New York Times*, February 21: D1, D20.

Hoogvelt, Ankie M. M. 1987. *The Third World in Global Development*. London: Macmillan.

———. 1997. *Globalization and the Postcolonial World: The New Political Economy of Development*. London: Macmillan.

Houtart, Francois and Francois Polet, eds. 2001. *The Other Davos: The Globalization of Resistance to the World Economic System*. London: Zed.

Huntington, Samuel, P. 1993. "The Clash of Civilizations." *Foreign Affairs* 72(3): 22–50.

Ibrahim, Youssef M. 1994. "Fundamentalists Impose Culture on Egypt." *The New York Times*, February 3: A1, A10.

Ihonvbere, Julius O. 1993–1994. "The Third World and the New World Order in the 1990s." In *Third World 94/95: Annual Editions*, edited by Robert J. Griffiths. Guildford, CT: Dushkin.

International Monetary Fund. 2001. "Balance of Payment Statistics." Retrieved from www.imf.org/external/up/sta/bop/bop.htm.

Iriart, Celia, and Howard Waitzkin. 2004. "Managed Care Goes Global." *Multinational Monitor* 25(10): Available at www.multinationalmonitor.org.

Jackson, Cecile. 1993. "Doing What Comes Naturally? Women and Environment in Development." *World Development* 21(12): 1947–63.

Jaffee, Daniel. 2007. *Brewing Justice: Fair Trade Coffee, Sustainability, and Survival*. Berkeley, CA: University of California Press.

Jahan, Rounaq. 1995. *The Elusive Agenda: Mainstreaming Women in Development*. London: Zed.

James, C. L. R. 1963. *The Black Jacobins: Toussaint L'Ouverture and the San Domingo Revolution*. New York: Vintage.

Jenkins, Rhys. 1992. "Industrialization and the Global Economy." In *Industrialization and Development*, edited by Tom Hewitt, Hazel Johnson, and Dave Wield. Oxford, UK: Oxford University Press.

Jordan, Mary and Kevin Sullivan. 2003. "Trade Brings Riches, but Not to Mexico's Poor." *Guardian Weekly*, April 3–9: 33.

Juhasz, Antonia. 2002. "Servicing Citi's Interests: GATS and the Bid to Remove Barriers to Financial Firm Globalization." *Multinational Monitor* 23(4). Retrieved from www.multinationalmonitor.org/mm2002/02April/Apri102corp3.html.

Kagarlitsky, Boris. 1995. *The Mirage of Modernization*. New York: Monthly Review Press.

Kahn, Joseph. 2002. "Losing Faith: Globalization Proves Disappointing." *The New York Times*, March 21: 7.

———. 2003. "China's Workers Risk Limbs in Export Drive." *The New York Times*, April 7: 3.

Kaldor, Mary. 1990. *The Imaginary War: Understanding the East–West Conflict*. Oxford, UK: Blackwell.

Kamel, Laila Iskandar. 1999. "The Urban Poor as Development Partners." *Cooperation South* 2: 127–33.

Kane, Hal. 1996. "Micro-Enterprise." *World Watch* 9(2): 11–19.

Karliner, Joshua. 1997. *The Corporate Planet: Ecology and Politics in the Age of Globalization.* San Francisco: Sierra Club Books.

Kemp, Tom. 1989. *Industrialization in the Non-Western World.* London: Longman.

Kennedy, Gina, Guy Nantel and Prakash Shetty. 2004. "Globalization of Food Systems in Developing Countries: A Synthesis of Country Case Studies." In *Globalization of Food Systems in Developing Countries: Impact on Food Security and Nutrition,* eds Gina Kennedy, Guy Nantel, and Prakash Shetty. Rome: Food and Agricultural Organization of the United Nations.

Kernaghan, Charles. 1995. *Zoned for Slavery: The Child Behind the Label* [Videotape]. New York: National Labor Committee.

Kikeri, Sunita and John Nellis. 2002. *Privatization in Competitive Sectors: The Record to Date.* World Bank Policy Research Working Paper 2860. World Bank, Washington, DC.

Kilvert, Andrew. 1998. "Golden Promises." *New Internationalist,* September: 16–17.

Kimbrell, Andrew. 2002. *The Fatal Harvest Reader: The Tragedy of Industrial Agriculture.* Washington, DC: Island Press.

King, Alexander and Bertrand Schneider. 1991. *The First Global Revolution: A Report by the Council to the Club of Rome.* New York: Pantheon.

Klare, Michael T. 2002. *Resource Wars: The New Landscape of Global Conflict.* New York: Henry Holt & Company.

Klein, Naomi. 2003. "No Peace Without a Fight." *The Nation,* March 31: 10.

Klenk, Rebecca M. 2004. "'Who is the Developed Woman?': Women as a Category of Development Discourse, Kumaon, India." *Development and Change* 35(1): 57–78.

Kloppenburg, Jack R. Jr. 1988. *First the Seed: The Political Economy of Plant Biotechnology, 1492–2000.* Cambridge, MA: Cambridge University Press.

Kneen, Brewster. 1990. *Trading Up: How Cargill, the World's Largest Grain Company, is Changing World Agriculture.* Toronto: N.C. Press.

Knox, Paul and John Agnew. 1994. *The Geography of the World Economy.* London: Edward Arnold.

Kohl, Benjamin and Linda Farthing. 2006. *Impasse in Bolivia. Neoliberal Hegemony & Popular Resistance.* London: Zed.

Kohli, Geeta and Kim Webster. 1999. "Female Circumcision: A Ritual Worth Continuing?" Unpublished term paper, Rural Sociology, Cornell University, New York.

Kolko, Joyce. 1988. *Restructuring the World Economy.* New York: Pantheon.

Kotkin, Stephen. 2007. "First World, Third World (Maybe Not in That Order)." *The New York Times,* May 6: 4.

Korten, David. 1995. *When Corporations Rule the World.* New York: Kumarian.

Korzeniewicz, Miguel. 1994. "Commodity Chains and Marketing Strategies: Nike and the Global Athletic Footwear Industry." In *Commodity Chains and Global Capitalism,* edited by Gary Gereffi and Miguel Korzeniewicz. Westport, CT: Praeger.

Kothari, Smitu and Pramod Parajuli. 1993. "No Nature Without Social Justice: A Plea for Cultural and Ecological Pluralism in India." In *Global Ecology: A New Arena of Political Conflict,* edited by Wolfgang Sachs. London: Zed.

Landsberg, Martin. 1979. "Export-Led Industrialization in the Third World: Manufacturing Imperialism." *Review of Radical Political Economics* 2(4): 50–63.

Lang, Tim. 1998. "Dietary Impact of the Globalization of Food Trade." *IFG News, International Forum on Globalization* 3: 10–12.

Lang, Tim and Colin Hines. 1993. *The New Protectionism: Protecting the Future against Free Trade.* New York: The New Press.

Lang, Tim and Michael Heasman. 2004. *Food Wars: The Global Battle for Mouths, Minds and Markets.* London: Earthscan.

Lappé, Frances Moore, Joseph Collins, and Peter Rosset, with Luis Esparza. 1998. *World Hunger: Twelve Myths.* 2nd ed. New York: Grove.

Lappé, Frances Moore and Anna Lappé. 2002. *Hope's Edge*. New York: Tarcher/Putnam.

Lappin, Todd. 1994. "Can Green Mix with Red?" *The Nation*, February 14: 193.

LaTouche, Serge. 1993. *In the Wake of the Affluent Society: An Exploration of Post-Development*. London: Zed.

———. 2004. "Degrowth Economics." *Le Monde diplomatique*, November: 15.

Leader article, 2004. "Shining Example." *The Guardian*, April 23: 3.

Le Carre, John. 2001. "In Place of Nations." *The Nation*, April 9: 11–13.

Legrand, Christine. 2002. "Argentina's New Poor Battle Against Hunger." *Guardian Weekly*, July 11–17: 30.

Lehman, David. 1990. *Democracy and Development in Latin America*. Philadelphia: Temple University Press.

Lehman, K. and A. Krebs. 1996. "Control of the World's Food Supply." In *The Case Against the Global Economy, and for a Turn toward the Local*, edited by J. Mander and E. Goldsmith. San Francisco: Sierra Club Books.

LeQuesne, C. 1997. "The World Trade Organization and Food Security." Talk to UK Food Group, July 15, London.

Lewin, Tamar. 1995. "Family Decay Global, Study Says." *The New York Times*, May 30: A5.

Lewis, Paul. 1997. "IMF Seeks Argentine Deal Linking Credit to Governing." *The New York Times*, July 15: D1, D19.

Li, Tania Murray. 1999. "Compromising Power: Development, Culture, and Rule in Indonesia." *Cultural Anthropology* 14(3): 295–322.

Lietaer, Bernard. 1997. "From the Real Economy to the Speculative." *International Forum on Globalization News* 2: 7–10.

Lipton, Michael. 1977. *Why Poor People Stay Poor: Urban Bias in World Development*. London: Temple Smith.

Lissakers, Karin. 1993. *Banks, Borrowers, and the Establishment: A Revisionist Account of the International Debt Crisis*. New York: Basic Books.

Llambi, Luis. 1990. "Transitions to and Within Capitalism: Agrarian Transitions in Latin America." *Sociologia Ruralis* 30(2): 174–96.

Lohmann, Larry. 1993. "Resisting Green Globalism." In *Global Ecology: A New Arena of Political Conflict*, edited by Wolfgang Sachs. London: Zed.

London, Christopher. 1997. "Class Relations and Capitalist Development: Subsumption in the Colombian Coffee Industry." *Journal of Peasant Studies* 24(4): 269–95.

Lorch, Donatella. 1995. "Ugandan Strongman a Favorite of World Lenders." *The New York Times*, January 29: A3.

Lynas, M. 2001. "Selling Starvation." *Corporate Watch* 7 (Spring). Available at www.corpwatch.org.

Maass, Peter. 2001. "Emroz Khan is Having a Bad Day." *The New York Times Magazine*, October 21: 48–51.

MacKinnon, Ian. 2007. "Palm Oil: The Biofuel of the Future Driving an Ecological Disaster Now." *The Guardian*, April 4.

MacShane, Denis. 1991. "Working in Virtual Slavery: Gulf Migrant Labor." *The Nation*, March 18: 325, 343–44.

Madden, Peter and John Madeley. 1993. "Winners and Losers: The Impact of the GATT Uruguay Round in Developing Countries." *Christian Aid*, December: 17.

Madeley, John. 2000. *Hungry for Trade*. London: Zed.

Magdoff, Harry. 1969. *The Age of Imperialism*. New York: Monthly Review Press.

Mamdani, Mahmood. 1996. *Citizen and Subject: Contemporary Africa and the Legacy of Late Colonialism*. Princeton, NJ: Princeton University Press.

———. 2003. "Making Sense of Political Violence in Post-Colonial Africa." In *Fighting Identities: Race, Religion and Ethno-Nationalism: Socialist Register 2003*, edited by Leo Panitch and Colin Leys. London: Merlin.

Mark, Jason. 2001. "Brazil's MST: Taking Back the Land." *Multinational Monitor* 22: 10–12.

Marsden, Terry K. 2003. *The Condition of Rural Sustainability*. Wageningen: Van Gorcum.

Martin, Hans-Peter and Harold Schumann. 1997. *The Global Trap: Globalisation and the Assault on Democracy and Prosperity*. London: Zed.

Matthews, C. 2006. "Livestock a Major Threat to Environment." *FAO Newsroom*, November 29. Available at: www.fao.org/newsroom/en/news/2006/1000448/index.html.

Maybarduk, Peter. 2004. "A People's Health System." *Multinational Monitor* 25(10). Available at www.multinationalmonitor.org.

McBride, Stephen. 2006. "Reconfiguring Sovereignty: NAFTA Chapter 11 Dispute Settlement Procedures and the Issue of Public-Private Authority." *Canadian Journal of Political Science/Revue canadienne de science politique* 39(4): 1–21.

McDougall, Dan. 2007. "Success in a Slum." *Guardian Weekly*, March 16–22: 29.

McGreal, Chris. 2006–07. "Continent Waits to See Cost of Lavish Embrace." *Guardian Weekly*, December 22–January 4: 6.

McKay, Steven C. 2006. *Satanic Mills or Silicon Islands? The Politics of High-Tech Production in the Philippines*. Ithaca: Cornell University Press.

McMichael, A. J. 1993. *Planetary Overload: Global Environmental Change and the Health of the Human Species*. Cambridge, UK: Cambridge University Press.

McMichael, Philip. 1993a. "World Food System Restructuring under a GATT Regime." *Political Geography* 12(3): 198–214.

———. 1993b. "Agro-Food Restructuring in the Pacific Rim: A Comparative-International Perspective on Japan, South Korea, the United States, Australia, and Thailand." In *Pacific-Asia and the Future of the World-System*, edited by Ravi Palat. Westport, CT: Greenwood.

———. 2001. "The Impact of Globalisation, Free Trade and Technology on Food and Nutrition in the New Millennium." *Proceedings of the Nutrition Society* 60(2): 215–20.

———. 2003. "Food Security and Social Reproduction." In *Power, Production and Social Reproduction: Human In/security in the Global Political Economy*, edited by Stephen Gill and Isabella Bakker. London: Palgrave Macmillan.

———. 2005. "Global Development and the Corporate Food Regime." In *New Directions in the Sociology of Global Development*, edited by Frederick H. Buttel and Philip McMichael. Amsterdam: Elsevier.

McMichael, Philip and Chul-Kyoo Kim. 1994. "Japanese and South Korean Agricultural Restructuring in Comparative and Global Perspective." In *The Global Restructuring of Agro-Food Systems*, edited by Philip McMichael. Ithaca, NY: Cornell University Press.

McMichael, Philip and David Myhre. 1991. "Global Regulation versus the Nation-State: Agro-Food Systems and the New Politics of Capital." *Capital & Class* 43(2): 83–106.

McMichael, Philip and Laura T. Raynolds. 1994. "Capitalism, Agriculture, and World Economy." In *Capitalism and Development*, edited by Leslie Sklair. London: Routledge Kegan Paul.

McMurtry, John. 2002. *Value Wars. The Global Market Versus the Life Economy*. London: Pluto.

Memmi, Albert. 1967. *The Colonizer and the Colonized*. Boston: Beacon.

Menon, Gayatri A. 2001. The Multivalency of Microcredit: The Cultural Politics of Credit and Citizenship in India. Unpublished Master's thesis, Development Sociology, Cornell University, New York.

———. 2007. "Securing Shelter in the Shadow of Violence: the Clandestine Politics of the Urban Poor in Mumbai." Paper presented to Living on the Margins conference, Cape Town, South Africa, March 26–28.

Menotti, Victor. 1996. "World Leaders Warn of 'Backlash to Globalization.'" *International Forum on Globalization News*, Fall: 1, 7.

———. 1998. "Globalization and the Acceleration of Forest Destruction Since Rio." *The Ecologist* 28(6): 354–62.

———. 1999. "Forest Destruction and Globalisation." *The Ecologist* 29(3): 180–81.

Meredith, Robyn. 1997. "Auto Giants Build a Glut of Asian Plants, Just as Demand Falls." *The New York Times*, November 5: D1, D8.

Middleton, Neil, Phil O'Keefe, and Sam Moyo. 1993. *Tears of the Crocodile: From Rio to Reality in the Developing World*. Boulder, CO: Pluto.

Mies, Maria. 1991. *Patriarchy and Accumulation on a World Scale: Women in the International Division of Labor*. London: Zed.

Milbank, Dana. 1994. "Unlike Rest of Europe, Britain is Creating Jobs but They Pay Poorly." *Wall Street Journal*, March 28: A1, A6.

Millstone, Erik and Tim Lang. 2003. *The Atlas of Food*, London: Earthscan.

Mitchell, Timothy. 1991. *Colonizing Egypt*. Berkeley, CA: University of California Press.

Mittal, Anuradha. 1998. "Freedom to Trade vs. Freedom from Hunger: Food Security in the Age of Economic Globalization." In *WTO as a Conceptual Framework for Globalization*, edited by Eva Harton and Claes Olsson. Uppsala, Sweden: Global Publications Foundation.

Moberg, David. 1999. "Bringing Down Niketown." *The Nation*, June 7: 15–18.

Moghadam, Valentine M. 1993. *Modernizing Women: Gender and Social Change in the Middle East*. Boulder, CO: Lynne Rienner.

———. 2005a. *Globalization Women. Transnational Feminist Networks*. Baltimore: Johns Hopkins University Press.

———. 2005b. "Editorial." *International Social Science Journal*, 184: 203–06.

Moghadam, Valentine M. and Lucie Senftova. 2005. "Measuring Women's Empowerment: Participation and Rights in Civil, Political, Social, Economic, and Cultural Domains." *International Social Science Journal* 184: 389–412.

Monbiot, George. 2006. *Heat: How to Stop the Planet Burning*. London: Allen Lane.

Montalbano, William D. 1991. "A Global Pursuit of Happiness." *Los Angeles Times*, October 1: F1.

Moody, Kim. 1999. *Workers in a Lean World: Unions in the International Economy*. London: Verso.

Moran, Theodore H. 2000. "Investment Issues." In *The WTO After Seattle*, edited by Jeffrey J. Schott. Washington, DC: Institute for International Economics.

Morgan, Dan. 1980. *Merchants of Grain*. Harmondsworth, UK: Penguin.

Mosse, David. 2004. "Is Good Policy Unimplementable? Reflections on the Ethnography of Aid Policy and Practice." *Development and Change, 35*(4): 639–671.

Muchena, D. T. 2006. "The China Factor in Southern Africa." *Openspace*, 1(4): 22–26.

Müller, Anders Riel and Raj Patel. 2004. "Shining India? Economic Liberalization and Rural Poverty in the 1990s." *Food First Policy Brief No. 10*.

Murphy, Sophia. 1999. "WTO, Agricultural Deregulation, and Food Security." Paper presented at the Globalization Challenge Initiative, December. Retrieved from www.foreignpolicy-infocus .org/briefs/v0114n34wto_body.html.

———. 2006. *Is a Green Revolution for Africa the Answer?* Minneapolis: Institute for Agriculture and Trade Policy, Brief no. 20, October 27.

Myers, Norman. 1981. "The Hamburger Connection: How Central America's Forests Became North America's Hamburgers." *Ambio* 10(1): 3–8.

Myerson, Allen R. 1997. "In Principle, a Case for More 'Sweatshops.'" *The New York Times*, June 22: 5.

Myhre, David. 1994. "The Politics of Globalization in Rural Mexico: Campesino Initiatives to Restructure the Agricultural Credit System." In *The Global Restructuring of Agro-Food Systems*, edited by Philip McMichael. Ithaca, NY: Cornell University Press.

Narayan, Deepa, with Raj Patel, Kai Schaft, Anne Rademacher and Sarah Koch-Schulte. 2002. *Can Anyone Hear Us? Voices of the Poor*. New York: Oxford.

Nash, Nathaniel C. 1994. "Vast Areas of Rain Forest are Being Destroyed in Chile." *The New York Times*, May 31: C4.

Ndulo, Muna. 2002. "International Trade, Development, and Africa." *Africa Notes* (Institute for African Development, Cornell University), September–October: 6–10.

Nepstad, D. 2006. "Diet for a Hot Planet." *Boston Globe*, November 22. Available at www.boston.com/news/globe/editorial_opinion/oped/articles/2006/11/22/diet_for_a_ hot_planet.

Neville, Richard. 1997. "The Business of Being Human." *Good Weekend* (*The Age*, Melbourne, Australia), August 23: 48–50.

New Internationalist. 2007. "Sand in the Wheels." May: 10–11.

Newman, Bryan. 2006. "Indian Farmer Suicides: A Lesson for Africa's Farmers." *Food First Backgrounder* 12(4): 2.

Noble, David. 2007. "The Corporate Climate Coup." *ZNet/Science*, May 8. Available at www.zmag.org/content/print_article.cfm?itemID=12771&section.

Nogueira, Ana, Josh Bretbart, and Chris Strohm. 2003. "Rebellion in Argentina." Retrieved from www.zmag.org/Zmag/articles/may02nogueira_breitbart_strohm.htm.

Norberg-Hodge, Helena. 1992. *Ancient Futures: Learning from Ladakh.* San Francisco: Sierra Club.

———. 1994–1995. "Globalization versus Community." *ISEC/Ladakh Project* 14: 1–2.

Ohmae, Kenichi. 1985. *Triad Power: The Coming Shape of Global Competition.* New York: Free Press.

———. 1990. *The End of the Nation-State: The Rise of Regional Economies.* New York: Free Press.

Olive, David. 2003. "Global Cooling." *Toronto Star*, April 6. Posted April 8, 2003 by mritchie@iatp.org.

O'Meara, Molly. 1999. "Reinventing Cities for People and the Planet." Worldwatch Paper No. 147, Washington, DC: Worldwatch.

Ong, Aihwa. 1997. "The Gender and Labor Politics of Postmodernity." In *The Politics of Culture in the Shadow of Capital*, edited by Lisa Lowe and David Lloyd. Durham, NC: Duke University Press.

Ong, Aihwa. 2000. "Graduated Sovereignty in Southeast Asia." *Theory, Culture and Society* 17(4): 55–75.

Onishi, Norimitsu. 1998. "Nigeria Combustible as South's Oil Enriches North." *The New York Times*, November 22: A1, A6.

———. 1999. "Deep in the Republic of Chevron." *The New York Times Magazine*, July 4: 26–31.

———. 2001. "Rising Muslim Power in Africa Causes Unrest in Nigeria and Elsewhere." *The New York Times*, November 1: A14.

Orlanda Pinnasi, Maria, Fatima Cabral, and Mirian Claudia Lourencao. 2000. "An Interview with Joao Pedro Stedile." *Latin American Perspectives* 27(5): 46–62.

Panitch, Leo. 1996. "Rethinking the Role of the State." In *Globalization: Critical Reflections*, edited by James H. Mittelman. Boulder, CO: Lynne Rienner.

Paranagua, Paulo A. 2007. "Caracas Runs on Easy Money." *Guardian Weekly*, February 9–15: 27.

Parenti, Christian. 2005. "Hugo Chávez and Petro Populism." *The Nation*, April 11: 15–21.

Paringaux, R.-P. 2001. "The Deliberate Destruction of Agriculture: India: Free Markets, Empty Bellies." *Le Monde Diplomatique*, September: 1–9.

Parrott, Nicholas, and Terry Marsden. 2002. *The Real Green Revolution: Organic and Agroecological Farming in the South.* London: Greenpeace Environmental Trust.

Patel, Raj. 2007. *Stuffed and Starved: Markets, Power and the Hidden Battle for the World Food System.* London: Portobello Books.

Patel, Raj, with A. Delwiche. 2002a. "The Profits of Famine: Southern Africa's Long Decade of Hunger." *Backgrounder, Food First* 8(4). Retrieved from www.foodfirst.org/pubs/backgrdrs/2002/f02v8n4.html.

———. 2002b. "What Does NEPAD Stand For?" Retrieved from http://voiceoftheturtle.org/show_article.php?aid=97.

Patnaik, Utsa. 2003. "Global Capitalism, Deflation and Agrarian Crisis in Developing Countries." *Social Policy and Development Programme Paper Number 15.* Geneva: UNRISD.

Payer, Cheryl. 1974. *The Debt Trap.* New York: Monthly Review Press.

Pearse, A. 1980. *Seeds of Plenty, Seeds of Want.* Oxford, UK: Clarendon.

Perkins, John H. 1997. *Geopolitics and the Green Revolution: Wheat, Genes and the Cold War.* New York: Oxford University Press.

Perlez, Jane. 2001. "U.N. Chief Calls on U.S. Companies to Donate to AIDS Fund." *The New York Times*, June 2: A1.

———. 2002. "For Some Indonesians, Echoes of 'Coolie' Nation." *The New York Times*, August 18: 10.

Perrons, Diane. 2005. *Globalization and Social Change. People and Places in a Divided World*. London: Routledge.

Phillips, Michael M. 2002. "U.S. to Push Service-Sector Trade in a Sweeping Liberalization Plan." *Wall Street Journal*, July 1: 5.

Phillips, Tom. 2007. "Despite a Crackdown, Illicit Logging is on the Rise in Lawless Areas of the Amazon." *The Guardian*, April 21. Available at www.guardian.co.uk.

Pilger, John. 2002. *The New Rulers of the World*. London: Verso.

Pitt, William Rivers. 2003. "Be Afraid . . . " *The Ecologist* 33(3): 21–22.

Place, Susan E. 1985. "Export Beef Production and Development Contradictions in Costa Rica." *Tijdschrift voor Econ. en Soc. Geografie* 76(4): 288–97.

Plehwe, Dieter. 2007. "What Kind of Development Knowledge? Probing the World Bank's Civil Society." *Globalizations* 4(4): 517–531.

Polgreen, Lydia. 2007. "Africa's Storied Colleges, Jammed and Crumbling." *The New York Times*, May 20: A1, 4.

Pollack, Andrew. 1999. "Biological Products Raise Genetic Ownership Issues." *The New York Times*, November 26: A9.

Pretty, Jules. 2007. *The Earth Only Endures: On Reconnecting With Nature and Our Place In It*. London: Earthscan.

Public Citizen. 2001. "Down on the Farm: NAFTA's Seven-Year War on Farmers and Ranchers in the U.S., Canada and Mexico." Retrieved from www.citizen.org.

Pyle, Jean L. 2001. "Sex, Maids, and Export Processing: Risks and Reasons for Gendered Global Production Networks." *International Journal of Politics, Culture and Society* 15(1): 55–76.

Quing, Dai. 1998. "The Three Gorges Project: A Symbol of Uncontrolled Development in the Late Twentieth Century." In *The River Dragon Has Come! The Three Gorges Dam and the Fate of China's Yangtze River and Its People*, edited by Dai Quing. London: M. E. Sharpe.

Rademacher, Anne and Raj Patel. 2002. "Retelling Worlds of Poverty: Reflections on Transforming Participatory Research for a Global Narrative." In *Knowing Poverty: Critical Reflections on Participatory Research and Policy*, edited by K. Brock and R. McGee. London: Earthscan.

Radford, Tim. 2005. "Most of World's Resources 'Used Up.'" *Guardian Weekly*, April 8–14: 12.

Raghavan, Chakravarthi. 1990. *Recolonization: GATT, the Uruguay Round and the Third World*. Penang, Malaysia: Third World Network.

Raikes, Philip. 1988. *Modernising Hunger: Famine, Food Surplus & Farm Policy in the EC and Africa*. London: Catholic Institute for International Affairs.

Ramesh, Randeep. 2006. "Indians Get First Taste of Supermarket Shopping, but Wal-Mart is Kept at Bay." *Guardian Weekly*, June 9–15: 16.

Rankin, Kathy. 2001. "Governing Development: Neoliberalism, Microcredit, and Rational Economic Woman." *Economy and Society* 30(1): 18–37.

Ransom, David. 2001a. "A World Turned Upside Down." *New Internationalist* 334: 9–11.

———. 2001b. *The No-Nonsense Guide to Fair Trade*. London: Verso.

Rau, Bill. 1991. *From Feast to Famine: Official Cures and Grassroots Remedies to Africa's Food Crisis*. London: Zed.

Raynolds, Laura T. 1994. "The Restructuring of Export Agriculture in the Dominican Republic: Changing Agrarian Relations and the State." In *The Global Restructuring of Agro-Food Systems*, edited by Philip McMichael. Ithaca, NY: Cornell University Press.

———. 2000. "Re-Embedding Global Agriculture: The International Organic and Fair Trade Movements." *Agriculture and Human Values* 17: 297–309.

———. 2001. "New Plantations, New Workers: Gender and Production Politics in the Dominican Republic." *Gender & Society* 15(1): 7–28.

Raynolds, Laura T., David Myhre, Philip McMichael, Viviana Carro-Figueroa, and Frederick H. Buttel. 1993. "The 'New' Internationalization of Agriculture: A Reformulation." *World Development* 21(7): 1101–21.

Razavi, Shahrashoub and Carol Miller. 1995. *From WID to GAD: Conceptual Shifts in the Women and Development Discourse.* Occasional Paper 1, (Geneva: UN Research Institute for Social Development, UNDP).

Reardon, T., C. P. Timmer, C. B. Barrett, and J. Berdegue. 2003. "The Rise of Supermarkets in Africa, Asia, and Latin America." *American Journal of Agricultural Economics* 85(5): 1140–46.

Reardon, Tom and C. P. Timmer. 2005. "Transformation of Markets for Agricultural Output in Developing Countries Since 1950: How Has Thinking Changed?" In *Handbook of Agricultural Economics,* edited by R. E. Evenson, P. Pingali, and T. P. Schultz. Oxford: Elsevier.

Redding, Sean. 2000. "Structural Adjustment and the Decline of Subsistence Agriculture in Africa." Retrieved from http://womencrossing.org/redding.html.

Reich, Robert B. 1991. "Secession of the Successful." *The New York Times Magazine,* January 20: 42.

———. 1992. *The Work of Nations: Preparing Ourselves for 21st Century Capitalism.* New York: Vintage.

Renner, Michael. 2002. *The Anatomy of Resource Wars.* Worldwatch Paper no. 162. Washington, DC: Worldwatch.

Research Unit for Political Economy. 2003. *Behind the Invasion of Iraq.* New York: Monthly Review Press.

Revel, Alain and Christophe Riboud. 1986. *American Green Power.* Baltimore: Johns Hopkins University Press.

Ricardo, David. 1951 [1821]. *On the Principles of Political Economy and Taxation.* 3rd ed. In *The Works and Correspondence of David Ricardo,* vol. 1, edited by P. Sraffe with the collaboration of M. M. Dobb. Cambridge, UK: Cambridge University Press.

Rich, Bruce. 1994. *Mortgaging the Earth: The World Bank, Environmental Impoverishment, and the Crisis of Development.* Boston: Beacon.

Richburg, Keith B. 2002. "Illegal Workers Do Europe's Dirty Work." *Guardian Weekly,* August 15–21: 29.

Ride, Anouk. 1998. "Maps, Myths, and Migrants." *New Internationalist* 305: 9.

Riding, Alan. 1993. "France, Reversing Course, Fights Immigrants' Refusal to Be French." *The New York Times,* December 5: A1, 14.

Rifkin, Jeremy. 1992. *Beyond Beef: The Rise and Fall of the Cattle Culture.* New York: Penguin.

———. 1998. *The Biotech Century: Harnessing the Gene and Remaking the World.* New York: Tarcher/Putnam.

Rist, Gilbert. 1997. *The History of Development: From Western Origins to Global Faith.* London: Zed.

Ritchie, Mark. 1993. *Breaking the Deadlock: The United States and Agriculture Policy in the Uruguay Round.* Minneapolis: Institute for Agriculture and Trade Policy.

———. 1994. "GATT Facts: Africa Loses under GATT." Working paper, Institute for Agriculture and Trade Policy, Minneapolis, MN.

———. 1999. "The World Trade Organization and the Human Right to Food Security." Paper presented at the International Cooperative Agriculture Organization General Assembly, August 29, Quebec City, Canada. Available from www.agricoop.org/activities/mark_rithcie.pdf.

Roberts, Timmons J. and Bradley C. Parks. 2007. *A Climate of Injustice. Global Inequality, North–South Politics, and Climate Policy.* Cambridge, MA: MIT Press.

Robinson, William I. 1996. *Promoting Polyarchy: Globalization, US Intervention, and Hegemony.* Cambridge, UK: Cambridge University Press.

———. 2004. *A Theory of Global Capitalism: Production, Class, and State in a Transnational World.* Baltimore: Johns Hopkins University Press.

Rocca, Jean-Louis. 2007. "The Flaws in the Chinese Economic Miracle." *Le Monde diplomatique*, May: 10.

Rocheleau, Dianne E. 1991. "Gender, Ecology, and the Science of Survival: Stories and Lessons from Kenya." In *Feminist Perspectives on Sustainable Development*, edited by Wendy Harcourt. London: Zed.

Rohter, Larry. 2002. "Amazon Forest Still Burning Despite the Good Intentions." *The New York Times*, August 23: A1, A9.

———. 2003. "Relentless Foe of the Amazon Jungle: Soybeans." *The New York Times*, September 17: 3.

Roodman, David Malin. 2001. "Still Waiting for the Jubilee: Pragmatic Solutions for the Third World Debt Crisis." Worldwatch Paper No. 155. Washington, DC: Worldwatch.

Rosenberg, Tina. 1998. "Trees and the Roots of a Storm's Destruction." *The New York Times*, November 26: A38.

Ross, Robert J. S. and Kent C. Trachte. 1990. *Global Capitalism: The New Leviathan*. Albany, NY: SUNY Press.

Rostow, Walt W. 1960. *The Stages of Economic Growth: A Non-Communist Manifesto*. Cambridge, UK: Cambridge University Press.

Rothchild, Donald and Letitia Lawson. 1994. "The Interactions between State and Civil Society in Africa: From Deadlock to New Routines." In *Civil Society and the State in Africa*, edited by John W. Harbeson, Donald Rothchild, and Naomi Chazan. Boulder, CO: Lynne Rienner.

Rothkopf, David. 2005. "Pain in the Middle." *Newsweek International*, November 21. Available at www.msnbc.msc.com/id/10019816/site/newsweek.

Rowley, C. D. 1974. *The Destruction of Aboriginal Society*. Ringwood, Australia: Penguin.

Rowling, Megan. 2001. "Sea Change." *New Internationalist* 341: 23–24.

Roy, Olivier. 1998. *The Failure of Political Islam*. Cambridge, MA: Harvard University Press.

Rueschemeyer, Dietrich, Evelyne Huber Stephens, and John Stephens. 1992. *Capitalist Development and Democracy*. Chicago: University of Chicago Press.

Ruggiero, Renato. 1996. "Trading Towards Peace?" Address to the MENA II Conference, December 11, Cairo, Egypt.

———. 1998. "From Vision to Reality: the Multilateral Trading System at Fifty." Address presented at the Brookings Institution Forum, Washington, DC, December.

———. 2000. "Reflections from Seattle." In *The WTO After Seattle*, edited by Jeffrey Schott. Washington, DC: Institute for International Economics.

Sachs, Jeffrey. 1998. "The IMF and the Asian Flu." *The American Prospect*, March–April: 16–21.

———. 2005. *The End of Poverty: Economic Possibilities for Our Time*. New York: Penguin.

Sachs, Wolfgang. 1992a. "One World." In *The Development Dictionary*, edited by Wolfgang Sachs. London: Zed.

———. 1992b. "The Discovery of Poverty." *New Internationalist* 232. Available at www.newint.org/issue232.

———. 1993. "Global Ecology and the Shadow of 'Development.'" In *Global Ecology: A New Arena of Political Conflict*, edited by Wolfgang Sachs. London: Zed.

———. 1999. *Planet Dialectics: Explorations in Environment and Development*. London: Zed.

Sadasivam, Bharati. 1997. "The Impact of Structural Adjustment on Women: A Governance and Human Rights Agenda." *Human Rights Quarterly* 19(3): 630–65.

Saldaña-Portillo, María Josefina. 2003. *The Revolutionary Imagination in the Americas and the Age of Development*. Durham, NC: Duke University Press.

Salinger, Lynn and Jean-Jacques Dethier. 1989. "Policy-Based Lending in Agriculture: Agricultural Sector Adjustment in Mexico." Paper presented at World Bank Seminar on Policy-Based Lending in Agriculture, Baltimore, May 17–19.

Salmon, Katy. 2001. "Where There are No Subsidies." *New Internationalist* 334: 22.

Sandbrook, Richard. 1995. *The Politics of Africa's Economic Recovery.* Cambridge, UK: Cambridge University Press.

Sanderson, Steven. 1986a. *The Transformation of Mexican Agriculture: International Structure and the Politics of Rural Change.* Princeton, NJ: Princeton University Press.

———. 1986b. "The Emergence of the 'World Steer': Internationalization and Foreign Domination in Latin American Cattle Production." In *Food, the State, and International Political Economy,* edited by F. L. Tullis and W. L. Hollist. Lincoln: University of Nebraska Press.

Sanger, David E. 1998. "Dissension Erupts at Talks on World Financial Crisis." *The New York Times,* October 7: A6.

Santos, B. de S. 2002. *Towards a New Legal Common Sense.* London: Butterworths.

Saul, John Ralston. 2005. *The Collapse of Globalism and the Reinvention of the World.* New York: Penguin.

Schaeffer, Robert. 1995. "Free Trade Agreements: Their Impact on Agriculture and the Environment." In *Food and Agrarian Orders in the World-Economy,* edited by Philip McMichael. Westport, CT: Praeger.

———. 1997. *Understanding Globalization: The Social Consequences of Political, Economic, and Environmental Change.* New York: Rowman & Littlefield.

Schemo, Diana Jean. 1997. "Rising Fires Renew Threat to Amazon." *The New York Times,* November 2: A6.

———. 1998. "Data Show Recent Burning of Amazon is Worst Ever." *The New York Times,* January 27: A4.

Schneider, Cathy Lisa. 1995. *Shantytown Protest in Pinochet's Chile.* Philadelphia: Temple University Press.

Schoenberger, Erica. 1994. "Competition, Time, and Space in Industrial Change." In *Commodity Chains and Global Capitalism,* edited by Gary Gereffi and Miguel Korzeniewicz. Westport, CT: Praeger.

Schott, Jeffrey J. 2000. "The WTO After Seattle." In *The WTO After Seattle,* edited by Jeffrey J. Schott. Washington, DC: Institute for International Economics.

Schwedel, S. and K. Haley. 1992. "Foreign Investment in the Mexican Food System." *Business Mexico* (Special Edition) 2: 48–55.

Segelken, Roger. 1995. "Fewer Foods Predicted for Crowded Future Meals." *Cornell Chronicle,* February 23: 5.

Seidman, Gay. 1994. *Manufacturing Militance: Workers' Movements in Brazil and South Africa, 1970–1985.* Berkeley, CA: University of California Press.

———. 2005. "'Stateless' Regulation and Consumer Pressure: Historical Experiences of Transnational Corporate Monitoring." In *New Directions in the Sociology of Global Development,* edited by Frederick H. Buttel and Philip McMichael. Amsterdam: Elsevier.

Sen, Gita. 1994. "Women, Poverty, and Population: Issues for the Concerned Environmentalist." In *Feminist Perspectives on Sustainable Development,* edited by Wendy Harcourt. London: Zed.

Sengupta, Somini. 2002. "Money from Kin Abroad Helps Bengalis Get By." *The New York Times,* June 24: 3.

Séréni, Jean-Pierre. 2007. "Hydrocarbon Nationalism." *Le Monde diplomatique,* March: 12.

Sharma, Kalpana. 2000. *Rediscovering Dharavi. Stories from Asia's Largest Slum.* New Delhi: Penguin.

Sharma, Devinder. 2007. "Big Box Retail Will Boost Poverty." *India Together,* February 16.

Sheller, Mimi. 2003: *Consuming the Caribbean.* New York: Routledge.

Shenon, Philip. 1993. "Saipan Sweatshops are No American Dream." *The New York Times,* July 18: A1, A10.

Shiva, Vandana. 1997. *Biopiracy: The Plunder of Nature and Knowledge.* Boston: South End.

———. 2000. *Stolen Harvest: The Hijacking of the Global Food Supply.* Boston: South End.

———. 2003. "The Living Democracy Movement: Alternatives to the Bankruptcy of Globalization." In *Another World Is Possible*, edited by William F. Fisher and Thomas Ponniah. London: Zed.

Shultz, Jim. 2003. "Bolivia: The Water War Widens." *NACLA Report on the Americas* 36(4): 34–37.

Silver, Beverly. 2003. *Forces of Labor: Worker's Movements and Globalization Since 1870.* Cambridge, UK: Cambridge University Press.

Simons, Marlise. 1999. "Cry of Muslim Women for Equal Rights is Rising." *The New York Times,* February 24: A1, A6.

Singh, Ajit. 1992. "The Lost Decade: The Economic Crisis of the Third World in the 1980s: How the North Caused the South's Crisis." *Contention* 2: 58–80.

Singh, Kavaljit. 2003. "Washington Reigns Supreme." *Tribune (London),* April 18. Posted April 26, 2003, by mritchie@iatp.org.

Singh, Kavaljit and Daphne Wysham. 1997. "Micro-Credit: Band-Aid or Wound?" *The Ecologist* 27(2): 42–43.

Sivanandan, A. 1989. "New Circuits of Imperialism." *Race & Class* 30(4): 1–19.

Sklair, Leslie. 1989. *Assembling for Development: The Maquila Industry in Mexico and the United States.* Boston: Unwin Hyman.

———. 2002. *Globalization. Capitalism & Its Alternatives.* Oxford, UK: Oxford University Press.

Skrobanek, Siripan, Nattaya Boonpakdi, and Chutina Janthakeero. 1997. *The Human Realities of Traffic in International Women.* London: Zed.

Skutnabb-Kangas, Tove. 2001. "Murder That is a Threat to Survival." *Guardian Weekly,* March 22–28: 3.

"Slavery in the 21st Century." 2001. *New Internationalist,* July–August: 18–19.

Smith, Jeremy. 2002. "An Unappealing Industry." *The Ecologist* 32(3): 40–41.

Smith, Stephen. 2002. "'Political Sharia' Poses Threat to Nigeria's Unity." *Guardian Weekly,* January 31–February 6: 30.

Sobieszczyk, Teresa and Lindy Williams. 1997. "Attitudes Surrounding the Continuation of Female Circumcision in the Sudan: Passing the Tradition to the Next Generation." *Journal of Marriage and the Family* 59: 966–81.

Soederberg, Susanne. 2006. *Global Governance in Question: Empire, Class and the New Common Sense in Managing North–South Relations.* London: Pluto.

The South Centre. 1993. *Facing the Challenge: Responses to the Report of the South Commission.* London: Zed.

Starr, Amory. 2000. *Naming the Enemy: Anti-Corporate Movements Confront Globalization.* London: Zed.

Stavrianos, L. S. 1981. *Global Rift: The Third World Comes of Age.* New York: William Morrow.

Stevens, William K. 1994. "Poor Lands' Success in Cutting Birth Rate Upsets Old Theories." *The New York Times,* January 2: A8.

Stevenson, Richard W. 1993. "Ford Sets Its Sights on a 'World Car.'" *The New York Times,* October 27: D1, D4.

Stewart, Douglas Ian. 1994. *After the Trees: Living on the Amazon Highway.* Austin: University of Texas Press.

Stiglitz, Joseph E. 2002. *Globalization and Its Discontents.* New York: Norton.

Stimson, Robert L. 1999. "General Motors Drives Some Hard Bargains with Asian Suppliers." *Wall Street Journal,* April 2: A1, A6.

Strange, Susan. 1994. *States and Markets.* London: Pinter.

Strom, Stephanie. 1999. "In Renault–Nissan Deal, Big Risks and Big Opportunities." *The New York Times,* March 28: A3.

Stuart, Liz. 2003. "Journey's End for Trafficked Humans." *Guardian Weekly,* February 13–19: 21.

Swift, Richard. 2002. *No-Nonsense Guide to Democracy.* London: Verso.

Swords, Alicia. 2007. "Neo-Zapatista Network Politics. Transforming Democracy and Development." *Latin American Perspectives* 34(2): 1–16.

Tabb, William. 2000. "After Seattle: Understanding the Politics of Globalization." *Monthly Review* 51(10): 1–18.

Tan, Abby. 1991a. "Paychecks Sent Home May Not Cover Human Losses." *Los Angeles Times,* October 1: H2–H3.

———. 1991b. "The Labor Brokers: For a Price, There's a Job Abroad—Maybe." *Los Angeles Times,* October 1: H1.

Tautz, Carlos Sergio Figueiredo. 1997. "The Asian Invasion: Asian Multinationals Come to the Amazon." *Multinational Monitor* 18(9): 1–5.

Templin, Neal. 1994. "Mexican Industrial Belt is Beginning to Form as Car Makers Expand." *Wall Street Journal,* June 29: A1, A10.

Thompson, Ginger. 2002a. "Free Market Grinds Mexico's Middle Class." *The New York Times,* September 4: 3.

———. 2002b. "Big Mexican Breadwinner: The Migrant Worker." *The New York Times,* March 25: A3.

Thompson, Tony. 2005. "All Work and No Play in 'Virtual Sweatshop.'" *Guardian Weekly,* March 25–31: 17.

Thurow, Lester C. 1999. "The Dollar's Day of Reckoning." *The Nation,* January 11: 22–24.

Tripathi, Salil. 2004. "Shine On." *Guardian Unlimited,* May 13. Available at www.guardian.co.uk.

Tripp, Aili Mari. 1997. *Changing the Rules: The Politics of Liberalization and the Urban Informal Economy in Tanzania.* Berkeley, CA: University of California Press.

Tsing, Anna Lowenhaupt. 2005. *Friction: An Ethnography of Global Connection.* Princeton: Princeton University Press.

Turner, Mandy. 2007. "Scramble for Africa." *The Guardian,* May 2. Available at www.guardian.co.uk.

Tuxill, John. 1999. "Nature's Cornucopia: Our Stake in Plant Diversity." Worldwatch Paper No. 148, Washington, DC: Worldwatch.

Tyler, Patrick E. 1994. "China Planning People's Car to Put Masses behind Wheel." *The New York Times,* September 22: A1, D8.

———. 1995. "Star at Conference on Women: Banker Who Lends to the Poor." *The New York Times,* September 14: A6.

Uchitelle, Louis. 1993. "Stanching the Loss of Good Jobs." *The New York Times,* January 31, Section 3: 1, 6.

———. 1994. "U.S. Corporations Expanding Abroad at a Quicker Pace." *The New York Times,* July 25: A1, D2.

———. 2007. "NAFTA Should Have Stopped Illegal Immigration, Right?" *The New York Times,* February 18: 4.

Udesky, Laurie. 1994. "Sweatshops Behind the Labels." *The Nation,* May 16: 665–68.

Ufkes, Fran. 1995. "Industrial Restructuring and Agrarian Change: The Greening of Singapore." In *Food and Agrarian Orders in the World Economy,* edited by Philip McMichael. Westport, CT: Praeger.

United Nations. 1997. *United Nations Development Report.* New York: Oxford University Press.

———. 2002. *Human Development Report 2002.* New York: Oxford University Press.

UNCTAD. 1996. *Trade and Development Report 1996* (Geneva).

United Nations Environment Program (UNEP). 2002. *Global Environmental Outlook 3 Earthwatch.* Retrieved from www.unep.net.

"U.S. Imperial Ambitions and Iraq." 2002. *Monthly Review* 54(7): 1–13.

Van der Gaag, Nikki. 2004. *The No-Nonsense Guide to Women's Rights.* London: Verso.

Vía Campesina. 2000. "Bangalore Declaration. October 6. Available at http://viacampesina. org/main_en/index.php?option=com_content&task=view&id=53&Itemid=28.

Vidal, John. 2001. "Brazil Sets Out on the Road to Oblivion." *Guardian Weekly,* July 19–25: 20.
———. 2003. "All Dried Up." *Guardian Weekly,* March 27–April 2: 24.
———. 2006. "Collapse of Ecosystems Likely if Plunder Continues." *The Guardian,* October 25: 13.
———. 2007. "Climate Change to Force Mass Migration." *The Guardian,* May 14. Available at www.guardian.co.uk.
Wacker, Corinne. 1994. "Sustainable Development Through Women's Groups: A Cultural Approach to Sustainable Development." In *Feminist Perspectives on Sustainable Development,* edited by Wendy Harcourt. London: Zed.
Walby, Sylvia. 2005. "Measuring Women's Progress in a Global Era." *International Social Science Journal* 184: 371–87.
Waldman, Amy. 2002. "Poor in India Starve as Surplus Wheat Rots." *The New York Times,* December 2: 3.
Walker, Richard. 2004. *The Conquest of Bread. 150 Years of Agribusiness in California.* New York: New Press.
Wallach, Lori. 2003. "What the WTO Didn't Want You to Know." Available at www.iatp.org.
Wallach, Lori and Michelle Sforza. 1999. *Whose Trade Organization? Corporate Globalization and the Erosion of Democracy.* Washington, DC: Public Citizen.
Wallach, Lori and Patrick Woodall. 2004. *Whose Trade Organization? A Comprehensive Guide to the WTO.* New York: New Press.
Walton, John and David Seddon. 1994. *Free Markets & Food Riots: The Politics of Global Adjustment.* Oxford, UK: Blackwell.
Waring, Marilyn. 1988. *If Women Counted: A New Feminist Economics.* San Francisco: Harper & Row.
Washington Post. 1999. "Coffee Drinkers: Where are Your Beans Grown?" Reprinted in *The Ithaca Journal,* January 5: 3B.
Watkins, Kevin. 1991. "Agriculture and Food Security in the GATT Uruguay Round." *Review of African Political Economy* 50: 38–50.
———. 1996. "Free Trade and Farm Fallacies: From the Uruguay Round to the World Food Summit." *The Ecologist* 26(6): 244–55.
———. 2002. "Money Talks." *Guardian Weekly,* May 9–15: 21.
———. 2006. "The Forgotten Other India." *The Guardian,* October 3. Available at www.guardian.co.uk.
Watts, Jonathan. 2005–06. "Rivals Awake to a Giant in Their Midst," *Guardian Weekly,* December 23–January 5: 36.
Watts, Michael. 1994. "Life Under Contract: Contract Farming, Agrarian Restructuring, and Flexible Accumulation." In *Living Under Contract: Contract Farming and Agrarian Transformation in Sub-Saharan Africa,* edited by Peter D. Little and Michael J. Watts. Madison: University of Wisconsin Press.
Weber, Heloise. 2004. "The 'New Economy' and Social Risk: Banking on the Poor?" *Review of International Political Economy* 11(2): 356–86.
———. 2006. "A Political Analysis of the PRSP Initiative: Social Struggles and the Organization of Persistent Relations of Inequality." *Globalizations* 3(2): 187–206.
Weinberg, Bill. 1998. "La Miskitia Rears Up: Industrial Recolonization Threatens the Nicaraguan Rainforests—An Indigenous Response." *Native Americas* 15(2): 22–33.
Weisbrot, Mark. 1999. "How to Say No to the IMF." *The Nation,* June 21: 20–21.
Weissman, Robert. 1991. "Prelude to a New Colonialism: The Real Purpose of GATT." *The Nation,* March 18: 337.
Wessel, James. 1983. *Trading the Future: Farm Exports and the Concentration of Economic Power in Our Food System.* San Francisco: Institute for Food and Development Policy.
White, Richard E. and Gloria Eugenia González Mariño. 2007. "Las Gaviotas: Sustainability in the Tropics." *World Watch* 20(3): 18–23.

Williams, Gwyneth. 1981. *Third-World Political Organizations: A Review of Developments.* Montclair, NJ: Allenheld, Osmun & Co.

Williams, Robert G. 1986. *Export Agriculture and the Crisis in Central America.* Chapel Hill, NC: University of North Carolina Press.

Wittman, Hannah. 2005. "The Social Ecology of Agrarian Reform: the Landless Rural Workers' Movement and Agrarian Citizenship in Mato Grosso, Brazil." Unpublished PhD dissertation, Development Sociology, Cornell University.

Wolf, Eric. 1982. *Europe and the People Without History.* Berkeley, CA: University of California Press.

Wolfensohn, James. 2000. "Rethinking Development—Challenges and Opportunities." *UNCTAD* meeting, Bangkok, February 16. Available at www.iatp.org.

Wood, Ellen Meiksins. 1999. "Kosovo and the New Imperialism." *Monthly Review* 51(2): 1–8.

Wood, Robert E. 1986. *From Marshall Plan to Debt Crisis: Foreign Aid and Development Choices in the World Economy.* Berkeley: University of California Press.

Woodall, Pam. 1994. "War of the Worlds: A Survey of the Global Economy." *The Economist,* Special Supplement, October 1: 24.

Woods, Ngaire. 2006. *The Globalizers. The IMF, the World Bank, and Their Borrowers.* Ithaca: Cornell University Press.

Woollacott, Martin. 2002. "Islamism after Copenhagen." *Guardian Weekly,* December 19–25: 14.

Worden, Scott. 2001. "E-Trafficking." *Foreign Policy,* Spring. Retrieved from www.foreignpolicy .com/issue_marapr_2001/gnsprint.html.

Working, Russell. 1999. "Russia's Patchwork Economy: Korean Companies, Chinese Workers and U.S. Entrée." *The New York Times,* March 18: D1, D23.

World Bank. 1981. *Accelerated Development in Sub-Saharan Africa: An Agenda to Action.* Washington, DC: World Bank.

———. 1989. *Sub-Saharan Africa: From Crisis to Sustainable Growth.* Washington, DC: World Bank.

———. 1990. *World Development Report.* Washington, DC: World Bank.

———. 1997. *World Development Report.* Washington, DC: World Bank.

———. 1998–99. *World Development Report.* Washington, DC: World Bank.

———. 2000a. *World Development Report.* Washington, DC: World Bank.

———. 2000b. *Voices of the Poor.* New York: Oxford University Press.

World Institute for Development Economics Research. 2006. *The World Distribution of Household Wealth.* Helsinki. Available from www.wider.unu.edu.

World Social Forum. 2003. "Charter of Principles." In *Another World Is Possible,* edited by W. F. Fisher and T. Ponniah. London: Zed.

World Trade Organization. 2001. "International Trade Statistics." Retrieved from www.wto.org/english/res_e/statis_e/its2001_e/its01_toc_e.htm.

WuDunn, Sheryl. 1993. "Booming China is Dream Market for West." *The New York Times,* February 15: A1–A6.

Yardley, Jim. 2007. "China Says Rich Countries Should Take Lead on Global Warming." *The New York Times,* February 7: A9.

Young, Gerardo and Lucas Guagnini. 2002. "Argentina's New Social Protagonists." *World Press Review,* December 11. Retrieved from www.zmag.org/content/showarticle.cfm? SectionID=42&ItemID=2735.

Zalik, Anna. 2004. "The Niger Delta: 'PetroViolence' and 'Partnership Development.'" *Review of African Political Economy* 31(101): 401–24.

Zalik, Anna and Michael Watts. 2006. "Imperial Oil: Petroleum Politics in the Nigerian Delta and the New Scramble for Africa." *Socialist Review,* April. Available at www.socialistreview .org.uk/article.php?articlenumber=9712.

Glossary/Index